MW01485099

Sunbelt Capitalism

POLITICS AND CULTURE IN MODERN AMERICA

Series Editors: Margot Canaday, Glenda Gilmore, Michael Kazin, and Thomas J. Sugrue

Volumes in the series narrate and analyze political and social change in the broadest dimensions from 1865 to the present, including ideas about the ways people have sought and wielded power in the public sphere and the language and institutions of politics at all levels—local, national, and transnational. The series is motivated by a desire to reverse the fragmentation of modern U.S. history and to encourage synthetic perspectives on social movements and the state, on gender, race, and labor, and on intellectual history and popular culture.

Sunbelt Capitalism

Phoenix and the Transformation of American Politics

Elizabeth Tandy Shermer

UNIVERSITY OF PENNSYLVANIA PRESS

PHILADELPHIA

Published by
University of Pennsylvania Press
Philadelphia, Pennsylvania 19104-4112
www.upenn.edu/pennpress

Printed in the United States of America on acid-free paper
10 9 8 7 6 5 4 3 2 1

Library of Congress Cataloging-in-Publication Data
Shermer, Elizabeth Tandy.
Sunbelt capitalism : Phoenix and the transformation of American politics / Elizabeth Tandy Shermer. — 1st ed.
p. cm. — (Politics and culture in modern America)
Includes bibliographical references and index.
ISBN 978-0-8122-4470-0 (alk. paper)
1. Cities and towns—Arizona—Phoenix—Growth. 2. Phoenix (Ariz.)—Commerce—History—20th century. 3. Phoenix (Ariz.)—Economic conditions—History—20th century. 4. Phoenix (Ariz.)—Politics and government—History—20th century. 5. Phoenix (Ariz.)—Social conditions—History—20th century. 6. Conservatism—Arizona—Phoenix—History—20th century. I. Title. II. Series: Politics and culture in modern America.
HT384.U62A68 2013
307.7609791'73—dc23

2012023970

Dedicated to the families we choose

Contents

Introduction

> Few Northeasterners realize the new prominence of the South and West or appreciate that a new political era is in the making.
>
> —Kevin P. Phillips, *The Emerging Republican Majority*, 1969

In 1969, Kevin Phillips earned national recognition for *The Emerging Republican Majority*, which reconsidered a persistent set of century-old regional voting patterns. In this celebration of Richard Nixon's 1968 electoral triumph, Phillips concluded that the Republican's victory symbolized the overthrow of an "obsolescent 'liberal' ideology." While public memory of the book has largely faded, Phillips's identification of a "Sun Belt Phenomenon" has had a lasting impact. In just five pages, the author defined a region that captured popular and scholarly attention for thirty years. Phillips, an amateur statistician turned White House aide, argued, "as of the present . . . the huge postwar white middle-class push to the Florida-California Sun country (as well as suburbia in general)—seems to be forging a new, conservative political era in the South, Southwest and Heartland." At the heart of this phenomenon were booming metropolises, which he described as "centers of commerce, light industry, military preparedness, defense production and space-age technology, vocational seedbeds of a huge middle class . . . a century removed from the Allegheny-Monongahela Black Country and the dun-colored mill canyons of the Merrimack."[1]

Phoenix, Arizona, clearly exemplified, as journalists Peter Wiley and Robert Gottlieb noted, "the prototypical Sun Belt city." The railroad hub had once been smaller in population than rival Tucson and also a third of the size of El Paso, the Southwest's largest city at the turn of the twentieth century. In these years, agriculture, mining, ranching, and tourism had structured Phoenix's economy. After World War II, the Valley of the Sun became a major center for high-tech consumer electronics, defense production, and research and development, new investment that sparked a population increase from 65,000 in 1940 to 440,000 in 1960. Today, the United States' fifth-largest city is at the center of a metropolitan region whose total population exceeds four million. A postindustrial service economy dominates this desert metropolis, symbolically represented by the presence of the headquarters for the University of Phoenix, American Express, and US Airways, as well as that other twenty-first-century economic phenomenon, the day labor collection points that daily take over the parking lots of the many home improvement megastores throughout the area.[2]

There was nothing inevitable about the town's spectacular growth. The activism, agency, and ideas of a well-defined mid-century cohort of local business elites and high-level industrialists were responsible for this political, economic, and social transformation. This subset of corporate executives and managers, who would emerge as a principal force in the postwar conservative movement, opposed the regulatory liberalism that Franklin Delano Roosevelt's administration embodied. Much attention has been devoted to their anti–New Deal politics at the national level, but they may well have been more influential in states and small cities, especially when they sought to escape regulations, taxes, and unions by dispersing their operations beyond the northeastern, midwestern, and Pacific Coast industrial strongholds. In the severely underdeveloped, commodity-dependent, Depression-ravaged South and Southwest, residents were desperate for investment, particularly local businessmen, who like outside investors were most often white men (commonly referred to as Anglos in the West). The major store-owners and professionals in these regions' small towns sought to diversify the local economy and build their fortunes. Yet their industrial recruitment efforts did not represent a grassroots movement. They were in fact the municipal "grass tops," as sociologist Philip Selznick termed the local elites whom liberals empowered to oversee the New Deal at the community level.[3] The small town gentry, the periphery's grasstops, were situated between the local working and middle classes and the elite investor contingent who resided in the country's manufacturing belt. This stratum of community merchants and professionals were often educated in elite eastern or California schools, belonged to national organizations of retailers, lawyers, or newsmen, and negotiated directly with leading manufacturers or bankers who sold products or made loans throughout the South and Southwest.

These businessmen were largely hostile to the emergence of the liberal, regulatory state. These southern and southwestern boosters, often organized within city Chambers of Commerce or similar business associations, were not laissez-faire ideologues; they instead developed their own state-dependent vision for the economic growth and social development of these heretofore remote regions. The ideas undergirding this nascent growth philosophy can best be understood as a homegrown, developmental "neoliberalism," a set of ideas that emphasizes the use of the state to facilitate commerce, often through decreasing regulations, taxes, and union rights. Much scholarship asserts that this ideology had its birth in early postwar think tanks, the later New York City fiscal crisis, and the first years of free-market globalization. Yet the proto-Sunbelt's business and political elite assembled many elements of this doctrine in their earlier quest for hypergrowth and political hegemony. Their ideas grew out of interwar municipal reform movements, which legally disenfranchised working-class and minority voters and hence ensured that the white upper class retained substantial political power. These efforts later enabled municipal and regional business leaders to challenge and undo liberal reforms at the community level.[4]

Local, regional, and national businessmen involved in these campaigns never championed a crude antistatism during the New Deal, World War II, or the postwar period. They instead embraced government power and planning in order to reconstruct a developmental state that would privilege industry by insulating it from the electorate, dismantling social welfare provisions, weakening organized labor's strength, curbing regulatory restrictions, and reversing the New Deal–era tax shift from homeowners to businesses. By the mid-1950s, industrial-relations experts, boosters, and CEOs considered such policies a part of southern and southwestern cities' investment environment, their so-called business climate. The requirements for being "business friendly" expanded continuously because interregional competition for lucrative, high-skill, high-tech investment enabled manufacturers to demand more tax concessions, regulatory giveaways, and state financial supports. Guarantees even grew to include publicly financed manufacturing facilities, roads, utilities, parks, subdivisions, and schools to serve industrialists who needed to attract and retain a well-trained workforce.

The business climate ideal, and the corporate welfare state that it required, represented a challenge to mid-century liberalism. Competition to generate the most favorable conditions for industry inspired a faith in the conglomerations' capacity to generate employment opportunities, which simultaneously subverted local needs for tax revenue, social investment, or assurance that new jobs would be good and permanent. Regional rivalries also eroded the legitimacy and potency of liberal economic doctrine in the northeastern, midwestern, and Pacific Coast manufacturing strongholds where local governments began to mimic Sunbelt legislation in the late 1950s. As a result, mid-century investment campaigns did diversify the southern and southwestern economies but nonetheless failed to engender the social and political liberalism which New Dealers had expected to accompany the urbanization and industrialization of these hitherto underdeveloped regions.

When compared to other Sunbelt cities, Phoenix proved both atypical and archetypal. The town, like other beleaguered southern and southwestern municipalities, might well have followed New Deal prescriptions for growth and development because liberals had power and legitimacy during the first half of the twentieth century. Massive infrastructure spending, the huge subsidization of agriculture, and federally protected unionization made Arizona solidly Democratic in the 1930s and 1940s. Interest in diversifying the area's economy was also widespread among Phoenicians. Many sought to end the city's dependence on agriculture and mining, thereby opening the door to a set of unionized, high-wage jobs not only in factories and mines but also in the high-profile service sector, namely, the city's hotels, bars, and clubs, as well as local government offices. Labor organizing accompanied a broad attempt to democratize municipal governance, exemplified by efforts to abandon the town's Progressive Era, "good-government" charter, whose citywide election rules had long marginalized working-class and minority voters. On the horizon was also a plebeian alliance against the racism that kept the town divided between the wealthy Anglo population north of the railroad tracks and the residents of African, Mexican, Asian, and Native American descent living on Phoenix's south side.

The Great Depression also proved a watershed moment for the Phoenix Chamber of Commerce. The association's affluent, white, male leadership had been generally uninterested in large-scale investment. A younger cohort of businessmen, most notably Barry Goldwater, rejected Arizona's pastoral present and embraced aggressive promotion to build a dynamic city that relied on distribution and high-tech manufacturing. But Goldwater and other ambitious Chamber men feared that liberals and unionists would dictate Phoenix's development. Although these boosters benefited from

New Deal efforts to develop the West, they also held that liberal policies extended the reach of the state too far into managerial offices and corporate boardrooms, taxed businesses and wealthy Americans too much, and created unreasonable expectations of social support among low-income Americans. Labor's recent organizing successes also heightened fears that the Phoenix business elite would lose their prestige, power, and moral authority to a coalition that they considered unnatural, illegitimate, and corrupt. These concerns spurred influential lawyers, bankers, newsmen, and retailers to organize themselves for a political and ideological assault upon Arizona's fledgling New Deal order. Their initial plans took place within the Chamber's offices and the city's philanthropic and social clubs, where they denounced the corruption and parochialism that they thought characterized both liberal Democrats and an older cohort of local politicians.

These Anglos, really the town's would-be rainmakers, sought to make their city into a major distribution hub, a garrison for the American military, a tourist destination for adventurers, sports enthusiasts, and urbane snowbirds, and, above all else, a preeminent manufacturing center. Light electronics, aerospace engineering, and general high-tech research and development topped the Chamber's priorities. These sectors were particularly attractive because boosters predicted that they would be both highly profitable and suitable for the physical realities of the arid, hot Arizona desert. Many of these business activists were avid outdoorsmen, jealously protective of the Valley, keenly aware of the area's limited water supply, and dedicated to preventing Phoenix from becoming a desert replica of smoggy Steelbelt cities.

They often, in fact, invoked the specter of working-class, smokestack-filled Chicago as a negative reference. Boosters objected to proposed investment from firms that needed a less-skilled labor pool and thus would provide employment for Phoenix's large minority and Anglo working classes. Chamber men instead sought to attract an educated, skilled, professional workforce, which, at the time, was almost guaranteed to be white and male. They never publicly declared themselves against investment that relied on an immigrant, low-skill, or low-wage labor pool but still tailored their boosterism to appeal to lucrative firms and Anglo, suburban family men to people Phoenix with residents who would share the commercial elite's metropolitan tastes and support their efforts to create an Anglo, technocratic Phoenix. This kind of industrial recruitment also protected their reputation for moderate civil rights policies, even in a city with well-defined color lines.

Chamber men had to embrace politics to turn this vision into a reality. These businessmen first went to war with organized labor over a "right to work" referendum, which they declared necessary for industrial peace, economic opportunity, and overall prosperity. City politics also dominated the Chamber's postwar agenda. Leaders organized the supposedly nonpartisan Charter Government Committee in 1949, a political machine that lasted for more than twenty years and enabled boosters to harness the electorate's support for refashioning Phoenix into a mecca for high-tech industries. This industrialization program relied, in essence, on providing whatever tax advantages, zoning variances, and municipal services corporations demanded in their negotiations to open branch plants and other facilities in the Phoenix Valley. Outside industrialists generally wanted guarantees that the trade union movement would remain weak, promises that taxes on industry would be low, water would be plentiful, and land deals would be generous.

Industrialists asked for even more during the 1950s and 1960s. Competition from other business-friendly metropolises gave CEOs greater leverage in these relocation negotiations. This trend was especially prevalent among the science-based industries, which needed a stable, highly skilled workforce. These firms demanded better public schools, access to technical education programs for their employees, and recreational and cultural opportunities to satisfy the families of managers and the many professionals employed in high-tech concerns. Such stipulations led to the transformation of a small, nearby teacher's college into Arizona State University (ASU), whose large, ambitious engineering department proved crucial in attracting a number of major defense firms and consumer electronics manufacturers.

Such recruitment statecraft defied easy political categorization. Racism, sexism, Christian moralism, and anticommunism were driving forces behind right-wing movements in other parts of the country during the early postwar period, but none of these traditions proved as important as the locally grown business critique of liberal governance and interventionist economic policy in Phoenix. Rainmakers were early, outspoken opponents of the New Deal state and its local iterations but were not hostile to state action per se, especially if it sustained their vision of a growing city that competed on a national level for the most advanced and sophisticated business enterprises. Many Phoenicians, including Chamber men, still saw little problem with segregated schools, residential redlines, antimiscegenation laws, or restrictive covenants barring Jews and other non-Anglo residents from the city's premier clubs and institutions. Even the most free-enterprise focused boosters often belonged to churches, synagogues, and Mormon temples. There was also an active John Birch Society chapter in the city and a newspaper that played on fears of Communist subversion in its attacks on modern liberalism. Yet divisive racial, religious, or anticommunist issues did not define this generation of local businessmen or prove decisive in their rise to power. Instead, or at least until the mid-1970s, both the Phoenix-based Arizona GOP and the city's powerful Chamber of Commerce had emphasized growth and development.[5]

The politics of promotion still failed to help boosters, including Goldwater, define themselves after Roosevelt's election. They first turned to the Republican Party to set themselves apart from liberals in their war against a staid political order and a local reform movement. Promoters perfected a language of freedom, democracy, and opportunity in their public campaigns for hypercompetitive investment strategies and a social order that placed businessmen in charge of the city. Indeed, they did not fully wrap themselves in a conservative rhetorical mantle until the mid-1950s, when the term "conservative" came to envelop the many different criticisms of midcentury liberalism. Accordingly, conservative will not be used in this book until business elites themselves began to deploy the phrase, in order to highlight how their specific usages defined their movement, statecraft, and worldview. Neoliberal will likewise only be offered as an analytical descriptor in order to emphasize how past policy decisions established the kind of statecraft now placed underneath neoliberalism's expansive framework.[6]

No matter what lexicon Chamber men adopted, their policies unquestionably transformed Phoenix. More than seven hundred manufacturing firms began operations in or relocated key facilities to the city between 1948 and 1964 alone. The specific closed-door negotiations that brought Motorola, General Electric (GE), Sperry Rand, Unidynamics, and Greyhound illustrate the extent to which the Chamber and the city council were willing to orient the state toward fulfilling the location requirements that high-ranking CEOs demanded. For example, though Motorola executives established a research and development laboratory in the Valley before the business elite took control of city politics, the firm's expansion in the area depended on the outright repeal of taxes on inventory and machinery used in manufacturing but also on the creation of ASU's engineering department. The head of GE also concerned himself with the university's maturation when he located the company's computer division in Phoenix, not high-wage, well-regulated, and heavily unionized California. Giveaways convinced

Sperry Rand to reestablish an entire division in the Valley because executives stood to profit handsomely from a lease that the Chamber brokered, a new factory for which boosters fundraised, and a business-backed moratorium on the sales tax levied on goods sold to the federal government. Unidynamics came to the Valley after a member of the Phoenix Chamber became governor and created a special task force to enable Arizona's executive branch to replicate, on an even larger scale, corporate-oriented policies. This new power over local and state governments later served to facilitate the Valley's metamorphosis into a postindustrial metropolis dotted with corporate headquarters.

Civic leaders in the South, Southwest, and Northeast had sought to emulate the Phoenix boosters long before service replaced manufacturing in the Valley. Rainmakers, for example, were invited to visit and make recommendations. They also had the ear of the executives who invested in central Arizona. Many of these magnates were also unhappy with liberal economic policies, including Lemuel Ricketts Boulware. GE's anti-union vice president had already become a celebrity of sorts among businessmen for his strategy to break the power of unions and then proved himself more than happy to keep his firm in the Valley and campaign on behalf of Phoenix Republicans. Chamber men's dealings with such corporate luminaries also propelled Arizonans into leading roles in right-wing business groups and political networks. Financier Walter Bimson became the head of the American Bankers Association. Lawyer Dean Burch held the chairmanship of the Republican National Committee as well as the Federal Communications Commission. And, of course, there was Barry Goldwater, whose rise to national prominence was based less on his Cold War anticommunism than on his high-profile renown as an opponent of organized labor and liberal economic policy. He was able to influence the nomination of two Phoenicians, William Rehnquist and Sandra Day O'Connor, to the Supreme Court. Both shared his views on the proper role of the state vis-à-vis the economy and made judicial decisions that further aided the rise of governance and fiscal philosophies antithetical to New Deal liberalism.

Phoenix's industrialization was hence a local story embedded within broad political, economic, and social upheaval. Sunbelt sprawl and its politics were neither inevitable nor territorially innate but outgrowths of tectonic, region-specific changes in twentieth-century capitalism. Creating the Sunbelt, in effect, meant upending the relationship between America's industrial strongholds and their hinterlands. Historians have long considered the prewar South and West to have functioned as domestic colonies in service to the country's burgeoning manufacturing empire. Residents relied on imported goods, entrepreneurs had little access to credit, and profits from outsiders' investments largely went back to corporate boardrooms and big-city banks in the Steelbelt. Agricultural and extractive markets in turn determined economic fortunes across the periphery, even for the small-town and urban ownership and professional classes, like the Phoenix Chamber elite, whose profits rose and fell alongside commodity prices. This colonial servitude had an effect on these regions' politics and society. Legislative apportionment, either dictated through state constitutions or determined by the leverage and economic power of absent investors and firmly entrenched estate owners, left many townspeople underrepresented. This malapportionment constrained city dwellers' ability to change the state tax codes and laws that discouraged homegrown industrialization initiatives. Virulent, legally enforced racism and segregation also divided the electorate and prevented concerted efforts to dethrone the landed elite and the contingent of transplanted capitalists.[7]

Depression and war provided opportunities for reclamation. In the arid states, the word "reclamation" has long been associated with the irrigation projects needed to make the territory flower. Now, signs alert residents that undrinkable reclaimed water maintains lush lawns and beautiful gardens. Yet reclamation represented something far more grandiose during the New Deal, when FDR promised that improved infrastructure would reclaim underdeveloped lands, untapped water supplies, and desperate citizens in the periphery. Many New Dealers hoped so, not only concurring with Roosevelt's 1938 assertion that "the South was the Nation's No. 1 economic problem" but also considering the West too in need of reconstruction. Prominent liberals were confident that regional folkways and politics could be transformed through a dramatic federal reconstruction of national banking, labor, and oversight policies as well as funding for local public infrastructure, social welfare, and consumer credit. World War II advanced this process, empowering liberals to dramatically increase investment in the South and West and to bring regional wage, hour, and racial work standards more fully in line with Steelbelt norms.[8]

Regional New Deals were never exercises in top-down reconstruction. Politically engaged executives, many of whom had never made peace with New Deal liberalism, and frustrated boosters, who looked askance at new federal agencies and programs transforming their towns, also wanted to recover their power to manage and govern in Washington, the Steelbelt, and the periphery. Top businessmen waged their large-scale reclamation efforts from the Capitol, where they used their positions within federal bureaucracies to craft key war production and demobilization policies. These generous contracts, tax breaks, and surplus sales generated windfall profits that funded business migration into Steelbelt hinterlands, where growing conglomerations profitably served emerging markets. The grasstops, for their part, ensured the high return on these investments by curtailing union rights, commercial regulations, and business taxes.

Hence corporate expansion, not homegrown, individual entrepreneurship, instigated the American periphery's industrialization. Firms were openly courted because even the most ardent critics of the colonial status quo considered manufacturing vital to a genuinely new South and West, which representative democracy, progressive taxation, and organized labor would guarantee. Yet the grasstops considered these principles deterrents to investment. Their arguments seemed increasingly salient when plants and military installations in defense boomtowns closed. Ensuing postwar desperation gave outside executives extraordinary leverage over these communities in crisis, where CEOs found the politically insurgent urban business elite eager to use their power to frustrate liberal economic policies. This partnership produced experimental, pragmatic policymaking that increased the size, scope, and power of government in order to attract and retain investment while steadily dismantling fledgling regional New Deal orders.

The resultant industrial flight eventually transformed the entire country. The Sunbelt was at one time a distinct region, which included those southern and southwestern metropolises that transcended their region's old commodity-based economies and traditional power structures. Such cities included Atlanta, Austin, Charlotte, Dallas–Fort Worth, Denver, Houston, Las Vegas, Los Angeles, Memphis, Miami, Phoenix, Raleigh-Durham, Reston, San Diego, and San Jose. Their manufacturing dynamism in turn aided their postindustrial metamorphosis: many are metropolitan epicenters of the now-dominant service, finance, knowledge, and real estate sectors. Their immediate hinterlands, dotted with smaller cities and towns, also belong to the Sunbelt because their limited growth represented the inequality and stratification endemic to mobile, mid-century capitalism. Less investment came to Birmingham, Alabama, El Paso, Texas, Greenville, Mississippi, Mobile, Alabama, and Ogden, Utah, where new industries tended to complement, not supplant, these areas' traditional economies and to supply the

Sunbelt's flagship cities. Textile factories, food processing plants, oil refineries, and smelting operations never generated the diversified economic base necessary to buoy these smaller communities when these businesses moved again in pursuit of cheap labor, less regulation, and low taxation. Such divestment eventually left the communities as devastated as the northeastern and midwestern manufacturing centers, which industrial dispersal had begun to gut two decades earlier.

Rustbelt reinvestment was, in turn, as spotty as Sunbelt industrialization. Chicago, Boston, and New York remained headquarter cities because executives used the threat of and reality of capital flight to push for the tax incentives and giveaways that transformed these metropolises into postindustrial centers of trade and finance. In contrast, the small textile towns, steel cities, and auto parts enclaves in the oxidizing Steelbelt had little else to sustain their economic livelihood. Those communities that have reemerged as eastern silicon or Big Pharma valleys, such as Allentown, Camden, and Pittsburgh, depended on a cadre of boosters, who looked past rebuilding the steel economies, pursued new types of investment, and increased their influence in local, state, and federal affairs in order to mimic Sunbelt wage, tax, and oversight laws.

Yet the statecraft developed to attract high-tech manufacturing, health care, and recreational investment still stood apart from the earlier policy framework that had enticed investors into the Steelbelt's periphery. Southern and southwestern boosters built new suburbs around small cities, transformed quasi-colonial states with new governmental bureaucracies and tax codes, and limited union power before industry fully arrived. Rustbelt burghers, in contrast, struggled to rebuild neighborhoods, redirect established government agencies and policies, and upend political structures that had given the working class a significant voice in protectionist and redistributive public policies. Thus, new retail, service, health, and knowledge jobs never replicated the standardized higher wages, benefit guarantees, or public services that labor liberalism had provided the working class. Just a fraction of the work in the nation's new service-dominated economy has been lucrative, let alone secure. The low-cost manufacturing that exists along the U.S.-Mexico border and draws immigrants into the American South has in fact so eroded wage and living standards that the Sunbelt has been compared to those developing countries, often once a part of colonial empires, in the so-called Global South.[9]

Capitalism's complicated inner workings thus serve as a prism to better interrogate the ideas and policies behind economic transformation. Indeed, the simultaneous emergence of the Sunbelt and the modern conservative movement demands a reconsideration of American politics and statecraft. Many scholars have taken contemporary, extremist statements to stand for the entire conservative perspective on state regulatory power. The most infamous is GOP strategist Grover Norquist's quip: "My goal is to cut government in half in twenty-five years to get it down to the size where we can drown it in the bathtub." He certainly embodies the worldview of some contemporary libertarians but does not represent the viewpoint of even the corporate Right or its helpmates on the local level, either today or throughout most of the twentieth century.[10]

This small versus big government rhetoric fails to capture that state expansion defined modern America, no matter the party in power. Enlargement was a bitter process, not a pluralist exercise, which grew out of industrialization. Governments across the world, for example, played a vital role in building the global cotton economy that defined the long nineteenth century. Policies to provide textile manufacturers with cheap workforces and raw materials subsequently increased the size and power of imperial central states. Progressives, liberals, unionists, and radicals in turn struggled to redirect the state's power to stabilize the economy, empower the citizenry, and build social welfare guarantees, the impulses behind mid-century social-democratic statecraft. Those more recent movements, commonly labeled "conservative" or "neoliberal," endeavored to reconstruct states, often increasing some governmental functions at the expense of others, as Sunbelt business climates certainly did. Hence the modern era's political divide never rested on the false dichotomy between statism and antistatism (often juxtaposed as liberal versus conservative) but depended on how state power was deployed, who the state was intended to serve, and what types of policies the state was pursuing or curtailing. Boosters, of the sort who would prove so influential in Phoenix and other Sunbelt boom cities, considered market restraints an imposition on individual initiative, economic development, and general civic progress. But they did not and do not necessarily reject a strong state or, as one political scientist famously quipped, "distrust their state." The grasstops and their executive-level kinsmen certainly detested liberal regulatory statecraft but nonetheless involved themselves in politics in order to construct governments that encouraged investment through the privatization of government services, the general reduction of business taxes, and the imposition of limits on trade union power.[11]

These businessmen worked in the trenches of policymaking. They crafted the growth and investment statecraft that freed the South and Southwest from colonial servitude without yielding to populist demands for stability, security, and representative democracy. Grasstops and investor policy experimentation hence complemented ideological reconsiderations simultaneously taking place in top think tanks and economics departments. The result was a region-specific, pragmatic, homegrown, developmental neoliberalism that eventually transformed the politics and market ethos of the entire country. This statecraft had the most immediate, dramatic consequences in domestic colonial outposts. The resultant slow, steady drain of jobs and investment from the manufacturing strongholds eventually empowered local promoters' corporate collaborators to regain control over local politics in places like Philadelphia and Ohio, and eventually New York City, where they instituted the Sunbelt strategies that they had helped to shape. Hence, by 1969, when Kevin Phillips sounded a death knell for modern liberalism and heralded the emergence of the South and Southwest's rebirth as conservative strongholds, it had become apparent that industrial development had indeed abolished the colonial character of these regions. Yet in the process American politics had also been reoriented toward an underlying principle that the government and the citizenry should be in service to a distinct stratum of American capital.[12]

PART I

Desert

Chapter 1

Colonial Prologue

"A very hot, desolate place," mused banker George Leonard. "There was a lot of development," he recalled. "They had some lar—fairly large stores in town. They had hotels. But, it struck me as probably as close to Hell as you could be while being on Earth." Leonard's stark recollections of 1930s Phoenix very much captured the town's status as a struggling frontier outpost. Arizona, after all, had only become a state in 1912. Two decades later, this capital city remained in many ways stranded between the great industrial cities in the Midwest and East and the emergent ports, playgrounds, and verdant agricultural valleys of interwar California. In the early twentieth century, Phoenix and the other little towns in the Salt River Valley—Tempe, Mesa, Glendale, Scottsdale, and Chandler—depended on agriculture, but Phoenix, the largest community, was also a center of politics, trade, and commerce and thus was enmeshed in, and in many ways a creature of, the state's mineral and ranching economies. The expanding city was likewise an exotic tourist destination for well-off Easterners. Many flocked to Phoenix and elsewhere in the Far West, eager to experience a slice of the Old West or reap the medicinal benefits of a dry and sunny climate.[1]

Salt River Valley communities were thus thoroughly entangled in the emergence of modern corporate capitalism. Early twentieth-century liquidity enabled industrialists to merge, consolidate, and expand their operations, which fixed the Northeast, Midwest, and parts of the Pacific Coast as an industrial core that relied on outlying areas for raw materials and customers. Manufacturers in imperial cities, such as Chicago, had deep, multifarious connections to suppliers in their hinterlands. Industry-specific supply, demand, and credit structured this periphery. The Windy City, for example, stood at the apex of "thousands of overlapping regions." "Each connected," historian William Cronon showed, "in myriad ways to the thousands of markets and thousands of commodities that constituted Chicago's economic life."[2]

These remote territories, regardless of whether they had yet to become states, were in a sense domestic colonies. Historians of both the South and the West have long asserted that the power dynamic and development differential between this industrial core and the South and West was an exploitative one, largely because agriculture, mining, and other extractive industries dominated economic activity in both regions. As Sheldon Hackney and C. Vann Woodward pointed out, all Southerners relied on imported goods, urbanites remained a small portion of the overall population, and industrial profits flowed north to corporate boardrooms and big-city banks. "Penalties for this type of industrialization are spelled out in the comparative statistics of per capita income, per capita wealth and wage differentials," asserted Woodward in 1951. "Social costs may be reckoned in terms of the South's lag in expenditures for public education, public health and public service." Only a massive program of New Deal investment and labor market reform during the 1930s and 1940s would begin to unshackle the South. The same was true for the West, which had also lacked the capital and infrastructure to support manufacturing. Nineteenth- and early twentieth-century federal programs, largely involving railroad building and reclamation, had never been enough to develop the Mountain West or even large parts of California and Washington. Only postwar defense spending, argued historian Gerald Nash, supplied the capital to fully fund locals' tireless efforts to "diversify their economy sufficiently to end their colonial relationship with the older East."[3]

Still, this label has been controversial. "*Colonial economy*," economist Gavin Wright expounded, "is just the right description of the South's condition: a distinct economy located within the political jurisdiction of a larger country, subject to laws, markets, policies, and technologies that it would not have chosen had it been independent." Yet Wright maintained that the South's distinct economy did not fit the pattern of American imperialism, which used money, people, and state power "to capture a territory like California and absorb it so thoroughly into the nation that its colonial origins are forgotten." Labor, capital, and migration thus defined this Southern economic exceptionalism. The labor pool was isolated and far less skilled when compared to the rest of the nation's workforce. Moreover, the great banking houses of New York and Boston also constricted credit, exerting the kind of imperial power that maintained regional servility. Indeed, post-Reconstruction industrialization had actually outpaced northeastern manufacturing's antebellum growth; it only appeared slow because Southerners needed, yet resisted, an even more substantial influx of outside investment to keep pace with population growth in the region. Equally important, capital outlays in the South generated relatively few developmental or educational dividends because a cadre of technically proficient factory innovators never flooded into the southern textile towns or logging camps to extend and enhance the inventive commercial culture that had become so characteristic of American production in small-town Indiana, Illinois, Wisconsin, and other states in the midwestern manufacturing frontier.[4]

Yet the urban Pacific Coast, not the South, was the true colonial outlier. The interior West, Phoenix included, had much in common with the supposedly exceptional South. The entire periphery lacked the capital to nurture hometown entrepreneurs, relied on a both fixed and migratory workforce isolated, largely as a function of race, from the nation's labor pool, and struggled to attract the technicians, engineers, and tinkers who fine-tuned American assembly lines. Both sections had little manufacturing, which dictated that fluctuating commodity prices largely determined sectional economic fortunes. The South was almost uniformly monocultural. Cotton, sugar, rice, or tobacco dominated whole stretches of this region's landscape, whereas ranching, mining, farming, and tourism structured the economies of the western states. Economic elites, whether absentee owners or old-line agricultural dynasties, controlled state politics through state constitutional provisions that replicated federal electoral constraints on direct elections and popular democracy. These colonial hierarchies were structured around race, class, and gender. In the South, an increasingly rigid Jim Crow order sustained a social and economic caste system that kept African Americans at society's lowest rung but also stopped poor whites and the small class of urban professionals and shop owners from challenging the rule of the New South's plantation and small industrial elite. A fixed biracial framework did not define the multiracial West, where homesteading, and success, along with Protestant familial norms, dictated whether ethnic whites or Mexicans would be considered fully white and American.[5]

Phoenix's Four C's

Interwar Arizona, vast in size but small in population, was unquestionably a colony along these lines. The four C's, cattle, copper, cotton, and climate, structured the state's economy, which effectively placed the land and its people in a form of servitude to outside commercial cities. This subordination retarded large-scale development and individual opportunity. Natural pastures and mild winters, ecosystems visually at odds with Arizona's famous deserts, supported central Arizona's livestock industry. Meat packing was nonetheless limited: most cows were either killed in the state and shipped in refrigerated trucks to California or sent alive by rail or truck to West Coast stockyards. Southern Arizona mining outfits extracted virtually every sort of metal, precious or base, with the notable exception of tin. Copper still ruled supreme. One historian labeled the small mining communities of Morenci, Jerome, Ajo, and Bisbee "isolated, mercantilistic colonies." This descriptor captured the power and influence operators had over miners, families, and towns. Few individuals could afford the costs and risks, both personal and financial, of starting and maintaining these operations, which left executives to direct extraction from far outside the West.[6]

Copper was big business. Industrialization generated an inexorable need for American copper, whose sales far outstripped those of gold between 1896 and the early 1930s (when economic paralysis curtailed demand). Arizona led the nation in copper extraction after 1907, contributing about one-third of the country's supply. But the industry provided little return for most Arizonans, including Phoenicians. Money flowed into the city's banks during flush periods, but local agricultural harvests still added more to the central Arizona economy than the few local foundries or the large southern Arizona mining firms. Mine owners had real influence over Phoenix via the state legislature, where representatives from southern districts formed a dedicated bloc to protect their shareholders and profit margins.[7]

Copper tycoons' power dramatized the nature of colonial servitude. Phelps, Dodge and Company, much like the South's textile enterprises, directed profits away from company towns but still maintained a tight grip on these communities, and these metal magnates played a heavy hand in Ari-

Figure 1. Aerial view of Phoenix circa 1920. Courtesy of the Arizona Historical Foundation, Subject Photograph Collection, folder 8, box 59.

zona's legislature and other western state assemblies, just as planters dominated many southern governments. Mining interests did have good reason to concern themselves with Arizona politics: even before the 1930s, these copper executives faced numerous legislative attempts to tax profits, regulate prices, empower unions, and improve working conditions.[8]

These policy battles took place in the state Capitol building, whose famed copper dome towered over much of downtown Phoenix. Arizona's capital had very much remained a laggard frontier town. Salt Lake City, Spokane, Denver, Omaha, and Topeka all had grown more rapidly and developed more industry before 1920. Indeed, Phoenix had not really risen above other Arizona communities in stature, wealth, or population. Rival Tucson predated Phoenix and had more established connections with the mining towns in the state's southern rim. In 1910, a mineral boom brought so many workers to two of the largest camps, Bisbee and Douglas, that their combined population exceeded the numbers living in the entire Salt River Valley.[9]

Phoenix's sluggish growth dramatized the ways in which climate and cotton, not copper or cattle, dominated the town's pre–World War II economy. Dry, mild winters made Phoenix a major destination for those with tuberculosis and other respiratory ailments. In the 1910s, Phoenicians proclaimed their home "the healthiest city in the known world." The health care industry expanded more during the next decade. Four institutions served visitors with lung diseases during the 1920s. The sick who could not afford treatment also flocked to Phoenix. Resident Elizabeth Beatty remembered "scattered tents and unpainted shacks, most of them floorless. In each was a sick person living alone or with other members of the family. In several cases, more than one member of the family was ill with tuberculosis." Thus locals usually embraced vacationers far more than they welcomed the sick. Writer Goldie Weisberg complained that the latter "were often just remittance men living in sanitariums," who were much less desirable than "the elderly gentlemen who like to play golf all year round . . . and . . . the ladies of all ages who like to applaud them."[10]

America's leisure class did rest and relax in Phoenix, especially when transportation options increased in the 1920s. Four new hotels opened in this decade: the San Carlos, the Jokake Inn, the Westward Ho Hotel, and the Arizona Biltmore. These retreats were impressive but still monuments to the town's colonial status. The Biltmore, part of the Bowman-Biltmore chain, was an immediate success when it opened in 1929. The property's six hundred acres included an inn, a golf course, and private residences. Even Chicago Cubs' owner William Wrigley Jr. became enamored with the area. He invested almost $2 million and also built a new private getaway for himself nearby. His home attracted other wealthy midwestern snowbirds, who also constructed vacation houses in the Salt River Valley and migrated in and out with the seasons, turning Phoenix into a winter destination for a significant slice of the nation's industrial elite.[11]

Agriculture, the most important facet of the Valley's narrow economy, also exemplified the dynamic between the imperial manufacturing centers and their multivariate hinterlands. A journalist called the Valley "the agricultural center of Arizona; and one of the most productive portions of our country." The "250,000, acres of fertile land from the desert," he declared in 1919, "mean production, profit, and contented life." Harvests yielded a bounty for export and local use: farmers cultivated 675,000 tons of alfalfa in the 1910s, 75 percent of which was consumed locally by residents who combined it with other grains or by ranchers who used it to fatten their cows and sheep during the winter. Milk cows, ostriches, turkeys, and chickens also ate cured green alfalfa so that they could produce dairy products and feathers for local and outside consumption.[12]

But everything depended on water. "The farmers dream of making a Utopia of the Salt River valley," the superintendent of local water projects explained, "and look to electric power to furnish them with the cooling breezes of the electric fan, and the comforts of electric lights . . . and many other electric devices." The national government played a heavy role in watering the state. Yet federal programs to build the necessary dams, canals, and reservoirs needed to reclaim the desert actually contributed to the rise of outsider-controlled agribusiness. Although, for example, the 1902 Newlands Act had been intended to benefit small farmers who moved west to homestead, these yeomen lacked the capital to invest in the vast water projects required to make the desert bloom. Homesteaders had long struggled to reap the benefits of the arid environment's mild winters, which forced them to sell their parcels to absentee owners. This ownership pattern made Maricopa County and Phoenix ineligible for federal funds. Forty-nine landowners, both large and small, subsequently formed the Salt River Valley Water Users' Association (SRVWUA) in 1903 to work around these restrictions and bring much needed water to the area. Stockowners, who operated out of Phoenix, worked with federal officials to make plans, draft repayment schedules, and distribute water. Their early efforts culminated in the construction of the Roosevelt Dam, which irrigated 250,000 acres by 1911.[13]

Water went largely to fields of cotton, a crop that exemplified the pitfalls of the limited colonial economy. World War I had created an enormous new market for Arizona yields because manufacturers, now unable to secure Egyptian harvests, needed high-quality Pima cotton. Fine, long strands were very durable and useful for textiles, yarn, and thread but also for tires, hot air balloons, and airplane wings. Cotton transformed central Arizona. Some 2,200 regular employees and countless seasonal pickers lived in company towns. Cotton grew on 75 percent of all farmland by 1920, displacing vegetable and fruit production as well as the local dairy industry, where the number of cows fell from eighty thousand in 1917 to just nine thousand by the start of 1921.[14]

Opportunity also attracted outside investors, who only increased the area's dependence on cotton. Indeed, the Goodyear Tire and Rubber Corporation's arrival epitomized how the frontier's exoticism and potential drew industrialists into the region, which they then exploited. "The desert, in the Biblical phrase, blossomed like the rose," Goodyear executive Paul Litchfield enthused once he saw how water transformed land "blanketed everywhere with sagebrush and greasewood, the twisted rope that is mesquite, the glistening paloverde." His firm made ready use of the Valley's cotton yields to fulfill military supply contracts. The company not only placed orders with

Figure 2. King cotton never reigned over Arizona as it did in large sections of the South, but the Pima variety still played a vital role in the Valley of the Sun's economy. Acres were dedicated to its cultivation, Goodyear built company towns, and many residents found work in fields and cotton gins in the late 1910s. Courtesy of the Arizona Historical Foundation, Subject Photograph Collection, folder 1 of 5 (4993, N4232), box 26.

local farmers but also leased land around Phoenix, in parts later known as Litchfield and Goodyear, to cultivate crops and to build gins and cottonseed oil mills. Litchfield bought himself a large parcel in the 1920s, when he built a house to stay in when his business interests gave him an excuse to leave Goodyear's Ohio headquarters.[15]

The ill effects of the cash crop had been realized by then. Peace effectively destroyed the cotton economy because demand fell sharply when the need for uniforms, tires, and airplanes dissipated. Egyptian cotton also flooded the market and drove prices down to about 28 cents per pound, less than half of the cost of production in the Salt River Valley. The Arizona Cotton Growers Association responded by lobbying Congress for a tariff on imported cotton, organizing farmers to hold firm at a specific price point, and sitting on their stock until the price rose. Farmers nonetheless failed to liquidate the 92,861 bales produced in 1920 for several years.[16]

Valley agriculture rebounded in the mid-1920s. Local bankers, with money from Los Angeles lenders, offered special loans with low-interest rates to farmers who agreed to plant anything but cotton. Farming groups also drove diversification. A reorganized Arizona Pima Cotton Growers Association reached a consensus in 1921 to plant just eighty thousand acres and only sell from their existing stock. Members also promoted use of Arizona cotton among home sewers in the area and advertised their surplus to textile mills outside the state. Growers, who had survived the cotton bust, turned their lands into orchards, vineyards, vegetable patches, citrus groves, grain fields, and poultry farms. They also embraced short-staple cotton. Meal and hulls fed livestock, and fibers were woven into textiles.[17]

The crop thus never reigned over central Arizona in the way King Cotton ruled over much of the South. The boom was too short lived, and the Salt River Valley's soil and climate provided profitable alternatives to cotton. Mining and ranching had also remained powerful forces in politics, so cultivation did not replicate the South's cotton-focused political economy structured around a large, disenfranchised African American workforce and an elite caste of politically powerful plantation owners. Valley growers had instead depended on Mexican immigrants. Many migrant laborers had come under exceptions to the Immigration Act of 1917, which allowed entry for those with promises of employment. This first Bracero program served the war effort directly but still did little to upend the region's status quo: this migratory workforce was new to neither Phoenix nor the West.[18]

Yet such a labor regime was novel in the South. Planters had largely made use of a standing pool of poor black and white laborers. A permanent contingent of southern migrant field hands began to form during World War I. Late nineteenth-century midwestern wheat and grain production had effectively pushed northeastern growers into truck farming, the production of fruits and vegetables for local markets. These yields needed to be handpicked. White ethnics, Italians in particular, had first worked these fields and orchards, but African Americans, who were unable to find industrial work during the Great Migration, also collected this bounty. Remuneration demands, general unrest, and labor shortages prompted owners to turn to local, state, and federal authorities to keep the workforce cheap, reliable, and plentiful. Policies included assigning farmworkers to fields, easing immigration from Canada and Mexico, and work-or-fight vagrancy laws, which legalized a coercion and intimidation directed mostly at people of color. The Everglades, only recently transformed to sustain large-scale agriculture, soon became the winter encampment for African American pickers. Migrants came to the area during the colder months, either from northern farms or Georgia cotton fields, and left to tend harvests elsewhere in the eastern United States when the Florida citrus season ended.[19]

Itinerant laborers rarely found employment in southern and southwestern factories. They certainly did not in Phoenix's small manufacturing sector, one largely structured around processing raw materials and meeting community demands. Roughly eleven hundred residents worked in the eighty establishments operating in 1937. Most businesses only served the local market. For example, the Tovrea Packing Company, Inc., exported just 30 percent of the meat it processed. There were three brick and tile manufacturers in the city, which largely provided the materials for the growing construction industry. The town's twenty-one small bakeries also fed Phoenicians from what local farms produced. Seasonal work could be found too in the air-conditioning and Venetian blind industry. Each summer, Phoenicians took jobs in the town's thirty firms that either made the parts for or assembled coolers.[20]

A few firms used Arizona's natural resources and bumper crops to meet regional and national demands. Ice was big business. Residents consumed only 20 percent of what was produced in Phoenix; the rest was shipped out with perishable products. Ice cooled, for example, the twelve thousand carloads of lettuce and four thousand carloads of cantaloupes that left Phoenix in 1939. The Desert Citrus Products Association used 20 percent of the grapefruit harvest for juice, which they shipped across the United States. The Arnold Pickle and Olive Company supplied other locales with bottled and preserved Valley produce. Local manufacturers also benefited from the state's extractive industry. Phoenix foundries made ready use of the metals mined in the surrounding areas. The Allison Steel Manufacturing Company, U.S. Pipe and Steel Company, and Goettel Brothers Sheet Metal Products Company stood out among the smaller outfits.[21]

Only a small percentage of Phoenix businesses had no connection to the four C's. One such industry was wholesaling. Phoenix's position between two major western cities, El Paso and Los Angeles, made it a natural stop along domestic trade routes. Barq's, Coca Cola, Dr. Pepper, Nehi, and Seven-Up all had bottling plants in the Phoenix area. There was also a distillery, the Arizona Brewing Company, and the Artisana Water Company, which bottled water. The N. Porter Saddle and Harness Company thrived on the rising fascination with the American West. Customers from Mexico, Canada, Europe, and the industrial United States prized the business's boots and saddles. Porter's fifty employees produced only about a hundred saddles a month.[22]

Boosters busied themselves guarding the pastoral qualities that attracted investors, tourists, and other consumers of western Americana. Local merchants founded the Chamber, briefly the Phoenix Board of Trade, in the territorial days to promote agriculture. The original bylaws pledged interest in "all matters regarding the welfare of the city of Phoenix and the county of Maricopa." "Talk Phoenix; write Phoenix; smile Phoenix; laugh Phoenix; praise Phoenix . . . enthuse over Phoenix . . . defend Phoenix; work for Phoenix and get your friends, enemies and neighbors to work also. Boost up loud, long and lively," one member demanded. The founders established just four committees (traffic, agriculture, membership, and information) to carry out their mission. Irrigation nonetheless dominated their agenda in the early years. Their first initiative was to circulate a federal petition to secure water storage facilities for cotton production. Later activities in the 1910s revolved around attracting farmers from the Midwest with assurances like "You can't lose when you put your money in dirt that yields all year round." Chamber members also kept tabs on the Valley's agricultural, mineral, and manufacturing output in order to distribute this information in promotional literature. Volunteers also politicked, to an extent at least, state and federal governments in order to protect Phoenix's farming interests.[23]

Promoters only tentatively pursued broadening the town's economic base. The Chamber, for example, initially ignored military pressure to build a permanent airfield after World War I. During the conflict, the army had to repurpose the local fairgrounds, a stopgap ill suited to defense needs. "The thing you people ought to boost now," an army commander explained to city business owners at the war's end, "is making this town a junction point for the airmail delivery service. Get the city to donate a field for the machines and build hangers . . . close to the city. Phoenix is the logical junction point for airplane service between El Paso and Los Angeles." Chamber men were not enthusiastic until the 1920 cotton crash put them in search of new developmental opportunities. Thus, when the army and the U.S. Postal Service made new overtures in 1923, members formed the temporary Municipal Airport Development Committee to assist officials in site selection.

Enthusiasts also worked with the Phoenix Realty Board to persuade the city council to buy the chosen spot in 1924. A year later, the Phoenix Municipal Airport began operations, already the largest airfield in the sparsely populated territory between Texas and California.[24]

These and other small interwar initiatives did somewhat increase the Chamber's activity and professionalism. Members searched for outside markets for Valley crops, which spurred a transportation improvement effort, such as the special Highway Committee's commitment to secure roads between Phoenix and every Arizona county seat. The workgroup also lobbied for federal funds to construct a highway to aid distributors. The new routes obtained subsequently increased the flow of pleasure- and health-seeking tourists. The Chamber, along with other local organizations, poured money into late 1920s advertisements to attract these vacationers to "the winter playground of the Southwest," "where winter never comes." Travelers supported the retailers, who used the association's resources to promote Phoenix as a shopping center. They wanted to attract customers from both Arizona and beyond and thus urged Valley locals, "Throw Away Your Mail Order Catalogue And Come To Phoenix." Merchants also sponsored campaigns, in concert with other organizations around the state, to encourage residents to "Use Arizona Products" or "Trade At Home." The Chamber also sporadically released the *Phoenix Gold Bond*, a helpful but barebones recitation of population figures, property assessments, freight rates, taxes, banking deposits, water projects, and crop reports.[25]

The Chamber nonetheless remained steadfastly provincial in these years. In 1925, just twenty-one men sat on its board of directors. A travel writer noted that "the staff consisted of no more than a half-dozen people, full and part-time, the budget was infinitesimal and Phoenix was pictured as a town attractive to dudes in love with the legend of the cowboy, health-seekers, and tourists who might desire relief from a harsh Eastern winter." Members in fact finally formed a fifth permanent committee in 1926. The team oversaw the "Valley Beautiful Movement," another limited tourism venture that simply urged resident to "grow grass and plant flowers," make Phoenix "the city of trees," and "Do Away With the Desert." Yet promoters still held onto the frontier ideal in this period, much to the frustration of their successors, one of whom complained that he "could hardly believe my eyes when I saw what was being sent out! Pictures showing Phoenicians in beards"—and not the modern clean-cut growths either; they were scraggly and reminiscent of the worst stereotypes of prospectors and down-on-their-luck miners.[26]

Colonial Color Lines

Booker T. Washington looked past these rustic qualities when he proclaimed Phoenix a model city in 1911. "Any one who has traveled thru [*sic*] this desert country, with its red mountains and yellow plains, has been imprest [*sic*] with the violent contrasts in the colors of the landscape," he wrote after his visit. "I was even more imprest [*sic*]," he added, "with the variety and contrasts in the colors of the different elements of the population." Phoenicians, in and around the city, fascinated him: a white, female hotelier relied on a local Chinese eatery to fulfill room service orders; Chinese restaurateurs anchored a vibrant Chinatown alongside a bevy of merchants; wealthy denizens hired Japanese servants and cooks, who also made a living selling produce out of trucks at the city's edge; a few African Americans owned farms, laundries, real estate firms, cafes, and barber shops, with Mexican Americans staffing some of these establishments, though many migrated in and out of Phoenix to work in mines or agricultural fields. "There are a greater variety of races and people who are struggling up out of a primitive and backward condition than in any other part of the United States," Washington surmised, "each race has been given all the opportunities that have been granted to the others."[27]

Washington's account was seductive but also flawed: the town was no pluralist Eden. Railroad tracks sectioned off the wealthier, predominantly Anglo, north side, which one reporter deemed "a hermetically sealed environment that prevented or retarded contact with the poor." A few pioneer families and newcomers, primarily from the Midwest, formed Phoenix's interwar elite. They interacted in long-established social and service organizations, including the Rotary, Kiwanis, and Lions clubs as well as the Chamber and the Phoenix Country Club. Transplants largely made their fortunes in the niche markets that sporadic growth established. George Mickle, for example, had recognized a need for neighborhood groceries when he arrived in the early 1910s. Pay 'n' Takit was the state's largest chain when he sold it to Safeway Stores in 1927. Mickle then invested sale profits in new ventures, including the Phoenix Title and Trust Company and one of the city's first skyscrapers. Other old-line and newly arrived entrepreneurs joined him in reshaping the Phoenix skyline with more towering buildings, which, by extension, made the downtown area a center for shopping, banking, and service. The well-to-do also established tony neighborhoods, including Country Club Estates, which surrounded its namesake's clubhouse, during this period.[28]

The women living in these exclusive, white enclaves were very much a part of the town's social fabric. The arts flourished because of their work. The Phoenix Women's Club, for example, organized drama, art, and literature classes for themselves and others. The organization's offshoot, the Phoenix Fine Arts Association, planned state fair exhibits, sponsored exhibits and lectures, and endeavored to build a gallery. Yet the Valley's ladies had far more pressing concerns than leisure. City services appalled them. They worked to better schools, juvenile services, and prisons. Prohibition and prostitution controversies also brought them into local and state politics, either to pass laws limiting liquor and vice or to ensure their enforcement.[29]

Many of these efforts reflected white, Progressive Era aspirations to tame the inner cities, where the immigrant and minority working classes lived. Phoenix's Anglo-run and -funded Friendly House, for example, was modeled after the Steelbelt settlement houses that had been run to "Americanize" new arrivals. Phoenicians had left this task to schools and churches before 1920, the year local principal Grace Court urged the Phoenix Americanization Committee to create a space that would offer vocational, homemaking, civics, and English classes as well as recreational activities to Spanish-speaking residents. "If Mexicans could be made to feel this was their home," she hoped, "greater results could be obtained along Americanization lines." The first director of Friendly House was an Anglo woman, who taught classes but also planned celebrations of Mexican holidays. The second director, Placida García Smith, had received a degree from Colorado State Teachers College and taken graduate classes in sociology at the University of California, Berkeley. This member of Phoenix's Mexican American middle class resided, like the institution's Anglo board members, north of the railroad tracks. She did not deviate from Friendly House's original mission; in classes, she stressed embracing American citizenship. "My name is Placida Smith," she always began, "a good American name and a good Mexican name."[30]

Even though Friendly House was just across the tracks from its sponsors' homes, it was in many ways a world away. Phoenix's working-class

Anglos and residents of Chinese, Japanese, Native American, Mexican, and African ancestry lived in this south side, often referred to as south Phoenix, though it is easy to confuse the area with poor, heavily non-Anglo South Phoenix, which was only annexed to, and hence incorporated into, Phoenix in 1960. Most denizens toiled in nearby fields, only returning to the city when the fitful agricultural economy no longer provided jobs. A handful of the more affluent citizens in the south Phoenix area ran businesses, including groceries and restaurants, for their less well-off brethren. All offered descriptions of Phoenix racism at odds with Washington's admiring account. "Phoenix," an affluent black mortician declared, "was unquestionably the Mississippi of the West." "The difference was that they didn't lynch you," one long-time resident explained.[31]

Opportunity, despite Washington's claims, was limited, even if Spanish-speaking residents found employment in all economic sectors of the city and the county. Though Anglos had formally founded Phoenix, residents of Spanish and Mexican descent had worked on farms or helped construct city buildings and basic infrastructure projects since territorial days. By 1911, the barrio stretched from the railroad tracks south to the Salt River. The enclave later expanded and then bifurcated into two neighborhoods. Reports still deemed the entire area, even sections with better homes, a "foul slum, the like of which can probably not be found elsewhere in the United States." During the interwar years, population density fluctuated alongside commodity prices. The catastrophic collapse of the cotton and mining industries in 1921, for example, stood behind concerted efforts to repatriate Mexican nationals and Mexican Americans. Many refused to leave Phoenix, a deportation center. Hundreds encamped along the canals, roads, and railway tracks that led into the town. They took whatever jobs they could find and returned to mines and farms when the economy rebounded.[32]

Asian residents also had limited avenues for advancement. Phoenix's Japanese denizens worked, primarily, in local agriculture. Arizona's 1917 Alien Land Act barred them from "acquir[ing], possess[ing], enjoy[ing], transmit[ing], and inherit[ing] real property or interest therein." Despite the law, the number of Japanese-run farms grew from sixty-nine (3,537 cultivated acres) in 1920 to 121 (16,237 cultivated acres) by 1930. In contrast, the majority of the Chinese population, which grew from 110 in 1910 to 227 by 1930, worked in the city. There was a small Chinatown in the south side, which included a handful of restaurants, stores, and laundries. Men reportedly gathered to gamble and smoke opium in the austere temple and community center. Some worked as domestics or took odd jobs. The more affluent Chinese owned and operated local businesses, which employed other Chinese residents. Shop owners offered cutthroat prices, which generated little profit, and worked grueling hours in order to compete with Anglo merchants. "Stores were opened almost twenty-four hours a day and seven days a week," one historian noted. "They worked industriously and lived in the most inexpensive way. It was quite common among them to live in the back of the store and sleep over a wooden board bed with one meal a day."[33]

But Native Americans barely subsisted. Like elsewhere in the greater West, they sold souvenirs to tourists, a practice that boosters often supported as a means to charm visitors. A 1923 federal program also brought Native peoples into the city in order to work in agricultural fields. One report explained that this project reflected "the strong hope of white people of this particular section that the Indians will displace alien Mexicans as the permanent resident labor supply for agriculture and industry."[34]

Race, commodities, and manufacturing were hence key considerations for Arizonans consumed by one of the interwar period's most divisive issues: labor. Many residents wanted to inscribe protections for unions and restrictions on management in Arizona's constitution. Unionists, progressive Democrats, former Socialists, small farmers, members of Arizona's tiny Labor Party, and a few moderates also united behind direct democracy proposals in order to curb the power of the corporations that dominated the mining, ranching, and agricultural sectors. As a result, the 1912 state constitution actually mandated employer liability, workmen's compensation, and elections for mine inspectors but also prohibited corporations from employing private police forces or using "freedom from self-incrimination" to keep their books closed. Progressives also managed to insert constitutional provisions for ballot initiatives and recalls. The labor movement made particular use of the referendum clause after Congress approved the document: in 1914 voters passed union-backed measures that made blacklisting illegal and stipulated that American citizens had to account for 80 percent of a business's workforce, at least for firms with a staff greater than five. Legislators also intervened to make strikes more effective. A 1913 law banned "injunctions" against strikes and picketing unless needed "to prevent irreparable injury to property." The bill protected workers' rights to assemble, receive strike benefits, patrol peacefully, strike, and participate in and call for secondary boycotts as long as workers' activities were not violent and did not damage private property. The U.S. Supreme Court declared this legislation and the foreign worker limitation unconstitutional in 1915 and 1921, respectively. Both decisions were well in line with the jurisprudence that hamstrung labor law reform before the New Deal. In Arizona, the rulings had the additional effective of curtailing such policy experimentation throughout the 1920s.[35]

The Court's edicts thrilled Arizona businessmen, many of whom considered the interwar era union movement illegitimate. The most disdainful had instigated the legal suits in the 1910s that eviscerated the progressive laws and constitutional provisions enacted after Arizona achieved statehood. Mine owners took the conflict into company towns. In 1917, Phelps Dodge Corporation managers deported more than a thousand hard rock miners and their families, many of whom had connections to the syndicalist Industrial Workers of the World, from Bisbee and other southern Arizona copper outposts in 1917. The nationwide impulse to limit union power and security through contract clauses animated much of this anti-unionism, particularly the strain found in Phoenix and its surrounding fields. In 1919, the Chamber, along with other Anglo, elite agricultural, commerce, and civic associations, publicly declared their opposition to contractual agreements that forced management to hire only union members. "We believe," a businessman asserted in the local press, "that the closed shop . . . is fundamentally in opposition to the best interests of the city, such a closed shop . . . curtails competition, develops ill-will, puts on inefficiency, stands for coercion, is against American freedom, and is a usurpation of American rights." From now forward, they maintained, the Valley would be an "open shop."[36]

Yet disagreements over this Labor Question were not distinguishable by party affiliation. Before 1950, voters had elected a GOP governor only in 1916, 1918, 1920, and 1928 and had never sent a Republican to the U.S. House of Representatives. Divisions were instead between the poor and the wealthy, the urban and the rural, and the statist and the antistatist.[37]

Such conflicts fractured the Arizona Republican Party in the 1910s. Progressive Republicans, who embraced Theodore Roosevelt and his New Nationalism, decried those who looked to William H. Taft and his programs of minimal regulation and restraint. The former found common cause with a minority of the state's Democrats, who considered themselves progressives and championed Woodrow Wilson. Yet most Arizona Democrats had not embraced Wilson's tepid liberalism, nor would they champion the economic and social philosophies undergirding the New Deal wing of the mid-century Democratic Party. For example, Barry Goldwater's uncle, Morris, was a self-proclaimed Jeffersonian Democrat, who founded the state's party but also instilled in his nephew steadfast political support for small government and a free market.[38]

The breakdown of the Arizona legislature exemplified these divisions. Representatives divided themselves between "majority" and "minority" blocs, but these terms did not refer to the state's two political parties, which caucused separately. Instead, what Arizonans called "Jeffersonian," "conservative," or "pinto" Democrats made up the "majority," often dismissed as the mouthpieces of the railroad barons, mine operators, utility company owners, bankers, wealthy farmers, and moneyed ranchers. The oppositional faction, in whose ranks were found the latter-day New Dealers, supported labor and mostly hailed from Tucson and Phoenix. The real fights in the legislature, then, were among Democrats. Republican representatives were few and far between and generally joined these coalitions in order to end stalemates.[39]

Colonial Economies

Though Arizona was far removed, physically and developmentally, from the North and the Midwest, the schisms within the state's politics mirrored the political divides and reconfigurations within the industrial core. From the Reconstruction Era through the Great Depression, a transformation of the American economy, from proprietary to corporate capitalism, generated much debate and forced a realignment of the major parties. In the South and Southwest, a similar set of conflicts engulfed the electorate. Realignment was nevertheless forestalled because outside investors and landed elites exercised enormous power over party apparatuses and voting booths. Moreover, citizens tended to vote for a party out of habit or tradition. They also had little choice: one-party rule was common in both the South and the West during this extended colonial era. Southern states were Democratic, of course, but western states, such as Republican Utah and Democratically inclined New Mexico, also tended to have a one-party tradition that persisted well into the Cold War era.[40]

This similarity underscores how much in common Phoenix and Arizona had with the rest of the American periphery. Narrow economic bases structured much of the South and Southwest. As a result, there was little individual opportunity and much economic volatility. Some residents accepted this status quo, others had just a passing interest in pursuing investment, and precious few desired the kind of manufacturing establishments that would divorce communities from commodity markets. Southern planters, by and large, feared new factories not dependent on their crops because such enterprises might offer wages high enough to rob them of their cheap, desperate labor force and undermine the Jim Crow hierarchy that structured southern politics and economic life. An Alabama senator, for example, told Congressmen that the New South's nascent coal and iron industry represented "more a curse than a blessing." "If industry . . . is to draw the labor from the cotton plantations continually by added temptations," he warned in the midst of Birmingham's postbellum growth, "I do not see how we are to conduct our great agricultural enterprises." Alabama agriculturalists also proved cool toward the city's development: Black Belt newspapers criticized "the railroads which penetrate the best cotton lands," the meager investment returns, and the low wages that did not allow workers "to live decently." Such hostility served to limit small-town promotional campaigns in the plantation belt, whereas shop owners and professionals in small towns in the Piedmont, upper South, and Gulf Coast areas did embrace new ventures, competing at a fever pitch for textile mills, lumber yards, and rubber plants. Goodyear, for example, opened a facility in Gadsden, a lucrative investment in a blighted Alabama hamlet as desperate as Phoenix, where Paul Litchfield was simultaneously expanding the firm's operations. Most of these interwar ventures offered low-skill work in repressive company-town conditions, which many Southerners still considered to be a form of salvation for the white working class.[41]

In contrast, large southern cities were primarily trading outposts. Atlanta, Charlotte, Memphis, and Miami, for example, survived largely on the flow of raw materials from the southern interior to the North and the finished goods that traveled back along these same trade routes. Atlanta's $340 million trading economy dwarfed its $41 million production sector in 1910. The urban South's small manufacturing sector had grown because boosters there, unlike their Phoenix counterparts, had actively sought a diversified economic base. Miami promoters' efforts stood out in this period. They declared the Chamber's 1907 incorporation for "the upbuilding [*sic*] of the City of Miami, the advancing of her financial interests, the establishment of factories, mills and enterprises of benefit to the community at large." Leaders also turned, like their southwestern contemporaries, to the federal government for help constructing the infrastructure upon which commerce depended. Miamians lobbied for the 1925 Federal Rivers and Harbors Act to provide funding for a South Florida harbor that would facilitate trade with Latin America. Their Charlotte counterparts had already made the Queen City the financial center of the Carolinas' textile and agricultural economy. A Good Roads Movement placed the town at the center of interconnecting highways, while bankers simultaneously consolidated operations, pushed mill men to deposit profits in their institutions (not Steelbelt financial houses), and convinced Federal Reserve officials to place one of the regional banks in Charlotte. Atlanta businessmen were also innovative, persistent boosters. Their sophisticated bulletin was a far cry from the *Phoenix Gold Bond*'s stark statistical tables. The *City Builder* included photographs, stories on various Atlanta events, commentaries on local and federal laws, analyses of rival business associations' initiatives, and reports on Chamber activities and goals, which included a new publicity bureau and trade "opportunity with the Orient."[42]

This interwar boosterism nonetheless failed to liberate the region. Factories merely supplemented the agricultural economy and thus protected the plantation elite from challenges to their power. Northern industrialists also had little quarrel with much of southern society, particularly planter hostility to regulation, taxation, and labor organizing, which kept the region's political-economic structure distinct from, yet in service to, the corporate manufacturing economy anchored in the Northeast and Midwest. Industrialists also resisted operating factories that needed skilled workers, whose power to negotiate higher pay could negate the benefits of the low-skill, low-wage South. As a result, few African Americans worked in these mills, which protected the region's rigid caste system. The planter class also stood firm against intensive industry that required a large, specialized workforce. They, and other white Southerners, had little interest in giving African Americans access to permanent well-paying jobs that would take them out of the fields and homes of white Southerners. Urban boosters also took no issue with the preservation of the region's racial order. The Atlanta Chamber, for example, emphasized that its interwar "Atlanta spirit" factory-recruitment campaign did not inherently challenge southern mores. Even the Memphis Ku Klux Klan shared this view and thus had no qualms about including a promise for a "Bigger and Better Memphis" in their 1923 political work.[43]

Promotional efforts in the Southwest likewise varied in scale and scope. Austin's Chamber actually opposed industrial investment throughout the interwar period, whereas El Paso, Albuquerque, and Tucson boosters tended to dedicate most of their resources just to attracting tourists and health seekers. The Tucson Sunshine Climate Club, a consortium of four hundred businesses and civic activists, raised $250,000 to promote the city in *Life, Outlook, National Geographic, Saturday Evening Post, Vanity Fair,* and *Vogue.* In their ads, boosters mentioned the warm winters, San Xavier del Bac Mission, and the Temple of Music and Art. El Paso businessmen trumpeted their place on the border and promised visitors easy and safe passage to Mexico. Albuquerque, Tucson, and El Paso, like Phoenix, thus remained relatively bound to the Southwest's traditional economies. Albuquerque was a central railroad hub; Tucson's fortunes rested on the fate of southern Arizona's copper mines; and El Paso was a distribution point for cattle, oil, copper, and other minerals.[44]

California boosters were the exception. They built centers of production and defense that placed southwestern outposts in the urban Pacific Coast's hinterland. San Diego, Los Angeles, and San Francisco all benefited from Washington's early twentieth-century determination to make the United States a naval power in the Pacific. The Spanish-American War and the conflict in the Philippines effectively dramatized the importance of the West Coast for national security. But coastal Californians also saw the potential for trade. They therefore demanded the federal government maintain a large navy after World War I and lobbied feverishly to secure the requisite military installations. Still, the Golden State was only militarized through the concerted efforts of Chambers of Commerce, naval and military affairs committees, and city officials who worked to convince residents that constructing fortress cities would prove lucrative. Business associations were key to urban California's industrialization. San Francisco elites, for their part, secured defense dollars and votes for prospective military outposts, whereas Los Angeles boosters turned their attention to aircraft in the 1930s. The Chamber's Aviation Department even worked with the editors of the *Los Angeles Times* to win public approval of the military's plans to build airfields in the area.[45]

Such competition drove the San Diego Chamber's wholesale transformation. The association pushed for railroad connections to the East, fought for Boulder Dam project waters, and employed city planners to control development. The scope of its operations far surpassed its Phoenix counterpart's activities. San Diegans started committees for business development, tourism, governance, legislation, taxation, safety, water, education, civic work, conservation, membership, research, publicity, foreign trade, agriculture, military investment, and industrialization, which even included an aviation subgroup. By the late 1920s, boosters courted baseball teams, assisted new investors, and publicized the virtues of their city throughout California and Arizona.[46]

The carloads of Phoenix cattle and crops sent to San Diego and other expanding West Coast port cities only dramatized the extent to which the Salt River Valley served urban California. Statehood simply had not provided the kind of credit, infrastructure, and labor pool that substantial manufacturing required. Yet Arizona and its capital were typical of the underdevelopment characteristic of the subtropical regions that would one day be dubbed the American Sunbelt. The pitfalls inherent in reliance on commodities, like Arizona's famed four C's, had long been evident, and the coming of the Great Depression only made them more apparent. Arizona cotton production was halved, and state cattle prices dropped from $43.50 to $10 a head between 1929 and 1932. The copper industry's disintegration had a ripple effect across the state: banks folded, 80 percent of miners were unemployed, the railroads laid off thousands, and the Phoenix and Tucson construction sectors collapsed, exacerbating the hellish conditions banker George Leonard encountered when he first arrived in the capital. Twenty percent of Arizona families, double the national figure, were on public assistance in 1933. When Arizona's corporation commissioner reflected on this devastation just a few years later, he could see but one cause: this "colony of Eastern interests" had for too long been enslaved by a "raw material economy."[47]

Chapter 2

Contested Recovery

Journalist Lorena Hickok's 1934 trip to investigate the Depression's effects on Arizona and its capital left her skeptical that either could recover. "So much for private industry's prospects for providing jobs for people," she scoffed in her letters to Roosevelt adviser Harry Hopkins. "If the mines are running, the state is prosperous, and everybody has work. If they aren't, the state is in bad shape, and there aren't any jobs. That's about the situation." But Hickok doubted liberals could provide Arizonans with a New Deal. "It's the same old story down here," she lamented. For white-collar people, "with white standards of living," relief levels were "anything but adequate," whereas, she confided, "Mexicans—or, East of the Mississippi, Negroes [were] . . . [a]ble, many of them, to get work, but at wages so low that they are better off on relief." "I've encountered it everywhere I've been on this trip: Alabama, Texas, Louisiana, New Mexico," she wrote, "in the whole Southern half of the United States you will find this to be the big relief problem today." "The work that is offered them pays darned little . . . it's practically peonage," she admitted, "but it's all they've ever known, and I doubt if the Relief administration is financially in a position to battle low wage scales all over the South and Southwest."[1]

Hickok's judgment encapsulated the political and social challenges facing those New Dealers who sought to transform Arizona and the rest of the impoverished periphery. Many liberals considered the Southwest to represent as much of a colonial quagmire as the South, which FDR singled out as "the Nation's No. 1 economic problem" in the National Emergency Council's famous 1938 report on the region. Stagnation, disenfranchisement, and unrest prompted Washington-based liberal policymakers to experiment with relief programs, construction projects, and reform measures (the policies that Hickok described in her correspondence) to guide these hinterlands' recovery, reconstruction, and growth. But many fought wholesale reclamation, including congressmen, high-ranking businessmen, and even industry-minded bureaucrats within the Roosevelt administration, who fiercely objected to programs intended to end peripheral economic servitude.[2]

Top-Down Reclamation

Overall, New Dealers did the most to fully reconstruct the country's industrial heartland. Although the Public Works Administration (PWA) spent money in all but three U.S. counties, the majority of projects and the lion's share of allotments went to the Northeast and Midwest, where Roosevelt era reforms raised living standards and transformed into active citizens the immigrant ethnic workers whose marginality in factories and communities had been so manifest during previous decades. Across the Steelbelt, New Dealers and their trade union allies utilized a new legal framework to bring millions of workers into powerful, industry-wide trade unions, which inaugurated the most dramatic rise in working-class living standards in the twentieth century and created a moment for tripartite governance. This corporatist power-sharing arrangement gave, at the very least, unions a voice at the table when business managers and government officials framed wage, price, and regulatory guidelines for large sectors of the U.S. economy.[3]

Liberals were well aware that the South and Southwest also needed to be drastically reconstructed. National Resources Planning Board (NRPB) officials, those federal bureaucrats charged with studying and making policy recommendations for recovery and development, considered both regions to be servile colonies. "Income derived from national resources" in the Southwest, researchers lamented, "is . . . less than the value extracted." "Except for payroll," noted others, southern "manufacturing activity fails to enrich the region." Yet New Dealers were not chastened. David Lilienthal, head of the Tennessee Valley Authority (TVA), contended that a fundamental transformation of the South "*can be done*, that the fog, and the fears its shadowy shapes engender, will vanish." Likewise NRPB officials asserted that the Southwest had "the essentials for greater growth and progress—large natural resources, and the man-power, equipment, and ability for expanding industry and improving conditions for living."[4]

The New Deal did much to lay the groundwork for economic diversification. Southern states each received more than two hundred PWA projects, with Georgia standing out with 518. Texas, a state belonging to both the South and the Southwest, led both regions with 912 programs and $109 million in allotments, more than five times the amount spent in Georgia. California benefitted from 807 undertakings and $103 million in expenditures. But Texas and California were outliers. The PWA gave no interior southwestern state more than $12 million. Utah had 182 projects, Arizona received 122, New Mexico was awarded ninety-six, and Nevada obtained only forty-two.[5]

Arid-state initiatives took the form of the kind of infrastructure investment that New Dealers considered vital for immediate recovery and lasting prosperity. In Arizona, for example, the Works Progress Administration built twenty-four schools, made improvements to two hundred more, and laid more than seventeen hundred miles of road before 1939, more than three-quarters of which were in rural Arizona. Government money also paid for golf courses, parks, and clubhouses throughout the state. New Dealers offered direct relief to Native Americans but also poured money into improving farms, pastures, irrigation systems, and soil conditions on reservations. Federal dollars flowed into Phoenix as well. The Maricopa County Civil Works Board oversaw construction of bathhouses and swimming pools and funded curb repairs and landscaping projects. The Civil Works Administration also funded a major overhaul of Phoenix's airport, Sky Harbor. The county leased the facility from owners in order to qualify for $133,213 in federal loans, which bettered airfields and terminals.[6]

But success hinged on citizen participation. A genuine wellspring of southern liberalism and radicalism aided New Dealers. African American and white Southerners took the opportunity to serve in the administration and fight for racial justice. Others worked outside the confines of the federal government and its programs. Activists formed the interracial Southern Conference on Human Welfare in 1938, which stood out in its criticism of Jim Crow. White and black Communists challenged the National Association for the Advancement of Colored People (NAACP) to attend to the needs of sharecroppers and also organized workers for the new, militant Congress of Industrial Organizations.[7]

Such grassroots-federal partnerships seemed embedded within TVA, the most iconic, controversial symbol of the New Deal for the South. "We aren't just providing navigation and flood control and power," FDR explained.

"We are reclaiming land and human beings." TVA promised cheap, hydroelectric power, which liberals considered critical to economic growth and an improved standard of living. Rural areas, both in and outside the South, had long struggled to electrify, but private power companies simply had too much control over both power-generating technology and the distribution network to enable local governments to provide this basic public service. Liberals wanted TVA to function as a public competitor. Initial rates were nearly half the national average, which spurred municipal governments to apply for federal funds to build the transmission infrastructure needed for access.[8]

TVA's David Lilienthal considered these power lines a conduit for the social liberalism embedded within the New Deal. As he put it in his 1944 appraisal, *TVA: Democracy on the March*, "The physical achievements that science and technology now make possible *may bring no benefits*, may indeed be evil, unless they have a moral purpose, unless they are conceived and carried out for the benefit of the people themselves." His "grass roots" revolution depended on experts to balance the general social welfare with the interests of business and "the active daily participation of the people themselves" to protect their resources and check federal power. "To process the raw resources of nature is a major job of private industry," he submitted, which "cannot rest upon industry's good intentions alone. Private industries are rarely either in a position . . . to see specifically what is needed to protect the basic public interest." Lilienthal thus envisioned small farmers distributing expert-improved, federally funded fertilizers, community land-use associations determining equitable rental agreements for government property, and area cooperatives managing profits from the federal hydroelectric infrastructure. Lilienthal enthused that TVA represented a revolution in national and southern politics because it "settled" the conflict over public power: the common folk, engineering staff, and TVA workforce had triumphed. "Democracy is on the march in this valley," he crowed.[9]

Liberals never constructed a western TVA, but New Deal projects still provided the sizable investment that the West had needed to transcend its colonial status. Federally funded initiatives irrigated twenty million acres of land in the mountain and Great Basin states. Hoover Dam, begun before but finished early in the Roosevelt administration, harnessed the power of the Colorado River to divert water and power to Arizona, California, and Nevada. Federal loans also enabled Arizona towns to begin their own projects, including the Roosevelt Irrigation District near Buckeye and the Roosevelt

Water Conservation District near Mesa. Such undertakings increased regional settlement and farming opportunities in what a National Reclamation Association president declared to be "a new West—a bountiful dwelling place—using the natural resources of a pioneer empire."[10]

Power projects also raised the standard of living for both rural and urban Southwesterners. Though there was no western federal competitor, TVA had helped standardized prices. Providers of electric power reduced rates across the country to compete and to counter claims that more TVA-inspired programs were effective, necessary, or desirable. This maneuver actually generated record earnings for these power companies because lower prices increased consumption even though profit margins were smaller. Meanwhile many municipalities applied for federal moneys to build their own power plants. Such investment turned deserts into agricultural fields and brought electricity into Arizona homes. As in the South, cheap power represented a step toward southwestern economic independence because it provided the basis for the development of new industries to process raw materials into locally produced manufacturing goods. "After years of exuberant squandering," PWA director Harold Ickes enthused, "our people are insisting that our public lands, our forests, our water, our soil, our metals and minerals, our wildlife, and our natural recreational assets be used without waste."[11]

Southwestern liberals and radicals, like their southern equivalents, were also vital to the propaganda effort that put regional reconstruction on the nation's moral agenda. The Farm Security Administration, for example, funded Dorothea Lange's work. She consciously photographed workers of Mexican, Filipino, and Japanese descent alongside white Dustbowl migrants, her most famous subjects, to capture the economic exploitation, racism, and nativism that defined Golden State agribusiness. Social conditions in the fields feeding urban, coastal California also defined the work of lawyer Carey McWilliams. This leading member of the antifascist Left exposed the exploitative conditions on California's giant farms (his 1939 *Factories in the Fields* influenced more than one generation of reformers) but also fought anti-Semitism, nativism, and employer violence as the head of California's Division of Immigration and Housing. Class and racial democracy were foremost on McWilliams's mind when he openly declared in 1935 that California was "the state of the union which has advanced furthest toward an integrated fascist set-up."[12]

Not all arid-state capitalists were reactionaries, and liberals nurtured those who proved cooperative in efforts to reconstruct the region. Indeed, the industrialist whom journalists considered the "New Deal's favorite businessman" was Henry Kaiser, whose federally funded construction projects set a new standard for western development. The upstate New York native moved to the West Coast in 1906. His relationship with the federal government began in 1927, when his California-based paving outfit won a $20 million contract to build roads in Cuba. New Dealers rewarded his enthusiasm, compliance, and ingenuity throughout the 1930s. His firm played a major role in constructing the Hoover, Bonneville, and Grand Coulee dams, undertakings that necessitated accommodating his business practices to liberal reforms, most notably the 1935 Wagner Act. He continued to take federal funds and cooperate with New Dealers during World War II, when he started shipyards and other war production enterprises along the West Coast. Kaiser and his son also stood out during this period for their investment in employee medical care, which led to the creation of a revolutionary health care plan, Kaiser Permanente, in 1945.[13]

Financiers aided Kaiser and other builders. The region's standout bankers, even those residing in California's fortress cities, lobbied the federal government for financial and investment policies at odds with the practices that had frustrated industrialization and impeded recovery. Amadeo Peter Giannini, for example, allied himself with New Dealers eager to transform the Far West's economy. This child of Italian immigrants had not been born into the nation's business elite but still displayed a keen entrepreneurial spirit, which first helped him succeed in his San Francisco produce business and then build his bank into the nation's largest before his 1949 death. Giannini had inherited the Columbus Savings and Loan's directorship from his father-in-law in 1902 and quickly grew resentful of the institution's refusal to serve a broader clientele, particularly California's working class, who needed modest loans, and small farmers, who required credit between seasons. His Bank of Italy, later Bank of America, embraced this low-income demographic. The institution, founded in 1904, opened branches throughout the state to expand financial opportunities for Californians, while Giannini continued to make loans to large film, auto, oil, agriculture, and food-processing enterprises. This business model—a sort of unconscious Keynesianism—informed his support for Roosevelt. The financier identified with FDR's promise to the forgotten American, an oath embedded within Giannini's banking philosophy. Giannini accordingly endorsed federal infrastructure expenditures, measures to protect homeowners, price supports for farmers, and the 1933 and 1935 Banking Acts, which also aided his expansion plans. "There is something wrong with a system that lets 14,000,000 men get out of work," he explained to reporters. Such public declarations gave him powerful friends in Washington, including the Reconstruction Finance Corporation's Jesse Jones and the Federal Reserve Board's Marriner Eccles.[14]

Eccles played an outsized role within the Roosevelt administration. This liberal Utahan inherited his father's small banking empire in 1912 and then built a fortune by financing industry and agriculture. The Depression hit this Mormon's interests hard, forcing him to call in loans, lay off employees, and cut back on production and service. Such orthodox banking practices troubled him, eventually making him an outspoken critic of the "underconsumption" that he considered responsible for the economic crisis. Eccles embraced deficit spending, easy credit, and consumer purchasing power. Despite, or because of, the unpopularity of these views within financial circles, FDR made Eccles chairman of the Federal Reserve Board in 1934. Eccles spent his fourteen years at the Fed championing full employment initiatives, stabilized prices, and low interest rates. The New Dealer was not a monetarist but instead favored governmental planning, fiscal stimulus, and a highly regulated banking sector. This approach never won over a majority of his fellow bankers, but it did provide the cost assurances that made the federal government's huge borrowings politically palatable in the late 1930s and throughout the war years.[15]

The most controversial, influential Roosevelt administration financier was Texan Jesse Jones, who headed the Reconstruction Finance Corporation (RFC). His growing antagonism to the New Deal proved a bellwether of how broad segments of American businessmen would react to liberal-led infrastructure spending. The Tennessee native had moved to Texas in his twenties and then made his name in banking through his aggressive efforts to transform Houston from a struggling railroad hub, dependent on the cotton market, into a port city of global importance. His boosterism in the 1910s put him on par with Atlanta, Miami, and coastal California Chamber men. Jones and other Houston financiers and lawyers pursued a taxpayer-financed ship channel that, in Jones's words, would turn the city into "the inevitable gateway through which the products of this growing southern and western *empire* can best reach the markets of the world." Infrastructure improvements spawned a diverse, dynamic manufacturing base, which proved profitable to Jones and his compatriots. Financial success also made him well known, but party politics really gave him power. He saw the benefits of Texas's short-lived Guaranty Law, an indemnity policy similar to other state interwar programs and a precursor to federal deposit insurance. He threw his support to Democrats who embraced such plans, including William Jennings Bryan and Woodrow Wilson, whose election enhanced Jones's influence in Texas and in Washington. He thus already had the respect of Texas congressmen and the admiration of Hoover administration officials when he lobbied to direct the RFC. Many were also acutely aware that his bank had actually remained solvent after the 1929 crash.[16]

Jones was never a New Dealer. Still, the Roosevelt administration promoted him from board member to chairman in 1933. His largesse saved scores of banks and railroads and also funded hundreds of factories and thousands of infrastructure projects. But the "economic emperor of America," as one journalist dubbed Jones, ran the RFC with an iron fist and a commitment, unlike Eccles and Giannini, to the traditional banking principles that had retarded western development. Jones rejected projects that he considered risky, no matter who in Congress or in the federal bureaucracy lobbied him. He funneled much money to Texas but never considered the RFC a tool to develop the South and Southwest or a bureau to offer a overarching plan for industrialization. Yet he also condemned those executives who did not understand the need for federal financial regulation to police, stabilize, and establish consumer confidence in banking.[17]

Negotiating the New Deal

Jones's ability to impact the implementation of New Deal economic policy from within the administration coincided with constant opposition from outside the executive branch. Indeed, dissent, resistance, and antagonism always dogged liberals. A core group of about one hundred U.S. representatives and thirty-five senators, such as Virginia's Senator Carter Glass, always considered experimentation "an utterly dangerous effort of the federal government to transplant Hitlerism to every corner of the nation." Others resented that their colleagues seemed unwilling to challenge Roosevelt. "I am getting sick and tired, as a working member of this House, being led, so to speak, with a ring in my nose," fumed Franklin Hancock Jr. (D-NC), who had initially supported the administration. These early stalwarts often called themselves Jeffersonian Democrats. Though their power was negligible during Roosevelt's first years in office, they increasingly worked with intransigent Republicans to stymie continued reform and reject modern liberalism's economic agenda. "Some of these men might better be termed reactionaries, others moderates," a historian argued. "Many spoke the language of Social Darwinism; others were Burkean conservatives. Some were agrarian conservatives; others were spokesmen for urban business interests." By 1938, they had united in a congressional coalition opposed to liberals' domestic agenda, specifically the federal bureaucracy's growth, deficit spending, support of trade unionism, and the development of the modern welfare state, vital components of the interior's political-economic overhaul.[18]

The South, as Glass and Hancock illustrated, was also a crucible of antiliberal sentiment. A tenuously allied Democratic Party had triumphed in 1932 yet had not surmounted the entrenched divisions between the southern agrarian wing and the northeastern industrial wing. Both factions wanted to challenge unfettered capitalism and provide the South with economic aid, but planter-class Democrats still opposed reforms that would disrupt the southern racial hierarchy. These Southerners had the votes to influence policy: the number of non-southern Democrats in the House during the 1930s and 1940s fluctuated wildly—from 217 in 1937 to seventy-three in 1947—while the number of southern Democrats stayed at around 115. Only an implicit agreement that New Dealers not fundamentally reconstruct the South enabled them to transform the industrial core. Hence major labor and welfare initiatives, including the Wagner Act, the Social Security Act, and the Fair Labor Standards Act, excluded agricultural and domestic work, the sectors in which southern African Americans primarily labored.[19]

Liberal respect for the balance between local, state, and federal power also empowered southern critics to undermine New Deal directives. Even technocratic modernizers like Lilienthal often balked at fully centralized national aid programs, desiring instead significant, local influence. As a result, many wealthy whites, who retained their opposition to federal intervention and hostility toward the industry that threatened to upend Jim Crow, were left in charge of local relief and welfare programs in the South. In fact, the grassroots never oversaw TVA; management was instead ceded to the "grass tops," sociologist Philip Selznick's moniker for this local elite. The NAACP accordingly damned TVA as "Lily-white Reconstruction" because community representatives provided service to white communities first. Most African American TVA employees, moreover, worked in low-paid, unskilled positions. "The grass-roots policy is merely a rationalization," a staffer complained, "a distinction . . . must be drawn between 'institutional grass roots,' and a 'popular grass roots' which would be less concerned with the prerogatives of established leaders. Unfortunately, in practice, the TVA has chosen the former."[20]

The project also failed to end power politics. The program was nearly sacrosanct in the South, yet the public-competitor experiment faced continued, open opposition from utility CEOs and hostile Wall Street bankers who considered the initiative a dangerous overreach. TVA did force firms to lower rates and had aided rural electrification initiatives, but power barons' aggressive lobbying efforts nonetheless thwarted plans for analogous projects in western river valleys to assist residents, existing businesses, and new industries.[21]

Major executives also fought New Dealers. Union salary scales and challenges to managerial authority increasingly infuriated CEOs, even those who had once supported federal labor and welfare reforms to control turnover, stabilize wage rates, and reduce the need for costly pension plans. Some embraced a modern form of welfare capitalism, which subverted liberal efforts to build a public social welfare system and end what economists have since deemed a quasi-feudal relationship between employees and managers. Directors, like those atop Sears Roebuck and Kodak, rejected Henry Ford's controlling paternalism in the 1930s, instead relying on the social and behavioral sciences to guide managerial practices, adopting impersonal administrative procedures, and offering modest fringe benefits to stymie unionism and cement employee allegiance to management, not the national government. Owners also prevented the expansion of federal welfare by adopting the New Deal's language of security to promote the company pension, insurance, and medical plans central to the postwar public-private welfare apparatus.[22]

Leading industrialists combined such private countermeasures with public campaigns against the New Deal. The du Pont family's political efforts, for example, represented an early managerial offensive that complemented the growing congressional opposition to the New Deal. The three du Pont brothers, who sat at the helm of the family's empire of polymers and plastics, had supported FDR in 1932 largely because of his determination to end prohibition (they hoped an alcohol duty would prevent income tax increases). These men repudiated the president and his programs by 1934. They, along with their friends in industry and finance, favored political action over private denunciation. These financiers, industrialists, and businessmen contributed generously to the du Ponts' American Liberty League, which in turn denounced the New Deal for generating class conflict, violating the Constitution, and abridging property rights. The league's lawyers also took the New Dealers to court in an effort to stop the implementation of the liberal legislation that could nationalize new wage, work, and living standards. The organization, however, faced much ridicule and then just faded into oblivion when its war chest could not thwart Roosevelt's 1936 reelection.[23]

Desert Imbroglio

American Liberty League partisans had nonetheless publicly expressed a powerful critique of the New Deal, one present and salient far beyond their New York offices. Conflicts over how to relieve and reclaim hinterlands were in some ways even more dramatic and decisive in the South and Southwest, where industrialists' power and liberals' legitimacy both hinged on residents' support. The use of federal funds and the enforcement of new rules, moreover, had a more immediate effect in blighted communities, which had been cash starved even before the Depression.

That certainly was the case in Arizona. The Depression catapulted liberal Democrats into new positions of power and authority in local affairs. It was true, as one resident complained, that "in far too many cases the Phoenix office of a Federal agency is merely a sub-office," subordinate to the regional headquarters that liberals had established in San Francisco, Denver, and Albuquerque. But still the government had spent $10 million in Maricopa County by the mid-1930s. By then, six thousand people worked for the state, the area's largest employer. Not unexpectedly, these new jobs and infrastructure projects strengthened the Democratic Party's hold on Arizona politics. Voter registration had been three to one against the GOP when Arizonans first cast an overwhelming vote for Roosevelt in 1932. The disparity increased to more than four to one by the end of World War II.[24]

The surge largely benefited the liberal minority who championed the New Deal. Carl Hayden, an Arizona Progressive with links to organized labor and big, federally funded, western water projects, continued to be reelected to the Senate. In the 1944 gubernatorial race, Sidney Osborn took every county and lost in just twelve districts out of a total of 432. Stability, opportunity, and industry summed up Osborn's goals for Arizona. "Give the everyday fella a chance, and the country will be safe," Osborn asserted. "We must look after 'em decently. I want to help look after 'em."[25]

Arizonans also replaced "pinto" Democrat Senator Henry Ashurst with New Dealer Ernest W. "Mac" McFarland. The lawyer had practiced privately and served as the assistant attorney general, county attorney, and judge of the Superior Court for Pinal County, whereas Ashurst was a career politician. He had held the second seat for twenty-eight years and seemed, at least to the state's few Republicans, to belong in the GOP, not the New Dealers' Democratic Party. To unseat Ashurst, McFarland presented himself to voters as a liberal who considered the government vital for economic security, especially for home ownership and old-age pensions. During the 1940 primary, McFarland lambasted his opponent for his long absences from the state and charged that he had lost touch with Arizonans who wanted a New Deal in the form of water projects, copper tariffs, farm programs, and industrial investments. McFarland secured the nomination, which effectively guaranteed his general election win. Barry Goldwater certainly recognized MacFarland's ascent as assured. He deemed Ashurst's loss a "catastrophe." "The one error of your life has been that you were not a Republican," Goldwater wrote. "This fact has prohibited those voters from Arizona who border on the intelligent from voting for you by virtue of the fact that they are Republicans."[26]

McFarland's most ardent supporters underscored the extent to which New Deal liberals, whom Goldwater so detested, had established an Arizona beachhead. One Phoenician reported to McFarland that he heard "the usual beefing about taxes" but assured the congressman that most Phoenicians seemed to realize "we are in a critical age." He did not question the liberals' programs or the great expansion of the state that they were overseeing but asked why business owners "can charge off trips around the world as business expense, whereas a young widow of a veteran who died in the Philippines cannot deduct the $40 monthly she must pay to a nursery school to care for her child while she works." This concerned Democrat and father held an interest in bettering government services and using the state to redistribute wealth to its citizens. He even asserted that the administration needed to go further in its efforts. "The Bureau of Internal Revenue needs a very severe shaking on a number of points," he contended.[27]

Yet some Arizonans were also distrustful of, if not outright opposed to, New Deal initiatives. Those at the helm of Arizona's four C's, for example, actually looked askance at programs designed to raise prices and increase production. Copper tycoons, for their part, resisted the National Recovery Administration's price controls and workplace regulations that stabilized markets and eroded regional wage distinctions. Ranchers eventually acquiesced to Agricultural Adjustment Administration oversight because markets had failed to rebound by 1934. Federal officials subsequently developed a drought-purchasing program to reduce supply, bolster prices, and stop overgrazing. Rapid recovery did not mitigate managerial hostility. Cattleman Henry Day, for example, accepted federal money yet raised his daughter, Sandra Day O'Connor, later a Supreme Court justice, to be skeptical of interventionist statecraft.[28]

Phoenix boosters displayed a comparable enmity to the New Deal, one that informed their efforts to launch a private recovery effort. "Skeptical is putting it mildly," a top lawyer later snorted. Yet Chamber men were not averse to the Salt River Valley's industrialization and diversification, particularly once they began to feel the full effects of the Great Depression. Only the dramatic drop in mine revenue, for example, led the Chamber's board to identify "the need of substitution [from] some other industry" in April 1933, when the leadership established a committee to explore broadening, if not replacing, the city's traditional economic base with increased tourism and manufacturing. And a select few were confident that they, not the New Dealers, could transform the Valley. "There was a definite feeling of destiny for Phoenix. Just no doubt about it," Frank Snell later recounted. "This was going to be a bigger and a better town. And I think [that] caused most everybody . . . to take an interest in civic matters."[29]

Top businessmen and professionals nonetheless found themselves divided, largely by age, on whether to embrace industry or defend Phoenix's bucolic past. A new set of young boosters stood in stark contrast to the Chamber's interwar leaders. Their predecessors had embraced an Arizona economy based on climate tourism, mineral extraction, and agriculture. This next cohort sought to displace these long-standing economic pillars with wholesaling, distribution, and large-scale manufacturing. In the 1930s and 1940s, Frank Snell, John Rhodes, Howard Pyle, Charles Stauffer, Wesley Knorpp, Eugene Pulliam, Walter Bimson, Carl Bimson, Paul Fannin, Harry Rosenzweig, and Barry Goldwater took control of and transformed the Phoenix Chamber of Commerce. Their embrace of urbanization, industrialization, and modernization defined them as modern men, not the "pseudo-conservative" or "dispossessed" figures whom Daniel Bell and Richard Hofstadter later identified and condemned as the postwar conservative movement's foot soldiers. These boosters actually came out of the city's most profitable businesses and industries, particularly its banks, law firms, newspapers, and stores.[30]

The Chamber men were not necessarily "Westerners" and cannot be captured by the term "cowboy conservative." This identifier wrongly assumes that an entrepreneurial libertarianism was somehow endemic to the region. Promoters, moreover, also hailed from all over the country. Some traced their families back to the state's territorial days. Others migrated to Phoenix with hopes of escaping the Northeast and Midwest, where unionists and New Dealers had a better foothold. A few also came for the weather and their health. Some of their firms, such as Goldwater's department store and Rosenzweig's jewelry business, had been established before statehood, while others were recent start-ups. Many of the organization's leading figures, including the Arizona natives, received their bachelor's, law, and business degrees from universities in the East and Midwest, including George Washington University, the University of Michigan, and Harvard University. Thus, their membership in, need for, and access to extensive alumni networks, professional organizations, and leading financial houses firmly established this coterie as the Phoenix grasstops.[31]

Status and power informed these Anglo professionals, high-level managers, and business owners' self-ascribed right to rule and industrialize. They had, for example, a keen sense of political, civic, and economic entitlement. "There was a feeling that we had work to do to make it a bigger and better town," Snell explained. Another called this broad effort to modernize the Chamber an attempt to make "something out of nothing," strengthen the local economy, and avoid another depression. Their sense of prestige and authority and a firm conviction that the New Deal represented a monumental challenge to both unified these businessmen. "You can't do it individually," Snell later clarified. "It was a network." Journalists, newspaper owners, and radiomen had a monopoly on news sources, which allowed them to set the debate over Phoenix's economic and political future. Lawyers drafted new legislation, including the state's right-to-work referenda, which they defended in the courts. Bankers financed the Chamber's industrial recruitment campaigns and broad political initiatives. Retailers were some of this movement's most famous spokesmen and most influential members. "They were the Chamber of Commerce," Snell explained. "You could count on them [to help with Chamber campaigns], I know that because I did." These shop owners also helped solidify the grasstops' connections to the nation's industrial elite because merchants naturally operated, more so than the others, within larger business matrices. Retailers had long-standing relationships with wholesalers, suppliers, and manufacturers in order to keep prices low and compete with mail-order catalogues, a tough competitor in sparsely populated states.[32]

Phoenix's business organizations and social clubs served to incubate criticism of the colonial status quo and of the New Deal. Churches, synagogues, and Mormon temples were far less important in this small western trading outpost because no single house of worship could accommodate a commercial elite comprised of Catholics, Protestants, Jews, and Mormons. "Men of position," as Snell clarified, instead operated out of clubs and Chamber offices. "The Rotary Club owned the town, the Kiwanians ran it and the Lions enjoyed it," Snell bragged. "You walk down the street," he continued, "and you couldn't go two blocks without meeting ten people that you knew well." Snell was particularly reverential toward the Arizona Club and its "round table," where rainmakers ate, played cards, and discussed the future. "It was the business people," he reminisced, "that sat around and solved all the problems of all the city and the nation every night . . . we really did talk about important things and many times they were carried out." These men, and their wives, also served in the most important charities and service organizations and relaxed at the Phoenix Country Club. Many considered the resort an important venue for the city's frustrated businessmen, including Denison Kitchel, who had been a registered Democrat but became an active Republican and then a Goldwater adviser in 1964. He remembered: "We happened to play tennis a bit and we'd meet on various occasions . . . we became interested together in the same type of problems." "A lot of people that were in that group did move on into more public activity," he added.[33]

This elite's desire to tame the desert was also reflected in the atmosphere of these private organizations. The Westward Ho Riding Club, later christened the Valley Field Riding and Polo Club, was incorporated in 1929. Thereafter the organization hosted breakfasts and evening events in its clubhouse, often with tableware and decorations that bespoke a mythic Indian or cowboy past. This tradition continued into the postwar period, when indoor festivities, approximately ten a year, dominated the events calendar. Diners enjoyed evenings of lobster, filet mignon, or barbeque, or attended a Mexican fiesta, Chinese summer party, or Hawaiian bash. The organization's jealously guarded exclusivity also represented the Anglo haut monde's sense of themselves as the city's natural leaders. These guardians of "Arizona Heritage" reluctantly allowed junior memberships to those under forty and resisted opening the organization up to recent arrivals. They even waffled on the sale of unused land in 1990 in order to retain their status as a

Figure 3. Members of the Valley Field Riding and Polo Club at a 1934 costume party. This and other exclusive organizations, like the Chamber and the Country Club, were key meeting places for the Phoenix business elite, who feared and resented liberal and left-wing reform efforts. Courtesy of the Arizona Historical Foundation, Valley Field Riding and Polo Club Collection, folder 11, box 10.

"private club" that could legally restrict membership without forfeiting their tax-exempt status. Membership was for wealthy couples. Candidates had to have a sponsor, two additional supporters, and the membership committee's unanimous support. Bylaws dictated that divorcing spouses decide who would retain membership. If the member remarried, the newlywed forfeited his or her membership and had to reapply as a part of a couple (likewise if a widow or widower remarried).[34]

Young boosters with a firm footing in these elite, Anglo civic and social circles struggled to gain control of the Chamber of Commerce during the 1930s and thus worked within and outside the association to shape, benefit from, and fight liberal reforms. For example, the Bimson brothers, Walter and Carl, deployed an illustrative pragmatism. They bitterly opposed much of the New Deal but still found themselves forced to work with liberals to gird the state's banking infrastructure, profit from federal programs aimed at saving the construction industries, and influence how financial reforms would be carried out in order to protect their profit margins. In the process, they began to conclude that economic diversification required an expansion of the state's governing apparatus in order to create conditions that might sustain substantial manufacturing enterprises and liberate Phoenix from the quasi-colonial status characteristic of those regions that were similarly yoked by raw materials markets.

The Bimsons' path to Phoenix was circuitous. They grew up in Berthoud, Colorado. Their father, a blacksmith, eventually purchased a bank, which is where Walter learned bookkeeping. After graduation from the Harvard School of Business Administration, he found work at one of Chicago's premier financial institutions, the Harris Trust and Savings Bank. The collapse of the global economy in the early 1930s had a profound effect on him. He became the treasurer of the Illinois relief fund. Nightly, he pored over the rapidly expanding literature on the economy in order both to understand the causes of the Depression and to find solutions. He also traveled to Europe in 1931 to see these new economic theories in practice. Statist European approaches appalled him, solidified his faith in private enterprise, and gave him a fierce hostility to both socialism and modern liberalism. Bimson also rejected many elements of what would become American-style Keynesianism. The banker dismissed outright the liberals' newfound support for large-scale fiscal spending. "Much of our income in recent years has been fictitious," he asserted. "It has resulted from tremendous borrowing on the part of the government." "Swivel-chair Planners of our generation," he feared, held "delusions" that growth could be "blue-printed" and "that government planning can take the place of individual initiative."[35]

Bimson championed an entirely private response to end the economic crisis. He urged his Chicago colleagues to welcome all depositors, not just the wealthy, as a way of forestalling greater state intervention in the economy. He pushed for Harris to create a "people's bank," which would serve small businesses and working-class residents cut off from the security and easy credit that banks provided large businesses and better-off Chicagoans. Bimson's ideas contained elements of Giannini's philosophy. Both advocated opening banks' doors to a new set of customers, yet Bimson rejected the kinds of federal prescriptions both Giannini and Eccles championed. Bimson theorized that federal regulation of banking and other economic activity would be unnecessary if his democratized lending institution fought the Depression with low-cost, easily obtained loans to businesses that needed equipment and debt consolidation. He also wanted to extend credit to individuals who needed to buy homes or automobiles. "It seemed wrong, within the conservative policies of this bank, that honest, hard-working citizens with legitimate needs for capital could not obtain loans unless they already had money and collateral to back them up," he later explained. He envisioned banks priming the economic pump through the kind of federal loans Jones approved during the 1930s. Bimson, then, embraced massive spending but rejected New Deal faith in a powerful state that could itself jump-start or stabilize the economy. He also shared the ideological outlook of many welfare capitalists: subvert popular acceptance of the liberal regulatory state, thereby bolstering the citizenry's faith in private enterprise, not the government.[36]

Bimson's employers ridiculed his ideas, which forced him to make Phoenix's Valley National Bank (VNB), not Chicago's Harris Trust, his laboratory. "I was brash," Bimson later explained, "I came because I wanted to be independent and run my own bank . . . [and] try some experiments that I couldn't carry out in that bank." He envisioned himself a remote challenger to the Steelbelt moneyed elite, who, from his perspective, had ignored the majority of Americans. "We were not interested in being exclusive, or discriminating, or restrictive, or high-hat, or silk stocking," he later clarified. "We wanted to do business with people—all of the people—with businessmen of all sorts and varieties." Phoenix's struggling financial infrastructure proved advantageous for the financier: many Arizona institutions had folded, and others had not fully recovered from the initial downturn. His familiarity with central Arizona also aided his ambitions. His annual trips to settle Harris Trust's accounts had already put him in contact with the Salt River Valley Water Users' Association, the Arizona Pima Cotton Growers Association, and large area businesses. Such connections made him, unlike Eccles and Giannini, a well-connected transplant from the investor classes that had historically profited from hinterland investments.[37]

Bimson nonetheless broke with those imperial banking traditions that had so limited credit access. Upon taking office on January 1, 1933, he immediately gave employees commands in line with his plans for a private New Deal: "Make loans!" "I want this period of automatic loan refusal to end and end now," he declared. "The biggest service we can perform today is to put money into people's hands." "This bank's credit capacity isn't what it will be, but we have some capacity, and I want it used," he ordered. "Use it to get buying under way, to get building under way, to get business and farm production under way." He imported his younger brother, Carl, an engineer, to direct

VNB's new installment policies, not just for homes but also for cars and other medium-sized expenditures. VNB offered customers easy paperwork, little red tape, and a low rate, which Carl monitored and refined in order to compete with plans that department stores and lenders extended. Walter traveled throughout Arizona to promote his financial philosophy and emphasize that his bank, not the state, was putting money into their hands. Both Bimsons defined this business philosophy as a kind of free-market altruism. Carl often argued that "what benefits Arizona benefits the Valley Bank." Walter scoffed at bankers who worried about his free-wheeling lending policies. "Immoral to show a man how he can buy a washing machine so his wife won't break her back over a washboard? Immoral to help an enterprising individual equip and start a small business of his own?" Walter rhetorically asked. "Nonsense!"[38]

Their pragmatism pushed the Bimson brothers to make use of the New Deal state and its coffers. Both feared state-driven recovery yet were not opposed to using this money as a short-term emergency measure to help rebuild Valley National and prime the state's pump. VNB was one of the first southwestern banks to take advantage of RFC funding. After VNB issued debentures against its strongest assets, the RFC issued the institution an $840,000 loan, which financiers then extended to Arizonans and their businesses. VNB was also one of the first firms to assure its deposits with the newly created FDIC, deposit protections that Jones had long championed.[39]

The Bimsons made the most use out of Federal Housing Administration (FHA) funds. Title I of the 1934 National Housing Act aimed to help the floundering construction industry by insuring 20 percent or $2,000 of a RFC loan for home repair and modernization. Eleven Arizona banks received FHA approval, but the Bimsons were the most aggressive in utilizing these funds. Financiers collaborated with New Dealers and Chamber men to advertise the initiative. Local radio stations promoted the program, and the Junior Chamber of Commerce sponsored a "Better Homes Show." Fifty Federal Emergency Relief Administration employees distributed literature across the city the week of the expo and talked to almost two thousand homeowners. This publicity campaign and the promise of free, live entertainment brought thousands to the Shriners Auditorium, where attendees visited booths showcasing new appliances, fixtures, and construction materials. At the final exhibit, property owners could apply for an FHA-secured loan. Carl also headed a team of VNB employees, who walked through Phoenix neighborhoods, met with homeowners, and pointed out how they could repair roofs, build pools, fix septic tanks, or install swamp coolers with these newly available moneys. He personally spoke at picnics, swimming pools, baseball games, and other public venues. The trained engineer even helped customers draft plans for major home improvements. Arizonans took out more than $86,000 in loans for home improvements by the end of 1934. A year later, the figure increased to more than $500,000, making the state a national leader in the loan program.[40]

Success prompted federal officials to employ Carl as an FHA spokesman. He vigorously promoted the program, even using VNB resources to offset travel costs. Yet his enthusiasm stemmed from the meaning that he gave the law, one very much in accordance with the Bimsons' worldview. "This Act," Carl told a Miami Rotary Club, "is being operated by business men [*sic*] for the benefit of business men [*sic*] generally throughout the United States." He claimed the New Dealers had called in "leaders in their respective businesses, and it was they who conceived the plan now known as the National Housing Act." When he sold the program to homeowners, he asserted: "This plan is based on old-fashioned and orthodox principles to bring together private capital, industry and labor—to do a long overdue job of brightening up American homes." "This is private money," he emphasized, "not government money."[41]

The brothers also endeavored to take advantage of the program on their own terms. They wanted to make more loans than permissible (FHA regulations prohibited banks from advancing more than half of their holdings for mortgages). The Bimsons traveled to New York and California to implore the major insurance companies with Arizona offices to buy $1 million in government-backed mortgages so the Bimsons could expand credit in the state. When Occidental Life Insurance Company of Los Angeles agreed to purchase the mortgages, the brothers announced their return from California with full-page ads promoting the consumer loans. Customers flocked to the bank.[42]

The Bimsons' banking practices also incorporated strategies to subvert, not just maneuver around, New Deal policies. Walter had an early showdown with liberals over VNB's expansion. Congress had stipulated at the New Deal's start that no bank could open new branches until the House and Senate had amended the Banking Act. This temporary moratorium frustrated Walter's eagerness to open additional offices as a part of his general efforts to revitalize Arizona with private capital. He took his stand against the New Deal in Casa Grande, where he had hoped to open a VNB office but instead settled on assisting local business owners in starting a "currency exchange." The firm provided a trained banker for this site, but Casa Grande's business community paid the manager's salary and the building's rent. Legally, this "bank" could not hold deposits or make loans. It was technically unconnected to VNB, but in practice the teller acted as a remote courier to VNB's Phoenix headquarters. He stayed in Casa Grande to receive deposits, collect loan payments, take credit applications, and handle many other routine duties. The employee then sent all deposits and credit applications to Phoenix and disseminated all moneys sent back to the community, which, on paper, owned the "bank."[43]

The Bimsons replicated the currency exchange program in five towns, which irritated Washington. But no laws prohibited this practice, much to the frustration of the Federal Reserve's board of governors and legal staff. They met with Walter more than once to discuss this scheme. When he presented his plan before the Federal Reserve Bank in San Francisco, officials expressed their displeasure but had no recourse to stop him. Additional queries angered the elder Bimson, who told administrators, "You'll find when all is said and done that it comes down to this: either those currency exchanges are branch banks or they are not. If they are, then grant the necessary permits and The Valley Bank will seek to purchase them from their present owners and operate them as branches hereafter. If they are not branches, then they lie outside the boundaries of your jurisdiction and we shall continue cooperating with them as at present." The Fed acquiesced to Bimson. He received two letters from the government after Congress lifted the moratorium. One declared his puppet banks illegal and ordered him to stop operations by July 1, 1934. The second communication included six applications to turn the currency exchanges into branches by the end of June.[44]

Walter's victory was more than a symbolic win in the broader business resistance to the New Deal. VNB's solvency, recovery, and expansion made the Bimsons powerful men in Arizona. For example, Walter had the personal influence to orchestrate the 1933 Arizona bank "holiday." Much of VNB's money was in California. When Walter learned that the Golden State's governor had closed the banks, the financier feared a run on his firm, which had already started to rebound under his "Make Loans!" directive. Both Bimson and Arizona governor Benjamin Moeur lived at the Westward Ho Hotel at the time. On March 2, 1933, at four in the morning, Bimson knocked on the governor's door, woke both him and his wife, and asked Moeur to shut down Arizona's banks on the spot. The statesman demurred but nonetheless granted Bimson an 8 A.M. meeting to discuss the matter with the state attorney general. Bimson arrived with a drafted decree and convinced the governor to sign before the 9 A.M. openings. Afterward, with a panic averted, both brothers had the ears of Phoenix officials, state legislators, and every governor, regardless of party.[45]

This influence further transformed the Bimsons' view of economic development. They had started to reshape, benefit from, and negotiate the expansion of the liberal regulatory state in their city, state, and country. This early political work thus underscored the difficulty of improving Arizona finance to match the Steelbelt's fiscal infrastructure, while ensuring that the area remained economically advantageous for boosters and outside investors. Carl, for example, chafed at old state and local laws that kept Phoenix at the margins of the American commercial "frontier." Short-term loan restrictions particularly rankled him. Each VNB branch needed to apply for a small-loan license because banks were not permitted to provide such services. With a license, each branch could loan a maximum of $300 dollars with 3.5 percent per month interest. But this jerry-rigged solution did not help the Bimsons finance personal loans for autos or home improvements. Moreover, the brothers could not make loans against a business owner's accounts receivable, which stymied their efforts to help Valley merchants, entrepreneurs, and professionals. To fully fulfill the "Make Loans!" directive, the brothers took their case to the legislature and profited handsomely from new statutes that permitted firms to issue larger short-term loans and make deals based on expected profits.[46]

The Bimsons also lobbied against the New Deal's redistributive statecraft, which neither brother ever accepted as a part of their populist boosterism. They joined other Arizona financiers in decrying state taxes on bank property as unfair and unequal. They asserted that these duties hampered bank-led recovery efforts because the taxes supposedly made it too costly for healthy institutions to absorb failing banks. Walter pushed the Arizona Bankers Association to study the problem in 1939, and its members subsequently discovered that Arizona levied more taxes on banks than any other state and had wildly different rates for real estate, deposits, capital accounts, and other income cases. When the association members took their case for reform to the legislature, they were actually frustrated by Governor Sid Osborn. This New Deal Democrat supported redistribution and subsequently vetoed tax code amendments twice. Arizona financiers persisted, which paid off in the form of a 1943 legislative override to allow the just-passed moratorium on bank share taxes and flat 5 percent levy on all bank income to take effect. Taken together, these changes vastly reduced Arizona banks' share of the overall tax burden and represented a tentative step toward reducing business contributions to state and local revenue.[47]

Buying Payroll

Other boosters across the South and Southwest also experimented with state power in the name of investment while the Bimsons busily constructed the framework for their postwar banking empire. As in Phoenix, a new coterie of industry-minded boosters came to the fore in regions bitterly divided over the New Deal. These small-town professionals, businessmen, and retailers aggressive pursued industry but still resisted adopting federal directives that would have placed local wages and working conditions on par with Steelbelt standards. The grasstops, Phoenix's rainmakers included, hence represented an effective veto on New Deal reforms in America's hinterlands. Unlike the Southern agriculturalists who for a time compromised with New Dealers in Congress, both regions' urbanites and townspeople actively challenged the passage, subverted the aim, and stymied the implementation of liberal laws and administrative regulations being formulated in the nation's capital.

Depression era boosterism nonetheless varied in scope and scale. The urban Southwest's most aggressive professional and ownership classes utilized their cities' existing resources by inserting themselves into politics and using their influence to direct municipal funds toward industrial recruitment. In San Jose, for example, the city council gave the Chamber public funds for a national publicity campaign in 1938. In an effort to join the ranks of San Francisco, San Diego, and Los Angeles, San Jose boosters targeted high-tech electronics firms to complement the Golden State's defense economy. The founders of Hewlett-Packard arrived in San Jose in 1938, and within ten years IBM, General Electric, and Kaiser also began operations there. In Austin, a new cohort of young businessmen challenged the Chamber's old guard, who had opposed industry during the interwar period. The upstarts forced the resignation of the organization's secretary, who had held the position since the 1910s, and embarked on a publicity campaign similar to San Jose's initiative. The new leadership worked willingly with liberals, including young U.S. Representative Lyndon Baines Johnson. Their relationship was reciprocal: boosters provided the money for his campaigns, and

LBJ repaid them with federal funds to improve the town's water supply, airport, and city hall. San Diego's grasstops recognized both cities for what they were: rivals. By the early 1940s, these Chamber men even began revising their policies in order to better compete for military projects and entice defense contractors.[48]

Southern efforts to vie for investment ranged widely during these years. In the plantation belt's perimeter, boosters experimented with community drives to raise capital for private economic development on the premise that such sacrifice would yield relief. In Dickson, Tennessee, which already had some manufacturing enterprises, workers contributed toward their employer's plant expansion by donating 6 percent of their $10 weekly salary. Smaller towns in the cotton South also pursued diversification. Albany, Georgia, promoters raised $10,000 from residents with a public subscription drive to underwrite a new hosiery plant. The deal hinged on investor assurances that they would hire local high school graduates if employees forewent salaries during a six-month training period. Urban Chamber men, like their Southwestern counterparts, more easily attracted nonagricultural investment if their cities already had a more diversified base, such as the Charlotte Chamber men who embraced federal programs to revive the devastated Queen City. The already established transportation and financial hub benefited from federal dollars to expand basic infrastructure, including the airport, which helped lure seventy-five new manufacturing outfits to the area before 1940.[49]

Mississippi's landmark 1936 Industry Act represented a watershed moment in this long-standing community tradition of simply "buying payroll," a common critique of zealous Southern boosterism. This legislation proved a pragmatic step toward a grasstops recovery effort that would subvert liberal reclamation. The law outlined an early systematic state program for industrial recruitment and economic diversification, which relied on enabling state officials and townspeople to finance investment campaigns and secure new industries, both of which addressed the structural inequities in the rural South's quasi-colonial relationship with outside industrialists. The bill justified the entire initiative as a means for the state "to protect its people by balancing agriculture with industry" because "the present and prospective health, safety, morals, pursuit of happiness, right to gainful employment and general welfare of its citizens demand, as a public purpose, the development within Mississippi of industrial and manufacturing enterprises."[50]

The architect of Balance Agriculture with Industry (BAWI), Governor Hugh White, harnessed the executive branch's power and credit capabilities in order to direct diversification from the grasstops. The former lumberman's program bolstered boosters' ability to negotiate with outside industrialists without challenging the stark differential between the Steelbelt and its hinterlands, which, in effect, mitigated the immediate threat to agriculturalists and investors. BAWI officials exercised tremendous control: they ran the promotional campaign in major newspapers and trade journals, waded through the three thousand responses, decided which proposals were feasible, and ran tours for prospective investors. Local residents had an important role in the process. Municipal governments made proposals, built the required facilities, and entered into contracts with businesses. Schemes filed with the Industrial Commission also needed a signed petition from 20 percent of registered voters. Officials demanded detailed plans that outlined the city's existing debts, tax rolls, and population figures as well as projected wage rates, types of job opportunities (with an emphasis on the number of skilled positions), tentative contract agreements, and estimated costs. Commissioners studied these proposals and provided locales with a "certificate of public convenience and necessity" that allowed the municipal government to raise money to provide for an investor's demands. Voters had to approve the necessary bond measures, which ranged up to $300,000, by a supermajority. Area leaders could then buy land and erect buildings, which were rented to the firm in a multiyear lease far below their actual worth (as low as $1 per annum). Some agreements even terminated with facilities being turned over to the parent corporation.[51]

The bitter fights between Mississippi agricultural elites, industry-minded boosters, and liberals over BAWI were emblematic of regional conflicts over relief, recovery, and reconstruction. Governor White shared New Dealers' faith in community control and economic decentralization and desire to undermine the southern planter class's authority. Executive bureaucracies thus sought to empower assertive boosters, such as Greenville's Chamber men, who considered BAWI crucial for transforming the town into the seat of a "budding southern industrial empire." Such eagerness informed White's insistence that the citizenry participate in recruitment. He authorized the Industrial Commission to contact manufacturers but also stipulated that local governments, bodies "close to their people," signal the initial interest in investment. Such guidelines circumvented the southern aristocracy's control over state and county governments. The three-person Industrial Commission likewise represented an affront to planter power because White ignored powerful agriculturalists and instead appointed successful, well-connected businessmen to this body. All had extensive contacts in the outside financial and manufacturing circles that had long relied on the South to supply them with raw materials and customers. The first three commissioners were Harry Hoffman, a railroad executive, Greenville's Frank England, the southern sales manager for an Indiana manufacturer, and Meridian's S. A. Klein, a broker, investment banker, and department store owner.[52]

BAWI proved highly controversial. A 1936 legal suit represented an early challenge, one based on an objection to the use of public funds to aid private enterprise (then illegal under Mississippi's constitution). Jackson lawyers, all closely connected to White, argued that these expenditures served a larger public purpose even though moneys were initially directed to private businesses. "The majority opinion," a state Supreme Court judge dissented after a five to one ruling upheld the law, "drives a steam shovel right through our Constitution." Other Mississippians were alarmed that buying payroll did not necessarily translate into economic recovery or accommodation to federal wage standards. A *Tupelo Journal* reporter decried salaries that remained well below federal mandates when he discovered that workers in a Columbia facility earned just 75 percent of the NRA-determined minimum wage. "Is that the class of laborers we want in Cleveland?" local residents of that Mississippi city asked before they rejected a proposal to bring a silk hosiery plant to the area. Opponents also resisted BAWI's underlying premise favoring rapid, business-first industrialization: "We insist that if a factory concern is not big enough to erect its own building, and doesn't want to come to Cleveland that bad, let them stay away. . . . Steady growth is better."[53]

Denizens could frustrate the ambitions of state officials and private investors, but BAWI practices also ensured that new businesses would not deliver the kind of grassroots transformation that Lilienthal and other New Dealers had considered the natural outgrowth of diversification. Liberals wanted to promote economic growth through industrialization to provide towns with payroll, but they also championed state protections for the citizenry through social welfare programs funded through higher taxes, trade unions to empower workers and enforce labor laws on the shop floor, and regulations designed to transform traditional southern business practices. BAWI undermined these New Deal aspirations as well as the mandates, written into the act, that projects would "relieve unemployment" and "not become a burden upon the taxpayers." Policies, in theory and in execution, actually exacerbated the regional exceptionalism that underlay the South and Southwest's domestic colony status. Contracts worked out between state officials, local governments, and private investors kept wages down, town finances shaky, and residents disempowered. Some investment schemes relied on bonds as large as $300,000, sums difficult for taxpayers to pay back because BAWI stipulations for a surplus labor pool, anti-union contract provisions, and tax giveaways slowed revenue growth. Officials also tended to reject outsiders' ideas for Mississippi-based businesses or enterprises unconnected to agriculture, which could have raised community wage scales.[54]

Assessments of BAWI accordingly ranged widely. Mississippi only issued twenty-one certificates. Eight deals fell through in final arrangements, and only seven ventures, mostly textile concerns, opened before 1940. Firms employed 2,691 residents, less than 5 percent of the state's industrial workforce. When White's term expired in 1940, legislators, with the new governor's approval, immediately repealed the Industrial Act. But Mississippians reconsidered the initiative's apparent failure during the war when five additional BAWI factories began operations, several textile firms broadened their output to include shells and tires, and Pascagoula's new shipyard became the state's largest employer. It and the eleven other BAWI plants paid more than $43 million in wages between 1939 and 1943 and employed 14 percent of Mississippi's industrial workforce. Southern business organizations subsequently took much interest in the defunct initiative, which prompted the Atlanta Federal Reserve to publish and disseminate a 1944 study of BAWI's origins, policies, and results. Mississippi assemblymen revived and expanded BAWI that same year despite economists' concerns about persistently low wages and failed negotiations. Southern promoters in other states, most notably Tennessee and Kentucky, also ignored these warnings and aped BAWI practices in their postwar state development programs.[55]

"Work for the Glorious Future of Phoenix"

Arizonans did not construct such powerful bureaucracies until years later. As in other arid states, industrialization depended on grasstops business associations, which benefited from the concentration of the state's populations in cities, like Phoenix, even as boosters struggled against the barons and managers of the extraction, processing, and shipping of western commodities.

The Chamber of Commerce was of the utmost importance to Valley businessmen. Indeed, the Bimsons' efforts to rebuild their bank, improve the Arizona economy, and thwart New Deal social reforms had coincided with their work to displace the Chamber's aging leadership.

The Royal Order of the Thunderbirds, a special honor fraternity within the Phoenix Chamber, represented an early, subtle attempt to redirect the larger association's activities. "We wanted something that young men would take an active part in and run," a founding member and later Chamber president explained. Five members started this special events group in 1938, with each selecting ten men a piece to fill out the organization's ranks. Barry Goldwater and Harry Rosenzweig were among the group's first members. Goldwater's younger brother, Bob, and Frank Snell joined shortly thereafter. The order selected men in their thirties and early forties, when they had achieved some local prominence and were able to spend time away from their work. Invitees only served five years as active members. They then earned Life Thunderbird status, which made working on the organization's behalf voluntary and thus opened up opportunities for new recruits to maintain the Thunderbirds' registry of fifty-five active draftees. True to the elite business world out of which this organization sprang, the Thunderbirds incorporated and appropriated Indian culture into their activities. They earned beads and feathers depending on how successful they were and how much they contributed to the order. They also decked themselves out with turquoise and silver jewelry and high-necked blue velvet jackets when they met with CEOs.[56]

In some respects, this group seemed to be just another tepid expansion of Phoenix boosterism. Like the Tournament of Roses Association of Pasadena, the Thunderbirds planned special promotional events in order "to work for the glorious future of Phoenix." The annual Phoenix Open golf tournament was the group's most publicized event. Though the city had hosted such contests earlier, it was the Thunderbirds, and Bob Goldwater in particular, who made the competition a major annual event to bring in more sightseer dollars.[57]

But founding Thunderbirds openly rejected the association's earlier limited agenda for irrigation, agriculture, and small-scale tourism. They accordingly set out to formally transform the Chamber into a much larger organization dedicated to the material and political work necessary to build an industrial metropolis. Snell played a pivotal role in the institution's overhaul. The grocer's son had grown up in Kansas City, matriculated from

Georgetown's law school, and had intended to move east to Connecticut to practice law. He instead came to Miami, a small Arizona copper outpost, at the behest of his uncle. He eked out a living in remote mining towns, but life in Phoenix intrigued the young lawyer more. "I came [in 1927] because I thought I did see a challenge both in the law business and in the growth of the city," he remembered, "It was still semi-sleepy desert town in a way. Cooling had not yet come and everybody loved it but I don't think we ever thought we'd ever be too big a city."[58]

Snell rose through the ranks of Phoenix's civic, business, and professional circles. He became active in both the Kiwanis and the Chamber of Commerce. He founded a practice with Mark Wilmer, who hailed from Wisconsin. Snell and Wilmer, L.L.P., represented many Phoenix business interests, including air-conditioning manufacturer Oscar Palmer, grocer turned lender George Mickle, large agricultural associations for cotton, citrus, and milk producers, Valley National Bank, and a private bus company openly hostile to union efforts to organize the city's transportation workers as well as eager to end municipal bus services entirely. Such relationships placed Snell at the center of the circle of business elites opposed to the New Deal and eager for industry. The litigator hence became a linchpin in Chamber, courtroom, and electoral challenges to liberalism.[59]

Snell brazenly decried Rooseveltian statecraft. He wanted to attract significant investment but openly lambasted liberal prescriptions that promoted the general social welfare alongside industry when he addressed Arizona business and civic groups. "You sell your Soul, your Liberty, Yourself, for the tempting rainbow of economic security," the lawyer warned. "I cannot join that rather audible and demagogic crowd that today is claiming there are no more chances left for the individual to forge ahead, and win his way in the world—and therefore we must overthrow our present economic system." "God save us from that sort of economic security, or Economic Democracy," he concluded in 1939. He conflated, like many other critics, these liberal experiments with both left-wing and fascist movements in Depression-era Europe. He deemed liberalism "Socialism for the Democrats in Washington," because they, from Snell's perspective, had adopted "exactly the program of the Socialists advocated 20 years ago—the only difference is the Socialists admit that such a program constitutes Socialism." Snell considered businessmen and professionals bulwarks against this creeping radicalism. He warned that Adolf Hitler had disbanded and prohibited "Rotary Clubs, trade associations and similar organizations . . . [because they] were breeding grounds of Democratic principles and policies" and thus encouraged Phoenix entrepreneurs to "stand up and be counted if we are to continue to be the masters of our fate rather than servants of an all powerful government."[60]

Snell's concerns colored his 1939–1940 stint at the Chamber's helm, a watershed fiscal year that redirected the organization's mission and modus operandi. He methodically addressed his compatriots' complaints that members did not take an active part in the organization, that the leadership had not given business owners an opportunity to be involved because "special interests and small groups have dominated the Chamber and its Board of Directors," that official events were merely "'hoopala' with no real or constructive purpose behind them," and that the organization was poorly administered. The association did have $18,000 in outstanding bills and just $8,000 in accounts receivable in 1939. Snell had the Chamber pay its debts, begin a membership drive, generate a list of three hundred associates eager and willing to become involved in committee work, and pass new bylaws to provide structure and accountability in all activities and programs. The old guard, as a result, started to lose control of key committees to the younger upstarts, including Barry Goldwater and Walter Bimson, who wanted to distance the town from its reliance on cotton, cattle, and copper.[61]

The Chamber also commissioned an important manifesto that outlined a vision for the city's future and the Chamber's preferred policies to underwrite economic recovery, prosperity, and growth. Boosters hired Arthur Horton, an Arizona State Teacher's College associate professor of social studies, to compile the three-hundred-page *Economic, Political, and Social Survey of Phoenix and the Valley of the Sun* (1941). Horton presented the tome as "an open-minded, disinterested, scientific, fact-finding survey as the basis for intelligent and constructive city planning in the future." The planning document actually provided edicts for Phoenix's economic diversification. The economist prepared most of the material on the area's natural, industrial, and financial resources but interjected reports from leading Chamber men, who articulated their personal opinions, plans, and predictions.[62]

The Valley's development was of the utmost concern. Horton emphasized water. "Property values, growth and good business are based upon future possibilities," he declared. "In the arid and semi-arid states WATER spells FUTURE. This water must be guaranteed for many centuries ahead." This resource would bring more than agriculture: irrigation would also generate jobs for two hundred thousand people and thereby stimulate all sectors of the economy. Water also delivered power. Electricity, Horton projected, would help private households but also attract industries unconnected to cotton, copper, or cattle. Paying for this modern infrastructure was another matter. Both Horton and Walter Bimson resisted reliance on federal moneys alone. The financier declared area banks capable of providing some working funds but nonetheless feared that local firms did not have the capital for more large-scale projects. In line with his earlier pragmatic acceptance of state funding, he recommended that fellow bankers exploit their connections to the federal government and the more established banks in the East to secure support for major improvements.[63]

The survey also championed a diversified local economy. Unlike the heads of BAWI's Industrial Commission, who had dreamed of industrialization but rejected plans for almost all manufacturing schemes unconnected to cotton, Phoenix Chamber men looked out at the arid desert and imagined the Valley and themselves capable of attracting and producing an entirely new class of products, output that would transform their town into a metropolis. The plan deemed travel, wholesaling, and manufacturing vital to the Valley's rebirth. "The natural thing to which to turn was the capitalization of our climate, our natural beauties, and the romance of the desert," Barry Goldwater explained. The retailer subsequently emphasized improving the association's national advertising campaign because: "The farmer has sold more produce. The hotels have filled more rooms. The merchants have sold more goods." Horton, for his part, also calculated that Phoenix was well positioned as a distribution and wholesaling hub. "Because of its central location, which is the most strategic in the commercial southwest between Los Angeles and El Paso, Texas," he noted, "Arizona is no longer isolated from fast commercial transportation facilities."[64]

Horton and his employers placed the most faith in defense and manufacturing. New Chamber leaders, unlike their interwar predecessors, embraced militarization, largely in the spirit of diversification. They celebrated Arizona as a prime location because it was relatively far from the vulnerable West Coast and shared a border with Mexico, which had been a crucial front in the previous global conflict. Boosters were also confidant that the Valley's orchards, vegetable patches, and cotton fields would be able to both feed and clothe American servicemen. With increased demand, copper mines would also surely reopen and move swiftly into production. Even in 1941, Chamber men had already made plans for demobilization, which emphasized retention, reconversion, and expansion of the new wartime industries. Phil Tovrea, whose family owned a major ranching outfit, warned that Phoenix had to develop a manufacturing economy. He considered California's fortress cities both rivals and models that thrived because of well-developed markets for mass-produced goods, excellent supply chains to serve outlying areas, and cheap electricity and raw materials. Thus Phoenix boosters, he emphasized, had much to do in order to transform the city into a desirable location for industrialists.[65]

Yet Chamber men found themselves unable to fully implement their plans until after World War II had ended. Their 1941 clarion call failed to move their representatives in Phoenix's city hall. Rainmakers begged commissioners to buy and read the survey to "determine the destiny of Phoenix and the Valley," but no substantive discussion of the findings appeared in the city commission's record. Officials only agreed to delay making a decision on purchasing the survey. The city did eventually buy forty copies, but only to help defray production costs.[66]

This defeat was hollow. Promoters had accomplished much during the 1930s. The Bimsons, for example, had already embraced federal funds to complement their loan policies, significantly involved themselves in state governance, and boldly stood up to New Dealers to defend their currency exchanges, while they aided other young upstarts who sought to take over and refashion the Phoenix Chamber. Such resistance to liberalism's march through the interior was hardly exceptional. Their grasstops counterparts across the South and Southwest had likewise experimented with the kind of policies that attracted outside investors hostile to the New Deal. Lorena Hickok had thus been right to predict in her 1934 reports on Arizona that Washington would struggle to raise wage and living standards. Yet the most substantial veto on liberalism was to be found not among Dixie agrarians but rather in the burgeoning alliance between the periphery's boosters and the nation's business elite.

Chapter 3

The Business of War

The Phoenix Chamber's 1941 survey had offered stark analysis of the Salt River Valley's colonial qualities alongside explicit warnings against liberalism's arid-state incursions. Barry Goldwater, for one, openly admitted in his submission that the "huge expenditure of public moneys . . . has been of extreme importance to retailing." Yet he also cautioned against such dependence on the federal government, already Maricopa County's largest employer: "It is sheer folly for any of our numerous branches of business to consider this money as a permanent source of income to business. If it continues," he ominously predicted, "it will be at the expense of business and is, so to speak, robbing Peter to pay Paul."[1]

Such fears shaped how the grasstops and investor classes responded to the liberal warfare state. Dramatic federal expenditures for defense and war production, price controls, protections for trade unionism, and executive orders against hiring discrimination and pay inequity enabled liberals to extend the general period of experimentation through the early postwar period. Yet the Roosevelt administration was hardly an economic dictatorship, as opponents so often charged. FDR's wartime state did have tremendous economic power, but it was often staffed at the very highest levels by businessmen and politicians hostile to the New Deal's continuation. Officials actually brought industrialists into federal mobilization agencies, where they established policies that guaranteed corporate profitability, often on the scale of a windfall, and also finalized deals favorable to private contractors. Boosters in turn bought payroll, courting manufacturers with the kinds of concessions that pleased manufacturers and appalled liberals. Defense investments only further encouraged the budding alliance between executives and promoters, especially among those businessmen, like Goldwater, who feared reliance on or subjugation to the federal government.

Wars on the Home Front

In May 1940, Roosevelt decreed that the bulk of war production would occur in the nation's interior, an order that both defense strategy and liberal ideology had inspired. Dispersed bases and war production factories would theoretically ensure that one strategic raid, bombing campaign, or blockade would not cripple the war effort. Later the federal government implemented policies that facilitated unionization of these defense industries, put maintenance of membership clauses in most collective bargaining contracts, and mandated fair employment practices covering millions of war workers. In the process, liberals would finally be able to lessen the South and Southwest's dependence on agriculture and mining, thus enabling a genuine grassroots revolution to take shape. Moreover, planning, which agencies like the National Resources Planning Board (NRPB) undertook, would collect economic data and recommend government action to ensure that reconversion to a peacetime economy would not lead to the rapid deindustrialization of these regions but rather continue to loosen the bonds between commodity producers and Steelbelt manufacturers.[2]

But formulating plans to advance New Deal liberalism during the conflict proved far easier than implementing them. Industry-friendly officials, many of them dollar-a-year-men still on the payroll of their own companies, controlled procurement. These civilians staffed key units at the War Production Board and other mobilization agencies. Both they and military leaders favored the corporate status quo when it came to awarding contracts. The great, established industrial corporations of the Northeast, Midwest, and Pacific Coast were therefore chosen as prime contractors. Executives often bristled at opening plants outside these areas, generally conceding once their existing facilities could not keep pace with need. Yet the factories eventually built in the South and Southwest during the war boom were shuttered almost as quickly as they were constructed, especially as orders slackened or were canceled.[3]

Yet communities, not corporations, suffered. Corporate taxes may have been high during this period, but profits nonetheless soared. Administrators signed generous individual contracts with suppliers but also embraced "cost-plus" clauses to ensure defense would be profitable to manufacturers still struggling to recover from the Depression. Agents later ensured that cancellation would be equally lucrative. The federal government paid up to 90 percent of nullified agreements, sold surplus inventory and factories at well below cost, and provided large tax breaks for investment in new or retooled plants and equipment, all of which generated record after-tax profits (approaching $10 billion a year in 1943, 1944, and 1945).[4]

Political warfare facilitated such corporate profitmaking and insubordination. Businessmen used defense as an opportunity to recapture the prestige and political influence that they had lost during the Depression. Production was now vital, patriotic actually. Industrialists could thus more easily attack not only strikes but also labor rights and, by extension, liberal planning initiatives and government regulations. All represented obstacles to generating the output necessary to triumph over the Axis Powers. Indeed, antilabor, anti–New Deal groups, like the National Association of Manufacturers (NAM), became far more active during the war, eager to cultivate a reconversion era when they might disarm the economic controls developed by the warfare state and reduce the legitimacy won by unionists and government planners during the previous decade. Congressional critics even succeeded in abolishing the NRPB in 1943. As a result, this overarching federal, central planning agency would no longer study, prepare for, or oversee reconversion for cities, states, or citizens, much less ensure FDR's "Freedom form Want" or Truman's "Right to Work," which he defined as a guarantee of a job. Intransigent CEOs also found a champion in Jesse Jones, now commerce secretary, who feuded with liberals like Vice President Henry Wallace, who wanted peace to usher in a "century of the common man." Jones was far more attuned to the needs of industrial ownership, envisioning his own postwar planning committee, but one staffed by representatives from top banks and manufacturers.[5]

Boosters in and at War

Turmoil in Washington did not stop local boosters from buying payroll during World War II. The Phoenix Chamber, for example, was well primed for the opportunity defense represented: key leaders had already been experimenting with the kind of economic enticements and organizational overhauls necessary to attract investment and support substantive manufacturing.

Rainmakers also profited from their ties to outside investors, especially Paul Litchfield. The Goodyear executive scoffed at War Department officials who questioned his capacity to fill contracts from a facility in Phoenix. This laggard town, they insisted, clearly lacked the requisite labor pool. "Much of the work could be done out-of-doors. Planes could be flown and tested every day of the year," the snowbird reasoned. "Arizona was far enough inland to be safe from enemy raids, such as might threaten plants on the Pacific Coast." Administrators were hardly in a position to press the point in the early years of the war effort: they had depended on Goodyear to help build America's air fleet since the interwar period. This major military supplier hence had just as much power as the top executives who insisted on using their existing Steelbelt facilities.[6]

Litchfield alone could not bring other plants or military installations to the Salt River Valley. Recruitment instead required cooperation between local citizens groups, liberal politicians, and federal policymakers. Chamber men, for example, found their Democratic senators eager to have the federal government invest in Arizona. Senator Ernest McFarland was particularly enthusiastic: "Arizona must look to its industrial development to secure its economy and insure a prosperous future," for the state could no longer rely on "agriculture alone as our major industry; we must develop industries." Senior Senator Carl Hayden shared this desire, lobbied on his state's behalf, and advised citizens how to best campaign for bases. Yet he admitted that he could not send the army to Arizona at "a mere snap of my fingers." The War Department and defense contractors held the true decision-making power.[7]

Phoenicians excelled at courting these power brokers. Arizonans secured lucrative contracts for the state's minerals, cattle, and crops, which helped build ships and feed the troops. Airfields still topped the agenda for the Phoenix and Tucson business groups who made repeated visits to Washington's war production planning agencies. Like Litchfield, these citizen lobbyists asserted that sunny days, dry conditions, and open skies made the state an ideal location for flight schools. Phoenix city commissioners worked in concert with Chamber men, congressmen, and Civil Aeronautics Authority (CAA) bureaucrats to establish these installations in Arizona. In November 1940, the city manager persuaded the commissioners to issue a decree authorizing him to work with both the CAA and the Chamber to finance Phoenix's militarization. Such cooperation entailed hammering out agreements with property and business owners on land needed for airfields, such as a deal to have the city pay half of a telephone company's relocation costs, projected to be $2,000, when the firm vacated needed facilities and plots adjacent to Sky Harbor Airport. Commissioners considered the agreement a collaborative coup and issued public "thanks to the press, public officials, State Legislature and other governmental units and public bodies, including the Chamber of Commerce, Municipal Aeronautics Commission of the City of Phoenix, private corporations and individuals."[8]

These joint efforts wrought large-scale military investment. The Southwest Airways Corporation built the first central Arizona field to train American, British, and Chinese pilots for the air corps, but the city's elected officials and business leaders selected and purchased the site in order to lease it to the army. Construction was swift. Luke Field was operational in just eleven weeks and soon became *the* single-engine advanced pilot training facility. Need was so high that cadets had to be sent to auxiliary fields as well as civilian-owned operations. By war's end, more than 145,000 trainees had come to Arizona to earn their wings.[9]

Residents, elected leaders, Chamber men, and congressmen also helped make Phoenix a center of defense production. The Valley's "Big Three" built airplane parts, small planes, flight decks, and pontoon bridges. The Aluminum Company of America's (ALCOA) facility just outside the city was the country's largest aluminum factory. AiResearch managers took control of a government airplane parts operation near Sky Harbor in 1942 and soon had twenty-seven hundred employees, many of whom lived in housing projects that the state built. Goodyear operated its established rubber plant and a new aircraft facility in the area. Litchfield openly lauded this most recent start-up as "another step toward decentralization of America's program for the production of vital defense materials." At its peak, seventy-five hundred workers produced aircraft parts in the factory.

Phoenix also became a training site for the skilled workforce required to keep the nation's new air fleet operational. Employment opportunities attracted thousands. "We had recruiters in all areas of the country looking for labor to staff this plant," one Goodyear executive remembered. "We trained cotton pickers galore out of Tennessee, Mississippi, Arkansas, Kentucky. . . . We had a lot of women that were well worth their salt in the plant. I was amazed at some of the younger women whose husbands were overseas. They were very adaptable. They were really sincere." A massive training program for aircraft maintenance work also schooled thousands of civilian technicians, who were supposed to head west for employment in California's shipyards and aircraft industries. Most found jobs in Arizona's expanding

Figure 4. Governor Sidney Osborn spoke at Luke Field's 1941 dedication ceremony, a wartime investment this liberal Democrat considered vital for Arizona's broad economic recovery. The installation proved such a boon to Phoenix that Osborn would single out aeronautics as a critical industry for postwar economic growth. Courtesy of the Arizona Historical Foundation, Sidney P. Osborn Photograph Collection, folder 9.

airfields. By the end of 1942, Arizona's twelve vocational centers had already produced more than eleven thousand graduates.[10]

Liberal politicians and Republican business leaders celebrated Phoenix's militarization. "More industries will come. We want them," liberal governor Sid Osborn declared when Goodyear executives announced they would expand their operations to include aircraft. "With all our potential water power and natural resources, we can make conditions increasingly attractive for them," he promised. "That will be my, and Arizona's[,] continuing effort." Sylvan Ganz, then president of the Phoenix Chamber, remarked, "The ice has been broken . . . from now on Phoenix will become increasingly important, and properly so, as an industrial center." "This is exactly the type of enterprise for which the Phoenix Chamber of Commerce has been striving and for which it will continue to strive," he enthused.[11]

Factories and airfields sparked Phoenix's recovery. The construction industry could not keep up with the demand for defense worker housing. Shortages prompted Chamber men and city commissioners to beg residents to take in homeless laborers. Need also resuscitated Phoenix's construction sector. The New Deal had funded the private homes and public schools and hospitals that postwar real estate magnate Del Webb built, but generous cost-plus contracts during the war truly transformed his balance sheets. His company erected all 126 buildings at the Phoenix Military Airport and employed twenty-five hundred men just to finish Higley Field's runways and buildings. Webb recognized the boon that defense provided: "Construction is no longer a private enterprise but rather a subsidiary of the federal government." The downtown also thrived, representing, according to a reporter, "the desert's greatest oasis" for military personnel and defense laborers living outside city limits. "They had about eight men in a tent. One man from the tent might come to town and buy for eight people," the mayor remembered. "They'd just walk through town and buy everything there was—meat and cigarettes and liquor." "Saturday nights at Central Avenue, Washington Street was almost as busy as pictures you see of crowded streets in New York," the owner of the Luhrs Hotel reflected. "Hotels were jammed full. Theatres and everybody else was making business. A boom business."[12]

The Chamber's young upstarts seized the opportunity offered by this retail renaissance, continuing their efforts to reorganize the association. Fear drove them to plan for the postwar closures that could devastate Phoenix. F. W. Asbury, who led the group in 1943 and 1944, created a committee to strategize. Those involved issued dire warnings of competition from boosters in other cities, whose intent to attract new industries could rob Phoenix of postwar investment. Such concerns heightened rainmakers' certainty that they were best prepared to lead. "The new era would be one of peace," the Chamber's president Herbert Askins stressed, "in which the chamber would provide leadership for the city and state in order to make Phoenix and Arizona a better place to live and work."[13]

Future stewardship underlay 1945 changes to the Chamber's bylaws. Revisions formalized more than a decade's worth of private remonstrations against the Chamber's interwar leadership, closed-door discussions of industrial potential, and public denunciations of liberalism. A strong restatement of the organization's purpose came in article III. The Chamber now assumed the power to "promote and foster the civic, economic, and social welfare of its members and the City of Phoenix, the Salt River Valley, and the state of Arizona, and to acquire, hold, and dispose of property, and to do any and all things necessary or suitable to those ends." This property clause was critical for the Chamber's industrial program. Phoenix's vast, undeveloped surrounding lands were a major draw for the military commanders and defense contractors that moved to the Valley. During the war, both the Chamber and the local government had to work out complicated, costly deals to buy property from either private owners, the city, the county, the state of Arizona, or the federal government. Under the revised framework, the Chamber could simply buy parcels and sell them directly to firms, which streamlined recruitment by circumventing government agencies and stockpiling desirable plots. This maneuver very much complemented the pragmatic, experimental boosterism designed to overcome the policy restrictions that had discouraged investment without threatening the buying-payroll principles that attracted investors interested in cost-effective relocations. Other organizational adaptations also increased the Chamber's influence and effectiveness, including new membership qualifications, changes in the duties of the board of directors, a $32,000 budget increase (bringing it to $70,000 a year), and new paid staff positions for the management of the association's day-to-day operations. Committee numbers tripled, which furthered the process of placing the Phoenix association on par with the most vigorous interwar Chambers. Specific departments now addressed industrialization, retailing, conventions, public relations, membership, and statistical information. The Post-War Development Committee even had subgroups, which included task forces for aviation and tourism.[14]

Chamber leaders also refined publicity and communication. The association published and distributed the first comprehensive directory of Phoenix and Maricopa County manufacturers and distributors in 1946. This listing made its way to members, other Arizona business groups, chambers of commerce in major western cities, and select wholesale and manufacturing enterprises outside the state. Hired advertising consultants recommended that other promotional materials should limit the dry tables and charts used in the *Phoenix Gold Bond* and feature color pictures of the surrounding area, like those used in the Atlanta Chamber's bulletin. Advisers maintained the expense would prove negligible in the long run because national publications could save and then use these images on slow news days. A new monthly newsletter, first entitled *Whither Phoenix?* and later changed to *Phoenix Action!*, was a vital part of, as president Askins described, "our revitalized Chamber of Commerce." The publication, still less sophisticated than Atlanta's well-established bulletin, chronicled ongoing initiatives, concerns, and recruitment campaigns.[15]

But hiring a salaried general manager topped the board of directors' professionalization agenda. In 1944 demobilization fears, lawyer Frank Snell recalled, inspired a search for "a very high, competent, effective, honest, respectable director" to help the Chamber "hold on to all the business we've got and, also, to begin to sell this community." Lew Haas first met with Phoenix boosters on a business trip on behalf of a Los Angeles–based trucking company. His resume impressed rainmakers: he had served as the *San Francisco Chronicle*'s business manager as well as the San Francisco Chamber of Commerce's representative in Washington, D.C., and its executive director. Phoenix businessmen begged him to take the job for just six months in order to aid in their institutional renovation. Haas, according to his wife, considered the offer an intriguing challenge, largely because the previous generation's parochialism confounded him. Still, he only accepted the offer because the desert eased his daughter's asthma.[16]

Haas's paternal concerns were only matched by his energetic, systematic boosterism. "The president is the show horse for the Chamber," a later president explained; "[Haas] was the workhorse." He founded the Chamber's Industrial Development Committee, on which the most energetic and influential businessmen served. All dedicated themselves to any program that would attract more industry to the Valley. The Chamber's traveling representatives also reported to Haas, even though most were on Valley National Bank's (VNB) payroll, for it was the general manager who met with city council members and had the ear of the governors' and state legislators.[17]

Haas reached out to politicians because he, like other influential Chamber men, considered Phoenix's industrialization dependent on a broad transformation of Arizona. "We believed," the president who hired Haas summarized, "that by united action in matters which should benefit the state we will be furthering the interests of every community, including Phoenix." Haas thus urged members to look west to the massive, well-organized San Diego and Los Angeles Chambers. He declared that Phoenicians needed to work with, not compete against, other Arizona towns and business associations. Only through cooperation, he argued, could they counter better organized West Coast affiliates. Transportation between Arizona towns was of particular concern. Haas contended that the state had already lost firms to New Mexico and California because their highways were better. He noted that cities in southwestern Arizona were also more a part of Los Angeles's hinterland than of Phoenix's. Winslow, for example, was just two hundred miles from the capital, yet businesses found it faster to send trucks to faraway Albuquerque and Los Angeles than to Phoenix.[18]

Chamber efforts to take advantage of the war boom in the Salt River Valley paralleled those of other revitalized business organizations in the South and Southwest. Opportunity for bases and factories, for example, had prompted organizational overhauls analogous to the internal changes that had transformed the Phoenix Chamber under Snell and his successors. Miamians expanded their relatively impressive interwar efforts through an Industrial Development Committee because a 1942 visit to the Los Angeles association had convinced them that "Miami could not build much further on the resort industry alone." The Miami committee's self-appointed chairman directed members to "[get] our house in order [by] approaching every Governmental sub-division to secure every possible industrial concession and cataloging all such assets," feting every visiting industrialist to find out "what this city should do to interest him and his friends in locating manufacturing projects here," and "hunting for industry, one unit at a time." Miami boosters also unanimously agreed to completely revise their existing area survey, catalog existing business "concessions," and "study . . . the present vocational training program . . . and need for its expansion to meet our industrial growth."[19]

This recruitment initiative coincided with an internal professionalization of the Miami Chamber. Publicity Committee members weighed in on Miami and Dade County promotional advertisements, developed a Publicity Board to better disseminate materials, and used their contacts to develop "publicity stories in trade magazines, house organs, national magazines of civic and fraternal organizations, and foreign newspapers and magazines." Miamians also adapted to industrialists' needs once they had secured investment. The Chamber organized a wartime Special Labor Committee after local managers complained that African American laborers' absenteeism slowed output in both commercial and defense industries. Subgroup members sought to regain control of streets and shop floors through campaigns "to make Negroes realize . . . that their first job is BEING a No. 1 American." Strategies included "compulsion to get the Negro loafer off the street," "have some representative leader . . . sell them on the idea that they are a responsible part of the organization," and long-range vocational training.[20]

Investment campaigns also necessitated that increasingly better organized associations fully engage with local and federal politics. Dallas Chamber men, for example, had spent the 1920s envious of Houston's growth and its powerful booster class. They had thus been dedicated to comprehensive governmental reform in these years, an effort that culminated in substantial 1930 city charter revisions. Reform provided Chamber men with more influence over city affairs, though they largely performed the business of governance through their successful and popular civic association, the Dallas Citizens Council, not their Chamber. In comparison to Phoenix rainmakers, Dallas promoters were far better positioned in their local government to lobby for wartime investment and secure the local inducements necessary to bring industry to the area. During 1940 lobbying efforts, Dallas Chamber men enticed investors with assurances that union density was low, that the weather was good, and that the town generally put business needs first. They also offered North American Aviation (NAA) executives a desirable location and promised to direct $25,000 from city funds toward the airport improvements that the firm needed. Boosters also reached out to other governing bodies: the Dallas County Commissioners' Court constructed the roadways between the city and plant, while policymakers in nearby Grand Prairie provided utilities.[21]

A similar crusade established the town of Marietta's Bell Bomber plant. In 1941, Cobb County's seat was an agricultural community in Atlanta's hinterland with just 38,300 residents, mostly farmers. Atlanta Chamber men, among the interwar South's most aggressive promoters, urged their rural neighbors to campaign for a military airfield. Marietta's grasstops, particularly its lawyers, were at the forefront of providing land incentives and other inducements to persuade the Bell Aircraft Corporation and the military to build Air Force Plant No. 6, soon the world's largest aircraft assembly facility. Atlanta's mayor and its most prominent professionals, who would form a fifty-member Marietta Chamber in 1942, embraced whatever was necessary to secure the desired defense dollars and industrial work. Labor needs were an especially pressing issue, so they worked closely with Georgia lawmakers to find federal funding for a training facility. Atlanta boosters lauded this investment in a skilled workforce: "Every person in Cobb county who wants to work at the bomber plant can obtain the training to fit him to work there." Yet local officials and business leaders remained opposed to federal or union efforts to more effectively raise wages and more fully reconstruct this part of the South. Such hostility sustained Bell's discriminatory hiring policies, well known among its twenty-five hundred African American employees (out of a total workforce ranging between eighteen thousand and twenty-eight thousand). Only a third held skilled positions.[22]

The Atlanta boosters involved in this deal exemplified the ways in which the peripheral, urban grasstops networked within a set of larger national business matrices. The city's significance to the South and outside investors made the Chamber important to leading executives. The U.S. Chamber of Commerce's president even spoke at a June 1941 luncheon about the need to "Build America Strong" through a "Moratorium in Industrial Strife" and "sound, patriotic, unselfish leadership." Atlanta boosters were also as well connected as Phoenix rainmakers. Michigan native Charles Palmer, who openly championed "diversification" "to get out of cotton," had attended Dartmouth, served in the U.S. Calvary on the Arizona-Mexico border, and started a small real estate firm in Santa Barbara, California, which a visiting Georgia Coca-Cola executive persuaded him to leave in 1920. Palmer invested in Atlanta's downtown office district while serving a variety of leadership positions in the U.S. Chamber of Commerce, Southern Conference of Building Owners and Managers, and National Association of Building Owners and Managers in the 1920s.[23]

The Atlanta Chamber's internal structure also highlighted how many boosters eventually came to conflate boosterism with governance. The Chamber's 1940s letterhead included, for example, the raison d'être: "To Help Make Atlanta the Best Governed Community in the South." At this time, the association already had in place the kind of organization committees that the Phoenix Chamber had only just started (bodies dedicated to industry, better business, information gathering, publicity, member relations, agriculture, and legislative research). Delta promoters increased the number of bureaus during the war in order to oversee apportionment, aviation, budgeting, education, fire prevention, health, housing, labor, metropolitan planning, population growth, public finance, recreation, traffic, and waterways, all of which prefigured the ambitious work that chambers elsewhere took on during peacetime.[24]

Reorganization and promotion reaped dividends. More than $60 billion was spent in Western states; nearly half this total came from defense contracts. The entire region secured 15 percent of all outsourced agreements. At one moment during the war, two-thirds of domestic army and navy bases were in the South. Labor-intensive projects, such as military bases, airframe factories, shipyards, and munitions, were sited in the South, whereas the Southwest housed these and other more sophisticated, high-tech initiatives, including facilities to develop and build radar and navigation systems. Marietta's Bell Bomber plant exemplified this regional rule. The fabrication facility stood in stark contrast to the sophisticated airplane parts factories operating in Phoenix. Intraregional differences were also acute. Federal dollars tended to flow to more populous areas. Forty-five percent of all new Far West war production plants, for example, were in California, generally around Los Angeles and San Francisco. Smaller towns, like Phoenix and Marietta, also secured funds, factories, and employment opportunities. Civilians subsequently poured into these communities for defense work. Richmond and Vallejo, California, quadrupled in size (to roughly a hundred thousand by war's end). Across the South and Southwest, downtown merchants, grocers, bar owners, restaurateurs, and hoteliers reaped the benefits of the deals to open military bases and manufacturing facilities. These towns blossomed on weekends, when workers and service personnel in nearby plants and camps went in to rest, relax, and shop. "This whole draft business is just a Southern trick," one officer quipped, "something put over by Southern merchants to hold the big trade they get from the training camps."[25]

Desperate Reconversion

But demobilization threatened to destroy this newfound prosperity even before war's end. Federal reconversion policies best prepared large corporations in established manufacturing centers for peace. Executives at General Motors (GM), for example, had stored most of the equipment once used to build its cars and trucks, which enabled its Michigan factories to quickly reconvert to civilian production. Management also benefited from a substantial federal tax refund that compensated defense firms for canceled contracts and the money spent to retool plants and equipment. Under such conditions, GM and other conglomerates tended to abandon their Southern and Southwestern facilities, many of which had been built without forethought as to how they could be refashioned for postwar use.[26]

Impending industrial desertion threatened to devastate cities, such as Marietta, Denver, Dallas, and San Diego, that had mushroomed in size and population through wartime spending. "Where are you going to find jobs for returnees?" Denver's Defense Council director wondered. "We often hear 'what have we been fighting for?'" Workers had reason to worry. Marietta's twenty-eight-thousand-person workforce shrank drastically even before the war ended, and few employees remained when the army turned the facility into a warehouse for surplus machinery. The situation was also dire in the West. NAA halved its Dallas staff between 1943 and 1945. All lost their jobs when executives vacated the facility after the Japanese surrender. Aircraft industry employment in Southern California also dropped dramatically, peaking at 2.1 million in December 1943 and falling to 1.23 million by July 1945. By 1946, only eight thousand San Diegans still manufactured airplane parts. The payroll produced by this sector had also plummeted from a high of $311 million to roughly $100 million.[27]

Such severe economic dislocations generated an intense debate about how the periphery might prepare for the postwar era. NRPB officials attuned to the needs of the Southwest had advocated planning to ensure continued industrial investment and better public services. Appointees studying the South prioritized accessible capital, vocational training, higher education, minority and poor white enfranchisement, progressive taxation, and more public infrastructure. Officials contended that such policies would facilitate a set of social and political partnerships, involving government, business, and ordinary citizens, to attract skilled, high-wage employment opportunities and establish national work and living standards.[28]

Substantial collaboration took place. Before the NRPB's demise, Twentieth Century Fund researchers catalogued almost two hundred domestic organizations actively working on reconversion policies. Twenty percent were government agencies. Most voluntary associations were research and educational institutes, business groups, trade unions, and farming associations. But coordinated planning persisted even after Congress defunded the NRPB. Atlanta Federal Reserve economists noted that regional groups formed at the board's behest, such as the Southeastern Regional Planning Commission, continued to operate. Committees tied to other federal agencies also strategized for a prosperous peace. The Department of Agriculture's Interbureau Co-Ordinating Committee on Postwar Programs included regional administrators from ten different federal departments. Delegates primarily synchronized research conducted in five different universities across the South in order to commission proposals and recommendations to avoid future problems in farming, conservation, and land use.[29]

But federal efforts were far from coordinated, systematic, or comprehensive, which enabled business organizations to play a sizable role in how reconversion unfolded. The American Management Association, Inc., for example, discussed postwar problems at all of its divisional conferences, which brought together ten thousand executives from across the country for each meeting. The group published extensive guidelines for how to make the most of generous federal demobilization policies; titles included "Blueprinting the Planning for the Postwar Job in the Factory," "Finding and Planning the Postwar Sales Structure," and "Population Shifts and Postwar Markets." NAM honed its arguments against liberal statecraft in the committees formed to fight inflation, shape contract termination agreements, ensure business's continued place in federal agencies, and advise individual manufacturers negotiating payouts, plant deals, and equipment sales.[30]

The Committee for Economic Development (CED), a national organization of prominent financial and industrial concerns, stood out among these private associations for its undertakings at the national, regional, and local levels. Commerce Department officials and businessmen serving in the federal government's Business Advisory Council conceived the panel as a workgroup for rapid economic reconversion. Jesse Jones selected most of the organization's original board of trustees, who guided CED after its September 1942 incorporation. The founders' faith in expert management represented an extension of the technocratic corporatism within the Progressive Era's National Civic Federation and Herbert Hoover's associative state. "The Challenge which business will face when this war is over cannot be met by a laissez-faire philosophy or by uncontrolled forces of supply and demand," one affiliate declared. "Intelligent planning, faith in the future and courage will be needed." Members championed the use of the federal government to guarantee high employment, largely through budgetary, tax, and fiscal policies. "Private business has little to do with maintaining high levels of employment, and . . . there is little that local governments can do," the CED's first chairman proclaimed.[31]

Local activities clashed with such Keynesian declarations. "When I started this job, I thought we were going to hatch a hen egg. It has turned out to be an eagle," the chairman quipped. CED established deep connections with small business associations and municipal governments nationwide and focused on directing the power of both, often overlapping, groups of residents to campaign for industry with the same kind of aggressive buying-payroll policies that underwrote Mississippi's Balance Agriculture with Industry. Collaborations with boosters prioritized the expansion and professionalization of municipal associations and governments to enable these towns to compete aggressively for private investment. At the local level, this advice reinforced the free-enterprise principles that CED's board of trustees warned federal policymakers were inadequate. Thus community guidance further reinforced what the grasstops had learned through their pragmatic experiments to attract and sustain substantial industrial investment.[32]

Expert efficiency infused the CED's systematic efforts, a spirit well suited to the organizational overhauls taking place within local business associations. CED leaders divided their operations among several districts, which mapped onto the Federal Reserve Branch Banks' regions. County and community chairpersons (sixty-eight in the Atlanta division's territory) worked directly with local companies negotiating with the federal government and provided resources for towns eager to use empty factories to diversify their economic base. Atlantans, who consulted with CED's area committee, listed but one objective: "High level of post-war employment." The Jacksonville, Montgomery, Mobile, Sarasota, and Birmingham Chambers also reported coordinating with the CED. The Birmingham group openly asserted, "We are following [CED's] outline, adapting it . . . to local needs and conditions" in order to attract "the new types of manufacturing that will come with new products such as plastics, glass products, etc." The Jacksonville association was equally active, starting thirty subcommittees within its industrial commission, six dedicated to aviation and only twelve focused on agriculture.[33]

Boosters and outside executives largely dictated the terms for new or continued investment because they had the necessary money, organizational infrastructure, and influence. Dallas Chamber men, for instance, campaigned for new investment through an aggressive publicity effort that showcased the city, its largely nonunion workforce, and NAA's empty facility. After Chance Vought Aircraft Company executives had made their interest known, they gave Dallas boosters an eleventh-hour ultimatum for a runway extension at Hensley Field. The city council, then marbled with businessmen, quickly allocated funds for the 1947 improvements. The deal provided a whopping forty-five thousand jobs, but Chamber men had happily bought all this payroll without guaranteeing the kinds of workplace rights, wage guarantees, or long-term security that New Dealers held to be sacrosanct and promoters and investors considered abominable.[34]

The Phoenix grasstops, like their Dallas counterparts, were also ready to make such overtures to new investors by war's end. Haas had already helped the Chamber's new leadership irrevocably alter the organization, even if the full effects would not be seen for a few years. Between the Chamber's formal reorganization in January 1946 and the start of the 1948 fiscal year, membership grew from roughly eight hundred to almost twenty-eight hundred. Annual income subsequently rose from $38,000 to $140,000. The new leadership's demands for political engagement sharply increased during these years. Goldwater, for one, spoke openly about the need for the business community to move beyond the limitations of voluntarism. "Every unit of organized business in this country should do all it can to maintain and strengthen our system of free enterprise," he asserted. "We can become a model for the rest of the country" if we "take a firm stand against evils which threaten our communities."[35]

Yet these words and boosters' plans placed the Chamber at odds with liberals who hoped reconversion would extend the New Deal into the postwar years. McFarland, for his part, continued liberal efforts to ease businesses' demobilization, guarantee economic rights for the citizenry, and promote higher national living and work standards in Congress. He outlined amendments to the Taylor Grazing Act that allowed the government to compensate cattlemen who lost their leases when the government canceled agreements in order to build new military bases. He also ensured that private citizens and companies would be allowed to buy government property no longer needed after the conflict ceased. He even assisted the Tucson city council's purchase of the local federally built airport. The terms of the sale were quite generous: the town paid nothing but agreed to maintain the facility and possibly give it back if hostilities resumed.[36]

The freshman senator was most well known for his leading role in drafting the G.I. Bill of Rights, a series of entitlements very much in keeping with the New Deal's ethos. He worked with representatives from the American Legion, the Veterans of Foreign Wars, Disabled American Veterans, and other groups to ensure the 1944 Servicemen's Readjustment Act would serve to "prevent men from being stuck behind an apple cart on every street corner, to protect them from having to hitchhike all over the country, with no money in their pockets for a meal." McFarland predicted the entitlements would guarantee the majority of Americans "the privilege of owning property." He lauded the legislation's provisions for small business loans as not only vital to veterans but also "essential to the national welfare as a matter of course" because he considered both homeowners and entrepreneurs the great counterweight to the corporations, unions, and and state bureaucracies engaged in tripartite power-sharing arrangements.[37]

State leaders also promoted liberal policies that would have facilitated the state and region's full parity with the industrial core's regulatory apparatus. Osborn convened a December 1944 meeting for western governors at the Westward Ho Hotel so they could discuss how to continue the region's industrialization once the war ended. He embraced a new "Age of Flight." "The airplane," he enthused, "has conquered distance and overcome the physical boundaries and hazards which past generations have found barriers to their progress, economic welfare and, even at times, to their civilization and spiritual well-being." "We see the tremendous advancements being made in our factories and plants, in the research laboratories and offices, and on our farms and ranches," he continued. "We are witnessing a preview of the West's opening opportunity in a great period in expansive history." "We must be leaders, not laggards," he concluded, before issuing his plans to fully open up western regions to both tourism and commerce.[38]

Phoenix mayor Ray Busey also embraced manufacturing. Efficiency, order, and modernity were key themes in this liberal's plans to transform the city and its government. "We are on the eve of a great expansion: annexation, water, sewers, airport, recreational facilities, transportation, modern ways of management and operation—and PLANNING," he declared. Yet Busey also discovered that decades of colonial servitude had left the municipal government unequipped to build a modern industrial metropolis. He dedicated himself to a thorough investigation of "the 'bugs' of every type" in order to "[get] all these public functions properly operating to the benefit of the public." Revenue collection, vital to bolstering public services, topped his concerns. "Each taxpayer must bear the burden of City taxes in proportion according to what he or she actually owns in taxable property," he asserted. "Operations will be instituted to collect as well the taxes which should have been coming in to the City treasury." Busey, true to liberal reliance on the grassroots, also looked to "civic-minded men and women" to donate "their time and talents" so that "every department of the City will be thoroughly studied and operated on."[39]

Busey was also committed to using state power to attract industry. He even earmarked city funds to pay for the Chamber's advertisements in national magazines because he considered such moneys a legitimate expense to recruit investors "to feed the people who are already here." Moreover, he reached out to the Chamber before the military ceased operations at Luke Field in order to acquire the land from the federal government. The mayor, like other liberals who embraced corporatist strategies, urged cooperation between the state and business. Busey, excited by the installation's postwar potential, urged the city manager to "apply to the War Department, but we should take up with our four representatives and do everything humanly possible, take it up with the Chamber of Commerce . . . really get behind this thing." He celebrated his advisers' collaboration with the association because their efforts had secured "more payrolls, more industrial concerns that will make us more safe in the future from an economic standpoint."[40]

Liberal policymakers and Chamber men had reason to devote time, money, and manpower to reconversion. Phoenix defense plants, many deemed federal surplus, started to shut down in the fall of 1945. The Garrett Corporation, which parented AiResearch, chose to leave the Phoenix facility when the government cancelled $36 million in contracts (a Los Angeles facility filled the remaining work orders). Goodyear Aircraft ceased operating in mid-1946; the Litchfield Park plant became a storage site for naval aircraft no longer in service. City officials and boosters later struggled to find an occupier when Goodyear sold its interests in the enterprise in 1947. ALCOA's CEOs had wished to remain in Phoenix, but the government refused to sell the site to the company, bowing to pressure from the firm's rivals, who charged that the sale would give the company a monopoly on the market. There was limited interest in buying the site's machinery, though no other business sought to purchase the plant.[41]

The grasstops considered themselves, despite their wartime activism, unprepared for reconversion. They subsequently sought advice from industrial snowbirds, like Litchfield, and also prominent CED officials. One of the group's principal advisers, Paul Hoffman, the celebrated president of Studebaker, addressed Chamber men frankly about "Your Postwar Future." But rainmakers already knew that they had reason to worry. Their rivals in Tucson had already begun municipal improvements with the hope that continued development of the roads in and around the city would make it desirable to wholesalers, distributors, and manufacturers. The already established California manufacturing juggernaut was also a major competitor. San Diego's business community had raised almost $250,000 during the final years of the war for the purposes of improving its infrastructure and attracting new industry. The *Arizona Republic*'s October 1944 coverage of San Diego's success offered a stark warning for all residents, not just businessmen: Phoenix was not prepared to hold onto, much less attract new, production facilities.[42]

This impetus to compete for new industry, coupled with the mid-1940s reality of corporate divestment, only exacerbated regional urban crises. Across the South and West, the grasstops and their investor allies had the power to craft the policies necessary to guarantee the corporate welfare that underlay their vision for dynamic, manufacturing metropolises. Yet they still fought to increase their influence and implement their plans, struggles that produced local political turmoil within the dramatic postwar fight over who would fully reclaim Phoenix and the rest of the urban periphery.

PART II

Reclamation

Chapter 4

The Right to Rule

Phoenix's haute monde had much success attracting postwar investment. Produce companies, for example, opened new warehouses and packing sheds. One of the largest, the Mission Frozen Food plant, represented a million-dollar investment, a welcome addition to a city being weaned off defense spending. Manufacturers too were moving into the Salt River Valley. A Central Arizona Light and Power Company vice president, Albert Morairty, and a Chamber activist and Reconstruction Finance Corporation representative, Roy Wayland, convinced Aviola Radio Corporation executives to relocate some of its Los Angeles–based operations to the AiResearch plant, an opening that promised work for fifteen hundred. Chamber men even persuaded Reynolds Aluminum Company CEOs to use ALCOA's facility to produce window frames and furniture tubing.[1]

Rainmakers nonetheless struggled to retain and attract investment. By the mid-1940s, they had already tentatively moved past voluntarism to take advantage of but also stymie the liberal regulatory state. In the process, they had completed much of the ideological groundwork for a homegrown neoliberalism that embraced government power to free industrialists from regulation and taxation. Yet Chamber men could not fully implement the policies that would come to define the Sunbelt's corporate welfare states. Success proved fleeting, at least in part, because Phoenix unionism remained strong. The Teamsters struck Aviola in April 1946, and by July 1947 the firm had begun to pull out of Phoenix. CIO unionists then organized Reynolds Aluminum employees into Steelworkers Local 3937. Fourteen hundred walked out in August 1948 after negotiations over a change in the wage agreement broke down. The firm's president then threatened to close the plant. A prominent rabbi, the Chamber's general manager, and the head of the Chamber's Industrial Development Committee, with some reported support from the governor, intervened in the negotiations between Reynolds and its employees. Unionists held out for six weeks until they finally accepted management's proposed twelve-cent wage increase, which kept Reynolds in the Valley.[2]

Strikes and organizing drives demonstrated to the grasstops that the trade union movement was a potent counterweight to businessmen on their shop floors, in managerial offices, and, most important, in politics. The Chamber's attempt to resolve the conflict at Reynolds, without substantive state involvement, harkened back to an older, increasingly fruitless bipolar model of labor-management relations. But now federally protected unionism sustained a robust labor movement, which drove businessmen, at both the local and the national levels, to reconquer the political sphere and use governments to restrict union power.

Labor was a tangible threat. Militancy had helped upend long-standing political regimes in the industrial Northeast, Midwest, and Pacific Coast. Similar reform campaigns, emerging from both unions and nascent civil rights movements, made headway even in the proto-Sunbelt. But after a sharp struggle, boosters there proved victorious in turning back labor power and influence both in city hall and on the shop floor. Their success was predicated on a politics of growth and on policies that privileged business expertise in managing city affairs, prioritizing the needs of outside investors above general social welfare protections for local residents, and demonizing trade unionism as an affront to opportunity, affluence, and economic dynamism. As a result, a wave of anti-union laws and municipal charter reforms were enacted across the developing Sunbelt, which, taken together, provided boosters far more control over their hometowns and states by the mid-1950s.

Business Anti-Unionism

Hostility to unionism, among economic elites as well as the larger public, was a complex, shifting phenomenon. Organized labor represented both an ideological and a material challenge to business owners and managers, who fought trade unionism to avoid losing power and control over their enterprises. Their campaigns conflated legal, legitimate union activities with graft and racketeering, which served to besmirch the entire American labor movement, not just those locals and unions with mob connections. For a brief time during the late 1920s and early 1930s, the term "racketeering" had linked extortion to union trade agreements. The word quickly became synonymous with organized crime, but without any explicit connection to labor. "Racketeer" was thus deployed against business owners hostile to government-supported trade agreements as well as unionists eager to enter such arrangements. When used against laborites, the label became practically interchangeable with "Communist," which exemplified how mutable both words had become. This conflation also represented the knee-jerk, ideological reaction among elements of the American business community who saw no difference between the most banal demands for better wages, benefits, and hours and the more far-reaching calls for a corporatist or social-democratic reorganization of the American economy. Trade unionism also affected business's bottom lines. Guaranteed cost-of-living adjustments, pension plans, and health care programs were big-ticket items during postwar contract negotiations, the cost of which management often passed on to consumers.[3]

Contractual membership agreements proved lightning rods for those distrustful of the new economic order. The closed shop dictated that employers hire only workers who were already members of a trade union, whereas union shop provisions stipulated that managers could hire anyone they wanted, but that as a condition of their employment, these new workers had to join the union holding collective bargaining rights soon after they began work. Employer opposition to these forms of "union security" was constant throughout the first half of the twentieth century. Most in management cited the ostensible threat to individual liberty, which turned the issue into a moral and economic dilemma. For example, in a 1901 drive against the closed shop, both the National Association of Manufacturers (NAM) and the National Metal Trades Association claimed the campaign was essential to the health of American industry and the liberty of the working man. A year later, muckraker Ray Stannard Baker published an article entitled "The Right to Work," an early use of this iconic phrase, in order to denounce closed shop and union shop protocols. The journalist preyed on *McClure's* middle-class readers' fears that organized labor had grown so powerful that it could deprive workers of their livelihood, which seemed the case during the 1902 anthracite coal strike when strikers attacked miners crossing picket lines. World War I then transformed the open shop issue into a symbol of patriotism and freedom, generating an anti-union hostility that continued during the era of the open shop "American Plan," which large corporations sponsored in the early 1920s.[4]

The New Deal transformed labor politics of this sort. The 1935 National Labor Relations Act empowered the federal government to force management to bargain with those unions certified by a new government institution, the National Labor Relations Board (NLRB). Senator Robert Wagner (D-NY) sold the measure as a means to inaugurate an era of industrial peace, a truce that he and others maintained would raise purchasing power and thereby aid economic recovery. This legislation proved redistributive because recognized unions could now bargain for wage and benefit increases that enabled workers to consume what they produced. Although the new law did not cover public employees, domestics, or farmhands, the white working class—and those women and African Americans who managed to secure factory jobs—benefited enormously from it for decades to come.

Liberals improved upon this New Deal for labor during World War II. The National War Labor Board (NWLB) actually strengthened labor's place in an emerging system of tripartite corporatism, which balanced the power of business with the strength of a secure labor movement and an involved liberal government. A key facet of this wartime labor relations regime was the "maintenance of membership" contract clauses that the NWLB ordered for all unions that adhered to the wartime no-strike pledge. These provisions gave newly organized employees, or those organized under an older contract, fifteen days to withdraw from the union (few took advantage of this escape clause). After this inaugural period, unionists had to remain members in good standing. Failure to pay dues or abide by union rules meant expulsion from the local and termination of employment. This arrangement pleased labor leaders, who had agitated for such security for years. These protections gave their unions permanency and strength because almost total organization of a workplace was now possible, often in branch plants and production facilities where it had once been difficult to persuade management to bargain in good faith.[5]

Union growth and legitimacy only intensified managerial anti-unionism. Southern Democrats and Steelbelt Republican congressmen, welfare capitalists, and NAM members all expressed their opposition to organizing as part of their private and public remonstrations against New Deal and wartime liberalism. Managers and small businessmen across the country were also concerned, if not outwardly hostile. This cohort, a stratum below

American Liberty League affiliates, had more leeway to challenge organizers by chipping away at union power and security from the local level. They lobbied state legislators, for example, to craft policies that curbed union security, powers that the Wagner Act did not devolve onto the states. One of the earliest encroachments was Wisconsin's 1939 Employment Peace Act, which limited organizing tactics and also strengthened protections for employers, not unions, during drives. This law served as a model for other state assemblies; six states (Arkansas, Colorado, South Dakota, Idaho, Texas, and Kansas) passed similar acts in 1943. Congressmen also introduced successful legislation to limit sit-down strikes during the war and later modeled the crippling postwar amendments to the Wagner Act, popularly described as the Taft-Hartley Act (1947), after the state-level Peace Acts.[6]

Section 14(b) of the act's 1947 revisions soon emerged as the new focal point in the continued struggle over labor's legitimacy. Another clause prohibited unions from making membership a requirement for employment, but 14(b) specifically allowed states to prohibit contract clauses that required new hires to join a local; this legal language was often simplified as a ban on union or closed shops in state ballot initiatives. These so-called right-to-work (RTW) campaigns gave the phrase a meaning far different from the one Truman had intended when he spoke of postwar guarantees for full employment. Electoral contests instead proved to be referenda on organized labor's security, power, and legitimacy.[7]

State-level efforts depended on support from powerful executives, business groups, and political organizations, which highlights the important collusion of national CEOs and the grasstops. Two Steelbelt Republicans, Ohio's Senator Robert Taft and New Jersey's Representative Fred Hartley, introduced the legislation that provided this legal framework to prevent peripheral assimilation to the industrial core's labor standards, a critical distinction between liberal and business-driven industrial reclamation. Influential business associations, often headquartered in manufacturing strongholds, were vital to hinterland electoral campaigns. The American Farm Bureau Federation, NAM, U.S. Chamber of Commerce, National Labor-Management Foundation, and De Mille Political Freedom Foundation poured their resources into financing local campaigns across the country to end what they called "compulsory unionism," years before RTW supporters founded the energetic, well-funded National Right to Work Committee in 1955.[8]

These organizations and their affiliates were involved in the first RTW referenda, which occurred before Taft-Hartley's passage. In 1944, such propositions were put on the ballot in Florida, Arkansas, and California. Passage would, in effect, mandate a statewide open shop: owners of unionized businesses could hire anyone, without a commitment that he or she belonged to or would eventually join a union. The text of the Florida, Arkansas, and California ballot measures, modeled after the Wisconsin Labor Peace Act, relied heavily on appeals to liberty and freedom and argued that a "person has the right to work, and to seek, obtain and hold employment without interference with or impairment or abridgement of said right because he does or does not belong to or pay money to a labor organization." This same language soon became ubiquitous when legislators in other states drafted similar bills.[9]

The Labor Question in Arizona

Arizona voters passed the first southwestern RTW law in 1946 through a voter referendum. Controversy surrounded union power because Depression era organizing had turned Arizona's fields and factories into the frontlines of labor-management conflict. Thus, this bitter 1946 campaign represented one of the first public fights over how and who would direct the desert's postwar reclamation.

Congress had unshackled Arizona unionism from its interwar judicial restraints in the 1930s. The state Supreme Court then complemented federal laws by protecting closed shop agreements indirectly in 1939 and directly in 1944. Arizona unionists needed this assistance. The struggle to organize central Arizona farms was as brutal as the conflict embroiling California's agricultural heartland. A Communist organizer even asserted that he had almost been lynched during the Cannery and Agricultural Workers Industrial Union's membership drives and strikes. Such hostility forced laborites to request that federal arbitrators intervene in these disputes. When the large Tovrea Meatpacking plant had fired organizers, the rank and file retaliated with a boycott and a complaint to the NLRB, which listed a litany of unfair labor practices. Investigators found irrefutable evidence of managerial intimidation and coercion and thus concluded their study with a demand that the company follow the new law of the land in 1938.[10]

Intervention and activism facilitated the Arizona labor movement's maturation. Numbers grew from 16,600 in 1939 to 57,400 in 1953 (density thus increased from 17.4 percent to 27.7 percent). Such growth made it possible for Arizona unionists, like their brothers and sisters in the Steelbelt, to plunge into state politics. A true reformist impulse existed among segments of this radicalized Arizona working class. Wade Church, the president of the Arizona State Federation of Labor in 1944 and 1945, supported local Townsendites' "$60 to 60" pension ballot initiative. He also advocated racial tolerance within all union locals and urged labor to band together against postwar anti-union legislation. Phoenix American Federation of Labor (AFL) and Congress of Industrial Organizations (CIO) public employee locals even put their rivalry aside in the public sphere. They cofounded the City Employees Unity Council, which served as a political arm for these unions.[11]

Arizona unionism was still as much radical as it was bread-and-butter. The CIO had important footholds. In the copper belt, the International Union of Mine, Mill, and Smelter Workers (Mine-Mill) proved a militant, Communist-led successor to the Industrial Workers of the World and Western Federation of Miners. Trade Union Unity League and Cannery radicals made their way into Arizona cotton fields and migrant labor camps. The CIO's United Public Workers vied with the AFL's American Federation of State, County, and Municipal Employees (AFSCME) for the allegiance of Phoenix city workers, competition that did not prevent police officers, firefighters, and administrative secretaries from obtaining far better wages, benefits, and protections.[12]

Most Phoenix locals were nonetheless rooted in the AFL craft tradition. The Pressmen and Typographical Workers prepared city newspapers. The Millmen and the Fresh Fruit, Vegetable, and Agricultural Workers organized mills and packinghouses, while the Motion Picture Operators, Musicians, and Stage Hands represented those workers in the performing arts. The building trades were also well organized. There were Brick Layers, Brick and Clay Workers, Carpenters, Electricians, Painters, Plasterers, Plumbers, Roofers, and Sign Painters locals. Conductors, Switchmen, Street and Railway Workers, and Chauffeurs and Teamsters unions represented those in transportation work. Phoenix's small metallurgy sector was also well organized and included, by the early 1940s, the Boilermakers and Helpers, Hod Carriers, Iron Workers, Latherers, Machinists, Operating Engineers, and Steel Metal Workers locals. Bakers, Barbers, Black Smiths, Brewery Workers, Butchers, Cleaners and Dyers, and Cooks, Waiters and Bartenders unions also had beachheads in the service sector. These unionists generally concerned themselves with setting trade standards and monitoring city politics. Their seeming parochialism nonetheless rankled local business elites as much as the CIO's industry-wide militancy because AFL business agents and organizers played a vital role in setting and enforcing work standards, building methods, and trade jurisdictions, all of which gave the craft unions of that era real power when it came to governance of the workplace.[13]

The Hotel and Restaurant Employees and Bartenders Union certainly had this kind of influence. Cooks, barkeeps, and waiters had formed Local 631 in 1933, but the local was not effective until the union sent Don Baldwin, who had been a machinist and Teamster organizer, to revitalize the affiliate completely. Part of his strategy was to pressure bars and restaurants to join the Phoenix Restaurant Association (PRA), which had 126 members in good standing. Yet only thirty-two establishments displayed the union card, which symbolized an eatery's adherence to union-mandated standards. Rates were abysmal: some nonunion houses paid waiters and waitresses just a dollar a day, less than half a Local 631 dishwasher's salary. Baldwin agitated for nonunion bars and eateries to join the PRA so that the association could stabilize both wages and prices. Setting the cost of food and beverages helped owners, but managerial membership really aided Local 631, which not only got a union shop clause in its 1941 contract but also won an eight-hour workday and increased pay across the wage scale. A few establishments refused to join the PRA or to bargain with the Bartenders local, most notably the high-profile Westward Ho Hotel and Hotel Adams. Both were favorite watering holes for Barry Goldwater and his Chamber associates and also resort destinations for the wealthy snowbirds who provided the grasstops entrée into national business and political networks. Baldwin engaged in boycotts and picketing in order to force these fiercely anti-union establishments to join the PRA and hire union help. Such pressure complemented new federal workplace regulations and facilitated the substantial spurt in union membership during the Phoenix downtown's wartime renaissance: Local 631 rolls increased from nine hundred in 1941 to thirty-five hundred by 1946.[14]

The Right to Work in Arizona

Federal legislation, union militancy, and labor's legitimacy united area businessmen. The most aggressive were determined to reclaim the political influence and right to rule that they had enjoyed during the 1920s, when the U.S. Supreme Court had invalidated much pro-labor legislation. The Associated Farmers of Maricopa County, for example, was anchored in the Valley's earlier open shop movement but also shared some of the violence-prone outlook of the more notorious California Associated Farmers depicted in Carey McWilliams's *Factories in the Fields* (1939). The central Arizona farmers' chapter formed in the late 1930s, at the apex of the conflict over Tovrea's labor practices. These self-described "redblooded American men" had an impressive membership list that included farmers and ranchers but also Phoenix bankers (including Walter Bimson), lawyers, hoteliers, and retailers (Goldwater being the most prominent). Large meatpacking, agribusiness, and shipping interests, along with the area manufacturers of ice and feed, contributed the most to the organization's coffers. Leader Kemper Marley, a cattleman, deemed the organization a bulwark against Communism: "We swear that Maricopa County will not be ravished, her businessmen and enterprises broke and ruined, and her private citizens denied the right to work if they want work. We are not going to allow imported 'muscle men' or roughneck 'good squads' to dictate the operation policies of any legitimate business enterprises in this area, or to insult our women, or to intimidate our neighbors." Members' efforts to quell unionism included public denunciations, legal challenges, and violent confrontations. Marley frequently warned residents about troubles to the west. "Look at Harry Bridges' gang of thugs and Communists," he demanded, "who have sworn to . . . wipe out our very basic existence." Leaders persuaded local authorities to quell unrest in the fields, with the sheriff proclaiming himself ready to "dispatch a large force of men to any sector of the valley to quell any uprising and throw the ringleaders in jail." Constituents also concerned themselves with urban disquiet, including strident demands for picketing restrictions to frustrate Local 631's campaigns.[15]

This anti-unionism, infused with warnings of subversion, graft, and decline, continued to animate Phoenix and Arizona politics throughout the 1940s. But Chamber men, not farmers or ranchers, emerged as the spokesmen for and instigators of this intensifying assault on labor's security and power. Well-known retail prince Barry Goldwater's antipathy toward organizing stood out. His notoriety came from his family's department store, Goldwater's, his 1940 trip down and filming of the Colorado River, and his Jeffersonian Democrat Uncle Morris, who started Arizona's Democratic Party during the territorial period and later served in the legislature as both Speaker of the House and president of the Senate. Barry's image of himself as a compassionate capitalist defined his managerial style. He opposed organizing drives in his store and tried to prevent union inroads by offering sizable benefits, including life insurance and medical care. A newsletter, "As Pedro Sees It," kept employees abreast of company policies and spread Goldwater's own particular philosophy of management-employee relations. He used one bulletin, for example, to dismiss rumors that employees did not receive benefits until they turned sixty-five, when, in fact, they only had to work for twenty years to begin drawing on their account. He also relied on this publication to spread his own political and economic philosophies, such as reprints of Carl Bimson's arguments that liberal economic policy would generate uncontrolled inflation. Issues also featured numerous announcements, articles, news items, and cartoons of "Pedro," a Mexican American wearing a sombrero and a poncho.[16]

Goldwater's managerial policies, both purported and in practice, offer a window into the worldview behind the grasstops' multifaceted industrialization initiative. Paternalistic, with all its racial, gender, and class implications, best described the business culture of Goldwater's. The press lauded Goldwater as a model employer. One reporter, for example, envied the fourteen employees that the merchant treated to a fancy dinner when he opened a new store in Prescott. "Perhaps it's pretzels and beer for run-of-the-counter sales ladies," the writer noted, "but it's champagne and chicken if they're on *Goldwater's* payroll . . . and a chance to 'dine out' with the dashing bon vivant, Mr. Barry Goldwater." "Pity the poor working girls? Not if they work for Goldwater's."[17]

This welfare capitalism looked far different from the shop floor. Goldwater and his closest peers in the Chamber would later define themselves as being against southern reactionaries. Some businessmen, like Goldwater, considered Jim Crow laws personally repugnant but saw little difference between southern mores and the de facto and de jure racism surrounding them. Other boosters paid lip service to equal opportunity just to attract investors. The association's membership nonetheless had deep prejudices, which fed into their sense of responsibility for and rightful control of their town and businesses. Goldwater's, for example, hired minorities in the 1930s but not to man cash registers. These employees worked away from customers, in all likelihood, as in other splashy department stores, to keep the Anglo clientele comfortable. Yet the retailer's drawings in "As Pedro Sees It" also indicate that Goldwater may not have considered minorities capable enough for sales jobs or, as a local Phoenix civil rights activist and lawyer later told interviewers, the retailer "was blind" and "didn't pay attention." Goldwater used "Pedro," a bumbling, lazy figure, for comic relief. An editorial on misplaced economic fears was next to a cartoon that depicted "Pedro" laughing as he says, "I am worried seek [*sic*]." Goldwater also reprinted parts of Elbert Hubbard's "If I Worked for a Man" to make clear the relationship he sought with the "salesgirls." "If you work for a man, in heaven's name work for him. If he pays wages that supply your bread and butter, work for him, speak well of him, think well of him, stand by him, and stand by the institution he represents," Hubbard commanded. "I would not work for him part of the time, but all of *his* time. I would give undivided service or none."[18]

The store's training play, "The Death of a Customer," offered perhaps the best example of the culture behind the counters at Goldwater's. High-level managers and the Goldwater brothers wrote this morality tale in which a customer died dramatically in Barry's office after a salesgirl was snobbish, wrote an illegible receipt, abused the elevator, left the customer waiting for forty-five minutes during an unscheduled break, ignored the client while on a forbidden personal call, and committed a host of other sins. The final act was a trial, over which the Goldwater brothers and their store manager presided in black judges' robes. The defendant appeared before them in chains, with tattered clothes, unkempt hair, and no makeup, and listened as Barry admonished her in an unscripted speech about her transgressions.[19]

Anti-unionism was also woven throughout Goldwater's *Phoenix Gazette* editorials attacking liberalism. He had not been hostile to the early New Deal, especially toward modernizing key financial institutions and the West. Goldwater's even displayed the Blue Eagle in its windows and advertising until 1934. Later Rooseveltian reforms, especially those that extended the federal government's power and strengthened the union movement, increased the retailer's hostility. In "Scaredee-Cat" (1939), he lashed out at bureaucrats, laborites, and businessmen, whom he denounced for not challenging the "minority groups who are causing the tax increases" and "wagging their tongues where they will do the most good: in political offices." His disgust for the "American businessman," "the biggest man in this country . . . afraid of his own shadow," was palpable. "He is the man who condemns, and sometimes justly so," Goldwater charged, "the politician over his luncheon tables and his desks and in his other very private conversations, but never in the open where his thoughts and arguments would do some good toward correcting the evils to which he refers in private."[20]

Goldwater despised liberals even more. The year before, in "A Fireside Chat with Mr. Roosevelt," he had offered a powerful, public statement of a

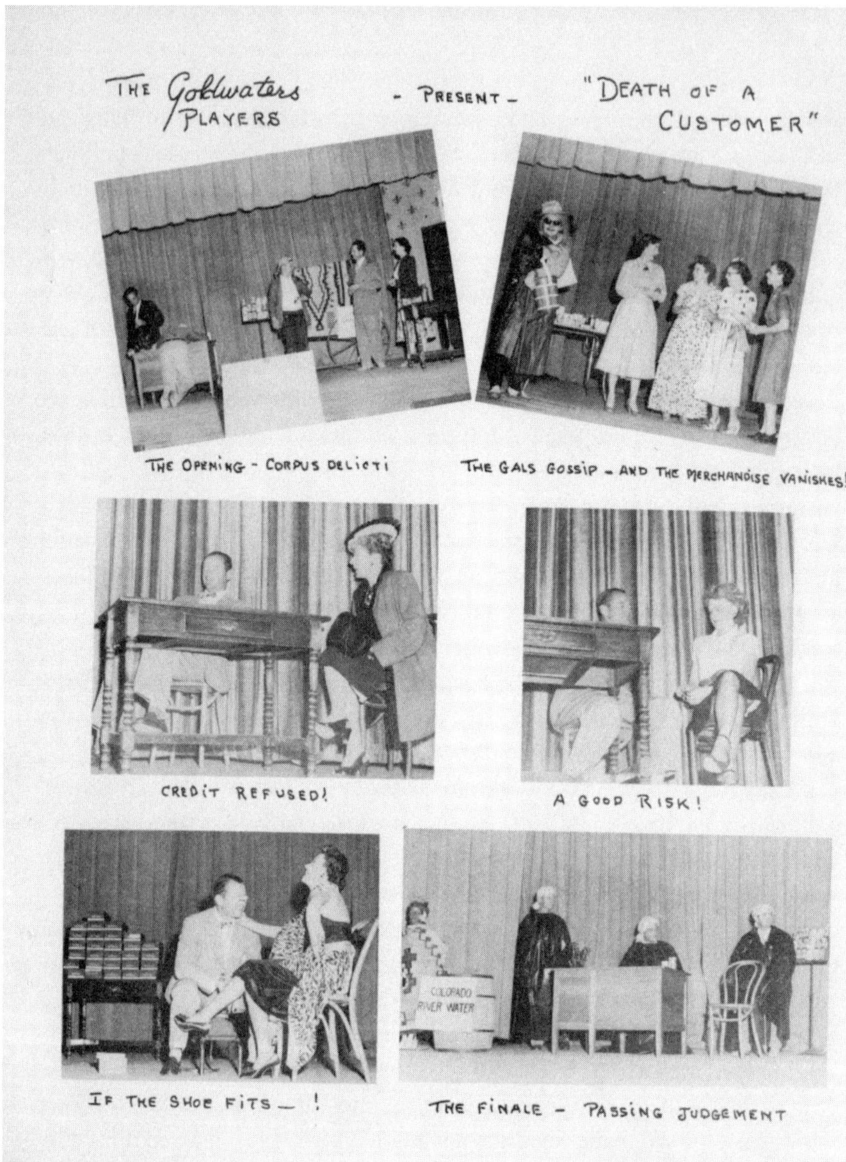

Figure 5. Photographs from the 1949 production of Goldwater's training play "Death of a Customer: An Original Training Play in Three Acts." The Goldwater brothers and their store manager scripted farcical, ribald antics into this training play to teach employees how not to behave on the job, lessons illustrative of the racialized, gendered, managerial worldview of Goldwater and his Phoenix contemporaries. Courtesy of the Arizona Historical Foundation, Saufley-Goldwaters Stores Collection, folder 14, box 1.

worldview openly hostile to much of the New Deal. "Just where you are leading us?" Goldwater had asked in 1938. "Are you going further into the morass that you have led us into," he continued, "or are you going to go back to the good old American way of doing things where business is trusted, where labor earns more, where we take care of our unemployed, and where a man is elected to public office because he is a good man for the job and not because he commands your good will and a few dollars of the taxpayers' money?" "Your plans called for economy in government and a reduction in taxes," he declared. "In five years my taxes have increased over 250 per cent and I fear greatly that 'I ain't seen nothin' yet'!" The worst move, from Goldwater's standpoint, was Roosevelt's "turn[ing] over to the racketeering practices of ill-organized unions the future of the working man. Witness the chaos they are creating in the eastern cities. Witness the men thrown out of work, the riots, the bloodshed, and the ill feeling between labor and capitol and then decide for yourself if that plan worked."[21]

Goldwater's columns bolstered Frank Snell and the Bimson brothers' efforts to stoke outrage against local and national New Dealers. George Mickle, whose buildings housed the Chamber at the time, wrote to Goldwater personally to commend him for taking a stand in the pages of the *Phoenix Gazette*. Lender George Ford praised the merchant's writing as "logical, fearless, and as far as it goes, truthful." "Compared with the average citizen, as your writing shows, you are a goliath," Ford gushed. "I say to you openly and fearlessly and would publish it now if possible, I hold the masses in contempt and their leaders and masters." Goldwater's words even inspired compatriots in more industrialized areas. "If business men [*sic*], over the United States would follow your example and publish articles of the kind," Henry Morgan of the Springfield Fire and Marine Insurance Company's Pacific Branch asserted, "it would in my opinion have a very beneficial effect."[22]

Goldwater had not yet embraced strategies to quell union militancy and to court workers that involved the state, much like the Chamber men who had tried to intervene in the postwar strikes at Aviola and Reynolds. Goldwater, for example, disliked *Arizona Labor Journal* editorials against the Office of Price Administration's 1946 disbandment. OPA was of particular concern to retailers, who disliked the agency's successful use of price controls to stop inflation before and immediately after the war. But Goldwater was equally concerned about class resentments and considered coverage an "attack on merchants." Yet his letters were not inflammatory. He instead wrote respectfully, "not in criticism of your journalistic efforts in this matter, but rather to express my views and those of the majority of reputable merchants throughout the country."[23]

Such private pleas were a far cry from the public indictments Goldwater and other Chamber men made during their efforts to pass a right-to-work law. This effort represented a forceful break at the local level with the bipolar model of union-managerial relations that the Wagner Act made obsolete. These efforts to legally restrict union security at the state level began during World War II. Boosters had long supported the open shop, but the NLRB's ruling against the Tovrea meatpacking operation stoked their anger. "Some one in Phoenix must make a stand in refusing to enter into the closed shop type of agreement," chain-store grocer A. J. Bayless demanded in letters to Valley businessmen. Pressure to limit union power only intensified, which led legislators to introduce several bills in both the House and the Senate in 1945. Most died in committee, but two proposals became the backbone of the RTW controversy. Senate Bill 6 stipulated that hiring for positions in state agencies could not consider union membership. Senate Bill 61 declared that no person's employment should be contingent on belonging to a local. Nine months after submission, the Senate defeated Bill 61 twelve to six. But public interest in the two measures and widespread concern over returning servicemen's needs led to the placement of the issue before voters.[24]

The coalition behind this drive paralleled the alliance within the Maricopa farmers' association. The success of the Labor Peace Acts and the early RTW referenda in other states had inspired retailers, hoteliers, and professionals in Phoenix and Tucson to collude with rural mining and agriculture interests to put a law weakening unions on the ballot. Chief among the supporters was Goldwater, who cashed in on his celebrity by reaching out to other merchants to make sure they supported the bill. Phoenix lawyers also aided the cause. They drafted the legislation and spoke on the issue publicly. Captains of commodities also supported the measure in the pages of *Arizona Farmer* and *Pay Dirt*. Farm and mine owners argued once again that the open shop kept subversives out of a far too powerful labor movement and a vulnerable state. Support was strong: 84 percent of Arizona Small Mine Operators members backed the anti-union legislation. Large copper outfits did not openly champion the proposition for fear of work stoppages but still provided behind-the-scenes aid for the public fight waged by the Arizona Farm Bureau, the Chamber, and the GOP.[25]

But the referendum's cause célèbre was a conflict within the Phoenix construction trades, not Arizona's mine shafts or agricultural fields. In 1945, highly decorated serviceman Herbert Williams started a welding business with five nonunion employees who had also just returned from the war. When his firm lost a job in Phoenix, Williams blamed unions and their closed shop agreements. The contractor claimed that locals refused new members until all of their current affiliates had jobs and alleged that organizers discriminated against veterans by privileging card carriers who had not gone off to war. He and his employees worked with lawyer George Hill, another returning serviceman, and other Arizonans to sidestep the legislature by putting the union security issue on a ballot initiative that relied on the 1944 Florida and Arkansas RTW statutes for its legislative and legal language. Williams and other union opponents put themselves forward as the Phoenix Veterans Right to Work Committee (VRTWC) and made patriotism, individual freedom, and corruption the campaign's key themes. Goldwater became one of the group's most prominent public spokesmen, also heading the VRTWC's efforts to enlist support from other businessmen, although the nonveterans among them stayed out of the spotlight.[26]

The 1946 initiative, like other union security referenda, forced a public debate over the philosophy that would guide postwar development. The VRTWC threw charges of dictatorship, Communism, and racketeering at unions and in the process publicly articulated the Chamber leadership's arguments against liberal labor policy. "Communists Aid Labor Bosses in Fighting Right-to-Work Bill" was the headline in one pamphlet. This handbill also connected the union and the closed shop issue to racketeering. A cartoon featured a bumbling, rumpled, cigar-smoking, overweight "labor boss" pressuring a worker "how to vote" with his "political theories" and "political philosophy." The burly, overall-clad unionist stood before a voting booth and declared: "Look, Mister! When I'm in There, I'm My Own Boss!" The cartoon's intention was clear: organized labor was an undemocratic institution riddled with both mobsters and Communists. Such charges dogged the Bartenders leadership. "Immediately following V-E day, Don Baldwin, secretary-treasurer of Local 631 . . . attempted to make Phoenix druggists sign union contracts forcing all employes [*sic*] to join unions," one newsletter alleged. "Druggist McCrary asked the union leader: 'What will happen to the boys I previously employed when they return from the Army and want their jobs back?' 'They will join the union or else they won't work!' Baldwin is quoted as saying." RTW ads in Spanish newspapers also decried the leverage that enabled leaders to collect dues while denying Mexican Americans jobs.[27]

Such arguments spoke to a majority of the electorate. Labor's success in the Northeast and Midwest seemed to have made Phoenix vulnerable to a new kind of corruption that many voters feared would retard reconversion. "Times are too strenuous," Tucson's Anna Gemmell declared, "to let John L. Lewis, Phil Murray, Walter Reuther, or William Green wreck our economy." Others, such as E. V. Silverthorne of Gilbert, blamed New Deal legislation for this economic threat, proclaiming that "the wagner [*sic*] Act was the most onesided and weakest Law [*sic*] ever ground out by any Congress." "I can see no reason why Labor should not have the same restrictions that are placed on Management," he reasoned. Voters often rooted their skepticism about labor's strength in concerns for returning G.I.s. A Salt River Valley agriculturalist who owned a large farm with many field hands asserted in a legislative hearing: "I have no quarrel with organized labor in any way, shape, or form," but "I think it is the only democratic thing to do . . . we should have the law on the statute books of this state which will permit those boys when they come back to go into any kind of a job without being required to join the union."[28]

Rank-and-file RTW supporters often focused their anger on the specter of the federally protected trade union movement. United Mine Workers member Luther Wofford was "100% for unionism but I want to tell you and I would like to go on record that I am absolutely against the labor racketeer." "When it comes to a point where a man or group of men can step up to another man and say, 'You can't work here unless you join our union,'" he declared, "that is un-American." William Coxon worried that there were "infamous people who sometimes head our organizations who ought to be cast out of them for the good of the rank and file." The former unionist also held that when "we say that a man must belong to a union, then it is a despotic monopoly." Phoenix unionist Dove Riggins begged the governor, "Stand with the working man. We depend on you to make that Work to Right [*sic*] Bill a law" because the measure would "cut their scheming out."[29]

Labor struggled in the face of these public denunciations. The Arizona political landscape seemed ready-made for a powerful trade union movement able to withstand this RTW push: a strong contingent of voters had long supported organizing, union density was high, and the Democratic Party's registry had grown. Yet the state labor movement had nonetheless fragmented. AFL leaders lamented that the Arizona branch of its political organization, Labor's League for Political Education, failed to endorse or publish a list of pro-union candidates. CIO strategists had similar problems.

Officials did not organize an Arizona division of the umbrella organization's political task force, CIO-PAC, until 1951. State leaders hoped it would "get labor in Arizona all going in the same direction." They had reason to be skeptical: unionists often seemed to lack champions from the state's majority party. "There are two types of Democrats here," a CIO stalwart lamented. "Both are controlled by the same interests."[30]

Laborites thus scrambled to defend their right to security. Unionists active in the state federation's Labor Defense Committee organized a Citizens' Committee Against the Right to Starve to defeat the RTW bills even before the issue had been formally placed on the ballot. Baldwin headed the Phoenix-based group and coordinated with other statewide associations opposed to the measure, including the left-wing American Veterans Committee and the more staid Veterans of Foreign Wars. Both chafed at the open shop supporters' assertion that they represented all former G.I.s. Without membership protections, RTW opponents warned, Arizona workers would be at the mercy of management, who could easily cut the good wages, benefits, and working conditions for which unionists had fought. Within these claims was a defense of the New Deal path toward postwar economic progress. Campaign literature stressed, "This proposed amendment does not, will not and cannot, create jobs." "The few extra dollars of spending money in the pockets of the working men and women, the most numerous class," unionists asserted, "mark the difference in this country between prosperity and hard times." "Those are the same few dollars that would be lost to the worker through the collapse of collective bargaining and wage guarantees if this proposed amendment were passed." "The amendment can and will destroy jobs," labor leaders concluded.[31]

Critics also declared the proposition unpatriotic and unsound. "We have two million organized boys fighting over there," the retired secretary of the Prescott painters argued. "I don't want them to return and have them find organized labor busted up in our beautiful State." "The open shop . . . only creates bitter feeling, disruption and [a] very low standard of living," Joe Rodríguez, a Phoenix Painter's member, declared. "If it was to be enacted . . . one of the most chaotic and dangerous conditions would develop in America to the point where I am sure Mr. Hitler and Mr. Hirohito would thank Heaven that such developments took place." "These two bills," an electrical worker proclaimed, "destroy the true rights of collective bargaining." Unionists themselves refuted claims that security clauses harmed workers, managers, or customers. "They have a closed shop in Phoenix," the president of the Arizona State Culinary Workers Alliance noted. "It has worked splendidly for the interest of the worker. It certainly hasn't hurt the public, their fares are as cheap as anywhere else." Stewart Udall, whose family was well known for its involvement in the Democratic Party, agreed: "A century of American history has written the lesson in bold-face type that the open-shop is a shop of violence, poor working conditions, subsistence wages, and abused human rights." The compulsory open shop, Udall continued, "would invite all manner of union-busting activity and might place the individual worker's welfare on no better footing than the mere good-will of management."[32]

Despite these vigorous protestations, organized labor was soundly defeated in November 1946. As elsewhere in the South and Southwest, arguments attacking labor's strength and ill-gotten gains prevailed. The proposition passed in every county. Fewer than fifty thousand voted against the measure, with more than sixty-one thousand in favor (56 percent).[33]

The fight was hardly over. Phoenix's Westward Ho Hotel became the epicenter of the conflict's next phase. The hotel had great symbolic significance. Many Chamber-oriented fraternal organizations met there, and the association had once used clubrooms for meetings. Local 631 leaders also prized the establishment. They had struggled to force the owner, who disdained both the union and the PRA, to negotiate. Antagonism only escalated after the new RTW legislation outlawed many of the protections that had enabled the local to grow so rapidly during the war. Employees struck thirty-six hours after voters approved the proposition, which turned the Bartenders' picket lines into demonstrations against the law. Owners declared publicly that they would permanently replace all striking workers, unionized vendors refused to make deliveries, and newspapers reported intimidation, violence, and vandalism aimed at replacements. The protest stretched into the early months of 1947 when several of 631's contracts with other businesses expired. Emboldened managers offered the union the same wages and benefits but refused to keep the security clauses or recognize the local as *the* bargaining agent for culinary workers and wait staff. The number of protests around the city grew and only ended after two weeks of selective protests forced owners to rehire striking workers and begin arbitration. Westward Ho's management remained steadfast: the owners only agreed to bargain just before the venue was scheduled to host, and hence stood to lose, the fall 1947 National Reclamation Association conference. Local 631 did not win recognition, but strikers, who had been out of work for almost a year, were rehired.[34]

Other unions also protested the statute's passage. Construction workers across the state, but especially in Phoenix, began talking about a general strike immediately after the proposition passed in 1946. More than two hundred workers walked out in July 1947 after the Del E. Webb Construction Company, fatted from defense work, refused to enter into a new wage agreement. The builder had contracts throughout the state, but the conflict hit Phoenix the hardest after the city building trades also declared the firm an unfair employer. Workers returned after four weeks, but arbitration still dragged on for months, ending with employees winning a twenty-cent hourly wage increase. Then Local 78 of the Fresh Fruit, Vegetable, and Agricultural Workers struck the Arizona Vegetable Growers Association for three months in 1947. More than three thousand laborers shut down the thirty-four sheds on Grand Avenue for three months over wages and union shop clauses. A fight erupted between strikers and scabs within a week. More than two thousand protestors surrounded the packing sites when replacements crossed picket lines. Outraged workers burned one of the sheds, which prompted liberal Governor Sid Osborn to declare martial law and call in the Arizona National Guard. Rancor continued for three months until growers offered a 10 percent wage increase and workers capitulated to an open shop contract clause.[35]

The "right to work" nonetheless remained an incendiary issue. Framers had neglected to insert enforcement provisions, which effectively made the original law a paper tiger (Local 631 as well as some construction locals still benefited from near union shop and closed shop conditions). Legislators quickly submitted and ratified a new bill, which enabled the courts to enjoin locals to force compliance and also permitted suits against unions for violating the law or urging others to do so. This hastily passed amendment lacked an emergency clause and would not take effect until ninety days after the legislative session ended. This oversight allowed unionists to circulate petitions to place the changes on the 1948 ballot. Laborites gathered more than ten thousand signatures, four thousand more than they needed but still far below the AFL's goal of forty thousand. The referendum also guaranteed that rules would not go into effect until after the vote. Organizers mobilized members to put an outright repeal of the 1946 statute before voters in 1948 and took their case to the courts. The AFL sued the American Sash and Door Company in February 1947, claiming that the new law was unconstitutional because the Arizona statute denied unions and employers the right to contract freely, discriminated against unionists, abridged the freedom of assembly, violated the Wagner Act, and denied workers equal protection.

These efforts failed. Citizens did not repeal the statute in 1948. Union density had increased to 24.1 percent (about forty-one thousand) but the number favoring the RTW law had climbed to 59 percent (more than eighty-six thousand). Voters also approved the new penalties the legislature had drafted; meanwhile the Arizona Supreme Court reversed its long-standing support for closed shop clauses in the wake of Taft-Hartley's passage. The U.S. Supreme Court justices then upheld the ruling in the *American Federation of Labor v. American Sash and Door Co.* (1948), which dashed the national organization's hopes of stemming state-level RTW campaigns and striking down section 14(b).[36]

Regional Reactions

The RTW controversy had a large impact on the South and Southwest, although this anti-union movement had different characteristics in each region. Southern union-shop fights were less about creating conditions favorable to the relocation of northern industry than about preserving the political power of the agricultural elite and the Jim Crow order. The southern aristocracy played a prominent role in elections because they faced multiple postwar challenges: a growing industrial class, an insurgent trade union movement, and a push for racial equality from African Americans and militant CIO organizers, whose organizational strategy attacked the system of white supremacy that structured the South's government, economy, and society. Mississippi planters, one reporter asserted, hated unionists as much as integrationists, noting that "whenever the talk turned to labor unions, the conversation was violent and burdened with hate and fear." "Who are the men who run this union anyway? . . . Baldenzi, Rieve, Cheepka, Genis, Jabor, Knapik, and Rosenburg," open shop proponents asked. "Just a bunch of pot-bellied Yankees with big cigars in their mouths. . . . If they come in you will share the same restroom with Negroes and work side by side with them." Farming elites found allies among southern manufacturers, who benefited from the Jim Crow order the planters had created because sharecropping and tenant farming ensured a reservoir of desperate workers who were willing to accept low wages and poor working conditions in mills and factories. Southern boosters also embraced these statutes because they fiercely guarded the wage and power disparities endemic to the region and attractive to investors.[37]

Yet racial demagoguery did not infuse southwestern RTW conflicts. As in Arizona, top-down, business-led campaigns generally capitalized on fears of labor's strength in the industrial Northeast and on Capitol Hill and conflated them with local labor-management conflicts. Proponents stressed that the Wagner Act was a dangerous law that fostered class conflict and allowed labor to grind industry to a halt. The villains were the labor "racketeers," whom New Deal policies had empowered and now protected.

Local business groups in the retail, tourism, service, agricultural, and extractive sectors were the leaders in these anti–New Deal counteroffensives. In all of these sectors, save agriculture, unions had been successful in organizing either in the West or somewhere else in the United States because of the protections the Wagner Act afforded labor. Owners and managers, like their Phoenix counterparts, feared the surge in union membership. In 1939 union density had ranged from 11.7 percent in New Mexico to 24.8 percent in California. By 1953 New Mexico still lagged behind with just 14.4 percent of the workforce organized, but union density in other developing states ranged between 26.8 and 37 percent. Such growth generated spectacular displays of labor's new strength. The International Brotherhood of Teamsters made impressive gains in the entire region by replicating the leapfrog tactics organizers had used in the East. The United Auto Workers made inroads in anti-union Los Angeles during the late 1930s after General Motors opened a plant in a white working-class suburb to service the West Coast car market and profit from open shop conditions. But managerial hostility did not stop organizers, who enrolled almost 95 percent of GM employees by February 1937. This victory was among the first that transformed Los Angeles from a company town into a city where organized labor had at least a foothold in almost all of the metropolis's major industries. Unions even established postwar service sector beachheads, notably during and after the massive Oakland "work holiday" in 1946. The retail clerks union, backed by a hundred thousand AFL unionists, shut down the city for three days, eventually forcing city retailers to offer the union a citywide contract. Labor even moved into the tourism sector. Unionized Reno culinary workers and bartenders went out on strike during 1949 contract negotiations for better wages and benefits, a stoppage timed with the all-important Fourth of July celebrations. Militancy proved a feature in southwestern mining: Local 890 of the International Union of Mine, Mill, and Smelter Workers struck the

Empire Zinc Corporation in 1950. Anglo and Mexican American miners and their families held out for more than a year in Hanover, New Mexico, a demonstration lionized in the famous left-wing film *Salt of the Earth* (1954).[38]

Business support for RTW became either a stopgap against earlier encroachments, a preemptive strike against unionization efforts before they began, or an ideological counterattack against any owner's loss of shop floor authority. Casino operators, who struggled to control organizing drives in the growing tourist and retail industries, forged ties with other open shop supporters in the Nevada Citizens Committee. This association accordingly swelled to two thousand members in both the northern and southern chapters just a year after the Fourth of July strike. Representatives from the old western economies also lobbied hard for the anti-union bills. Ideology largely drove growers' stand with other businessmen because unprotected laborites had only limited success in their continued campaigns in fields and orchards. Agriculturalists nonetheless sided with the mine operators, who argued that outlawing "compulsory unionism" was necessary because unions were becoming too strong.[39]

These counteroffensives represented attacks on union security and modern liberalism. RTW supporters, like those in Arizona, made frequent references to wartime industry-wide strikes as proof that organized labor was capable of bringing the economy to a halt, which implicitly dismissed labor's right to help craft economic policy. Accusations insinuated that an empowered trade union movement created industrial conflict, thereby endangering postwar affluence. Critics also deemed legal, normal trade union activities examples of corruption and racketeering. The slovenly gangster, not the shadowy Communist subversive, subsequently loomed large in closed shop literature. The Nevada Citizens Committee, for example, took out a half-page ad with an angry, fat, ruddy-faced labor "boss" chewing on a cigar, furrowing his brow, and wearing a gangster's hat and a pricey suit. The copy asked readers to consider why organized labor opposed the "right to work": "IS FREEDOM OF THE INDIVIDUAL UN-AMERICAN? Is his idea of forcing you against your will to join a union—American? That's what he wants—that's all he wants—complete power! He would be glad to take over—DO YOU WANT HIM TO?"[40]

Such denunciations hamstrung the southwestern trade union movement just as much as these charges had frustrated the Arizona rank and file. Laborites' arguments to protect union security clauses largely heralded the prescriptions for economic security imbedded in the Wagner Act and in

Keynesian social spending. Organized labor nonetheless struggled to form a popular front against the RTW threat. The Taft-Hartley Act had already weakened and splintered the labor movement. In the Southwest, Mine-Mill unionists, frustrated with their international's refusal to pledge that they were not Communists, divided the once powerful union. Locals abandoned the international "on grounds . . . that the International is dominated by Communists." Rivalry between AFL and CIO locals was also a problem. Attempts to unify Nevada labor organizations for political campaigns or lobbying efforts only seriously began in 1945. Yet the various unions and organizing bodies united only in 1956.[41]

RTW supporters consequentially won over a substantial number of voters across the emergent Sunbelt. Early propositions did fail in California in 1944 and New Mexico in 1948, but roughly 40 percent of voters considered restrictions necessary. A narrow majority, just 51 percent, passed Nevada's 1952 bill, but the percentage increased throughout the 1950s when Silver State unionists continued to place the measure before residents. The easiest antilabor victory came in Utah. Assembly members were so confident that the public favored the measure that they did not bother to turn it into a ballot proposition. The final tally split across party lines, with all Democrats in the legislature (six in the Senate and twenty-seven in the House) opposing the measure and all Republicans supporting the new statute (thirteen in the Senate and thirty-three in the House).[42]

These statutes proved pivotal to the grasstops-investor alliance to direct demobilization from within these domestic colonies. Labor had become bigger, more powerful, and more secure during the New Deal and World War II. Unions, moreover, demanded the kind of job security, stability, and remuneration that limited managerial power and company profits. And not just in the Steelbelt; locals fought for their rights in the South and West too, much to the frustration of boosters like Goldwater and investors like Aviola who considered organizing a tangible and philosophical threat. But Arizona's right-to-work statute did more than just maintain the enticing wage differential between the Steelbelt and its hinterlands. The law weakened union security and power, which freed Chamber men to increase their influence over politics and governance.

Chapter 5

Grasstops Democracy

"You get mad enough to punch noses. Then you punch doorbells," Barry Goldwater crowed in celebration of the National Municipal League selecting Phoenix as one of eleven All-American Cities in 1950. This recognition came just a year into his first term on the city council. Goldwater had reason to be pleased: the award was more for him and his grasstops running mates than for the town. The Chicago-based organization enthused that these "citizens refused to quit," displaying perseverance that had "turn[ed] the rascals out" and even converted a budget deficit into a surplus.[1]

Goldwater's foray into city politics had been as much a part of industrializing and reclaiming Phoenix as the right-to-work campaigns. The retailer had been angry for more than a decade. He had watched in horror as Phoenix workers organized Valley fields and businesses, picketed new industries and his favorite watering holes, and formed political associations to turn out the rank-and-file vote. But he had done far more than knock on doors. His efforts to revitalize the Chamber and pass union shop restrictions had done much to stymie the Arizona labor movement. But right-to-work laws were far less effective against the liberals and small-business owners who fought the grasstops for control of city hall. The town's charter also stymied boosters, who found that they needed to do far more than just run for office. They had to actually rewrite the rules by which leaders were elected, city affairs were conducted, and taxes were collected.

Such struggles over governance had been at the core of American big-city politics since Reconstruction. These battles continued through the Progressive Era, when northeastern white, upper-class reformers famously denounced "machine politicians," "ward bosses," and "special interests" for impeding efficiency and progress. Samuel Hays's classic 1964 study emphasized that these so-called good-government efforts and citywide elections had enabled urban elites to marginalize all but the more affluent and well-connected voters. The kind of clean, professional management that the National Municipal League so admired was thus predicated on an elite belief that cities would prosper if business leaders controlled municipal politics.[2]

Analogous movements in the South and Southwest were delayed and ineffective partly because of their towns' small size and porous class hierarchies. The urban upper classes in these regions faced potent challenges from outside their caste, including the areas' petit capitalists, who resisted radical, liberal, and even elite civic reform. These businessmen were not grasstops professionals, owners, or managers, who, by definition, had strong connections to regional and national alumni, banking, and business associations. The stratum of smaller shopkeepers and proprietors, who dominated interwar city halls, tended to slip back and forth between middle- and working-class status. Phoenix café owners, for example, rejoined the Bartenders' rank and file if they could not make a profit, as did erstwhile contractors affiliated with the building trades. This urban tier tended to value free enterprise, property ownership, and hard work but embraced proprietary capitalism, not the emergent corporate strain structured around the large, bureaucratic conglomerates that boosters privileged. Phoenix's petit-capitalist set, who filtered in and out of city politics in efforts to secure lucrative supply contracts, certainly fitted this description. Hence they represented as much of an affront to the Chamber's large-scale investment efforts as radicals, liberals, and unionists, who also attempted to maneuver these small-business owners out of power.[3]

Musical Chairs

Phoenix Chamber men created one of the most powerful, long-lasting, industry-attuned postwar municipal machines. The city's first charter, passed in 1885, had established a weak city government during a time when most residents looked to private companies, not the municipality, to provide water and power. Phoenix had four wards. Residents of south Phoenix voted in the third and fourth, while the more affluent Anglo population living across the railroad tracks chose representatives for the first and second districts. Councillors had to reside in, own property in, and pay taxes in Phoenix. They received reimbursement for expenses and time, not a salary. Public service was, nevertheless, profitable for elected officials and petit capitalists running small supply stores or construction crews. Councillors decided with whom the city contracted under a closed-bidding process, which promoted fierce competition for seats from among the middle-class stratum. These Phoenicians ran in or spent money on elections for their preferred candidates, who often received some type of additional remuneration for their votes.[4]

Residential demands for public services and utilities inspired the first charter revisions. Progressives in both parties faced stiff opposition from the circle of councilmen who drifted in and out office and from voters who refused to support the bonds necessary to invest in the city's infrastructure or buy existing utility companies. Reformers used the specter of patronage and corruption and the promise of efficiency and growth to persuade voters to pass charter amendments. "Many cities had been compelled to adopt [commission government] as a matter of self-defense of its citizens against corrupt political machines and grafting politicians," the *Arizona Gazette*'s editors asserted. This change, the *Arizona Republican* editors promised, would mean "the employment of the best men we can hire to run this large business, men of capacity and honesty." At-large election provisions were a critical issue. Supporters made no secret of their wish to employ this policy to disenfranchise working-class voters. "The third and fourth wards are composed of a class of people who do not meet with the high ideals of those here present," the Good Government League's secretary stipulated during a 1914 public meeting.[5]

Subsequent reforms increased the local government's scope and power. Voters endorsed by a margin of three to one a 1914 proposal that gave all policymaking decisions to a mayor and four commissioners. Candidates ran in nonpartisan citywide elections for staggered, two-year terms. The unpaid city council also hired an uncompensated city manager with the stipulation that he or she be a city resident. This chief administrative officer made almost all appointments to city offices, had the power to fire employees, prepared the annual budget, made contracts with vendors, and oversaw all public services.[6]

Implementing reform proved far more difficult than ratifying revisions. Phoenix's elite had been involved in the mayor's commission to draft a new charter but stayed out of politics after its passage. Thus, petit capitalists remained in control and continued fighting over who would sell the city paint, hardware, and concrete, prosaic goods in sharp contrast to the wares and services that the grasstops stratum of department store owners, bankers, lawyers, and newsmen provided Phoenicians. City contracts, moreover, also provided the profits that small businessmen, often allied with craft unionists, needed to keep themselves in politics. Thus the first city manager, William Farish, encountered fierce opposition from local business owners and politicians when he demanded businesses pay their taxes and participate in an open bidding process. Commissioners also resented Farish's ability to hire and fire city employees and opposed his plan to pay for public infrastructure by dismantling the costly kickback system that discreetly awarded contracts and dictated the contours of municipal politics. Officeholders not only rejected Farish's proposals but also ousted him in 1915, an election year when a budget shortfall necessitated a scapegoat.[7]

Farish's dismissal stymied progress. A new citizen's committee called for more charter revisions that enabled the commissioners to select all major appointees (the city manager could make recommendations only for minor offices). Thus corruption continued. Petit capitalists spent thousands in annual elections because commissioners divided up orders into small increments, which gave them control of three-fifths of the $1.2 million the city spent on such expenditures annually. Officeholders also continued to blame their emasculated appointee for many of Phoenix's problems. Staggered, two-year terms for commissioners led voting blocs to be reformulated almost yearly, often coinciding with the city manager's dismissal (there were twenty-three managers between 1920 and 1940). "Phoenix government resembled a game of musical chairs," one historian later commented. "Few mayors or commissioners remained in office for more than one term, and city managers came and went with them." Indeed, most expected to be fired after Election Day. "I knew that today was City Commission meeting day—bloody Tuesday, and this is why I wore my burying suit," one opined before his termination. "Henceforth you [should] simply chalk the names of new temporary officials on their office doors, thereby saving the hard earned taxpayers' funds now spent on gilt paint."[8]

Turnover and profiteering robbed south side residents of much needed public resources and services. They turned not to the city government but instead to the voluntary associations that wealthier non-Anglos ran in order to ameliorate the effects of racism and poverty and, in some cases, challenge the existing racial order. Wealthier African Americans confined to south Phoenix owned banks, mortuaries, construction companies, real estate agencies, insurance companies, eateries, saloons, pool halls, barbershops, and hotels, all of which served black patrons. Chinese Phoenicians, also barred from Anglo institutions, created the Chinese Chamber of Commerce, Free Masons, Merchants Association, Salvation Society, and Chinese Boy Scout troop. In the 1930s leading Chinese businessmen led a movement to abandon their Chinatown in order to eradicate Anglo perceptions of a Chinese ghetto and to find new business opportunities within city limits. Affluent Mexican Americans, who resided on both sides of the tracks, also ran community organizations, including La Liga Protectora, Alianza Hispano Americano, Sociedad Benito Juarez, Sociedad Porfirio Diaz, and the Mexican Chamber of Commerce. One of the most long-standing service organizations for Mexican Americans was the Anglo-run and -funded Friendly House, modeled after northeastern settlement houses. Director Placida García Smith's programming emphasized vocational training, not citizenship. During the Depression, for example, she focused on finding Spanish-speaking men jobs in construction or landscaping while she pushed women into domestic service. She openly assisted repatriation efforts and in 1933 lauded her organization for having helped send 130 families back to Mexico.[9]

Voluntarism waned when working-class Phoenicians and their wealthier Anglo allies endeavored to force governments to provide city residents with a real New Deal. Father Emmett McLoughlin led the charge to provide Phoenix with a public housing authority. He toured his south Phoenix parish with a *Phoenix Gazette* reporter in order to publicize the horrific conditions. "South of the tracks," he declared in the late 1930s, was "a foul slum, the like of which can probably not be found elsewhere in the United States." McLoughlin used the resultant notoriety to pressure the legislature to pass a 1939 law creating municipal public housing authorities. The chaplain went on to chair Phoenix's Public Housing Authority, which quickly drafted a plan to raze slums and build three public housing facilities, two in south Phoenix, the Marcos de Niza Project for Mexican American and Mexican residents and the Matthew Henson Project for African American residents, and one in east Phoenix, the Frank Luke Jr. Project for Anglo denizens.[10]

An impulse to fight racism, segregation, and discrimination animated this political engagement. Phoenix's Latin American Club, like other similar associations across the state, struggled for social and economic justice, exemplified by efforts to turn the Latino vote out for those candidates committed to Mexican American civil rights. Leaders charged that the wealthy Anglo commissioners who dominated the city ignored Mexican Americans.

"There is out and out discrimination" in hiring, argued president Luis Cordova in 1939. "[Mexican Americans] are also tax payers of the City of Phoenix [and] . . . entitled to a certain representation in City Government." To resolve these issues embedded within segregated, stratified Phoenix, a multiracial alliance coalesced in 1943. The Greater Phoenix Council for Civic Unity's (GPCCU) largely middle-class membership dedicated themselves to ending "discrimination in Phoenix and surrounding communities . . . by means of education, consultation, cooperative planning" and "cooperat[ing] with local, state, and national groups." GPCCU grew from just a handful of members to more than four hundred within a year. Soon after, newly founded chapters of the Urban League and National Association for the Advancement of Colored People complemented this organization's work.[11]

The small, heavily Anglo, Phoenix Communist Party also launched popular protests in these years. The very presence of these radicals, no matter their negligible influence in city hall, made clear that the Valley might well have hosted a vibrant Popular Front coalition. Communists and their fellow travelers espoused a grounded Marxism that connected the desire for radical change with the day-to-day needs of a growing city. They placed candidates on the ballot for all levels of public office, though no member ever came close to winning. They were also the first to publicly campaign for election-law changes that would enfranchise more minority and working-class people in city elections, appearing before commissioners in 1939 to appeal for charter reforms and a return to aldermanic districts "so that every section of the city and population shall be represented." Communists explained their support in the Popular Front's social democratic language: "The poorer people of the city have no opportunity to elect commissioners representing their section." City officials were unmoved. They refused to discuss the matter, dismissed the proposal outright, and never set a date for future consideration.[12]

Communists did not retreat. They later advocated a reconversion program that included full employment through the rehabilitation of defense plants for civilian use, the desegregation of emergency housing for veterans, and the continuation of federally funded child care. "If private industry cannot provide jobs for all," leader Karl Wilson declared in his 1947 commission run, "then the government must fill the breach with socially useful programs, such as street improvement, hospitals, libraries, parks, slum clearance, and low-rent housing projects." Radicals also took the struggle to the streets. As was the case elsewhere in the country, the Phoenix Woolworth's refused to hire African Americans as clerks in its store or allow them to sit at its lunch counter. In May 1946, more than a decade before the more famous sit-ins, fifteen African American and Anglo Communists picketed the store. Placards read: "Frontline for Democracy," "We Fought for Democracy Overseas, Yet Can't Eat in Woolworth's," "Woolworth's Pays Low Wages—Its Workers Are Not Unionized," "Arizona Needs Fair Employment Practice Law," and "Arizona Needs Civil Rights Law."[13]

Neither racial injustice nor electoral reform concerned petit-capitalist politicians who nonetheless embarked on some initiatives that fitted comfortably within the New Deal reformist impulse. Inept corruption best describes historical assessments of the interwar city government. But scholars have largely relied on newspapers' accounts, which leading members of the Phoenix Chamber owned, operated, and used as a means to guarantee grasstops power. These accounts ignored what commissioners did to revive Phoenix during the Depression. City officials made use of federal funds to modernize key components of Phoenix's infrastructure. A sewage system transformed sludge into fertilizers and reclaimed millions of gallons of water for farming. The municipal government also responded to citizens' complaints about air pollution, which hung over the city most mornings during the 1930s. The city's Engineering Department organized a successful campaign to persuade residents and businesses to cut back on the usage of wood and coal until a natural gas pipeline was finished.[14]

A Card Room Coup

Nonetheless, petit-capitalist governance rankled ambitious Chamber men. And the wartime boom only exacerbated tensions. Thousands of aircraft technicians and pilots trained in the Valley. But while sunny days pleased their instructors, increasing venereal disease and prostitution rates alarmed military officials. "There were nine houses of prostitution running, containing fifty inmates, two disorderly bars or joints which were headquarters for prostitutes, and one disorderly 'massage parlor,'" reported a federal investigator. Retailer Harry Rosenzweig later claimed that city commissioners profited from these activities because madams "would be arrested once a month . . . and they just automatically went down and paid the fine, only the fines went in a bag, and every month the council cut it up."[15]

City officials had, in fact, all but accepted the presence of prostitution. They endeavored to stop infections, prevent madams from buying off police officers, and funnel potential bribes into city coffers. Each month, every call girl had to post a $300 bail bond with the city clerk, which she displayed in her quarters to prove compliance. Women also received twice-monthly physicals from a city doctor, who provided prostitutes with another certificate to display. Jail awaited any courtesan or madam who attempted to circumvent these rules. But this municipal effort to manage the profession failed to satisfy the military, which threatened to declare the city off-limits to enlistees if prostitution and disease persisted. Alarmed city officials ordered the police to close down numerous houses of prostitution in 1942. Almost all quickly reopened, though without the "glaring neon signs" advertising them.[16]

A November 1942 riot in a largely African American neighborhood exacerbated the strained relationship between military officers and Phoenix commissioners. African American troops had been drinking in the area. One struck a young black woman on the head with a bottle. When an African American military police officer tried to arrest the assailant, he brandished a knife, which led another M.P. to open fire. One person was wounded. The other 150 troops out and about in the neighborhood became uneasy when buses arrived to take them back to their camps. In the commotion, witnesses remembered, a "lone shot from somewhere" rang out, which started a riot and led soldiers to quickly scatter. Phoenix patrolmen and military officers cooperated to find those involved. "They'd roll up in front of these homes" in personnel carriers, a bystander recounted, "and with the loudspeaker they had on these vehicles, they'd call on him to surrender. If he didn't come out, they'd start potting the house with these fifty-caliber machine guns that just made a hole you could stick your fist through." M.P.s arrested 180 men, killed three, and wounded eleven. Four days later, top brass forbade their charges to visit Phoenix. Luke Field's head officer claimed, perhaps to calm racial tensions, that it was not the "Thanksgiving Riot" that had prompted the ban; rather, the "venereal disease rate among military personnel" had been the culprit. No matter the reason, the restriction represented a real threat to downtown commerce, especially during the holiday shopping season. Commissioners were justly alarmed, promising "an immediate drive on all loose women."[17]

Chamber men used the issue to defame petit capitalists running the city. "We didn't get stirred up on morals too much," Frank Snell later clarified, "but when they were going to close the town, from an economic standpoint, that became important." Republican commissioner J. R. "Bert" Fleming, a businessman who aligned himself with the Chamber, saw the ban's larger implications: "War industries on the point of locating in Phoenix will decide that such conditions do not make for 100% production and that it will be safer to settle in a different city." "It will also make the recruiting of workers . . . difficult," he warned. "Women folks will not want to set out for Phoenix when other cities appear more desirable for their families." He also feared that downtown stores might lose as much as half a million dollars in sales. "For the betterment of Phoenix," he subsequently demanded, "I call on [the majority bloc] to resign your office."[18]

Newspaper owners emerged as an instrumental force in this power struggle, which solidified their place within the Chamber's long-term industrialization drive. "One of the big backers and helpers were some of the newspaper guys," a member later explained. The *Arizona Republic* had always been a mouthpiece for the state GOP (the paper had been called the *Arizona Republican* until owners bought the Democrats' *Phoenix Gazette* in 1930). Both the name change and the new acquisition were largely symbolic. Editors Charles Stauffer and Wesley Knorpp shared management of the dailies and used them to publish remonstrations against the New Deal, including Goldwater's inflammatory columns. They also controlled these newspapers' editorial content, which gave them a bully pulpit to rally the citizenry behind their cause and promote their preferred candidates during the war and afterward.[19]

Indeed, Stauffer and Knorpp helped orchestrate the coup that briefly gave the grasstops control over city hall. Knorpp had a vested interest in the matter: he served on the Phoenix Civilian Defense Committee, which concerned itself with the army's frustrations with crime and prostitution. The *Arizona Republic's* coverage attacked commissioners for "making no sincere effort to eliminate what has been called everything from 'a disgraceful situation' to much worse." The editors asked, "Are the people going to remain passive or are they going to demand that something drastic be done to remedy the situation?" This reportage set up Snell's 1942 "Card Room Putsch." More than fifty businessmen, led by Snell, Knorpp, and Chamber president C. E. Gollwitzer, attended the preliminary meeting to decide on their preferred appointees. Shortly thereafter seventy-five Chamber members attended the December 15 showdown at the Hotel Adams. These "representatives of the citizens of the community," as the *Republic* deemed them, assailed city officials into the early morning for the general "lack of confidence in government" throughout Phoenix and demanded the commissioners appoint their picks for city manager, chief of police, city clerk, and city magistrate. The commissioners capitulated in the wee hours of the morning, influenced partly by the few days left in the Christmas shopping season. They appointed an insurance man clerk and magistrate, a local businessman city manager, and a Maricopa County sheriff police chief. The military rescinded the ban three days later, with a threat to reinstate the quarantine if venereal disease rates rose again.[20]

The coup cemented local politics as a component of the Chamber's industrialization program and further sharpened grasstops' arguments for their innate right to rule. The *Republic* issued sweeping praise for the boosters' efforts: "Chamber directors have made it the solemn duty of all citizens and taxpayers to take a greater interest in and a more definite position with respect to the government of the community than has been the case heretofore." Coverage also emphasized the need for more business-focused reforms to attract investment. "The progress and growth of Phoenix depends entirely upon the type of city it is," the editors cautioned; being "a wide open town . . . would not make Phoenix the kind of community in which home-loving, law-abiding folk would desire to live."[21]

But boosters struggled to retain their newfound power. The 1914 charter gave commissioners staggered two-year terms. Grasstops candidates could only hope to win two seats at a time, which made it difficult to institute the broad policy changes the Chamber deemed necessary. They also needed to court a divided electorate. Residents actually had a range of political affinities, as evidenced by the nearly two hundred write-ins for open commission seats in 1945 (Snell, an African American community activist, and the head of Phoenix's Communist Party all received endorsements). The electorate's disparate and shifting allegiances mirrored, and partly influenced, the mutable alliances between officeholders in a town in which liberals, petit capitalists, Chamber men, unionists, and civil rights activists all sought to stymie their numerous opponents, form majority blocs, and pass substantive reforms of some kind or another.[22]

Constant realignments frustrated the grasstops. The city commission, with organized labor's support, took a stand against the emboldened Chamber in early 1943. One unionist angrily declared that "the City Hall had moved to the Adams Hotel." The Bartenders' Don Baldwin argued that card-room conspirators "represent only the business interests of this City and are interested only, not in good government, but in filling their pockets with that filthy lucre. . . . All of them . . . not only asked for a special privilege but they demanded it." Such support emboldened commissioners to publicly rebuke Snell, Knorpp, and Gollwitzer for their "excessive pressure." Within a month, the mayor, with the support of the commission's majority bloc, ousted Chamber-endorsed appointees and reinstated their predecessors.[23]

Chamber men subsequently formed the Phoenix Citizens Good Government Council (PCGGC), which Gollwitzer deemed the "godchild of the Phoenix chamber of commerce." Their first two candidates, Republican Chamber men Bert Fleming and Fred Wilson, won office in the 1943 election, formed a new majority bloc with another sympathetic commissioner, and replaced the city manager, clerk, and police chief within a year. Fleming's administration previewed the Charter Government Committee's business-attuned statecraft. PCGGC commissioners reduced deficits by both cutting services and resisting city employees' demands for higher wages but spent funds to upgrade Sky Harbor airport, draft plans to increase the water supply, and devote resources to curb gambling and prostitution. Their policies were controversial with local Democrats, who disliked the commission's "reactionary Republican leadership."[24]

Gollwitzer and Snell still considered the card room coup and the PCGGC a great success. In his 1942–1943 fiscal year report, Gollwitzer celebrated the Chamber's work to lift the military ban, protect the local economy, and inaugurate a new commitment to Chamber participation in municipal affairs. In a later interview, Snell admitted that the Hotel Adams insurrection was "the most undemocratic thing I ever did" but "very effective because as soon as [the military commanders] got word of it, the off limits was raised and we were back in business." He considered the takeover "just hitting the surface" but nonetheless instrumental in drawing "a fine group of people" into city politics "to prepare Phoenix."[25]

Liberals regrouped around 1946 mayoral candidate Ray Busey. The paint store owner straddled the line between the petit-capitalist old guard and Phoenix's nascent Popular Front. He had close ties to Father McLoughlin and the Phoenix Housing Authority, sat on the boards of St. Monica's hospital and the Phoenix Union High School District, and participated in efforts to integrate public parks and swimming pools. He had also endeared himself to labor. Congress of Industrial Organizations (CIO) unionists even put his name forward when the Maricopa County Democratic Central Committee pondered possible mayoral contenders. Busey's Greater Phoenix

Ticket, which included the Arizona Education Association's executive secretary and a veteran who had been Arizona's deputy U.S. marshal, ran on a reform platform that promised to implement changes to "restore representative municipal government." Candidates attacked the entire system: "You have no representative you can go and talk to on the city commission. Unless you live in a little preferred area." They also emphasized industry and growth, but not through business-first, buying-payroll principles. "We had dreams about Phoenix," Busey later explained. "We wanted Phoenix to be the economic center of the Southwest." He championed industrialization through a social, not a corporate, welfare state, which would attract new investment, build the city's infrastructure, end segregation, enfranchise south Phoenix residents, and utilize regulations and tax codes that prioritized public services. He was not alone in this vision for a local postwar New Deal to oversee growth from the grassroots. "The City of Phoenix will become one of the great cities of our nation," a running mate proclaimed, but "must not only become a city of unrivalled opportunity for those who will build businesses and industries. . . . Phoenix must become a city unexcelled as a community for people, all the people, to work in and live in."[26]

Liberals triumphed in the April 1946 election. In one of the highest voter turnouts in Phoenix history, Busey replaced Fleming as mayor, while the entire Greater Phoenix Ticket became the new majority bloc on the city commission. Under Busey, elements of a postwar New Deal seemed to be taking shape. The city entered into an agreement with Salt River Valley Water Users' Association to construct more spillways at the Horse Shoe Dam to serve the growing city, not just surrounding farms. A new public water treatment plant provided residents with thirty million gallons of water a day. Liberals also secured housing for African American and Mexican American veterans after minority servicemen had returned to find limited options. Federal Housing Administration officials had not authorized any projects in south Phoenix, nor did they challenge Phoenix realtors who redlined whole sections of the city. Most government-subsidized apartments also went to Anglo servicemen and their families. Close to a hundred black ex-soldiers had to move into a deserted Civilian Conservation Corps camp near South Mountain. Raymond Martínez, commander of a local chapter of the American Legion, later chastised the city for building housing for Latino veterans near a municipal dump. When officials moved this project into an Anglo neighborhood, residents demanded the project be closed. Busey was outraged: "We would have to break with all humanity if [the project] were stopped." Homeowners sued, but Busey never buckled. City attorneys won the subsequent court case, which kept the complex open.[27]

The same charter restrictions, shifting alliances, and political trench warfare tactics that frustrated boosters also prevented Democrats from instituting sweeping reforms. A holdover PCGGC commissioner signaled that he would refuse to cooperate with the new liberal bloc even before Busey took office: "I shall maintain that same independence of judgment in consideration of city affairs which I enjoyed and exercised during . . . the Fleming administration." The mayor found himself similarly frustrated with another PCGGC commissioner elected in 1947. "Neither you nor your good Government Club have made one constructive suggestion," Busey asserted during an open session. "Your total ideas have added up to nothing more than jumbled-up attempts to obstruct whatever is being done." Busey was partly responsible for this quagmire. An illness as well as his trips to promote Phoenix as a mail and transportation hub kept him from numerous commission meetings. Upon his return, he derided commissioners for reneging on promises of "an expanded water, sewer, airport, and City limits program." "Petty bickerings [*sic*] and small-time arguments for political gain have kept most of you busy at everything but those things you pledged yourselves to do," he lamented.[28]

Annexation facilitated the unraveling of a postwar New Deal for Phoenix. The development of residential communities and industry outside the city's borders long concerned Busey. Phoenix's planning director reported in August 1946 that 10 percent of the city's land stood vacant after the war, which partly influenced the construction of factories and subdivisions outside city lines. He recommended that town limits extend two miles around the entire perimeter in order to increase tax revenue and ensure proper planning so that these spaces did not develop haphazardly. Two 1946 and 1947 annexations followed these general recommendations. Busey then embraced a more expansive 1947 initiative to bring in all surrounding suburban areas. He warned that Phoenix would become "a hodge-podge of separate incorporated communities" and declared unpoliced sprawl "harmful to persons residing outside the city as well as in the city." His program was systematic. An appointee supervised all aspects of the annexation scheme, including oversight of public employees who circulated petitions. Neighborhood canvassers promised suburban-fringe residents that tax increases would be negligible in comparison to the reduced costs for improved water service, sewage disposal, fire protection, and police presence. All would lower insurance premiums. Busey also created the Greater Phoenix Council to work with Phoenix authorities in developing the 1947 annexation plans. Members included civil engineers as well as business leaders, even Barry Goldwater, who desired economic diversification even if his compatriots were not dictating policy. This alliance between experts, liberal officials, and businessmen, similar to wartime recruitment partnerships, brought the Phoenix Country Club, Carnation Dairy Company, and a residential area west of Central Avenue into Phoenix. Soon ten thousand new residents and five hundred more acres were added to the town.[29]

Physical enlargement floundered when officials attempted to annex industrial zones. Busey was out of office during the program's manufacturing-focused phase because illness had stopped him from running for reelection in 1947 (though he continued to appear at council meetings to defend the initiative). Implementation instead fell to newly elected, Busey-endorsed mayor Nicholas Udall, who hailed from a well-known family immersed in Democratic Party politics. Udall first targeted a six-hundred-acre tract, where warehouses, the Santa Fe Railroad yards, and the profitable Palmer Manufacturing Corporation operated unburdened by municipal building codes, zoning regulations, and taxes. But three key businessmen, Charles Meeker, C. A. Elquist, and Oscar Palmer, organized the West Phoenix Business Association to stop usurpation. "Phoenix has the most inefficient government," Elquist argued. Palmer balked at the additional taxes, which the city estimated to be between $3,000 and $4,000. "Any camel can carry so much," he warned. "We pay $27,000 more than we would in Little Rock and $37,000 more than in Wichita Kansas. We can't possible [*sic*] add $12,000 more to our load."[30]

Palmer's personal defiance transformed expansion politics. He presented Chamber directors with figures detailing his firm's contribution to the city's overall payroll, financial assessments of annexation's effect on his bottom line, and promises of lower operating costs from Texas and Arkansas promoters. He threatened to move unless the city abandoned expansion, eliminated taxes on manufacturing, or modified zoning ordinances. He also laid off 250 employees. Firing half his seasonal workforce convinced rainmakers, many of whom had supported incorporating residential areas, that the liberal annexation initiative was a mistake. A Valley National Bank (VNB) executive warned commissioners that if they wanted to attract, let alone keep, industry, they had to "give prompt attention to the whole subject of taxes on inventories, manufacturing, machinery, and industrial equipment."

The controversy sparked widespread public discussion. Twenty-five Palmer employees beseeched officeholders to abandon the proposal. "I have had several people contact me by telephone and in person," a homeowner reported, "[telling] us their troubles with assessments [that were] unfair and inequitable." "Something is going to have to be done to enable industry to stay in here," a contractor warned. "I can't pay City taxes on all my equipment and operate within the City." At least one commissioner eventually advocated "this idea of bringing in industry here by lowering the taxes, the machinery tax, the inventory tax." "Palmer," the representative reasoned, "would . . . serve as a guinea pig . . . because he is the biggest manufacturer here, and he will leave if we don't do something about it."[31]

Reformation

This annexation controversy proved but one component of a broader 1949 electoral referendum on industrial recruitment, business rule, and good governance. Busey had triggered this imbroglio when he ambitiously demanded charter reforms in October 1947. He advocated reestablishing the ward system to reenfranchise south Phoenix residents and allowing candidates to declare their party affiliations. Such solutions to Phoenix's political quagmire were firmly rooted in his faith in the grassroots to deliver democracy. "Successful government must spring from the people themselves," he declared. "Then, and only then, will it represent individuals in all neighborhoods and all walks of life." He also firmly rejected Progressive Era claims that partisanship wrought corruption and bossism, assertions both petit-capitalist and grasstops businessmen made to justify the status quo or substantive change. But Busey lost this battle because his Greater Phoenix Ticket running mates were less dedicated to reform and city commissioners publicly fought him and his plans. He also, like New Dealers before him, filled key policymaking posts with antiliberal businessmen.[32]

The mayor faced opposition from the start. Commissioners bristled when they learned of Busey's gambit, reading in the local press that he had hired attorneys, one of them labor lawyer and Arizona American Federation of Labor higher-up Wade Church, to revise the charter. "I, personally, as a taxpayer would not be willing to trust the judgment of either of those gentlemen in revising the City Charter," one representative fumed. Busey lost his majority on the city commission within weeks. A new bloc had formed, composed both of PCGGC commissioners and of Busey's former allies. Together, they selected a new city manager, James Deppe, the PCGGC's executive secretary. Although ostensibly a nonpolitical appointee, Deppe, a small-time electronics and appliance salesman, proved a skillful operative who continually flitted between one majority bloc or another on the city commission. He, for example, repeatedly clashed with Busey, brokered backdoor deals that circumvented the open-bidding system, and made appointments, including the police chief, without alerting the mayor.[33]

Deppe and the commissioners could thwart Busey's reform efforts because the mayor had failed to take into account the power of the grasstops, who opposed his efforts to enfranchise the grassroots. When Busey convened a Charter Revision Committee in October 1947, he had proudly announced that its membership would "represent almost every faction of the social structure of this great city." He named unionists, liberal Democrats, and minority residents as advisers. He also tapped ten boosters, the most notable being Snell and the Chamber's president, lawyer Charles Bernstein, who headed the Charter Revision Committee. Promoters wanted to be involved in this initiative, explained jeweler Newton Rosenzweig, because Phoenix was at a "crossroads. . . . Nothing much could be done without major changes in our charter." Busey afforded the workgroup great freedom, perhaps too much, because the businessmen soon assumed the lion's share of the work. "I never met them one time after they started," Busey later lamented. "I think that was another thing that one should never do. . . . They had minds of their own."[34]

The committee's recommendations accordingly followed the major tenets of good-government municipal reform: there would be no district voting or party influence. Voters instead considered business-backed charter changes, which replaced the four-member city commission with a six-member city council. All representatives, including the mayor, would be elected in at-large, biennial, nonpartisan contests. Primaries would be held in conjunction with national elections in November, which would give candidates a month to prepare for December general contests. The November 1948 proposals also allowed officials to hire a nonresident for the city manager post in order to recruit an able, experienced professional, who would theoretically rise above the corruption and factionalism that plagued municipal government.[35]

Revisions passed by a margin of two to one, a grasstops victory partially guaranteed by confusion and disarray among opponents of these changes.

Newly elected mayor Nicholas Udall was partially to blame. He proved himself more a conciliatory opportunist than a principled liberal. He had run for mayor in early 1948 by promising harmonious governance, resolving to keep Deppe as city manager and advocating a strong executive-mayor government, which would have given Udall tremendous power over the city's day-to-day operations. But both the city commissioners and Chamber men on the Charter Revision Committee opposed his plans. The former considered Udall's scheme as much a threat to their tenure and power (not to mention the spoils system) as Busey's ideas, while boosters advocated entrusting a professional city manager to run the town, not a local politician faced with biennial reelection. Fearing that neither proposal would pass, Udall relinquished his support for a strong elected, not appointed, executive less than two months before voters were set to decide on a new charter. The electorate was bewildered, and the resultant political paralysis sparked open protests and a rejection of what seemed like politics-as-usual. "Somebody is trying to do something behind the scenes," a voter surmised. "I am one who would like very much to bring it out in the open." "The present mayor and commissioners promised an end to this turmoil," a minister lamented, "but we again are faced with unexplained trouble." "You folks should pay more attention to running the City as a business," one resident complained, "instead of playing a lot of petty politics." "If you guys don't play ball," another warned, "we will get petitions to get all of you out."[36]

But passage did little to end the municipal infighting that angered residents. Voters had not elected a new mayor or city council and would not do so for a year, which left implementation of the changes to the same elected officials who had benefited from and worked within the old government system. The majority of commissioners united against Udall, just as they had against Busey, because Udall had ultimately supported the Charter Revision Committee plans. The majority bloc was thus able to pick its preferred candidates for the two additional city council seats and retain Deppe as city manager.[37]

The commissioners' defiance was but one reason for Chamber men to start a new nonpartisan slating group, the Charter Government Committee (CGC). The name purposefully linked the ticket to the popular reform measure and distanced the slate from the controversial, increasingly divided PCGGC, which had backed candidates and appointees, such as Deppe, who proved less attuned to grasstops concerns while in office. The CGC started small. Only eleven residents met in the summer of 1949 to discuss the upcoming council race. Young partisan professionals and Chamber stalwarts were the first to fill the organization's roster. Dix Price, president of the city's Young Democrats, remembered the venture as an act of bipartisanship: "I met the president of the Young Republicans on the street and he said to me 'Dix, we ought to get our two organizations together and bury the hatchet as far as city government is concerned and pick some good people and re-do the city charter and send this thing on its way." This coalition joined with an already organized group of businessmen to form "one massive citizens' committee." "They had the money and the time," Price explained, "the Young Democrats and the Young Republicans had the enthusiasm and the ideas." This select group's membership grew steadily, reportedly to more than three hundred members by the 1960s, almost all residents of Phoenix's wealthy northern neighborhoods (only twenty-four lived in Phoenix's south side).[38]

Barry Goldwater and Harry Rosenzweig figured prominently. The retailers were childhood friends, who played outsized roles in rebuilding the Chamber, city government, and Arizona GOP. Harry and his older brother Newton belonged to Phoenix's small enclave of Jewish merchants. Their father began Rosenzweig's as a pawnshop in the late 1890s and then developed his business into a chain of jewelry stores that also sold expensive silverware, china, and crystal. Harry shared Goldwater's passion for business and politics and dragged his brother into both causes. Harry served on the Chamber's board and also financed the key cultural components of the association's industrialization drive, including the Phoenix Little Theatre, Phoenix Symphony Association, and Phoenix Art Museum. He left his real mark in the founding of an aggressive, anti–New Deal, business-oriented state GOP. As a fellow Republican remembered, Harry and Goldwater "were really the center of what became the new Republican Party." When Goldwater went to Washington, Rosenzweig stayed behind and guided the GOP, serving as chairman between 1965 and 1975.[39]

Goldwater and Rosenzweig entered politics because they considered this work a part of a businessman's obligation to be politically engaged. "You both will probably think me seven kinds of a dirty bastard when you hear that I have decided to run for councilman," Goldwater wrote to his store managers. "I don't think a man can live with himself when he asks others to do his dirty work for him. I couldn[']t criticize the government of this city when I myself refused to help." He remained convinced, as he had been when he wrote the "Scaredee-Cat" editorial, that businessmen must govern:

"I know Phoenix will have two years of damned good government that I hope will set a pattern for the coming years and the coming generations."[40]

Both merchants proved vital to the cause. They helped the CGC win a slice of the south-side electorate by cashing in on their stores' positive image with non-Anglo residents and by campaigning in these neighborhoods on the promise that the CGC would bring more job opportunities to these struggling Phoenicians. Goldwater and Rosenzweig also claimed or received credit for selecting the inaugural CGC slate. Rosenzweig said later that he rebuffed initial requests to run but then agreed if he could pick the ticket. "I'd wanted people of stature," he explained. Reportedly he had initially reached out to a sympathetic trade unionist, an overture in spirit with the Chamber's reconversion era attempts to broker a private peace with labor. But pressure from union leaders led Jim Vickers to decline the invitation.[41]

Rosenzweig subsequently chose from Phoenix's haute monde. The CGC endorsed the reelection of commissioner Charles Walters, a prominent lawyer as well as Goldwater's fraternity brother during the year the retailer spent at the University of Arizona. The other candidates were Democrat Margaret Kober (wife of Goldwater's doctor and member of Planned Parenthood, the Phoenix Junior League, and the Community Chest), Chamber members Hohen Foster (who was also a partner in a local bottling company and a Democrat), and Frank Murphy (a successful insurance salesman). The final slots went to Rosenzweig and Goldwater; Rosenzweig reportedly convinced Goldwater to take the position after draining "the biggest bottle of Old Crow that I could find." Of these endorsees, four had been at the CGC's inaugural meeting: Hohen Foster, Frank Murphy, Harry Rosenzweig, and Margaret Kober. Rosenzweig was nonetheless keenly aware of the need to present voters with a "balanced" pool, which necessitated one woman and nominees of six different religious affiliations. Including a Jew, Catholic, and Mormon also reflected the spiritual diversity of the Phoenix grasstops. The illusion of bipartisanship and nonpartisanship was also a mainstay of this and later CGC tickets. Known Democrats, including the well-regarded Udall, appeared on the ballot, but half of the nominees were staunchly antiliberal Republicans, which was not an accurate reflection of the partisan split in Phoenix at that time.[42]

Udall had cause to join the CGC. Although he had sprung from a long line of Democrats and had been ousted from his job after Snell's Card Room Putsch, he also had close connections to many of Phoenix's most antiliberal businessmen, even attending the same high school as the Goldwater and

Rosenzweig brothers. Udall had also found himself more frustrated with commissioners, including his former running mates, than with the businessmen who had fought industrial annexation and his strong-mayor charter proposal. He had already sided with grasstops plans to guarantee some measure of strong-executive reform and was hence displeased when commissioners ignored his pleas to appoint interim council members who favored the just-passed charter amendments. City manager Deppe also rankled Udall, just as he had Busey. "I think Mr. Deppe has been under undue influence of outside forces," Udall told commissioners in the summer of 1948. "Because I have not agreed with these outside forces, they have marshaled various pressure groups against me."[43]

The 1949 election set grasstops and petit-capitalist businessmen against each other. Multiple independent candidates did run for mayor and the council, but the main contenders were the CGC slate and a Civic Achievement Group (CAG) ticket, which represented those small-business owners who had kept power since the 1914 charter revisions. Indeed, CGC endorsees considered these small businessmen as much an obstacle to the construction of an industrial metropolis as liberal Democrats and union leaders. "They just weren't big people," Kober remembered. Walters described them as "renegades." Goldwater asserted that these "incapable people" could not have provided "the type of government that a fast-growing community like Phoenix should have." The Democrat-dominated slate included Thomas Imler, W. F. Tate, Leo Weimick, Wallace Caywood, F. A. Ford, R. C. O'Hara, and Paul J. West. They stood in stark contrast to CGC nominees: West was a used car dealer, O'Hara sold refrigerators, and Tate owned a paint store. Several CAG candidates had ties to those resisting the already passed reforms. Tate had served on the last commission, joining other council members to name appointees to the empty seats over Udall's objections. The slate also wanted to retain Deppe.[44]

The CGC charged both CAG candidates and those associated with the city government with corruption. The CAG, one editorialist railed, was "dominated by the four Councilmen who have kept the present manager in his job despite the fact that he was reappointed in open defiance of the voters' mandate in approving the Charter amendment last November." The rest, editors claimed, were "tailenders who . . . were found as a means of solidifying the attempt to maintain status quo at City Hall." Deppe was another favorite target. Daily attacks on his less-than-two-year record in office eventually led CAG members to distance themselves from the city manager and promise to fire him if their ticket beat the CGC slate. W. H. "Doc" Scheumack, a paint store owner long active in city politics, seemed the most nefarious. His fundraising on CAG's behalf dogged him and his preferred ticket. CGC candidates and *Republic* newsmen labeled him a boss who had the city government in his pocket. He questioned, in a last-ditch effort to stop a CGC victory, how the newspapers could ever call a lowly paint retailer "the most powerful man in America."[45]

The press continued to be the Chamber's greatest weapon in municipal affairs. Knorpp and Stauffer had sold the *Phoenix Gazette* and *Arizona Republic* to Eugene Pulliam in 1946. The long-time snowbird and Indiana-based publisher would become one of Phoenix's most influential businessmen and a standout among the postwar conservative movement's coterie of media moguls. Born in Kansas to Methodist ministers in 1889, he traveled the Plains as a child. His parents instilled in him a missionary zeal, which he channeled into his journalism. He first embraced Progressivism, voting for Theodore Roosevelt in 1912, while writing against corporate greed, municipal corruption, and the Klan. His travels through Depression-ravaged Europe, like Bimson's trips, transformed his politics and led him to repudiate Rooseveltian liberalism. He decried the Democrats' platform as socialist. "It doesn't work," he warned, "because under it there is no freedom." In 1940, he supported Wendell Willkie, hoping that "the reckless, wasteful expenditure of federal funds is beginning to defeat the New Deal." The newspaperman's iron fist and influence soon became legendary. Colleagues called him BSC Pulliam, "Buy, Sell, Consolidate," because he had a small news empire both in the Midwest and, after his initial foray into Arizona, in the Southwest. Pulliam papers were notorious for their bias. When *Time* magazine ran a story on him, the piece opened with a famous Phoenix joke: "Pulliam asks one of his managing editors: 'What did Barry Goldwater say today?' The editor replies: 'Nothing.' 'Fine,' says Pulliam. 'Put it right on page one, but keep it down to two columns.'"[46]

Pulliam guaranteed grasstops' control of Valley news. FDR's daughter Anna and her husband, John Boettiger, had begun the *Arizona News* in 1947, hoping to create a mouthpiece for Arizona liberals. But Pulliam waged a two-year battle against the Boettigers for advertisers and subscribers. His assault may well have precipitated not only the paper's sale two years later but also the 1948 disintegration of the Boettigers' marriage. A year after their split, Bob Goldwater and Newton Rosenzweig joined the board of directors, further solidifying grasstops control of the local media.[47]

Pulliam was enormously influential. Kober remembered that he "struck at anyone he didn't like. . . . He was a rough-and-tumble guy." "That old Pulliam, when he called you on the phone, and he said, 'I think we ought to do this,'" Goldwater enthused, "you knew goddamn well we were going to do it. Wonderful man." "It couldn't have worked without Gene Pulliam," remembered a CGC founding member. Pulliam's 1949 editorials supported the reform ticket unabashedly. The publisher even refused to cover the opposition adequately or run its ads. The CAG subsequently charged that the CGC were the puppets, not of a paint seller, but of an out-of-state newspaperman eager, as one CAG candidate charged, to "import a manager . . . [because that] is the only way they can gain control of city hall."[48]

Pulliam could not deliver a win alone. Support came from the wealthiest areas in the city, where the majority of CGC members lived. Some of their most important backers may well have been part of the mob, the very people the reformers promised to drive out of town. Famed gangster Gus Greenbaum ran a gambling racket in Phoenix. Arizona government officials wanted him and his friends either out of town or in jail, yet Goldwater and Rosenzweig were far more tolerant. The senator even evidenced his long friendship by serving as a pallbearer at Greenbaum's 1958 funeral. Their connection was not altogether surprising. CGC merchants, newsmen, lawyers, and bankers had little patience with the petty, city hall corruption that they considered a threat to Phoenix's future. Greenbaum stood in stark contrast to this lot, as he had important connections across the country and had grand dreams and enterprises, which matched in scale and scope, if not in ambition, the plans that Rosenzweig and Goldwater had for central Arizona. After Rosenzweig asked for help, Greenbaum gave him a thick packet of money every week until the CGC triumphed in 1949. Though the jeweler handled the transactions, other candidates knew of the mobster's involvement. In order to make sure the victory was not questioned if the CGC won, the gangster also promised to leave Phoenix and return to Las Vegas. Candidates later admitted that the charges they lobbed at CAG nominees were unfair and untrue. "There was no connection to with [*sic*] organized crime," Goldwater confessed. Walters explained, "It was not a problem."[49]

Regardless, promises to eliminate graft, corruption, and incompetence made up the core of the CGC's 1949 electoral offensive. Campaign literature made four basic promises: "Put the Charter Amendment into effect, guarantee a trained City Manager, end political bossism in City Hall, and ensure efficient and economical government," boilerplate goals that fitted well within the general complaints that these and other good-government boosters had deployed against the New Deal and its supporters during this mid-century reform era. Throughout the election, CAG candidates therefore struggled to sidestep implicit and explicit accusations that they were dishonest and corrupt. "I can't take orders from a boss—any boss," countered one CAG endorsee. "That's the reason I'm in business for myself." Imler also feared bossism's specter and publicly proclaimed that Scheumack "is not interfering nor does he dare to interfere with me in any way, shape, or form." Caywood defended his service record: "There have been more improvements in the city in the past two years since James T. Deppe became city manager than I saw in the previous 15 years." The CAG credited commissioners with expanding the airport, improving parks and recreation, ridding Phoenix of its fly problem, and clearing slums, all of which were projects the city undertook and finished with the help of federal dollars.[50]

CGC candidates deflected these assertions by harnessing the very language of grassroots democracy that New Dealers utilized. The grasstops connected minding the people's will with a broad promise for good governance. The committee's chairman asserted, "Good government is dependent on the interest of the citizens," while *Arizona Republic* newsmen asserted, "Political machines fatten on public indifference. They melt away in the heat turned on by an aroused populace." "When you don't vote," CGC contenders threatened, "the political boss system, with its vicious machine, retains control of your city government.... The boss system demands its pound of flesh first. You and your needs are secondary." Goldwater gave no credit to policymakers who used federal funds to remake Phoenix into a metropolis. Instead, responsibility for any progress lay with the voters, who had been desperate for reform in 1948, and business leaders, who now promised to manage the city better than the old cohort of petit-capitalist politicians. Votes for the CGC slate, then, represented residents' ability to actively clean up city hall by empowering the businessmen to protect the citizenry and direct development.[51]

Yet CGC enthusiasts characterized themselves as civic-minded burghers, not managerial elites, who worked for the public's welfare. Newspaper editors described the group as a "citizens' movement against the political-boss domination of City Hall." The formal organization, the editors claimed, was merely the "nucleus" of a larger populist crusade, which was "really an extension of the civic activity which led to the study and revision of the City Charter and later to the successful effort for popular approval at the polls."

Journalists assured readers that these men and women were "broadly representative of the city's best citizens" and had "been selected with freedom from city politics as the prime requisite." No one need worry that the CGC seemed small, editorialized the *Arizona Republic* early in the campaign. "In the very near future it will expand from its present size of 29 members to more than 100," which thus indicated that the organization would not "set up a behind-the-scenes dictatorship."[52]

Such despotism, insurgents declared, was against the CGC's commitment to placing Phoenix on a "Sound Business Basis" through expert-driven revenue and budgetary reform. "Most Phoenicians realize that they are paying the highest tax bills in the city's history," *Arizona Republic* editorialists asserted. "They know, moreover, that they are not receiving full value for their tax dollar." Ending city hall corruption would thus lower taxes because "the city council . . . will give you the kind of government and the kind of services you need and deserve—and your costs will be lower." The CGC also promised to fire city manager Deppe, because his machinations were an affront to their plans for efficient, professional, low-cost governance. He just "doesn't know enough about municipal administration," *Republic* staffers summed up.[53]

Four ballot initiatives endorsed by the CGC were critical to its campaign and its larger vision for a modern Phoenix. The first three proposals focused on increasing the city council's power and efficiency. Candidates supported tough restrictions on passing emergency measures: approval would require a five-sevenths, not a four-fifths, majority, which also reflected the increased size of the council. The other propositions made the city health officer a civil servant and mandated that the judge who presided over the police court be an attorney. All of these measures focused on efficiency, control, and professionalism, which were the buzzwords of the CGC's campaign, the driving principles behind the Chamber's internal transformation, and pragmatic responses to the need to refashion government in order to facilitate industrialization.[54]

The final proposition was the tax referendum designed to keep air-conditioning magnate Oscar Palmer in the Valley. This initiative nonetheless represented another derivation of the Chamber men's longer assault on taxes and redistribution. Even before the annexation crisis, the organization's Industrial Development Committee had drafted proposals to extend the piecemeal changes that bankers, led by the Bimson brothers, had lobbied for at the state level. Ideas included lower freight rates, new zoning laws, bonds for urban development, and changes to the tax code. In 1949, voters entertained proposals eliminating inventory taxes, both for raw goods used in manufacturing and for finished products ready to be shipped, and reducing fees on equipment used in manufacturing. These measures were intended to satisfy Palmer but also attract industrialists and wholesalers, the types of investors the Chamber had identified as critical to growth in their 1941 plans for Phoenix. CGC supporters publicly deemed these levies, as they had union security protections, bad for the economy because "these taxes cause production costs to be higher here than in other areas, making it undesirable for manufacturers to locate here. Thus these two taxes have been keeping many manufacturers out of Phoenix, thereby robbing us of jobs for people and of increased prosperity." "The amount of revenue which will be lost in this proposed tax structure revisions," Chamber literature explained, "is so insignificant that it will be replaced manyfold by new manufacturers who set up their businesses here."[55]

Boosters threw their organization's weight behind passage. The finance committee raised almost $2,000 for campaign literature and the "More Jobs for More People" task force set up and then aired a series of talks. The Public Relations Committee prepared a manual to ensure boosters presented uniform arguments. "New industries mean more jobs and a readjustment of the tax structure is necessary to make Phoenix competitive when it seeks new industries," speakers explained. Representatives warned voters that Arizona had already suffered the ill effects of such levies: they publicized a manufacturer's declaration that he had left Arizona because the state inventory tax cut into his profits too much.[56]

Phoenix liberals and labor leaders were wary of these proposals. An independent candidate for council, Sam Levitin, railed against the referendum because it could destroy the necessary tax base for schools and other public programs. "We need industry, jobs, and payrolls," he allowed. "I hope the day will never come when we sacrifice our schools. Small homeowners and taxpayers cannot support repeal of the inventory tax as long as it is a part of the program to destroy our schools." The Phoenix Central Labor Council also declared publicly that it did not support the amendment because the Chamber refused to promise that such a policy change was not part of a broader program to reduce worker benefits, wages, and security in the name of industrial recruitment. "Who is it that really needs tax relief?" members of the Home Owners Protective Alliance asked. "Is it the manufacturer who prospered during the past few years, or is it rather the small home owner who is on the verge of losing his property because of vacancies and low rentals[?]" Protestors called these exemptions "an evasion of our duties as citizens pledged to support the government." They fumed that "the tax burden has been gradually shifted onto the backs of the home owner and the small taxpayer." "Insurance companies and absentee owners do not pay any state income tax. And now manufacturers and industry are asking for more tax exemptions!! Are home owners and small property owners alone to bear the full cost of city and state government?" they asked, before asserting: "Tax relief should begin with the people who most need it."[57]

These voices were a distinct minority in November 1949. A plurality endorsed all CGC endorsees and their ballot recommendations. Twice as many voters went to the polls, 53 percent of those registered, than in the previous election to pass the charter reforms. In the northwest portion of Phoenix, the CGC as a slate won almost 72 percent of the vote, in the northeast section just below 65 percent, in the southwest precincts just over 55 percent, and in the southeast area just under 54 percent. Goldwater's win was the most impressive: he earned 73 percent of votes cast (16,408 votes out of 22,353). Rosenzweig also did well, with just under fifteen thousand votes, which barely edged Kober's 14,498 vote count. Murphy, Foster, and Walters all won more than twelve thousand votes apiece, and Mayor Udall won reelection with almost 60 percent of the vote. Citizens also passed, by a margin of three to one, the pro-business tax ordinance that labor feared. Still-seated commissioners immediately went ahead with plans to annex the Palmer's tract, then valued at $1.75 million. Yet none of this satisfied the manufacturer. Palmer proclaimed that his business "cannot exist in the city" and closed down operations, only returning in the 1950s after he saw the later fruits of the 1949 sweep: an industry-oriented political machine that dominated city politics through the early 1970s.[58]

Mid-Century Municipal Warfare

Phoenix was but one of many cities transformed by mid-century municipal upheaval. But such reforms had quite a different character in the Steelbelt, where the liberal contingent of the Democratic Party was strong and organized labor was influential. Both rejected the good-government principles that governed the country's industrial heartland. An immigration influx into developing manufacturing metropolises and pitched battles over New

Deal reforms had extended such reform efforts through the Progressive Era and into the postwar period. In 1918, for example, commercialists and industrialists united as the Detroit Citizens League, which led to a campaign, steeped in the language of business-friendly efficiency, to institute at-large elections for city council seats. This change wrought electoral victories for executives and their preferred candidates in political contests throughout the 1920s.[59]

The Great Depression and New Deal facilitated the collapse of such regimes. As in Phoenix, Chicago's white ethnics turned away from the voluntary associations that had once provided them with the kind of social services, benefits, and assurances that they increasingly demanded the city and state offer. Their 1930s efforts effectively enabled them to guarantee themselves a New Deal. Executives would even aid other postwar reform initiatives to oust the earlier coterie of leaders, whose corruption collided with social democracy, efficiency, and free enterprise. Instilling these last two principles into Philadelphia politics, for example, compelled Republican executives, lawyers, and bankers to partner with liberals, Democratic Party ward leaders, unionists, and African American residents to pass 1951 charter reforms that empowered the mayor and City Planning Commission, not the city council, and also vastly expanded civil services.[60]

An empowered rank and file, not laboring under right-to-work restrictions, ensured that unionists would have a significant voice in, if not rule over, these municipalities. That was certainly the case in midsize industrial towns like Youngstown, Toledo, and Yonkers. In late-1940s Yonkers, fifteen thousand workers, roughly 90 percent of wage earners, were unionists, mostly in the radical United Electrical Workers and the Textile Workers Union of America. Members of both unions formed the Non-Partisan Committee in the late 1940s to, as one activist declared, "change the political climate in the city" and transform it into "a decent place for union people to live." They won three seats on the twelve-person city council in their first race. The rank and file were likewise influential in far larger northern metropolises, where their votes proved vital to the election and governance of New York's Robert F. Wagner Jr., and Cleveland's Anthony Celebrezze.[61]

In contrast, municipal reform during the first half of the twentieth century in the South and Southwest put a generation of business boosters at the helm of numerous cities. They prevailed by emphasizing urban growth, economic dynamism, and the kind of political reform that helped unite professionals, top business owners, and upwardly mobile suburbanites. As in Phoenix, they marginalized an older generation of political operatives, stymied the social-democratic reform efforts that homegrown New Dealers and their labor allies undertook, and conceded as little as possible to those demanding civil rights for minorities. Grasstops reclamation of the South and Southwest thus stood in sharp contrast to the labor-liberal reconstruction of the Northeast and Midwest. Elites in the emerging Sunbelt sought to reengineer local government as the handmaiden of rapid industrialization, but without eroding the labor cost and regulatory differential that had been central to the relationship between the nation's manufacturing core and its commodity-driven periphery.

Municipal reform in fact unfolded in a remarkably similar fashion across the South and Southwest. In Atlanta, for example, the early twentieth-century charter provided for a weak mayor, powerful city council, and ward voting, which gave working-class whites a sizable influence in city affairs. This voting bloc—half were trade unionists—elected mayors throughout the 1900s and 1910s who defended striking transit workers, advocated public ownership of utilities, and rewarded blue-collar Atlantans with city appointments. But the Chamber elite wanted to rule in order to assist the association's "Atlanta—500,000 in Ten Years" campaign designed to attract a hundred thousand additional residents by 1930, largely through "securing the location of hundreds of new enterprises." Business leaders spent much of the 1920s and 1930s fighting for control over city hall, an effort that relied on changing public perceptions that the association was "run by a clique" and making elected representatives ex-officio members of the Chamber's board of directors. But their success obtaining office and then wielding their power proved fleeting until 1936, when lawyer William Berry Hartsfield defeated a perennial, petit-capitalist mayor.[62]

Hartsfield's hold on city hall lasted almost thirty years. He was a dedicated booster, who destroyed the ward system and then created a civil service program that limited traditional patronage practices. Hartsfield's power was based solidly on the Atlanta business community, who provided the financial support, advice, and payroll that would keep the city growing. This "kitchen cabinet," as one historian described the network, paralleled the Phoenix Chamber, whose close connections gave this grasstops network remarkable cohesion and influence. "We had gone to the same schools, to the same churches, to the same golf courses, to the same summer camps. We had dated the same girls. We had played within our group, married within our group, partied within our group, and worked within our group," one explained. Their power, a lawyer emphasized in a 1950 interview, lay "under the crust" where this white, elite brotherhood buoyed "men that are put forward to get things done. They do not have real influence. They make no decisions without taking advice."[63]

Reform came to smaller southern cities after the war when newcomers complained about the lack of services and demanded better roads and schools. Returning servicemen often directed these campaigns against the long-entrenched leadership who proved unfit or unwilling to respond. Sid McMath, for example, led veterans in a concerted effort to transform Hot Springs, which aided his later bid for Arkansas governor on a platform that emphasized economic growth. A coalition of Georgia businessmen bested Augusta's entrenched political machine, which these veterans deemed the "Cracker Party." In 1946, deLesseps S. "Chep" Morrison defeated New Orleans Mayor Robert Maestri, who had a long-standing relationship with the city's well-established dynasties. Morrison was from an old Creole family but symbolized, as *Time* declared, "the bright new day which has come to the city of charming ruins" undergoing a metamorphosis from sin city to Pan-American commercial trading hub.[64]

Victorious southern boosters still had comparatively less overall control over their cities than did their southwestern counterparts. The Supreme Court weakened southern regimes when justices consistently ruled against white-only primaries in the mid-1940s. These decisions triggered registration drives in the urban South, most notably Atlanta, where activists tripled the number of black Fulton County registrants in just three weeks. This increase forced the white political elite to respond to these constituents' demands, particularly the affluent and influential who had spearheaded the voting campaigns. Both Democratic candidates went after the African American vote in the 1949 mayoral race. Appeals included direct bids in newspapers and before civic groups as well as sit-downs with community leaders, who demanded more city jobs and services. Hartsfield won and subsequently brought black elites into a biracial ruling coalition. African Americans were still, for all intents and purposes, junior partners and second-class citizens in an alliance that would be replicated throughout the urban South.[65]

Southern municipal regimes still had much in common with southwestern systems. Arid-state municipalities also abandoned commission-style governments and embraced an appointed and disproportionately powerful city manager. Charter revisions tended to mandate at-large elections, which marginalized broad segments of the local electorate because working-class and minority communities' chosen candidates needed more than half the votes cast in a city to win just one seat. In practice, such electoral rules privileged affluent, white neighborhoods (like north side Phoenix enclaves), where turnout also tended to be much higher. This population segment hence had the dominant voice in city affairs across the urban South and Southwest. Southwestern boosters did not, by and large, have to (and did not) court minority voters until the mid-1960s because their disenfranchising policies occurred largely outside the national spotlight on southern race relations.[66]

Voting clauses also provided the basis for true political machines. The most famous municipal regimes, urban historians have long asserted, were not the uncontested, all-powerful administrations that the term implies. Even in Progressive Era, machine-run Chicago, the Fifth Ward's African American residents had been able to elect politicians able to critique, sometimes influence, policy. Such opposition was rare in postwar southwestern councils. Most representatives came from Anglo, elite, business-led nonpartisan slating groups. In Dallas 157 out 182 city council members elected between 1931 and 1969 had the Citizens' Charter Association's endorsement, between 1955 and 1971 San Antonio Good Government League candidates only lost four city council races, and the Albuquerque Citizens' Committee never lost a race between 1954 and 1966.[67]

Such endurance offers an important counterpoint to the supposed exemplar of postwar urban corruption, the so-called Daley machine that controlled Chicago from 1955 to 1977. Mayor Richard J. Daley oversaw the early stages of the city's transformation from manufacturing power to postindustrial metropolis. Patronage and coercion dominate descriptions of his administration, but his continued success relied on the support both of working-class white ethnics, who benefited from the forty thousand municipal and county jobs that required reciprocity in the form of fundraising, tithing, and voting, and of Republican businessmen, who chafed at political nepotism yet championed the Loop's development through corporate investment and real estate development.[68]

The Sunbelt's grasstops defined their governance against such practices. Boosters instead relied on legally disenfranchising citizens in the name of businesslike governance. Yet their promises of additional payroll in many ways represented a kind of patronage even if stalwarts did not directly provide job opportunities. Promoters stressed only that their reelection was the sole guarantor of higher employment and more investment.

Such promises were certainly a part of the CGC's inaugural run. Candidates in fact made these vows throughout the committee's twenty-five-year reign over Phoenix city hall, a tenure that far exceeded almost all other business machines in the South and Southwest. The Chamber men effectively reclaimed Phoenix from the commodity markets, small-business owners, liberals, and radicals through a charter that limited representation of the working class, both Anglo and minority, who in any event found their capacity to organize curtailed by their defeat during the 1946 right-to-work controversy. Goldwater had nonetheless still been "mad" three years later when he ran for city council because weakening unions had not provided political hegemony for his generation of urban boosters. But the CGC had done far more than ring doorbells to prevail in 1949. Yet they would find themselves doing even more political work in order to build the political machine that could sustain the policy experimentation necessary to provide the governmental supports that outside investors demanded but without the oversight that they detested.

Chapter 6

Forecasting the Business Climate

"You don't get these companies without them being convinced that this is the right place to come. Develop the economic facts, watch the taxes," Frank Snell explained in an interview, noting that levies should be "fair but not burdensome." He left out competitive in this instance, but cutthroat best described Snell and the other rainmakers' approach to luring investors to the Salt River Valley. The Chamber actively monitored investment conditions, weighed them against their rivals' competitive advantages, and ruthlessly sought to undercut their opponents, all of which relied on the kind of professional acumen and political power gained from the organization's overhaul and reengagement with public affairs.[1]

No booster described such work as buying payroll by the mid-1950s. Instead, the grasstops, both in the Valley and across the industrializing South and Southwest, came to explain recruitment as a part of creating what they called a favorable "business climate" that would prove attractive to manufacturers and other job-creating investors. Promoters openly courted industrialists seeking to escape the taxes, unions, and regulations that were such an integral part of the system the New Dealers and their labor backers had constructed during the 1930s and 1940s. Maintaining an attractive "business climate" sounded far less crass than "buying payroll," a phrase long used to denigrate the subsidies and tax holidays that so many southern cities offered northern firms on the lookout for a low-wage haven. But the sophisticated mid-century business climate was an investment strategy just as politically charged and socially malignant. Interregional and interurban jockeying to generate the most favorable conditions for firms both depended upon and celebrated the corporate capacity to generate thousands of new jobs. Nothing else, the grasstops warned, mattered. Thus maintenance of Sunbelt booster regimes, including Phoenix's Charter Government Committee (CGC), implicitly maligned local needs for tax revenue, social investment, and economic stability, thereby redirecting state and local governments to place corporate welfare before social services.

Defining the Favorable Business Climate

Postwar industrial mobility served to substantially increase efforts to define, measure, and compare manufacturing advantages. Yet few academic investigators or private consultants ever fully agreed on what specific issues played the largest role in managerial dispersal or relocation decisions. The presence or absence of a state right-to-work law, for example, remained an intensely debated issue within the industrial-relations field. Taxation's impact on capital migration was just as controversial. New Deal liberals still working under Commerce Secretary Henry Wallace dismissed such levies' importance to executives in 1947. But in hard-pressed New England, where textile and light-manufacturing plants were shedding jobs in the mid-1940s and after, some Massachusetts legislators charged that high taxes "ha[d] retarded business development." And economist John Strasma, a renowned, prolific dispersal expert found that tax rates did matter to industrialists. He noted in a 1959 study for the Federal Reserve Bank of Boston that there was a significant spread between the highest and lowest taxes that states and cities levied on manufacturing firms: corporations could expect as much as a 10 percent reduction in their income depending on where they operated in Massachusetts throughout the 1950s. There was a 17 percent differential nationwide.[2]

Strasma's research, along with other studies, led experts to describe taxes as a part of a larger "climate," which industrial scouts naturally sought for their corporate clients. Investigators asserted that low levels of taxation and unionization along with the availability of good public services, those necessary for a firm to operate and retain its workforce, greatly influenced locational decisions. Experts then began to consider this "business-friendly" ethos as both a set of material advantages and signs of a nebulous but still advantageous industry-first mindset.[3]

Executives considered this research invaluable. Many smaller firms contracted with the Fantus Factory Location Service for advice on potential sites, while major manufacturers increasingly routinized in-house relocation surveys and procedures, often designating a vice president to be in charge of plant location or expansion by the late 1950s. Executives evaluated potential plant relocation sites continually. Business journalist Thomas Kenny reported, in a survey of 107 businesses, that a third annually analyzed their current locations based on "shifts in markets, changes in raw materials and product mix, deterioration of labor relations, and many other factors." He also emphasized the importance of "good schools and a cultural environment that [attract] high-level technical people." Such intangibles might well prove decisive. "Our final decision in a location is made by an unscientific walk around town to look at the parks to see if the grass is cut, at the schools to see what shape they're in, at the churches and the homes themselves to see if they're painted and well kept," one businessman explained. "These casual observations can reveal as much as all the inducements and welcomes extended."[4]

CEOs often described locational advantages in both tangible and symbolic terms. Complaints about revenue collection, for example, generally framed these business expenses in terms of a larger objection to liberal economic doctrine. "Taxes keep going up and destroy incentive to build or improve property," one manager argued, "just as Massachusetts state taxes destroy incentive of individuals." Manufacturers often incorporated their frustration at rising labor costs with their broad profit-focused and philosophical concerns. "The state method of excise tax assessments . . . are the most ridiculous we have ever seen," one CEO fumed. "Massachusetts does not seem to do anything concrete in encouraging business firms to expand due to the high tax rates on property, the labor market is very costly and there is no enticement for a firm to gain any real benefit." Some industrialists considered their material frustrations a part of a larger political challenge to profit and power. "Property taxes are important," one tycoon admitted, "but greater importance is given to Massachusetts politicians['] desire to initiate and implement legislation which will get them votes from the labor unions." "The legislators must be made to realize that they cannot kill the 'Goose that lays the golden egg,'" he warned. "Workmen's compensation increased giveaway [*sic*], lack of a right to work law, and other factors of a similar character are causing us to consider moving out of Massachusetts."[5]

Incentives might well pique such investors' interest, but, above all else, manufacturers had to be able to serve their markets. Indeed, surveys found that the ability to maintain or increase their customer base was the initial deciding factor in relocating to or staying in an area. Of course the existence of an adequate market might also deter a business from moving. "We are a local business, thus our plant cannot be located elsewhere," one small manufacturer reported in one of Strasma's investigations.[6]

The business climate ideal nonetheless reshaped the entire postwar political landscape. Corporations that had a national clientele and the ability to transport products found lucrative opportunities in the South and West. The resultant growth generated new markets that made the move even more profitable. National competition also guaranteed that manufacturers tied to a specific regional clientele were able to pick and chose among locales. For example, General Foods had numerous options within a 250-mile radius of New York when executives sought to consolidate northeastern operations. Fantus recommended Dover, Delaware, where local and state politics had left area taxes the lowest in the region, suppressed wage rates, rendered utilities relatively cheap, and offered adequate living standards for the needed workforce. General Foods chose the town in 1962, by which time large companies routinely presumed tax breaks, anti-union regulations, publicly funded streets and schools, and other giveaways to be the price municipalities had to pay to maintain or attract investment.[7]

Such expectations were no longer confined to the South or Southwest because the business climate ideal had became part of the policy discourse in the North and Midwest, and along the California coast as well. San Diego Chamber members, for example, initiated an aggressive recruitment program to diversify the fortress city's economy once they noticed the loss of military investment to Arizona, Nevada, and smaller California cities, including San Bernardino and Santa Barbara. Decline also forced rusting communities to compete, often through quasi-public associations dedicated to subsidizing local business and recruiting outside firms. Liberal Philadelphia city officials entered into such a partnership with the local Chamber of Commerce in 1958 in order to stem the outflow of manufacturing dollars. The newly created Philadelphia Industrial Development Commission (PIDC) intervened in the local industrial mortgage market, a plan inspired by southern boosters' use of industrial revenue bonds to underwrite private investment. This practice was illegal in Pennsylvania at the time (as it had been when Mississippians first passed Balance Agriculture with Industry), so Philadelphia officials acted as an intermediary for firms intent on buying vacant land or refurbishing abandoned factories. An IRS exemption for such quasi-public agencies helped PIDC to buy, improve, and then transfer the title of such properties to private firms. Boosters also tried to pass right-to-work laws throughout the Steelbelt. Trade unions prevailed in these referenda, but capital flight nonetheless eroded wage levels. As early as the late 1950s, the southern advantage in labor costs and taxes had already begun to decline relative to the Steelbelt.[8]

Maintaining Phoenix's Second Climate

Municipal reforms and organizing restrictions enabled Phoenix's politically empowered business elite to be as inventive as their rivals. Their specific policies relied on close attention to their competitors' business climates and prospective investors' needs, desires, and demands. These rainmakers shared the general sentiment that residents should respect industry as the "goose that lays the golden egg," but the grasstops still struggled to meet high-tech manufacturers' demands, even with the resources of Phoenix's largest banks, biggest retailers, and mightiest law firms. The Chamber's long-term success thus hinged partly on the influx of new members, who worked for new corporate arrivals. For example, in the early 1950s, an AiResearch manager with close connections to the military headed the Chamber's Manufacturer's Committee, which organized efforts to repeal taxes on local production facilities and aided firms in securing contracts with the armed services.[9]

Boosters constantly monitored their and their rivals' competitiveness. Even in 1960, arguably the apogee of the CGC's reign and the Phoenix Republicans' control of their party, the Phoenix elite so feared competitors that they turned to a local consulting firm, Western Business Consultants, later Western Management Consultants (WMC), in order to better equip themselves to bring industry west. The city government, Valley National Bank (VNB), and the Del E. Webb Corporation underwrote the company's investigations into the area's economic potential. Surveyors offered dire warnings: "Other areas in the West and South . . . offer the same basic locational advantages to people and industry as does the Phoenix Area and Maricopa County." WMC had no illusions as to why the city had been able to draw so many manufacturers: Phoenix, like other investment-starved desert towns, was relatively close to Los Angeles. Roughly a third of area manufacturers had a California market. "Unless local planning and preparation for growth is at least equal to that of competitive areas," analysts asserted, "a significant share of the plants which might have been established, and of the migrating population which might have settled in the County, will go elsewhere."[10]

WMC polled Phoenix's investor class to better guide policymakers. Consultants noted that the weather, schools, and recreational opportunities mattered most to the largest businesses, which catered to a national market and tended to be involved in the aerospace, computer, and electronics industries. These sectors' executives needed to convince highly skilled workers that there was an acceptable quality of life in Phoenix. These CEOs also valued Phoenix's proximity to California, its pro-business tax code, and the Arizona right-to-work law, all of which were even more important for smaller manufacturers with regional or local markets. The primary metals and apparel manufacturers, who also serviced the Los Angeles hinterland, emphasized the short drive to California, Phoenix's ample, cheap labor supply, and transportation availability, whereas the smaller firms focused mainly on being able to best serve Maricopa County.[11]

Both industrial satisfaction and discontent in the Valley proved instructive to boosters fine-tuning investment strategies. More than half of those firms employing more than twenty persons held that there were "better labor relations" and "more favorable wage scales" in Phoenix than elsewhere. Companies in the apparel, aerospace, and electronics factories nonetheless complained that the area lacked the kind of skilled labor pool they needed. Manufacturers additionally fretted over land costs, transportation options, the area's labor supply, taxation, air pollution, and water availability. Large aerospace and electronic executives, for their part, bemoaned the state of the city's physical and knowledge infrastructures. Water shortages were of particular concern, but most complained about the educational resources that their professional, skilled workforces needed. Indeed, of the firms surveyed, 27 percent asserted that they hired skilled workers, but only 16 percent of this total had success finding qualified local engineers. Almost a third reported problems attracting skilled workers, scientists, and engineers to the desert.[12]

Assuaging these and other managerial concerns relied on governance, also essential for transforming peripheral buying-payroll efforts into more complex business climate policies. The first chairman of the Chamber's Industrial Development Committee even warned board members: "Industry must have the assurance it will receive a fair deal from the locality in which it locates." He thus prioritized convincing voters to support the Chamber and CGC because elected representatives in local government could either hinder or enable promoters' ability to promote Phoenix and compete for outside investment.[13]

Political stability was imperative. The CGC, like other booster regimes, encountered few serious challenges in the 1950s. In 1951 former mayor Ray Busey and other Democrats sought to oust the Republicans and scrap the at-large elections that favored Chamber rule. Their Council for District Government ticket, all south Phoenix residents, stood in stark contrast to the business elite directing the CGC. A small businessman, who also belonged to the plumber's union, headed the ticket. One candidate had been a prospector but now served as the county's deputy treasurer. Another nominee was a retired conductor and security guard. The slate also included a Mexican émigré who managed an auto body shop and chaired the Mexican Chamber of Commerce. The CGC's opponents infused the election with class rhetoric. One claimed Phoenix was "being ruled and dictated to by the people from the County Club." Like Busey, they also demanded that candidates be allowed to identify with a party, a strategy that would have helped the all–Democratic Party ticket win many more votes. CGC candidates called their challengers "disgruntled political has-beens." "We have cut expenses, reduced taxes, eliminated graft, and increased the efficiency in every department," Margaret Kober asserted. "But everything this administration has done *can* and probably will be undone if your incumbent Council members are not re-elected." Voters once again responded to the CGC's finely tuned promise of good governance. The slate won handily, with Goldwater reelected by a four-to-one margin.[14]

To maintain the governing authority necessary to build a business climate, CGC leaders adapted to their opponents' charges of bossism and elitism. In contrast to other slating groups in the Southwest, the association pursued minority support relatively early. Organizers continued, as Goldwater and Rosenzweig had done, to campaign in the south side but also instituted a policy of naming at least one non-Anglo candidate. The first, Adam Díaz, ran on the 1953 ticket. "You are probably the most representative of all City Councils to serve in our community," CGC founder Dix Price enthused. "You represent every part of the town, all groups of great religions, and all political philosophies of this community." In the ensuing years, Anglo businessmen still dominated CGC rosters and slates, but members continued to anoint one non-Anglo candidate and an Anglo woman to serve alongside them. The CGC, for example, backed V. A. Cordova in 1955. The first Asian American, Thomas Tang, won a seat in 1959.[15]

These successful candidates did not represent a diversified CGC. Díaz, for example, grew up on Phoenix's outskirts and began his career at the Luhrs Hotel as a relief elevator operator. "I was part of the family," he later elaborated. He credited owner George Luhrs with urging him to work with the Americanization-focused Friendly House. His employer even gave him the opportunity to campaign on the organization's behalf among Phoenix's wealthiest citizens, including Walter Bimson, who occasionally made donations to Friendly House at Díaz's behest. Luhrs also gave Díaz tremendous leeway to participate in politics. Goldwater and Price first approached him about joining the CGC in 1949 because they were eager to include someone well known and active in south Phoenix civic affairs. The draftee hesitated because he did not want to miss work during the lengthy afternoon meetings, which took place in the building's Arizona Club. Luhrs gave his blessing and guaranteed that Díaz's pay would not suffer. Luhrs also accommodated his protégé's 1953 campaign schedule and even paid him when he was absent on Mondays and Tuesdays for council duties. Díaz initially considered his participation an opportunity to aid Phoenix's Mexican American residents, and he was, in fact, able to expand recreational opportunities in south Phoenix. Yet he refused to run for reelection two years later. "I felt inadequate, really and truly, because I didn't have the educational background," he later explained. "Many times I had difficulty in expressing myself as well as I would have liked to."[16]

Díaz's experiences elucidate key facets of the racially moderate ethos that infused so many booster regimes and recruitment campaigns. Southern and southwestern urban elites tried to manage desegregation from the grasstops, both to avoid federal intrusions into local and state affairs and to assure industrialists that racial strife would not threaten their investments. Southern "moderates," for example, sought to control desegregation of schools, workforces, and public offices. Such policies facilitated limited advancement, while subverting charges of racism and sexism. Grasstops reformers were in fact able to use compliance to covertly resist federal intervention by making the need for more involvement less readily apparent, a strategy not unlike the maneuvering that stymied David Lilienthal and the Tennessee Valley Authority's attempts to stoke a grassroots revolution.[17]

Race and racial subordination played quite different roles in the South and the Southwest. When sociologist Floyd Hunter asked an Atlanta Chamber of Commerce man what were the two biggest issues confronting Atlanta in 1950, he received this response: "I will give you one—segregation. You

Figure 6. Past and present Charter Government Committee officeholders gathered at the Phoenix Country Club luncheon to celebrate city manager Ray Wilson's 1962 retirement (only Barry Goldwater, then in the Senate, and two deceased members, Preston Brown and Faith North, were absent). The few men of color and Anglo women present reflected the selection committee's efforts to appear socially progressive. Courtesy of the Arizona Historical Foundation, Margaret B. Kober Collection, folder 7, box 1.

can slice that one in two and have two. . . . That is *the* issue." Racial matters therefore imbued the Atlanta Chamber's recruitment work and governing strategies. A 1946 committee roster designated a race relations committee to "develop [a] pattern for improved relations between the races. Work for adequate schools emphasizing the need for a vocational school. Encourage better health through better housing, recreation and better hospital and treatment facilities. Offer opportunities for self-improvement and advancement, thus increasing the earning level." A 1948 report on five years of Chamber activities crowed that members "coordinated local activities in

[the] interest of additional Negro parks. Supported expanded educational facilities for Negroes. Aided in planning new areas for Negro housing. Secured Negro policemen for Negro areas." The president even emphasized in a 1949 board meeting that "development of Negro housing areas [was] perhaps the most important thing needed for the development of Atlanta."[18]

Legally enforced segregation existed in the Southwest as well, but it received far less national publicity, and thus appearing racially moderate was not as central to maintaining arid-state business climates. This region's grasstops did not by and large form biracial ruling coalitions or dedicate special task forces or committees to race relations. San Diego promoters, for example, considered housing a critical recruitment issue, but their concerns were limited to shortages that frustrated investors, not the image or reality of residential segregation.[19]

In comparison to other Southwest elites, Phoenix boosters actually stood out for their efforts to seem racially moderate or even progressive. They approved of the token desegregation of public schools, perfunctory increase in public sector employment opportunities for minorities, and selection of non-Anglo candidates for council slates. Rainmakers also celebrated the inclusion of women and non-Anglo men in business and civic affairs in a manner analogous to Atlantans' claims that their commercial city was "too busy to hate." The Chamber, for example, hailed Walter Ong, a Chinese American chain store grocer, as Phoenix's 1956 Man of the Year. Non-Anglo residents did play a role in the Chamber and CGC. Ong headed the Chamber in the 1970s, and Díaz brought important public services to the south side in the 1950s. The grasstops nonetheless later admitted that an Anglo elite had really run the town in the early postwar period. "They were a part of the power structure in the community," explained one booster. "The women not so much, but the men were."[20]

Lip service and sly resistance were not enough by the mid-1960s. Civil rights activists' efforts to obtain legal protections and then enforce the 1964 Civil Rights Act and 1965 Voting Rights Act forced southwestern promoters to confront these issues. "Voting privileges are enjoyed by all of our people regardless of the race, creed, or color," the mayor assured federal officials conducting a 1960 Civil Rights Commission investigation. "We have accomplished so much on a voluntary basis," he concluded, "we should continue to solve minority discrimination problems in that manner." But during these hearings, representatives from the Phoenix Urban League, National Association for the Advancement of Colored People (NAACP), and other organizations offered a scathing set of counterexamples detailing discrimination and de facto segregation: "In downtown Phoenix, . . . only 3 of the stores had Negroes in employ, except as custodians, maids, or in general unskilled categories"; "Phoenix has 5 Negro policemen, out of a force of 400"; "there is a large group of Mexican-Americans who are not getting an education. There is a large group of American citizens who are not voting because they are not even registered for this purpose."[21]

Such attention to inequality outside the South spurred a revolution in investment-focused governance among business associations and their political machines. San Diego boosters, for example, organized the Management Council on Urban Employment in the mid-1960s to "actively" engage with "urban problems and minority employment." The education committee met with local leaders and considered their recommendations to improve schools following "disturbances" in African American neighborhoods. The meeting ended with the formation of a new subcommittee to focus on teachers, courses, and postsecondary opportunities for black San Diegans. Chamber attention to race relations increased in 1968, when the Industrial and Business Development Committee called for "more definitive programs" and meetings devoted to "discussion of these problems as related to the San Diego area." The subgroup even invited the president of San Diego's NAACP to speak before them. Tom Johnson's explanation that San Diego was "no different than other cities which have had riots" startled members, who deemed his "provocative and stimulating" 1968 talk a "keen insight into this problem area." Unrest in Phoenix neighborhoods also took rainmakers by surprise in the 1960s. They responded with council investigations, new members to the workgroup that selected candidates, and slate nominees who had made themselves known in years prior as outspoken critics of the CGC.[22]

Yet most of this work to maintain control of Phoenix and run the town was hidden from voters. CGC members, like their Atlanta contemporaries, always endeavored to distance themselves publicly from the Chamber and the emergent Arizona Republican Party. But the connections were obvious: the CGC often met in the association's offices because members were also high-ranking Chamber men. Frank Snell, Harry Rosenzweig, and Newton Rosenzweig all served as Chamber president. Each ticket also had at least one Thunderbird. Other CGC councilmen and mayors also held the presidency, including popular mayor Sam Mardian, a builder, and two-term councilman Allen Rosenberg, a banker. Barry Goldwater had been the organization's vice president. Founders even admitted in later interviews that the entire project was rooted in state GOP politics and the effort of local businessmen to influence municipal government. "Larger operators were some of the businessmen and so on who [were] the then leaders of the community," an early CGC endorsee remembered. "We probably would not have been allowed today to do what we did then," recalled Charles Walters, a longtime Chamber official and member of the inaugural slate. "We used to meet and talk out affairs over things of that nature and we pointedly did not want to have a big ruckus going on and we would try to solve the matters off the record." "And it was very successful," he added. "We had a lot of fun," Nicholas Udall remembered. "We used to meet, the six men, the lady didn't go with us, but every Monday night we would go to the old Central Drive-in at Central and Roosevelt and have a late snack and post-mortem, and so forth." "Charter Government as it went along was the nucleus of what turned out to be the Republican Party," Walters noted; many CGC stalwarts "were the same hard workers in the Republican Party."[23]

Higher-ups later acknowledged the organization's exclusivity. "It was all done in secret," a founder remembered, "and behind—or [in] the smoke-filled room, we would go after them and get them—persuade them to run." "We had no on-going organization. We had no by-laws. We had no dues. We had no permanent staff," Newton Rosenzweig recounted. "It was very much ad hoc." The CGC's lengthy roster far exceeded the Selection Committee's register, which listed those responsible for putting together the ticket every two years. Kober later explained that only toward the end of the CGC's reign did it grow to as many as twenty-two members. These selectors insisted on term limits for its candidates but imposed no such restrictions on themselves. "We'd start up all over again," Newton Rosenzweig clarified, "but it was generally pretty much the same group that came together." As late as 1963, the only person not still in the inner circle was Goldwater, who had moved away from local affairs as his national prominence grew. The only other council member from the 1949 election not sitting on the executive committee was Kober, who was the vice chairperson of the Selection Committee.[24]

By the mid-1950s, Phoenix's most influential businessmen, like their Atlanta counterparts, worked mostly "under the crust." Rosenzweig and Goldwater were the only two original CGC architects to also serve as councilmen. Haas, Snell, and Pulliam as well as the Bimsons never held public office. The CGC's candidates (doctors, attorneys, bankers, builders, retailers, executives, insurance men, and women volunteers) nonetheless understood well the principles behind grasstops industrialization. When voters questioned their motives, CGC partisans reiterated that their slate was for nonpartisan good government for the betterment of all Phoenicians. "We are interested in building Phoenix and in doing it the proper way," a councilman once explained to constituents. Nor did the registered Democrats serving on the city council in the 1950s challenge the Republican-dominated Chamber's agenda. Their presence was more a function of the quixotic nature of Arizona party politics than it was a tribute to their liberal political beliefs. These "pinto" Democrats were hardly the heirs to desert New Dealers like Busey.[25]

Councillors' affiliation was also negligible because city manager Ray Wilson had extraordinary power over Phoenix's growth. The CGC imported him from Kansas City in 1950. He spent his twelve-year tenure enforcing the spirit of the new charter, crafting policies that further separated the electorate and their chosen representatives from the everyday tasks of running the city. Much of the new city manager's initial work involved formalizing bureaucratic procedures so that department heads would "conduct their affairs in a uniform and orderly manner." By consolidating twenty-seven departments into twelve, Wilson brought almost every department under his control. Only the Civil Service Board, Parks and Recreation Department, and Phoenix Housing Authority remained outside his purview. Wilson was careful to issue frequent reports on his activities to voters, which stressed the CGC's focus on efficient, modern, businesslike governance. He, for example, deemed office mergers critical to trimming the budget. Government was "a business," he asserted in a report celebrating the "rigid economies in expenditures and . . . systematic collection of all revenues due the city" that had brought Phoenix out of debt.[26]

The physical record the council created speaks to how much Wilson personally oversaw. The earlier commission had held lengthy meetings, during which representatives debated public policy, fought over appointments, authorized payments, haggled over city unions' demands for higher wages, heard arguments for new fire trucks and parks personnel while citizens asked for liquor licenses, requested new zoning ordinances, applied for permits, and protested property tax evaluations. Meeting minutes for a single year during the 1940s filled at least two oversized, five-hundred-page volumes. Chamber men had struggled to gain an audience in these years, when Lew Haas had to personally appear before the group to give detailed reports on the Chamber's activities, particularly the use of city funds earmarked for advertising. He then made himself available for continued questioning long after meetings ended. The general manager also had to formally *ask* the council to pass specific ordinances, including the tax proposals that the Chamber drafted in light of Oscar Palmer's demand for reduced levies. Thus when Haas submitted a set of proposals to the commission in June 1949, asking they "be immediately drafted and enacted," officeholders hesitated, moved for further study, and eventually left the matter up to voters.[27]

This relationship changed dramatically once the CGC came to power. Wilson, for example, now appeared before the Chamber's board of directors to explain proposed city budgets, and in the years after 1950 key decisions were made long before they reached the council for formal approval. Councillors' public duties were vastly reduced even as Phoenix's population grew tremendously and staff increases warranted a new, larger city hall by the mid-1950s. Small issues continued to dominate forums, including the approval of liquor license applications, review of contract bids, entertainment of rezoning requests, and the discussion of annexation proposals with property owners. But the council was largely divorced from the nitty-gritty work of industrialization. The body, for example, had little involvement in working out the key components of the deal with Sperry Rand though Chamber fundraising initiatives hinged on settling the lease between the firm and the city. A 1956 mayoral invitation for "informal discussion" of the deal proceeded rapidly after a Chamber member urged settlement because "it gets harder and harder to raise money as we go into the Summer." A councilman motioned for immediate approval. Brief discussion followed, which included updates on the background work the Chamber had finished on the type of bonds, zoning classifications, and insurance policies needed. Council approval came swiftly thereafter.[28]

The municipal government was thus deeply entwined with the Chamber. The association's tax and budget committee, for example, provided city officials with detailed studies of Phoenix's finances, collections, and proposed budgets. This subgroup also drafted feasibility studies and plans for consolidating municipal departments and placing them under the city manager's control. Promoters also involved themselves with later city annexation initiatives. Although public employees carried out the formal, legal incorporation of these areas, Chamber men provided the groundwork for the city's rapid territorial expansion by funding and writing the initial planning studies.[29]

Such private support left elected representatives to simply provide the necessary, legal rubberstamp to land and tax agreements already negotiated by the Chamber and, of course, to hear the complaints of Phoenicians unhappy with zoning regulations or annexation procedures. The Chamber, in turn, needed the city to deal with these day-to-day problems of governance, while promoters crafted the overall economic expansion program. The council thus operated as a sort of pressure release valve that acknowledged and then stifled protest from liberal Democrats, unionists, and others who continued to oppose CGC rule.

The Political Climate

Yet Chamber men also needed to be attuned to their critics living outside city limits. Although boosters could do much to promote land deals and facilitate tax breaks within Phoenix, the state government held more power over the revision of labor laws and tax codes. Chamber surveys also revealed that industrialists considered elections at the state level "indicative of Arizona's attitude of 'independence from big Government.'" "The continuing national publicity that both Goldwater and [John] Rhodes are receiving was generally known by these people," an analyst reported, "they openly expressed admiration for both men and for their conservative business attitude." Valley congressmen served both promoters and investors. Goldwater met with defense contractors, apprised Haas of their needs, and distributed Chamber promotional materials. Boosters thus considered political victories a part of their broad push for investment. The association's 1948–49 lengthy list of accomplishments even highlighted lobbying efforts that cajoled state legislators to pass new zoning and planning regulations and to amend the workmen's compensation law.[30]

Chamber men accordingly considered resurrecting the Arizona Republican Party vital. "I don't think the future of *Goldwater's* means a thing," Goldwater told friend, reporter, and future governor Howard Pyle, "unless we insure the political future of Arizona and the country." Phoenix booster Republicans often declared their activism a patriotic effort to provide voters with a genuine choice on Election Day. "The Democratic Party had ruled Arizona with an arrogance that offended me," Goldwater expounded. "My decision to register as a Republican was an act of defiance," not against his family, who had a hand in the state Democratic Party's founding, but against one-party rule. Business newcomers also emphasized their desire for a "two-party system" to explain their vigorous participation in party politics.

Pulliam, shortly after he took control of Phoenix's newspapers, published an editorial proclaiming: "The citizen has no choice." "This is not a plug for the Republican party. It is not a plug for the Democratic party," he asserted. "It is a plug for good government in Arizona and in the United States." Chamber men later described the GOP's reestablishment as one of the hallmarks of their careers. Goldwater deemed it "the one thing I could try to do for Arizona that would mean more to it than anything else." "I have a strong sense of pride in having been privileged to lend a hand in maturing two-party government in Arizona," Pyle remarked in the mid-1980s, before adding that finally surpassing Democratic registrants was a "great feeling."[31]

Forging a viable challenge to Democratic rule had seemed an insurmountable task. Republicans met during the war at the Adams Hotel in, what one member recalled, "a room that was, ohhh, very, very small." John J. Rhodes found that little had changed after 1945. The Kansas native and Harvard Law School graduate had been stationed in Higley, Arizona, in 1941 and relocated to the Valley after the war. "I had been looking for Republicans," Rhodes remarked about his early days in Phoenix. "I found two or three, a couple of young lawyers in Phoenix and others." The litigator recalled that a justice of the peace had told him: "'You want to register as a Democrat, of course.' I said, 'No, Republican.' He said, 'Major, there aren't any Republicans in Chandler. . . . You're a nice young man and you might want to stay here and you won't amount to anything as a Republican.'" Rhodes ignored the jurist and instead joined the Chamber, founded a Young Republicans' Club, and campaigned for the 1946 right-to-work initiative.[32]

Yet the postwar Democratic Party was hardly the monolith that Rhodes described. "Primaries were hotly contested, sometimes bitter affairs," a pundit remarked. Runoffs bespoke increasing divisions between liberal and Jeffersonian Democrats. Some frustrated members began leaving the party during the Depression. For example, Phoenix National Bank executive Frank Brophy had initially supported Roosevelt and the New Deal. "I voted for him the second time because his first term, in the first New Deal, was extraordinary," Brophy explained. "They did some remarkable things. They cleaned up." The banker later broke with the Democrats because the 1938 Court packing plan "gave me a pretty good insight into what sort of man I later believed Franklin Roosevelt to be."[33]

New Deal influence within the Southwest compelled many Phoenix boosters to reinvigorate Arizona's GOP. The state committee chairman urged drafters of the 1945 platform to take a stand against the Democratic

Party's "extremely liberal communistic and bureaucratic ideals." He wanted the organization to "be the conservative party of Arizona and of America." The term "conservative" was largely absent from the lexicon of most boosters at this time, but militant Republicans were nevertheless dedicated to creating a movement emphasizing "the importance of property rights and human rights, and protecting both from impairment or destruction" by "government by minorities, . . . class or race prejudice, or . . . favoring one section of our population above any other." Individual freedom from "leftist labor bosses and certain beneficiaries of the public payroll" informed this desire for a "two-party system" with "a definite battle line between the two parties" so "the minority party . . . can hope to become the majority party." Yet at war's end, the commitment to "the shaping of the industrial and agricultural future of Arizona" was largely buried within these resolutions. But the intention was there, connected to a theory that an "increase in taxable wealth" would "permanently reduce taxes," and tied to a denunciation of "vote-seeking subservience to the radical elements of labor."[34]

The free market, not religious faith, defined these proceedings even though the most free-enterprise focused boosters often belonged to churches, synagogues, and Mormon temples. Theological differences did not divide Chamber men, define Phoenix business Republicanism, or lead its promoters to power because the grasstops had a wide range of spiritual convictions, shared an overarching opposition to New Deal liberalism, and sought votes and new investment at a moment when religion did not structure political discouse in the way that it would in later decades.

Boosters' spiritual convictions varied greatly. Goldwater, the son of a Jewish merchant, had been raised Episcopalian. His mother, a sporadic churchgoer, had introduced him to the divine in the Arizona wilderness, a baptism evident in his famous diaries from his 1940 trip down the Colorado River. "The tall spires near the rim of the canyon," he recorded, "look as though God has reached out and swiped a brush of golden paint across them, gilding those rocks in the bright glow of the setting sun." But his compatriot Howard Pyle professed his faith from the pulpit. This Baptist preacher's son would still occasionally preach but he daily put his principles into practice: he never drank, danced, or smoked (even in the ashtray-strewn rooms where Phoenix Republicans strategized). Federalism, not Protestantism, had led him to the GOP because members were dedicated to the principle that the "best government is the least government." Strategist Stephen Shadegg also regularly attended services. The former Democrat worshipped at Trinity Episcopal Cathedral and underwent both a political and spiritual conversion after World War II. He found inspiration from leading evangelical leaders, who convinced him that "the Church is not the governing structure or the ecclesiastical bodies, or the tracts, or the prayer book—the Church in the world is you." But Shadegg also considered more base anxieties, like taxes, a part of this higher concern about faith and freedom. Money, Shadegg stressed, was God's gift to the individual earner, not something to be taxed away for welfare programs. In Shadegg's reading, Jesus had offered compassion to individuals, not a bureaucratic promise to the masses. But Catholic Frank Brophy considered tax increases a symptom of a larger problem: "Communism," "International Finance," and "International Do Goodism" threatened "the political and economic freedom that we have known in the Western world during the past century." Only "Christian standards of morality" could counter the "satanic movement" at the center of the "disintegration of free institutions."[35]

These religious differences did not divide the Phoenix grasstops or color their early electoral efforts. Throughout the 1950s and 1960s, Shadegg strategized for Republican candidates, including Goldwater, and served on the Presiding Bishop Committee for Laymen's Work. Shadegg found the time to both campaign across Arizona and evangelize across the country, where he intertwined his distaste for liberal welfare programs and regulations with his devotion to Christianity. Shadegg could still count on Brophy's support for Republican causes, even though the financier feared that an "Episcopalian-academic-social-register-interventionist-school" had already corrupted Protestantism. Brophy was one of *National Review*'s deepest pockets, who remained steadfast in his support for the controversial John Birch Society and Goldwater, "one of the few redeeming features of the Republican Party nationally, and the same goes for the state party." Brophy wrote those words with conviction in 1963, more than a decade after Goldwater's first run for Senate. The candidate had seen fit to make but a few references to the Almighty in this race. Pyle too refrained from proselytizing while running for and serving as governor in the early 1950s. "My job," he clarified in 1951," is that of an opposition to the socialistic trends that are slowly but surely weakening the republic to which we pledge allegiance."[36]

Safeguarding free-enterprise inspired many of the young Republicans who took over the state GOP. Many ran for precinct posts in 1948, and forty won critical seats, enough for these business-minded Republicans to infuse the party with their politics. The 1948 state platform led with support for the recently passed Taft-Hartley Act as well as opposition to labor's efforts to repeal Arizona's right-to-work law. Other planks asserted that current taxes were too burdensome on state property owners. Only in the final sections did Republicans proclaim "support [for] a comprehensive program aimed at the development of aviation, both civil and military." Labor still topped the 1950 platform, yet anti-unionism was couched within a concern for investment, not militant calls for vigilance. The opening plank, for example, deemed workplace unrest harmful to the state's economic welfare and set the tone for proclamations that "future development of Arizona is dependent upon the industrial expansion of our state" and "industry goes where it is invited." Republicans accordingly promised new favorable tax laws, studies and statistics for potential new investors, and "counsel and advice in securing land or facilities for their use."[37]

Core members credited the right-to-work campaigns with building institutional momentum. "Getting that Act passed," one remembered when discussing his run for state Senate, "got me interested . . . in running as one of the Republican crusaders, as we called ourselves." Early drives rested on Goldwater and Rosenzweig's policy of "drafting" candidates hostile to the New Deal order, especially since many state and local positions were uncontested prior to their efforts. The Phoenix retailers theorized that they would capture the support of those who voted a straight ticket. Goldwater therefore picked from among the grasstops to fill out the ballot. He told Rhodes prior to the 1950 election, "I'm drafting you to run for Attorney General," which led to the following exchange: "'Mr. Goldwater, there is something you need to know. I don't want to be Attorney General.' And he said, 'Mr. Rhodes, there's something you should know. You won't be.'"[38]

Internal fights within the Democratic Party aided Republicans. Liberal Democrats actually encouraged defections during the postwar period in order to gain solid control over the state party. "We have much new blood in the Arizona Democratic party organization," a Democratic activist reported to Hayden. This official promised that these young Dems would help the "old guard" create "another Democratic stronghold." Those "Jeffersonian" Democrats who hesitated to reregister became increasingly nonplussed. "I am a registered Democrat," a Tucson resident admitted in 1950, "and hoping the Republicans offer a platform or plan a bit improved ove[r] the welfare and booze program of the Dems." Others hoped to instead "purge the Democratic party of those Democrats of convenience who crawled aboard in 1932." "Pintos" nonetheless increasingly turned to Phoenix Republicans, who attacked

Figure 7. Arizona Republicans courted Democrats wary or opposed to postwar liberalism. These so-called Jeffersonian Democrats, here out in force for Goldwater's 1958 reelection effort, were a crucial voting bloc in a state where Democratic registration at one time outnumbered Republican membership by four to one. Courtesy of the Arizona Historical Foundation, Personal and Political Papers of Senator Barry M. Goldwater, folder 5, box 730.

the federal government's increasing power. "I am registered as a Democrat," one Phoenician explained in a 1950 letter to Pyle, "but, I'd like to see you win. I liked what you said about Jefferson and the Jeffersonian philosophy of government. I liked what you said about 'too much government.'"[39]

The GOP effectively overhauled itself during the 1950s to court dissident Democrats. Organizational changes in many ways paralleled the Chamber's wartime refashioning. Stalwarts created a new bookkeeping system to better process contributions, kept IBM card files of registered Democrats and Republicans in Maricopa and Pima counties, completed systematic voting analyses on past major elections, held statewide fundraising drives, surveyed all Republican households, began clipping files on major events and issues, established a party newspaper, generated mailing lists for all members, helped start Young Republican clubs across the state, and sent officials to speak before audiences in each county. Party activists also campaigned outside their exclusive, Anglo neighborhoods, arguing, as they had during the right-to-work and CGC campaigns, that economic growth through free enterprise would best generate opportunities for minority workers. Conservative activists needed those votes: 17 percent of Arizonans had Spanish surnames, 9 percent were Native American, and 4 percent were African American. Pyle and Goldwater reached out to these voters in 1950. The merchant flew the GOP's gubernatorial candidate all over the state in the eight weeks before the election. The twenty thousand miles logged brought Pyle to rallies with diverse constituents, who had likely never encountered a Republican nominee in the flesh. The state GOP later supported the local affiliate of "Latinos Con Eisenhower," which convened at the Adams Hotel in 1952. At the same time, Republican candidates for state and national office, including Rhodes, personally campaigned in the barrio and supported Latinos seeking municipal office. Pulliam and his newspapers proved an asset to all of these efforts. Pierre Salinger, John F. Kennedy's press secretary, singled out the *Arizona Republic* as one of the worst examples of biased reporting during the 1960 presidential election. Republicans hardly minded. By 1960, the state party's growth and success had established it as a major force within the national GOP apparatus. The next year, the Arizona affiliate hosted the annual gathering of western Republican state parties for the first time. Goldwater, then chairman of the Republican Senate Campaign Committee, headlined the event.[40]

As in other GOP precincts across the country, women volunteers were effective shock troops in these electoral efforts and organizational transformations. Elite, Anglo, Phoenician women were, for example, omnipresent in the Chamber's advertisements and formal programs, the CGC's campaigns, and efforts to rebuild the Republican Party. Such work was not too far afield from their Progressive Era predecessors' involvement with the town's settlement house, school system, and arts scene. Only later, however, did postwar women insurgents, Sandra Day O'Connor included, emerge as Chamber members, policymakers, and politicians in their own right. But women across Arizona were still vital to the cause. Republican women's clubs canvassed neighborhoods, typed letters, stuffed envelopes, hosted fundraising coffees and lunches, and even "organize[d] some gals" on the party's behalf.

Winslow clubwomen hosted a Lincoln Day dinner for the entire town, showcasing a then novel color film of the 1952 inauguration that featured Goldwater as much as the new Republican president, Dwight D. Eisenhower. The Flagstaff chapter held an "old time dance" with "many more Democrats than Republicans there." Women also made a concerted and somewhat successful effort to win over non-Anglo Arizonans, who were urged to form their own clubs. Clubwomen also made themselves available to the national party for "any information and material you may choose to send us as a guide to better club work." "We need to know," the Winslow chapter's president enthused, "how we best can serve the Republican Party, how we may present ourselves to our community as an informed group of working women. We also need encouragement and consideration."[41]

The grasstops relied on rhetoric to complement these organizational efforts. As in the municipal contests, Phoenix Chamber men relied on charges of corruption, waste, and mismanagement to defeat liberal Democrats on a statewide level. Goldwater, for example, challenged McFarland for his Senate seat in 1952 by campaigning against FDR's legacy and Truman's record. The merchant attacked "Powercrats," whom he identified as a "small group of willful men who have recklessly exalted their personal power and seek to increase and perpetuate their selfish control over the free men and free women of America." The term was as loaded as his previous charges of graft because both hinted at liberal Democrats' seemingly expansive and illegitimate strength. Goldwater claimed there was only one reason for the power of "Harry S. (for Spendthrift) Truman": corruption. Goldwater contended liberals had introduced the "P's and Q's in federal government . . . Big Personal Profit Quietly and Quickly." He promised that Republicans would "put an end to waste . . . to overhaul and revise the existing machinery of government. . . . to put men in office who will regard that office as a public trust, and not as a personal possession for private looting." He pushed Arizonans to stop "big government" because "waste and wild experiments, and give aways in government . . . creats [*sic*] deficits and deficits create inflation and that in the end the ultimate consumer pays the total of government." Like so many other Arizona Republicans during the 1952 contest, Goldwater cast himself not as a "conservative" but as a descendant of Jeffersonian Democrats: "What has happened to the great Democratic party," asked Goldwater, "which historically and traditionally has always stood as the protector of the individual's freedom and the individual's liberty?" He deemed it now "subservient to the wishes of wilful [*sic*], power hungry men who lust for dictatorship, but not for freedom, men who have stated in their private letters that you and I are too damned dumb to make the right decisions."[42]

Goldwater and other business-minded Republicans won decisively in 1952. The senator-elect took a majority in fewer counties than McFarland did but still edged his opponent by seven thousand votes, with support from men and women voters, the young and the elderly, and white-collar workers and professionals. The Arizona GOP, bolstered by enthusiasm from numerous registered Democrats, made substantial gains in all levels of governance. Republicans increased their seats in the eighty-member lower house from eleven to thirty and gained four seats in the Senate, where they previously had none. Arizonans also elected Rhodes, the state's first Republican representative. Liberal strategists considered the 1952 results alarming. "From then on through the fifties," a Hayden staffer recounted, "I witnessed a steady swing to the right in the political climate of Arizona."[43]

The GOP did in fact grow rapidly. Membership rose steadily, while the number of Democrats declined briefly in the mid-1950s. Some political watchdogs blamed the surge in Republican Party voter registration on a wave of sun-seeking migrants from the Midwest, but that influx alone cannot account for the seismic shifts in Arizona's politics. Growth came in part from "pinto" defections, which also left both parties much more ideologically cohesive. Nonetheless, a marked influence in unaffiliated voters and the trickle of new Democratic registrants prevented the Republican Party from numerically eclipsing its rival until 1985 (Table 1).[44]

The party was competitive long before this tipping point. At the start of the 1950s, many observers speculated that Republicans could only eke out victories in three counties (Maricopa, Pima, and Yavapai). The other eleven were safe for Democrats. Yet by 1958, only five of these counties remained a sure thing for the Democrats. The GOP also seemed to have a solid lock on populous Maricopa County, where Phoenix continued to mushroom. Republicans did continue to struggle in rural areas, where party officials could not always find candidates to contest every election. Even in 1958, when some analysts already asserted that the state GOP had unheralded political legitimacy and influence, Republicans contested fewer than half of the open state Senate seats. Much changed over the next decade. In the lower house, Republican ranks rose from twenty-five (seventeen from Phoenix) in 1959 to thirty-five in 1964. Democrats lost control of both chambers in 1966.[45]

Although it would take a few years more, the GOP also came to dominate Arizona's legislative delegation in Washington. Goldwater's senatorial

Table 1. Registered Democrats and Republicans in Arizona, 1948–1985

	Democrats	*Republicans*	*Ratio (Dem./Rep.)*
1948	195,210	43,380	4.5/1
1950	225,114	50,191	4.5/1
1952	241,743	82,611	2.9/1
1954	214,814	87,690	2.4/1
1956	250,616	111,107	2.3/1
1958	267,881	117,047	2.2/1
1960	314,590	152,957	2.1/1
1962	326,003	173,282	1.9/1
1964	365,276	205,605	1.8/1
1966	351,266	213,897	1.6/1
1968	343,509	253,928	1.4/1
1970	335,327	263,574	1.3/1
1972	455,985	362,196	1.3/1
1974	466,908	370,759	1.3/1
1976	510,805	399,227	1.3/1
1982	509,629	488,003	1.04/1
1984	622,949	587,688	1.05/1
1985	575,330	583,406	1/1.01

Sources: Nancy Anderson Guber, "The Development of Two-Party Competition in Arizona," 43; Arizona State Library, Archives and Public Records, "Arizona Voter Registration, 1958 –1984," unpublished spreadsheet, sent to the author by request in an e-mail dated August 27, 2008; Howard Pyle, "Making History: Good, Bad, and Indifferent," March 6, 1985, p. 7 typescript, folder 6, box 12, Oral History Collection, Arizona Historical Foundation (Tempe, Ariz.).

Note: The precise figures for 1978 and 1980 are unavailable. A 1980 Republican State Committee newsletter indicated that GOP registrants continued to climb: "Democrats just 18 months ago enjoyed a 95,000 edge over Republicans in registered voters statewide, today that margin has been cut to 48,000!" Republican State Committee to Concerned Arizonan, June 1980, binder marked 1978 –1980, direct mail sample, unprocessed collection MS 90 —Arizona Republican Party, Arizona Historical Foundation (Tempe, Ariz.).

victories were based on his success in urban Arizona, which was heavily Republican, and Congressman Rhodes, who campaigned in Phoenix, easily won reelection throughout the 1950s. But the GOP failed to elect a candidate to the state's second congressional seat, which initially encompassed all residents not living in Maricopa County, until the 1970s. Senator Hayden also stayed in office until he chose to retire in 1968. Many of the leading members of the Arizona GOP had supported Hayden's continual return to Washington because the Senate workhorse was the driving force behind ensuring Arizona's share of the Colorado River's water. Hayden also distanced himself from his earlier politics, which made him somewhat more acceptable to booster Republicans. In the 1940s he had opposed Arizona's right-to-work referenda, fought the Taft-Hartley Act, and then voted to sustain President Truman's veto. Yet he never joined other Democrats in subsequent attempts to repeal Taft-Hartley or section 14(b), which gave states the authority to pass right-to-work laws. He assured concerned constituents that Arizonans had expressed their views on the matter repeatedly and he could not, in good conscious, ignore their decisions.[46]

Republicans and Democrats engaged in a protracted war for the governor's mansion during Hayden's final terms. Howard Pyle was a central figure in efforts to rebuild the struggling Republican Party. His father had been a boilermaker in Wyoming but had moved his young family to Texas, where he attended seminary school, and then to Phoenix. Pyle, Barry Goldwater, and future CGC mayor and Republican governor Jack Williams started broadcasting on Phoenix's KFDA radio station as teenagers. Pyle and Williams stayed in the radio business and became successful broadcasters. Pyle was known throughout the state for his skillful, moving coverage of World War II battlefronts, which included interviews with Arizonan servicemen and coverage of Japan's formal surrender. Pyle later admitted, "I knew absolutely nothing about politics," but Goldwater still managed to get the highly regarded newscaster into public office. The merchant wanted to run for governor in 1950 with the well-known Pyle as his campaign manager, a role intended to prepare the journalist for a 1952 Senate run.[47]

Pyle was a quick learner. He broke the gentleman's agreement with Goldwater and ran for the 1950 Republican gubernatorial nomination, campaigning on issues at the heart of both the GOP's revival and grasstops industrialization. Pyle attacked opponent Ana Frohmiller, the state auditor who had won twelve previous elections, for her support of the current state tax code and Arizona's liberal public assistance program, which he thought impediments to industrialization. He won a resounding victory in 1950 and also triumphed in 1952. While in office, he endeavored to impose the CGC's governing philosophy on the state. "It won't hurt us," he told voters in his reelection bid, "to think and plan and act as . . . if this were a private enterprise and we were operating it with a profit motive." Restructuring state government stood at the top of his agenda, not unlike the reengineering that boosters had undertaken to refashion the Chamber, the city government, and state GOP. Pyle called for consolidating operations, eliminating elections for some state offices, and cutting back on social services in the name of "increasing governmental efficiency." And the Jeffersonian Democrats dominating both legislative houses cooperated. "I'm still a Democrat; we're all Democrats," one opined. "But we vote here as citizens of Arizona." Pundits were shocked: "Nothing like this has ever happened before. Usually at the end of a session the Democratic members go home mad at the Democratic governor."[48]

But liberal Democrats campaigned on this complicity to convince voters to turn Pyle out of office in 1954. Self-proclaimed "Mr. Democrat" Ernest McFarland enlisted a slew of famous liberals, including Senator Lyndon Baines Johnson, to back his challenge. McFarland called Pyle's reforms "undemocratic" because they removed "the right of the people to select their public officials," implying that "you, citizens of the State, are incompetent to choose your public officials." Pyle responded by insinuating that labor bosses were manipulating his critics. Pundits never agreed on what cost Pyle the election. Some journalists blamed scandal and backdoor politics. He lost Maricopa County, particularly the city of Mesa, which had a large Mormon population, because he had ordered a raid on remote, isolated Short Creek, Arizona, where officials suspected residents practiced polygamy. Police arrested women and men, incarcerated some in faraway Kingman, Arizona, sent some children to foster homes, and left others with their young mothers. Many Mormons stayed home on election day, and others voted for McFarland, which left, as many reporters theorized, the incumbent without the necessary support in urban Arizona to carry the day. But others claimed Pyle lost because he was then out of favor with Pulliam, who failed to endorse the governor's reelection. "I was an independent thinker," Pyle later explained. "I was very determined not to be obligated to anyone."[49]

Democratic hold on the governorship proved fleeting. Propane magnate and Chamber member Paul Fannin easily defeated his Democratic opponent on a grasstops Republican platform in 1958. He held this office until 1965, when he left the governor's mansion to take Goldwater's place in the Senate. Control of the executive branch flipped back and forth in the ensuing decades, but Democratic victories never represented a repudiation of booster governance. Successful candidates generally made the same commitment to investment policies as their Republican opponents but also promised voters more consideration for civil rights and environmental issues.[50]

The influence Phoenix Republicans had over the politics of their state separated them from other Sunbelt boosters. Rainmakers depended on rural Jeffersonian Democrats' support in the legislature because Arizona law did not apportion seats by population. Yet agreement was limited to just a few issues central to the business climate, namely, the curtailment of social welfare programs, business taxes, and regulations. Phoenicians also prevailed because Tucson delegates sided with them on these matters, less so on policies that privileged Maricopa's industrialization over Pima County's growth. But Valley promoters navigated the legislature far better than their competitors, who were also uniformly underrepresented in arid-state governments. For example, Las Vegas boosters in sparsely populated Nevada had both rivals and allies to their north in Reno. Grasstops businessmen in both cities backed statewide tax and labor policies to help them compete for investment with other states, but they also stymied each other's efforts to fund city-specific advantages, especially the creation and expansion of a University of Nevada branch campus in Las Vegas. Southern Nevada promoters sought a research university to attract military and manufacturing investment, but their northern neighbors jealously guarded the supremacy of the University of Nevada's Reno campus. These northern boosters limited UNLV's growth because even as Las Vegas mushroomed in size, state legislators from Reno and rural counties controlled the state legislature.[51]

Malapportionment defined southern state politics as well. Georgia's infamous county unit system gave each county between two and six votes, which provided the more densely populated city of Atlanta and Fulton County with but four more votes than the least populous county. Such underrepresentation frustrated southern boosters, who sought to pass and implement the increasingly pro forma tax and union policies within the broad business climate ideal. Miami boosters thus listed "Home Rule" among "Bigtime Problems" in 1957, having fought for years "a system of government whereby strictly local matters were legislated upon by a state body once in two years." North Carolina's self-described "businessman in the statehouse," Luther Hodges, confronted this challenge when he endeavored to update state spending and taxation in the name of winning more outside corporate investment in the state. The former textile executive opposed increased corporate or individual taxes and instead proposed levies on tobacco and alcohol sales (not production), comparable to those in forty-one other states. Legislators, especially those representing agriculturalists, balked and passed taxes only on beer and wine.[52]

Such conflicts produced numerous legal challenges, which affected not only apportionment but also regional party realignment. Voters had sued repeatedly to challenge the status quo in the postwar period but never found relief in federal courts. Finally, in 1962, justices found in favor of Republican greater-Memphis resident Charles Baker, who sued Tennessee secretary of state Joe Carr because he was in charge of conducting elections. *Baker v. Carr* was just the first in a series of cases that paved the way for the actual realization of the one-man-one-vote principle, which was laid out in the *Gary v. Sanders* (1963) ruling that declared the Georgia County unit system unconstitutional. Enforcing this new representative standard was a slow, bitter process, which nonetheless transformed the entire region's politics and delivered real power to the metropolitan South, the incubator of the region's Republican parties.[53]

The decisions also transformed Arizona after Gary Peter Klahr, a twenty-one-year-old University of Arizona law student, filed a 1964 suit. A federal district court dictated that Arizonans had to have sixty representatives and thirty senators, half of each going to sprawling Maricopa County. The edict thrilled Phoenix Republicans. "I'm not pleased that the federal government has seen fit to tell us how our legislature should be made up," a CGC mayor opined. "But . . . I can't help but be elated that the urban areas are going to have at least proper representation." Indeed, this reconfiguration allowed Republicans to take control of both legislative houses in the November 1965 election.[54]

Yet Democratic-inclined Arizona's political realignment represented but one variation within a larger transformation of Sunbelt party politics. Malapportioned California, for example, had been a Republican stronghold, but conflicts between progressives, liberals, and conservatives splintered the state GOP, whereas in Arizona these factions had fractured the Democratic Party. Tensions came to a head in California when Republican William Knowland tied his 1958 gubernatorial bid to a failing right-to-work proposition. An energized union effort defeated this referendum and helped elect liberal Democrat Edmund "Pat" Brown, who oversaw the state's brief, midcentury social-democratic revolution in education, fair employment, and basic infrastructure. Eight years later Brown lost to Ronald Reagan, whose primary and general election victories relied on the Golden State's dedicated conservative suburbanites.[55]

Such suburban warriors were also critical to southern realignment. In the 1950s and 1960s white metropolitan voters found common cause with Republican presidential nominees, who preached at least a dime-store New Deal, if not an out-and-out repudiation of liberal economic principles, and a more middle-of-the-road approach to civil rights. Eisenhower won a majority in affluent white areas in the South in 1952 and even expanded the number of southern states in his next electoral tally. GOP nominees had mixed results in the South in the ensuing years because the metropolitan vote was more often than not a swing vote that matched the rest of the nation in its response to national issues, such as Vietnam, Watergate, abortion, law and order, and economic stagnation.[56]

Even though these residents had proved receptive to Republican overtures, Democrats nevertheless held strong at the local and state levels. Municipal elections were, as in the broader Sunbelt, still predominantly nonpartisan, but boosters running for state and federal office in the metropolitan South, unlike their Phoenix counterparts, ran in the Democratic Party even if their politics allied them more closely with national Republicans or conservative firebrands. Southern primaries were hence bitter contests between white liberals, who clung to the New Deal, white reactionaries, who fought desegregation, white suburbanites and businessmen, who detested liberal economic policies, and African American voters, who began to identify the Democratic Party as Roosevelt's Party and had no choice but to try and vote in its primaries in order to influence policy.[57]

Business climate politics, as in Arizona, still infused these postwar southern campaigns. Liberal Senator Claude Pepper lost the 1950 Democratic primary because of opposition from a newly emergent urban, business, white-collar, middle-class vote. He had supported organized labor, social security's expansion, more money for public housing, national health insurance, minimum wage laws, and Harry Truman's civil rights policies. His opponent, George Smathers, was a reactionary who derided Pepper's support for the trade union movement and civil rights, even calling Pepper a Communist. The incumbent won the rural white and African American Florida vote, but Smathers won the urbanized areas, particularly the vote of enterprising Southerners and recent northeastern and midwestern transplants, who identified as Republicans but had to vote Pepper out in the primary. This contest, then, was an important moment in Florida politics, which signaled an end to New Deal populism and the appearance of a new subset of Democratic voters who created a space within the party for the concerns of the industry-minded South and were emerging as uncompromising bulwarks against mid-century liberalism.[58]

Yet, in contrast to the Arizona GOP, southern Republican parties first emerged out of the suburbs, where residents chafed at the Democrat-affiliated urban business elite. Conflict arose over city leaders' efforts to bring these areas into city boundaries and thus impose the full range of urban politics, from taxes to busing, on these residents. The Republican moniker served as a way to unite the suburban rings against the cities' leadership. Only later would the nonmetropolitan South join these new parties in the national GOP's broad defense of states' rights and religious values. Equally important was the reciprocal process through which moderate and liberal whites, African Americans, and, later, Mexican Americans came to control the state Democratic parties. These slow tectonic shifts were evident in state voting patterns. In the southern periphery (Texas, Arkansas, Virginia, North Carolina, Florida, and Tennessee), Republicans posed a serious challenge to their opponents for Senate seats after 1961 and won 37 percent of those elections. But half the Republican senators elected were not able to win a second term. The GOP struggled even more in the Deep South where Republican challengers only won 13 percent of the Senate contests in the 1960s and 1970s. Even so, by the mid-1980s, a majority of white Southerners called themselves Republicans.[59]

Union and Tax-Free Oases

Gradual realignment and reapportionment also spawned further evolutions in regional conflicts over union security and taxation. The labor question had remained potent because right-to-work statutes, while clearly an ideological blow to the labor movement, nevertheless did little to stop an overall increase in the number of unionists. Utah's union density, for example, dropped from 26.8 percent to 16.4 percent between 1953 and 1960. Arizona's actually held steady at about 27 percent, but membership only grew from 57,400 to 90,700 during this period, years marked by substantial outside investment, hiring, and overall population growth.[60]

Efforts to pass additional right-to-work laws reached an impasse in these years, especially outside the South and interior West. The movement's electoral apogee was 1958, when propositions went before Washington, Ohio, Kansas, Idaho, Colorado, and California voters. Only Kansans passed the measure. The National Right to Work Committee, an organization founded in 1955 to unite various anti-union efforts, thereafter shifted its fight from the ballot box to the courts, while unionists would soon make a renewed push for congressional repeal of Taft-Hartley's section 14(b).[61]

Business climate competition nonetheless intensified labor-management conflict and kept the labor question in the courts and on state legislative agendas. Texans, for example, endeavored to have "fair share" or "agency shop" agreements covered under an already passed right-to-work law. They were responding to laborites who had negotiated these provisions in order to recoup the costs of representing workers who were not dues-paying members. Supreme Court justices ruled against unions in this 1963 challenge, deeming such membership stipulations akin to union shop clauses and thus illegal under existing right-to-work acts (unless the legislation specifically allowed such exceptions). This opinion had a profound effect on organizing in right-to-work states, where organizers endeavored to afford to represent members, bargain for better contracts, and fight continual courtroom challenges to their workplace rights.[62]

Labor issues also continued to roil Phoenix politics and Arizona jurisprudence during the early 1950s. City pharmacists were outraged at the power of Local 631, whose bartenders, cooks, and waitresses continued to picket many drugstores to force owners to recognize the union and maintain a de facto union shop. Drugstore owners responded by taking the union to court for violating the right-to-work statute. Jurists refused to enjoin Local 631 because the court held peaceful picketing legal. The setback propelled druggists to form a statewide association to gather signatures for a referendum restricting union capacity to boycott and picket. Restaurateurs, who had succumbed to Bartender pickets years before, aided the 1952 electoral campaign. A Westward Ho co-owner even headed the Committee for State Employees' Security, a business-dominated front group. "Don't Let the Bartenders Union Dictate Your Vote," their ads demanded. The proposition imposed restrictions on the types of strikes and pickets that Local 631 had used in the past, made it illegal for a local to picket an employer unless "a bona fide dispute regarding wages or working conditions" existed between management and "the majority of employees," empowered judges to enjoin unions engaged in either activity, and allowed affected parties to sue for damages. The statute passed by 63 percent. Conflict then spilled over into state courtrooms when businesses tried to enjoin striking unions and locals challenged the law. Jurists moved back and forth on these union security and power issues during the 1950s but ultimately sided with managers, ruling that picketing was more than an act of free speech.[63]

An increase in public employee unionism also forced boosters to adapt their anti-union policies to this next phase in municipal labor-management conflict. By the mid-1960s, these workers made up the majority of the Arizona labor movement (fewer than twenty thousand unionists worked in the private sector). The largest public employee unions were the American Federation of Teachers, International Association of Fire Fighters, the Phoenix City Employees Union (which had chosen to remain independent when the Congress of Industrial Organizations merged with the American Federation of Labor), and the American Federation of State, County, and Municipal Employees (AFSCME). Their membership was impressive because the CGC had refused to honor existing agreements when the inaugural slate took office in January 1950. The city manager justified his stance by citing the opinion of a Phoenix attorney who had unsuccessfully argued in a 1946 court case that it was illegal for the city to enter into an agreement with a trade union. Wilson and his successor maintained this position throughout the 1950s and 1960s, even as public sector organizing flourished elsewhere in the country: "I don't recognize any collective bargaining agreement. Each union official is welcome to come into my office at any time to discuss matters, but I don't negotiate wages or anything else with them." AFSCME Local 317 nevertheless endeavored to formalize grievance procedures with the city, particularly with regard to wage scales and job classifications, but leaders never challenged the municipal government to secure formal collective bargaining rights.[64]

Low taxes were as important to a favorable business climate as a docile labor movement. Some boosters had begun to consider antiquated peripheral fiscal structures inadequate for the task of industrialization during the 1930s but could not, as their principles dictated and their competitors ensured, impose tolls on businesses to pay for the modern infrastructure, such as roads, utilities, and schools, that potential investors demanded. Promoters instead came to rely on state governments to pass more excises, improve collection mechanisms, and increase burdens on small property owners and consumers. Prewar Bimson-backed banking measures were hence Phoenix-based precedents of the general postwar approach to financing corporate welfare.

Indeed, other businessmen proved equally inventive once municipal reform and party realignment gave them more political power. The Reno Chamber, for example, pushed a 1949 "free-port" bill through the Nevada legislature, which permitted manufacturers to avoid property taxes on goods officially "in transit" from or en route to California harbors. The assembly relaxed these rules throughout the decade, which allowed companies to process materials or engage in some manufacturing without fear of levies. Northern Nevada quickly became a warehousing, wholesaling, and manufacturing mecca. Boosters also skillfully raised revenue to offset cuts, often through sin and sales levies. In 1959, for example, Georgia taxed gas, alcohol, malt syrup, cigars, and cigarettes but not materials used for packaging and distribution, property imported into Georgia or acquired before April 1, 1951, or industrial materials used in any stage of product "processing, manufacture, or conversion."[65]

Georgia boosters' chief rival, Tar Heel Luther Hodges, was among the South's most innovative postwar tax collectors. North Carolina collected an additional $27.5 million in revenue after mandating that employers withhold and forward state income taxes directly to the government. This program, the governor noted, "added to the tax rolls many thousands of people who for some reason or another had never before made a tax return." Accumulation coincided with tax code revisions, the last changes having been made in 1939. Hodges had considered existing duties "a barrier," particularly a long-standing provision that assessed corporate income taxes on all profits. He instead championed a 6 percent tax on North Carolina–based earnings. Newspapers and a handful of legislators called the 1957 proposal a giveaway that would cost the state $7 million in collections, alarm bells that did not prevent the measure's passage.[66]

Local communities also offered additional incentives to complement the state-level concessions. These giveaways were in many ways analogous to buying payroll policies but were increasingly described within the more positive rhetoric associated with establishing a better business climate. Inducements included one-time deals to help a business start or build facilities, under-the-table agreements to not assess property at its full value, and repeals of taxes on industrial property. Consumers and homeowners thus increasingly bore more of the burden of paying for public and corporate infrastructure. Nashville's Chamber-controlled city council, for example, held city business taxes steady during its reign in the late 1940s and through the 1950s but raised revenue by increasing water and sewage rates in surrounding bedroom communities. Residents paid $300 a year for fire protection, the area's average monthly income.[67]

The refusal of large industrial companies to subject themselves to taxes fundamentally restructured fiscal practices and philosophies. Tax payments to nonfederal governments rose from $5.7 billion to $14.5 billion between 1950 and 1964 but still represented an overall drop in responsibility (from

39.9 percent to 34.6 percent; excluding employment taxes, the figure was 36 percent to 30 percent). Companies spent $500 billion on new plants during this period, much of this capital made available through business-first demobilization practices. Firms still experienced a general decrease in how much governments charged for these expansions. Such duties accounted for 22.6 percent of revenue in 1950 and just 18 percent in 1964. Individual property owners and consumers took on more of the burden: state and local governments collected 4.6 percent less property tax from business during this period, but individual property owners' contributions, as a percentage of total revenue, rose from 24 percent to 26.4 percent nationwide. Individual taxpayers paid a greater share of both state and local sales taxes (a jump from 11.7 percent to 14.7 percent) and also personal incomes taxes (which increased from 5 percent to 8 percent).[68]

This revenue revolution spread into the rusting Steelbelt as competition for investment reached fever pitch. By the mid-1960s, thirty-eight states had enacted statutes allowing municipal bonds for industrial development. Pennsylvania had actually banned such practices when Philadelphians started PIDC. Lawmakers embraced other business climate principles as well. Republican James Rhodes, who occupied the Ohio governor's mansion from 1963 to 1983, save for a brief interlude in the early 1970s, championed job creation through business climate principles, even proclaiming: "Profit is not a dirty word in Ohio." Slashing high business taxes topped his rejuvenation policies. Without reductions, he asserted, "We might as well hang signs at the state borders that say 'Industry Not Welcome Here.'"[69]

This industry-first philosophy also impacted federal policy. Businesses paid 46 percent of federal revenues in 1950 and just 40 percent in 1964. Reagan-era tax cuts maintained this downward trend at the national level but unintentionally reversed it at state and local levels because governments needed to tax business in order make up for decreased federal support. The amount companies paid in state and local taxes more than doubled during the 1980s and then continued to rise. For the 2006 fiscal year, business paid, on average, 39.9 percent of state taxes and 52.5 percent of local taxes. The amount paid in state taxes ranged from 26.4 percent (Virginia) to 92.7 percent (Alaska) and in local levies from 37.6 percent (Connecticut) to 79.1 percent (West Virginia).[70]

Phoenix Chamber men, like their peripheral counterparts, had also prioritized taxes when frantic reconversion efforts became sustained industrialization campaigns. Valley-based CEOs dictated that levies top the organization's agenda: managers consistently ranked the tax structure third in factors they considered when opening up new ventures. Only the labor supply and market proximity had a greater importance among respondents. Executives, even after a decade of CGC rule, expressed concern about property, sales, and end-of-year inventory levies as impositions that "could limit growth." A small subset complained in a 1964 survey, "City taxes out of line with benefits received" and "Taxes somewhat higher than state to east." Rainmakers fought to lessen business's overall contribution to state and local revenue. The Chamber contested the county inventory tax on wholesalers and retailers by organizing statewide support for a reduction or elimination of this duty. State county assessors cut the valuation substantially in January 1953. The revision, estimated to reduce bills by 22 percent, delighted businessmen. "This partial victory is only the fore-runner of many things we can and should accomplish," one crowed.[71]

Pyle's governorship fulfilled this prophecy. Chamber men found Democratic control of the legislative and executive branch stymieing, especially in their efforts to secure a "free port" law, similar to Nevada's statute. The proposal permitted Arizona warehousing outfits to receipt items from their final destination and only pay the sales tax if goods were sold within the state. Carl Bimson had promoted the 1949 bill after observing truckers waiting along the California-Arizona border until midnight on New Year's Eve to resume delivery in order to avoid the Golden State's high inventory taxes on incoming merchandise. Bimson theorized that the revision would strengthen Phoenix wholesaling because the town could easily serve Albuquerque, Salt Lake City, Denver, Los Angeles, San Diego, and San Francisco. Advocates, including many businessmen from across Arizona, convinced the majority of lawmakers that these duties made the state uncompetitive, but liberal governor Dan Garvey, who succeeded Democrat Sidney Osborn after his death, still vetoed the bill. Garvey's refusal ended discussion until 1951, when a similar act easily passed and was in no danger of a veto from Governor Pyle. Chamber men endeavored to take full advantage of this legislative victory. "I have discussed this law with representatives of the Santa Fe and the Southern Pacific Railway Corporation," a booster assured the governor, "and asked that they encourage their shippers to construct warehouses within the State."[72]

Increasing political power enabled Phoenix boosters to pass excise concessions to specifically attract aerospace, electronics, and computer manufacturers. Legislators signed off on a repeal of the tax on sales made to the federal government, an exemption on inventory, and a loophole that permitted businesses to subtract the amount firms paid to the federal government when figuring what they owed Arizona. These provisions were particularly valuable to high-tech companies: their inventories were often worth much more than the plant's equipment or property. These firms also made tremendous profits in sales of both military equipment and consumer goods, which made sales-tax exemptions vital to aggressively bidding for defense work and competitively pricing consumer products. Tax bills also did not increase substantially for the highly prized electronics and aerospace companies after the state raised property taxes from 10 percent to 25 percent in 1966. Most Phoenix manufacturers engaged in the kind of production that had considerable payrolls and profits, so their property taxes accounted for a small portion of their total tax bill. Industrialists could also claim their federal income tax as an exemption, further reducing what they owed Arizona. Thus, homeowners experienced the real dues increase needed to sustain the business-climate-driven corporate welfare state.[73]

Arizona's tax code was one of the most business friendly. In 1957, Arizona firms contributed just 32.7 percent of all state revenue, just 0.5 percent higher than the South's overall average and lower than the figures for New England, the Mid-Atlantic, and Great Lakes regions as well as for the United States as a whole. In 1962, property taxes on businesses represented only 4.9 percent of Arizona collections, far less than the averages in New England, the Great Lakes, the Plains states, and the Far West. Only percentages in the South were lower (just three states, Georgia, Florida, and Louisiana, claimed more revenue from such levies). Arizona property taxes were also less than in every other southwestern state but New Mexico because Arizona manufacturers exempted inventory from taxation (computers, semiconductors, and scientific equipment often accounted for more than half of these businesses' total property values). Arizona's corporate income tax was also lower than California's and Colorado's. Neighboring Utah and New Mexico had a lower rate but still did not allow companies to deduct their tax payments to the federal government. Arizona's tax code also privileged high-tech industries more than neighboring states did. Utah, New Mexico, and California levied more total dues on electronics and aerospace manufacturers (though Utah's overall taxes on computer manufacturers were still 98 percent of Arizona's). Economists also calculated that Colorado and California's income taxes were 70 percent to 80 percent of Arizona's duties on commercial printing outfits and sewing machine factories but were 12 percent to 25 percent higher for firms that produced computers, semiconductors, and scientific equipment. Accordingly, Colorado- and California-based high-tech outfits paid anywhere from twelve to twenty-five cents more on the dollar. Such a difference was quite significant for firms with multimillion-dollar profits and plants.[74]

This differential proved hard to maintain. All Sunbelt boosters, Snell included, did far more than "watch the taxes." They feverishly competed with each other to attract investors who demanded far more than duties that were "fair but not burdensome." Industrialists could find such general assurances almost anywhere by the 1960s. So they demanded more, which they could do because their grasstops allies had the political power, managerial control, and electoral backing to escalate competition into out-and-out combat.

Chapter 7

"Second War Between the States"

Journalists investigating the Sunbelt phenomenon in the 1970s described booster determination to compete for investment as a "new" or "second" "War Between the States." The competition to build the best business climate had indeed escalated since economists first coined the term. Even then executives expected systematic governance, political allegiance to a free-enterprise philosophy, anti-union legislation, and a business-friendly tax code. Boosters thus needed to offer more advantages to undercut their rivals. Industrialists insisted as much, especially those at the helm of lucrative high-tech firms. During the 1950s and 1960s, they increasingly demanded improved utilities, better public schools, technical education opportunities for their employees, and recreational and cultural amenities to satisfy the families of managers and the many professionals employed in science-based sectors. CEOs also stipulated that their enterprises contribute relatively little to the public coffers that financed their corporate security and welfare. This pressure consequently forced Phoenix Chamber men and their Sunbelt counterparts to brawl for investment. But bayonets had no place on this mid-century battlefield. Policy innovations were the weapons of choice, brandished in colorful brochures promising a town that "welcomes new industry" with low union density, less business taxation, and a free-market mindset to complement expanding physical, educational, and leisure infrastructures, all of which were publicly financed, privately promised, and politically guaranteed.[1]

Watering an Industrial Metropolis

Utilities were very much a part of booster arsenals. Water was of course universally important for businesses and suburbs, but it held particular material and symbolic significance for the Phoenix area's industrialization. The great irrigation projects that had watered the Salt River Valley in the 1910s were earmarked for agriculture. A 1913 law did allow towns near federal projects to contract for municipal purposes but forbade agreements between individuals, hence alderman made contracts for public services, such as fire fighting, but not for private residential use. The city government built a pipeline between the town and the Verde River in 1922, but this small project only supplied fifteen million gallons a day. New pipelines and larger reservoirs provided more water in the 1920s and 1930s but still left the city ill equipped for wartime production and postwar growth. Daily consumption in 1946 was at least a million gallons more than the city's reservoirs could hold. Rapid suburbanization only increased demand. Mayor Ray Busey subsequently pushed for a more extensive public water system but had to settle for a short-term solution in 1946, when the city built spillways in the Salt River Project (SRP) in exchange for access to the water captured behind the new system of gates as well as an additional twenty thousand acre-feet of water from the project's reservoirs.[2]

This stopgap proved insufficient. Farmland immediately surrounding Phoenix began to disappear as executives built branch plants and builders constructed subdivisions for successive waves of new postwar arrivals. Before 1948, Phoenix had expanded onto twenty-two thousand acres of irrigated land, but during the next decade it devoured an additional thirty-two thousand. Riparian rights did not transfer to home owners or investors, which left the unclaimed acre-feet in Salt River Valley Water Users' Association (SRVWUA) stores. Animosity ensued. Project coordinators endeavored to collect money to pay back the federal lien on the project but struggled to keep track of and deal with a tremendous influx of new home owners. Managers charged landowners equally to ease the task, which angered urban-fringe pioneers who paid as much as well-established farmers. Many suburbanites just simply refused to pay any share of the association's debt.[3]

A severe drought created an impasse in the summer of 1951. Farmers notified the city manager that water levels in the Salt and Verde rivers' reservoirs were dangerously low but refused to allocate more SRVWUA resources to the city (Phoenix had already been diverting roughly twice the agreed allotment). On July 4, 1951, the *Arizona Republic* warned that the Verde River reservoirs only had enough reserves for ten days. The start of the monsoon season and a tentative truce between agriculturalists and city leaders eased tensions and provided water to all residents (at a cost of $107,000). The crisis also opened up negotiations between the Charter Government Committee (CGC) and the SRVWUA. The resultant Domestic Water Contract, which dictated that Phoenix compensate the association directly for the suburbanites' delinquent payments (totaling more than $200,000), pay the amount due on all lands that had become a part of the city, and shoulder the cost of maintaining and operating the system. SRVWUA thereafter diverted residential shares to the city, which not only provided Phoenix with resources for public and private usage but also ensured a surplus because the amount of water allotted these once agricultural lands was far more than suburban tenants needed.[4]

The CGC's subsequent aqua initiatives epitomized Sunbelt neoliberalism. Phoenix bought private water companies and consolidated their mazes of pipes and wells into a municipal system. Watering Phoenix also forced the city to place before voters a series of bond measures to improve its aqua infrastructure. A Chamber-backed 1952 initiative provided $7 million for the Verde River system. Five years later, the city government requested voter approval of an additional $70 million, the majority of which officials earmarked for improvements to water and sewage systems to serve industrial zones and wealthy suburban areas.[5]

This neoliberal impulse also framed the Chamber's campaign against SRP, the public entity that managed water reservoirs, generated hydroelectric power, and sold kilowatts to residents. SRP represented an affront to Chamber men and the local private utility, Arizona Public Service (APS), which had several powerful boosters at its helm, including Frank Snell. Their intransigence was rooted in business hostility to public competitors, which had also plagued the Tennessee Valley Authority (TVA). Phoenix boosters were frustrated too that APS did not benefit from a 1937 referendum that waived taxes on public electrical and irrigation districts, a constitutional amendment in line with New Deal guarantees for affordable electricity. APS and SRP had agreed to divide the Valley between central Phoenix and surrounding farmlands, but sprawl strained this truce because SRP picked up urban-fringe suburbanites, who enjoyed the lower rates that the public utility maintained, at least partially, because of SRP's tax-exempt status. "This project competes with other business," *Republic* editorialists complained. Their 1958 demands for an end to SRP's special status also reflected the realities of the cutthroat business climate: state and local governments needed tax revenue to pay for industrialization. To attack SRP, detractors adapted the CGC's arguments that free-enterprise principles best served the grassroots, "carrying all they can stand in school taxes . . . [and] subsidizing a handful of farmers at the expense of home owners," while SRP went "scot-free" and "every other profit making business and institution in the state . . . [paid] its share of the tax load."[6]

Controversy erupted in November 1962, a month after an SRP rate decrease. The *Republic* published an ad asking: "Isn't it time the Salt River Power District paid its fair share of taxes on its electrical operations?" More denunciations followed, SRP officials theorized, to prepare the public for a brewing fight in the legislature over the costs, desirability, and fairness of public power. Project heads went on the offensive by publicizing rough estimates of the more than $800,000 SRP paid in various federal employment, state sales, and municipal use taxes. Ads proclaimed "The Salt River Project Does Help!" and offered "The Complete Story About the Salt River Project's Importance to YOU." SRP's general manager also publicly attacked APS for threatening the low rates "essential to carry out the purposes of the Project and to contribute to the continued growth of the area" as well as the Pulliam press for asserting that the City of Phoenix, SRP's largest water customer, did not need low-cost resources because "Phoenix can resell this water at any price it wants." "Just dump the cost of the tax you propose on the backs of small homeowners," he urged. "They can bear the burden, and who cares!"[7]

This skirmish divided the electorate and also forced boosters to reconsider their dependence on New Deal infrastructure to facilitate business-first industrialization. To craft the public utility's response, administrators reached out to Stephen Shadegg, a former Democrat and Carl Hayden strategist, who now managed Barry Goldwater's campaigns. Shadegg urged SRP officials to consider offering a payment in lieu of taxes to prevent SRP from losing its tax-exempt status. His involvement enraged Goldwater, who told him an agreement could not be reached because a Republican state senator planned to sponsor legislation to either revoke SRP's municipal status or rescind the loophole. Shadegg quickly pressured SRP administrators to send Governor Paul Fannin a proposal that included their stated willingness to make a payment in lieu of taxes and request that he appoint a blue-ribbon committee to investigate the matter. The governor's work group reached a consensus in ninety days: SRP retained its tax-exempt status but also made substantial remittances toward what it would owe in taxes to local and state governments.[8]

Boosters finagled more than a strained compromise when they embraced Hayden's federal solution to chronic water shortages. The senator was the architect of the federal Central Arizona Project (CAP), which delivered much needed water from the Colorado River. This public works initiative placed the state at odds with neighboring California, which received the lion's share of the river's water under older agreements. Consequently, the Golden State's powerful congressional delegation continually stymied the project until 1963, when the Supreme Court finally granted Arizona access to this riparian resource.[9]

CAP represented a conundrum for Phoenix boosters, who jealously guarded Arizona's magnificent rivers and canyons but never opposed water for metropolitan sprawl. Goldwater saw no inherent contradiction between the two. "A rough, fast, dangerous river," he celebrated in diaries from his 1940 trip down the Colorado River, "forever will challenge the ingenuity of man." The water's power and potential informed his pre-CGC stint on the Colorado River Commission, a state board that fought for Arizona's water rights and lobbied for federal projects, such as CAP. The merchant championed both. The riparian status quo "would wipe out many, many businesses whose relationship to farming is not evident to the unpracticed eye," he wrote to California customers in 1947, "destroying that much of our real property tax base."[10]

Goldwater would have still found himself at odds with Democrat Stewart Udall's initial plans for watering the arid states. Arizona's second representative served from 1955 to 1961, leaving Congress to serve as secretary of the interior under Kennedy and Johnson. In the House, Udall advocated that publicly owned Grand Canyon dams provide cheap electricity to consumers. This proposal frustrated conservationists and preservations as well as industry-attuned promoters. Federally underwritten public power seemed far too similar, even if just in spirit, to the TVA, which Goldwater considered an abomination. Although this viewpoint frustrated his southern champions who warned that TVA was a political sacred cow, Goldwater's *Where I Stand*, a 120-page manifesto for the 1964 election, advocated dismantling this "Federal 'white elephant'" by placing overlapping functions under the purview of existing bureaucracies and terminating or disposing of steam-generating plants and fertilizer programs. "There is no justification for continued Federal ownership of such commercial activities," he reasoned. He wanted private companies or local governments to buy TVA facilities, a privatization plan in line with later neoliberal strategies. As a last resort, Goldwater was prepared to establish "a special corporation" that would "take over these facilities . . . [,] offer stock for public sale and aim toward repayment of all government money involved in the shortest possible time."[11]

Such ideas and proposals informed the federal legislation that the Phoenix business elite supported. Hayden's CAP, unlike TVA, did not include provisions for generating electric power. Phoenix, and its urbanizing rivals in neighboring states, instead relied on electricity from the coal-fired power plants built on northern Arizona reservations in the late 1950s. The final water bill also funded the initiative through a federal loan to build the project with private contractors. This stipulation further divorced its development from TVA, whose construction had not been outsourced. Hence, in a similar fashion to the Bimsons' earlier embrace of Federal Housing Administration loans, these pragmatists rationalized their support for this large expansion of state power by arguing that the program would serve their economic goals and fall in line with their politics. "We never thought of it as the 'Feds' financing it," Howard Pyle explained, "so much as they were simply helping us to reimburse the 'Feds.'"[12]

Rainmakers fought for CAP at the local and federal levels. In 1964, the Chamber's board placed passage of the bill that authorized CAP high on the Chamber's list of major objectives for the fiscal year, just behind "strengthening the free enterprise system" and recruiting even more investment than in previous years. Members attended hearings in Washington, lobbied lawmakers to vote for the bill, and apprised other Phoenicians of congressional battles. Frank Snell also served on Arizona's legal team. Most important, booster Republicans supported Hayden's reelection in 1962. "It will take a unique combination of power to beat the project's enemies," *Republic* editorialists warned. "Such a combination rests in the hands of Carl Hayden." Stalwarts privately discouraged upstart Republicans, who wished to challenge him for the seat. "We would not have gotten the water," Pyle elaborated. "He was so familiar with the whole machinery . . . he was chairman of the Appropriations Committee and President Pro Tem."[13]

Hayden's 1962 GOP challenger thus came from outside the close-knit coterie of grasstops Arizonans. Party apparatchiks had planned to put up a token candidate, state GOP chairman Richard Kleindienst, but a little-known state senator, Evan Mecham, upset their scheme. The thirty-eight-year-old

Glendale-based car dealer represented a challenge to both Arizona's liberal Democrats and its businessmen Republicans. The Utah-born Mormon identified with the libertarian Americans for Constitutional Action, which had a small following among Phoenix's middle-class homeowners and small businessmen, those who had been left out of city hall for more than a decade.[14]

Mecham represented a particular strain of white populism. He supported CAP but also hoped that his victory would give the Appropriation Committee's chairmanship to Georgia's Richard Russell, whom Mecham respected as "a conservative Democrat" who would control spending far more tightly than Hayden. Mecham also advocated putting states in control of Social Security so as stymie the "Creeping Socialism . . . in the minds of those who want to take all the struggle and pain out of living, who will trade freedom for what appears to be security, who gladly eat the fruits of another's labor." He decried "professional politicians," including Hayden, who "belonged to Hyde Park, New York; Independence, Missouri; and Hyannis Port, Massachusetts"—not "a Conservative state." Mecham also assailed well-established booster Republicans because "they just went through the motions to fill the spot on the ticket." He hence considered his run as "not between Republicans and Democrats . . . but between those who urge further advances toward Socialism, and those who believe in the creative Conservatism of the American Constitution," which "dignifies the individual citizen." Mecham's "Let's Get Arizona for the People" program accordingly favored the sale of 11 percent of federal lands in order to reduce individual property taxes, so as to "give many people an opportunity to strike out on their own" and put the land to better use than "privileged interests who obtain Federal land leases for a few cents and acre . . . and sub-lease the land for profits up to 1,000%."[15]

Mecham's underfunded grassroots effort was a "positive program based on the principles of creative, conservative, constitutional Americanism," which included pledges to "get government out of business, stop aid to communist countries, and reduce taxes." When he first debated Shadegg, who had also entered the GOP primary without party leaders' consent, Mecham asserted: "The Republic was in danger of being destroyed by President Kennedy, the United Nations, Russia, the Common Market, and veteran Senator Hayden." Mecham included the Democrat among those "who do not believe in property rights and the free enterprise system" and were "selling socialism to the American people." Shadegg responded by defending Hayden as a "responsible member of the Democratic Party" and attacking his opponent's "oversimplified dogmatic answers," which belonged to "extremists of the far right." Mecham countered that his record as a state legislator had demonstrated "economical, creative conservative" statecraft to "keep spending to the point where taxes couldn't be increased, and Mr. Shadegg seems to think that is bad."[16]

Such accusations played well with the GOP's white, suburban base. Indeed, Mecham bested Shadegg. But the booster establishment then largely stood aside. Senator Goldwater had remained publicly neutral in the primary, with Shadegg later maintaining that the junior senator privately deemed Mecham "too extreme." Mecham's recollections corroborate Shadegg's assertion: the candidate remembered just one meeting after his primary victory, during which Goldwater, Fannin, and Kleindienst "inform[ed] me that we were on our own to run the campaign." Still, the upstart fared better than many expected in the November general election. Substantial Maricopa County support put the Republican just ten thousand votes behind Hayden, who returned to the Senate to finish his life's work of watering central Arizona.[17]

New riparian rights and aqua infrastructure transformed Phoenix and Maricopa County but also proved disastrous for the entire area in the decades to come. Agricultural fields and citrus groves gave way to suburban housing developments. By 1960, people finally outnumbered cattle in Maricopa County. "[The land]'s too valuable to remain in feedlot use," one inhabitant opined. Water usage subsequently doubled between 1955 and 1963, which exacerbated the chronic water shortages in the drought-prone Valley and also the long-standing conflict between metropolitan Phoenix and its agricultural hinterland. Farmers used almost 90 percent of the water consumed. Critics subsequently came to call them "Arizona's Welfare Queens" in the 1980s.[18]

But CAP proved unable to satisfy either growers or homeowners. Indeed, Marc Reisner predicted such disappointment in his history of reclamation, *Cadillac Desert: The American West and Its Disappearing Water* (1986). The still-incomplete CAP would surely be a "Sumerian scale" "ruin before its time," forcing Phoenicians "to do what their Hohokam ancestors did: pray for rain." Seven years later, federal officials declared the nation's most expensive reclamation initiative finished, thus inaugurating repayment of the $4.4 billion spent. Agriculturalists, whose enterprises were largely dependent on subsidies, found themselves unable to afford CAP water rates or federal repayments. Many subsequently folded or switched back to groundwater sources. CAP likewise disappointed many metropolitan users.

Tucson residents, who first received their share through an aqueduct in 1992, complained that taps delivered discolored, smelly, undrinkable water. City councillors accordingly halted delivery just three days after project waters first flowed into Tucson. CAP did, however, keep Valley swimming pools full, lawns watered, and golf courses lush during the drought-stricken 2000s, but water managers have openly stated that they have always been on the lookout for the "next bucket," industry slang for untapped water supplies.[19]

Land for an Industrial Metropolis

Land-use issues, like those involving water, also required reflexive policymaking to provide the infrastructure that industry needed without making the tax code uncompetitive. But new suburbs and corporate welfare guarantees were expensive, though city leaders largely blamed dwindling tax revenue on rapidly built subdivisions outside their jurisdictions. "We spent thousands of dollars a year," a Nashville mayor complained in 1946, "furnishing fire protection, water, sewers, and streets to 96,000 people outside the city who don't pay a dime toward the upkeep of the city." This suburban flight often devastated downtown business districts and transformed wealthy, Anglo neighborhoods into poor, minority enclaves. Many local governments attempted to ameliorate this crisis by annexing ballooning neighborhoods outside city limits. Policymakers disproportionately targeted wealthier, white districts in order to control sprawl, generate more income, and retain the white voting majority, which alderman considered their base.[20]

Metropolitan expansion varied by region. Midwestern and northeastern annexations often failed to yield substantial results. Regulations were strict, requiring at least a majority of property owners or residents to sign off on agreements. Long-established hamlets and burgs also tended to have entrenched community identities, which frustrated municipal attempts to bring residents under new jurisdictions. The Sunbelt grasstops enjoyed far more success. Their communities had all begun with smaller urban populations, which allowed for easier control of local politics. Postwar relocations and widespread housing shortages also forced longtime residents and new arrivals into quickly constructed developments outside city limits, where new suburbanites generally lacked personal investment in maintaining their young subdivisions' independence. Southern and southwestern states also had established fewer legal hurdles and required less popular approval to annexation. Georgia lawmakers did require a majority of both electorates to approve an acquisition, but North Carolina and Tennessee statutes provided for automatic incorporation of adjacent territories when the population of these outlying areas reached a set threshold. New Mexico relied on arbitration boards to broker agreements between city aldermen and suburban residents, usually in the city's favor, whereas Texas good-government types pushed through rules that allowed towns to redraw borders without property owners' consent.[21]

Boosters considered suburban annexations essential to industrialization. Promotional literature often highlighted population growth and census rank to assure investors that a town was already up-and-coming. Boosters also saw the annexation of affluent suburbs both as a path toward higher revenues, from consumer sales and individual property taxes, and as a program that would ensure the maintenance of a white, politically supportive majority in their expanding town. William Hartsfield, for example, lobbied for such absorptions to balance the increasing number of black Atlantans. "This is not intended to stir race prejudice," the mayor wrote to wealthy Buckhead homeowners in the early 1940s, "but do you want to hand them political control of Atlanta, either as a majority or a powerful minority vote?" Yet residents were unmoved until after the Supreme Court struck down Georgia's all-white primary in 1946, black Atlantans had begun impressive voter registration drives, and Hartsfield had secured his 1949 reelection by campaigning in better enfranchised black districts. But this new constituency approved of his 1950 "Plan for Improvement," which tripled the city's size and added a hundred thousand residents, most of whom were white. Indeed, the annexation initiative's passage slashed the town's black population from 41 percent to 33 percent. And Hartsfield had campaigned fervently to ensure victory. He won over white burghers with promises of development and prosperity and clinched African American support because of his race-moderate policies, which included installing street lights in minority neighborhoods and addressing black residents formally in official correspondence.[22]

CGC annexation initiatives were just as effective as Hartsfield's improvement plan. Phoenix boosters were convinced that more territory for their city constituted a sure path to urban greatness. "If Phoenix didn't annex land so it could grow and provide a center for the valley," a former assistant city manager asserted in the late 1960s, "this area would probably be just another concentration of little cities, none of which would amount to anything." Material requirements also drove promoters. Arizona had an average annual growth rate of 7 percent in the 1950s, but public spending outpaced revenue collection. Legislators passed a broad range of taxes to make up the shortfall generated by these increased expenditures and by the decreasing tax burden placed on businesses. In 1963, individual income, retail sales, gasoline, cigarettes, and liquor levies generated a record-breaking $22 billion in revenue, but Phoenix officials still needed new municipal duties and territorial acquisitions to keep pace with need.[23]

Spatial growth and industrialization had preoccupied the CGC council well before these shortfalls became a pressing issue. Goldwater, for instance, wanted the city to usurp property south of Phoenix, "dominated by warehouses and Southern Pacific properties." "It isn't the amount of money we can get out of taxes," he asserted in 1950, "they are there and can forever block proper development of Phoenix south to the river or south to the mountains which is where we have got to go." He advocated meeting with the Planning Department and the executives operating in this territory "to discuss this problem . . . because it is very, very vital. I don't propose to wiggle for them until they wiggle for us. Let's wiggle together." "I would rather see this City develop in an orderly fashion than have more industries come in and cause those conditions of no sewers and lack of sanitation," he elaborated. "If you bring industry in here, we have got to have more homes." But Goldwater had no intention of involving suburbanites in negotiations between city planners and investors. He considered expanded water, sewage, trash, police, and fire services more than adequate compensation for any new costs individual property owners incurred from absorption. Ignore their "squawks," the retailer warned, lest Phoenix "remain seventeen square miles for the next hundred years."[24]

Goldwater's ambitions became a cornerstone of a CGC annexation policy that epitomized neoliberal statecraft. Councillors relied on managed growth, not market-driven sprawl, to guarantee the revenue and power that Chamber men required to create an Anglo, industrial, suburban Phoenix. City leaders benefited from vast spaces between the capital and other Valley towns, which initially allowed every municipality to usurp suburbs before they became autonomous self-supporting communities. City Manager Ray Wilson's early consolidation of government departments proved critical because department heads could not take their case directly to councillors, or vice versa. Wilson could thus prioritize expansion and direct planners to study the issue as he saw fit. Studies concluded that undirected, uncontrolled suburbanization would not serve the central city, its suburbs, area manufacturers, or the Chamber's industrialization strategies. The already existing "irregular pattern of growth," Phoenix administrators warned, did not "conform to sound planning principles," which led them to conclude that "efforts should be made to expand the city limits to the south and northwest."[25]

Goldwater and other CGC higher-ups generally saw no inconsistency with this statecraft and their personal politics, which they only later fitted into the broad rubric of modern conservatism. A few were initially concerned with this extension of the local government's power. Attorney and councilman John Sullivan, elected in 1951, initially opposed this venture: "I thought it (annexation) was a private matter—if people wanted to come into the city, O.K." Wilson's assistant remembered that other appointees "were not all enthusiastic at first. . . . Sometimes we had to ride roughshod over people in finance or planning" because "they didn't want to move until other things were paid for." "We were afraid that would be too late," he explained, "that a ring of 'bedroom' towns would start to develop and we would wind up with a hundred jurisdictions in the valley." This argument turned Sullivan into one of Wilson's "leading supporters." "After being on the council for a while and reading some of the publications of the National Municipal League, and after taking a look at what was going on here, I changed," Sullivan recalled, "we could see it coming with Glendale, Scottsdale, etc."[26]

Such support enabled Wilson to adopt tactics central to Busey's ambitious annexation program. Wilson, like the liberal mayor, hired a full-time staff person to oversee annexation teams circulating petitions among homeowners. The first director of annexation, John Burke, was Phoenix's self-described "annexation worker." "I tried to get about one [signature] per block," he remembered. "I found I had to go out to help so much that I got about four more of my own group to circulate petitions." As in the Busey era, these difficulties pushed Burke to pay petitioners, a practice that existed in a political gray area before the Arizona Supreme Court ruled the tactic legal in 1961. Burke also furthered the highly regularized procedures Busey's administration had crafted, improved annexation promotional materials, and mandated meetings between new Phoenicians, councillors, and planners in order to discuss agreements and haggle over zoning regulations.[27]

CGC advocates of annexation both cajoled and threatened residents. State law dictated that a majority of property owners, as determined by total property values in a proposed tract, had to sign off on absorption agreements. City leaders offered small property owners the same arguments they used on Phoenix voters: efficient, businesslike government would prove a boon to all. "We had to show them," the assistant city manager explained, "their best interests lay, politically and economically, in the same area as those of the city. If we were stifled, they would suffer." "We would go out at night to meetings, sometimes almost every night for a while, and talk, show the good side of coming into the city, and so on." Brochures defended higher taxes, proclaiming: "Normal city services cost money," but annexation advocates, armed with charts and tables, stressed that "annexation would yield substantial dollar savings" and promised that residents could save "at least 50% in your fire insurance rate." But city representatives deployed sticks along with these carrots. In 1951, the council confined fire fighters to Phoenix city limits, which left many homeowners on the other side of the line without adequate protection. Suburbanites were also cut off from municipal water, which penalized South Phoenix denizens, who now had to rely on a private supplier who charged more than double the city's rates and often failed to maintain water pressure during early morning hours.[28]

These city annexation schemes were intertwined with Chamber expansion efforts. Mayor Nicholas Udall appeared before the association to ask for help and then discussed his progress with directors throughout the CGC's first term. City workers drummed up support in the neighborhoods on Phoenix's fringe and drafted the legal agreements necessary to formally assume these areas, but the Chamber's expansion committee often did the initial legwork. Volunteers evaluated properties and investigated tracts by collecting property descriptions, street addresses, and homeowners' names, freeing city officials to finalize other annexation agreements before pursuing new parcels. And of course, the Chamber actively propagandized within bedroom communities on behalf of the city.[29]

Winning over large industrialists preoccupied both city officials and Chamber men. "I did a lot of work with people from the industrial areas," a CGC mayor admitted, adding: "We never slight[ed] the residential areas." Planners needed manufacturers' support: liberal annexation efforts had floundered when industrialists had put their considerable weight behind stopping the city's expansion. Many postwar managers and executives had opposed annexation thereafter, even though city fathers now shared their antipathy toward redistributive tax policies and had already begun to shift the tax burden onto individual homeowners and consumers. Tensions between expansionist boosters and the area's caste of outside investors escalated in 1957, when planners moved to usurp a twenty-square-mile tract west of Phoenix, which had the largest concentration of industry in the Valley as well as forty-two thousand Arizonans. Investors quickly formed the so-called Industry Committee to study the proposal and survey their industrial neighbors, who uniformly opposed the plan. "We're darned sure not going to sign the petitions," an Allison Steel Manufacturing Company vice president stated. "We recognize the need for Phoenix to grow and prosper so as to remain the vital center of the valley," a Reynolds Metals Company attorney explained. He still demanded, "The city . . . [must] make some adjustments in its policies . . . [to] allow us to compete in the national marketplace or we cannot afford to risk annexation."[30]

Administrators desperate to annex homes and compete for investment spent almost a year wiggling for, not with, manufacturers. Lawyers for the recalcitrant industrialists drafted a complicated "Agreement of Intent," which not only solidified the end of any regulatory-redistributive impulse that had remained embedded within Phoenix expansion policies but also further oriented the city's laws and tax structures to favor investors. This contract, which city officials signed at the Westward Ho in April 1958, exempted these business owners from fourteen city ordinances and gave the same regulatory relief to all other Phoenix firms as well. Companies did not have to follow city building codes that owners considered too burdensome, and manufacturers and processors were guaranteed a ban on future city sales taxes, a moratorium on retail sales taxes on final sales, and the end of a city sales tax on goods sold to contractors.[31]

This pact further dictated that voters ratify these changes in order to make it illegal for officials to repeal these exemptions. Public servants and manufacturers promoted this referendum in the well-established language of business-led prosperity. Phoenix's finance director asserted that the influx of new companies and citizens would negate a predicted $120,000 revenue shortfall in the city budget because the agreement served as "an insurance policy for a sounder industrial climate." The mayor called the deal "one of the most successful steps toward the encouragement of industry . . . that any city in the nation has taken." "Tax laws placed out of the hands of changing political groups," an AiResearch manager assured Phoenicians, "will enable long-range industrial planning with the expansion of existing industry and the growth of new plants." This investor-grasstops partnership pushed the proposition through by a margin of four to one, although only 7 percent of registered voters participated.[32]

The referendum's passage proved pivotal in Phoenix's metamorphosis from a politically fractious colonial outpost into a neoliberal industrial juggernaut. The deal cemented Phoenix's investor class as enthusiastic champions of the city's geographical growth. Oscar Palmer promised that he would "never leave Phoenix," after he resumed operations. The air-conditioning magnate, who had foiled liberal annexation plans, had returned an avid proponent of continued expansion: "I can highly recommend to all industry that the costs [*sic*]of taxes in the city is far less than the benefits in city services, insurance, water, sewage, and other savings." Such support proved crucial for continued annexation because Arizona law allowed officials to collect signatures for acquisitions from large landholders only, save for a short-lived, mid-1950s, state-level change that forced planners to include personal property in calculating the signatures needed. The 1957 truce coincided with the repeal of this rule, which meant that expansion proponents only had to win over major property holders, who, given their partnership with the CGC and the Chamber, would not oppose proposals.[33]

Such policies frustrated small property owners. Suburbanites had proven themselves skeptics before the 1957 agreement, but they lacked organization and power. Yet they were outspoken. One denizen was as angry at the city council as he was at General Electric's (GE) management. The firm owned the majority of the land in a proposed annexation tract, which enabled the city simply to persuade the company to sign off on the deal in order to appropriate the entire parcel. But Leonard Grube recoiled at the thought of living under the city's jurisdiction and denounced both GE and the Phoenix city council for flouting personal property rights. Home owners "may not want the city Police cars giving minor traffic citations in their bailiwick. They may not want to pay city taxes. They may not want the city building inspectors sticking their noses in their room addition," he reasoned. "They may not want to help increase the City of Phoenix additional bonded indebtedness index."[34]

Such sentiment later roiled Valley politics, but in the late 1950s and early 1960s neighboring incorporated towns, not tax-fearing suburbanites, became the new obstacles to Phoenix's territorial acquisitions. Tempe, Chandler, and Glendale tended to not annex land between their limits and Phoenix's jurisdictions. The few conflicts that cropped up were usually ami-

Figure 8. Sparsely populated, rural Scottsdale (pictured circa 1949) would become an affluent bedroom community for the white, skilled, educated, professional workforce that Phoenix boosters sought to attract. Taxes and elections eventually pitted Phoenix and Scottsdale city leaders against each other as they tried to quickly annex the subdivisions being built outside their respective city limits. Courtesy of the Arizona Historical Foundation, Saufley-Goldwaters Stores Collection, folder 4, box 2.

cable, while acrimony riddled the bidding for the affluent neighborhoods between Scottsdale and Phoenix. Representatives from both towns circulated competing petitions and staged surprise late-night meetings to obtain the requisite signatures. Occasionally, officials even attempted to annex areas that rivals had recently absorbed. Phoenix's city government nonetheless won the overall war because it had the established wealth and bureaucracy as well as the support of the Valley's major news outlets.[35]

Like the rest of the Sunbelt grasstops, the CGC and its bedroom-community competitors did not seek to incorporate poorer, non-Anglo neighborhoods. Since 1948, South Phoenix residents, eager to have access to city services, had pressed to join its wealthier neighbor to the north. Requests went unheeded. Phoenix's future as a dynamic, industrial, middle-class, Anglo metropolis was foremost on the minds of both city leaders and Chamber stalwarts. Thus, South Phoenix only became a priority in 1959, when boosters looked eagerly toward breaking the five-hundred-thousand-person barrier before the census count began. The city proposed annexing South Phoenix with the heavily-Anglo South Mountain suburbs and Maryvale, the Valley's first master-planned community. The annexation came off on schedule, but South Phoenix's inclusion still did not guarantee that residents there would enjoy the level of water and sewer infrastructure the city provided wealthier residents and outside industrialists. South Phoenicians still paid higher rates to a private water company that failed to provide an adequate water supply, even three years after annexation. The council continued to ignore their pleas, leaving protestors to seek redress from state officials in 1962.[36]

The complaints hardly mattered to city boosters who considered their annexation program successful. During the first decade of grasstops rule, Phoenix's physical size increased more than tenfold while its population more than quadrupled. By 1960, 75 percent of Phoenix residents lived in areas that had been outside the city's borders a decade before. Such expansion made the city one of the fastest growing areas in the Sunbelt as well as the nation (Table 2).[37]

Yet expansion still failed to make up for the revenue shortfall incurred through metropolitan growth or industrial recruitment. Annexation secured more revenue from Valley residents, but federal analysts nonetheless noted that in the nation as a whole spending at the municipal level quadrupled between 1950 and the mid-1960s (totaling roughly $85 billion annually). Expenditures grew by almost 10 percent per year in this period, twice the nation's economic growth rate. Despite the income generated from better collection methods, higher personal taxes, or new consumer levies, expenses still far exceeded what local and state governments gathered from businesses and citizens.[38]

The Business of Higher Education

Educational outlays accounted for much of the dramatic increase in state and local spending and illustrate how industrial recruitment drove the post-

Table 2. Population and Territorial Growth of Selected Sunbelt Cities, 1940–1980

	1940		*1950*		*1960*		*1970*		*1980*			
	Land area (square miles)	*Population*	*Land area (square miles)*	*Population*	*Land area (square miles)*	*Population*	*Land area (square miles)*	*Population*	*Land area (square miles)*	*Population*	*Change in land area (square miles)*	*Change in population*
Albuquerque	11	35,449	47.9	96,815	58	201,189	82.2	243,751	95.3	332,920	766%	839%
Alexandria, Virginia	7.5	33,523	7.5	61,787	15	91,023	14.7	110,927	15	103,217	100%	208%
Atlanta	34.7	302,283	36.9	331,314	136	487,455	131.5	495,039	131	425,022	278%	141%
Austin	25.1	87,930	32.1	132,459	45	186,545	72.1	255,869	116	345,544	362%	293%
Charlotte	19.3	100,899	30	134,042	65	201,564	76	274,640	140	314,447	625%	212%
Dallas	40.6	294,734	112	434,462	254	679,684	265.6	844,303	333	904,074	720%	207%
Denver	57.9	322,412	66.8	415,786	68	493,887	95.2	514,678	110.6	492,686	91%	53%
Fort Worth	49.8	177,662	93.7	278,778	138	356,268	205	844,303	240	904,074	382%	409%
Houston	72.8	384,514	160	596,163	321	938,219	433.9	1,253,479	556	1,595,167	664%	315%
Las Vegas	N/A	N/A	N/A	N/A	25	64,405	51.6	72,863	55	164,674	120%	156%
Los Angeles	448.3	1,504,277	450.9	1,970,358	455	2,479,015	463.7	2,811,801	464.7	2,968,528	0.30%	106%
Memphis	45.6	292,942	104.2	396,000	129	497,524	217.4	657,007	264	646,356	480%	121%
Miami	30.3	172,172	34.2	249,276	34	291,688	34.2	334,859	34	346,865	13%	101%
Orlando	10.8	36,736	14.1	52,367	19	88,135	27.5	100,081	40	128,291	270%	249%
Phoenix	9.7	65,414	17.1	106,818	187	439,170	247.9	589,016	324	789,704	324%	1107%
San Diego	95.3	203,341	99.4	334,387	195	573,387	316.9	697,027	320	875,538	236%	331%
San Jose	14.8	68,457	17	95,280	56	204,196	136.2	461,212	158	629,400	968%	819%

Source: Data taken from U.S. Census

war founding, growth, and spirit of public, research-intensive universities. School expansion imported the kind of skilled engineers and scientists who, economist Gavin Wright noted, had failed to follow the meager prewar industrial investments made in the domestic colonies. The transformation of postsecondary schooling responsible for this postwar influx emerged out of a combination of closely interrelated purposes: the democratization of higher education and the professions, intense competition between communities for corporate investment, and the research and labor needs of the economy's most dynamic sectors.[39]

For their part, liberal educators and policymakers had considered higher education, for the liberal arts and sciences, crucial to personal fulfillment, career advancement, and social progress. "A region is dependent in no small way upon the products of its colleges and universities," National Resources Planning Board officials asserted in 1942, before lamenting that there were only 252 institutions of higher education, 171 of them private, in the Southeast (14.3 percent of the national total). Planners also found arid-state education lacking and thus recommended "vocational education in junior and State colleges. Develop technological research in universities. Encourage student and faculty self-government to foster a more responsible citizenry." New Dealers also emphasized "more scholarships to State universities, sufficient to cover minimum living expenses, so that qualified young people, remote from proper educational opportunities, can obtain a higher education."[40]

Business-minded industrialists and their scouts provided the political muscle and private funding for much of the educational infrastructure that was developed after World War II. Executives and experts demanded top-notch facilities because firms relied on Steelbelt science and engineering departments to bolster research and development, improve manufacturing operations, and produce well-trained new hires. Over time these demands reshaped public higher education, especially in those colonial regions undergoing rapid economic diversification. In states without existing research universities or engineering programs, local business groups, high-tech firms, and elected officials funneled public and private moneys into expanded or brand-new universities. This drive underlay a new Cold War urban ideal, the "cities of knowledge," which one historian characterized as "engines of scientific production, filled with high-tech industries, homes for scientific workers and their families, with research universities at their heart." California's Silicon Valley, with Stanford University at its center, exemplified this phenomenon. Immediately after World War II the school began an aggressive effort to recruit top engineering and scientific faculty from the Ivy League, vigorously pursued federal research funds, and dedicated sizable portions of its substantial endowment and land holdings into faculty housing and a pioneering research park.[41]

Postwar boomtowns also endeavored to become educational oases. Between 1957 and 1964, the national per capita spending on higher education soared from $82.47 to $137.38. Few Steelbelt states, where private and public schools were more developed, expended more than the national state-level average in this period. Southern states devoted far less per student, but the region's leaders (in Florida, Georgia, North Carolina, and South Carolina) disbursed just a few dollars more or less per student than New Hampshire, Massachusetts, Rhode Island, and Pennsylvania. Laggard states eventually increased outlays in order to compete. Mississippi, for example, made the pages of *Business Week* in 1966 when legislators there finally pledged themselves to the "modernization of laws governing the conduct of business," combined with a study leading to a "major new investment in educational program facilities and personnel." But the industrializing West still earmarked far more than Mississippi and the national average. Only Texas, Idaho, and Nebraska devoted less than the American mean. California, Nevada, Utah, Colorado, New Mexico, and Arizona each spent between 16 percent and 30 percent above the average in this era.[42]

Such expenditures were roundly celebrated. Experts considered community and vocational schools "a fruit of economic progress, but also a seed of economic progress—a valid capital investment." These institutions represented an intermediary step between "buying payroll" and large-scale industrialization because they "provided the needed skilled work force which will be necessary as communities exhaust their present labor pool and as they seek to enlarge not only the number of jobs, but also their economic base." Late 1950s Georgia industrial brochures subsequently trumpeted educational spending and the numerous black and white colleges. This inclusion also enabled them to emphasize racially moderate K–12 policies: "Educators and businessmen jointly drafted a master plan . . . to assure that each child, white and Negro, has . . . all modern educational advantages." Boosters assured investors that "businessmen are conducting a statewide campaign to recruit more qualified teachers" to ensure "a valuable additional source for capable industrial workers." Tennessee stood out in this period with direct state expansion of vocational schools. Legislators passed a 1963 bill that established a system of institutions in order to place one within thirty miles of every community.[43]

But high-tech executives privileged areas with research universities, which Phoenix lacked. Arizona State University (ASU) would thus be born out of a postwar alliance between investors, boosters, and liberal educators, who united behind a plan to expand Tempe's small teacher's college into a research-intensive university with a formidable engineering school. This coalition faced substantial obstacles: Phoenicians had few seats on the board of regents and faced hostility from farming and mining executives, who supported Valley promoters' intent to cut taxes and social welfare programs but nonetheless opposed public spending for education unless directly supportive of the agricultural or mineral research stations. Phoenix Republicans' legislative alliances were also tested by the Tucson delegates, who jealously guarded the status and funding of the University of Arizona (U of A), the state's flagship institution of higher education.

The partnership between businessmen and school officials took time to cultivate because rainmakers wavered on including postsecondary education as a component of industrialization. Their hesitancy had little to do with their distrust of federal aid for education, which both Fannin and Goldwater publicly opposed. Fannin called the 1958 National Defense Education Act "blind determination to reduce local government and individual initiative to dependence and ultimate subservience to a supercentralized Federal power," while Goldwater asserted in *Conscience of a Conservative* (1964) that Arizonans proudly rejected funds because residents could and would educate themselves. Liberal overreach, not more schooling, provoked this hostility from Fannin and Goldwater. Their Chamber brethren had established an Industry Training Advisory Committee by the mid-1950s. This workgroup studied demand for skilled workers, advocated curriculum changes to match area industrialists' needs, promoted these opportunities among residents, and advocated for public funding. Their reports proved critical in negotiations with high school and community college administrators, who first adopted specialized training courses for a range of fields, most notably electronics, in 1957.[44]

Liberal Grady Gammage, in contrast, fervently embraced higher education. The Arkansas farmer's son had immersed himself in books as a boy and worked as a grammar school teacher and principal after he finished high school. Tuberculosis prompted his move to Tucson, where he worked on the university's maintenance crew and took classes, first for his bachelor’s degree and then his master’s in education (he received his doctorate in 1940 after summer coursework at New York University and writing his dissertation back in Arizona). His politics and dedication impressed state educators, who lobbied the governor to place Gammage at the helm of Flagstaff’s teacher’s college, which had just twenty-six faculty members and 267 students when he arrived there in in 1926. Like other scholastic innovators during this period, Gammage dreamed of expansion and opportunity, which included offering evening classes for locals, creating twelve distinct academic departments, and formalizing hiring, promotion, and leave procedures that enlarged and replaced staff with graduate-degree holders. These policies led to the school’s accreditation as a class A four-year teacher’s college, one of the few in the West. His success brought him in 1933 to Tempe’s Arizona State Teacher’s College (ASTC), which was in danger of losing its accreditation. Only nine of fifty-two faculty members had a doctorate, several buildings had leaky roofs and peeling paint, and yearly enrollments were stagnant.[45]

Gammage struggled to win the necessary community support to transform the school. He met with the Phoenix Chamber in 1934 but found the grasstops, most of whom had advanced degrees from the University of Arizona or out-of-state universities, uninterested in the struggling Tempe school. State officials also proved hesitant. The Territorial Assembly had placed U of A under a ten-person board of regents but governed the Flagstaff and Tempe schools through a three-person board of education. These Depression era overseers were keen to cut costs, so it was only with great reluctance that they permitted Gammage to apply for Public Works Administration loans to build new dormitory, classroom, library, and athletic facilities as well as to purchase land for continued development. He championed the scheme in the name of employment, recovery, and opportunity, which soon won over Hayden, the governor, and the legislature. PWA officials allocated just $445,000 in 1935, which nonetheless enabled Gammage to construct a women’s dorm, add a heating plant, acquire ten acres of land, underwrite a sports stadium, and erect a new student center with an auditorium. Enrollment surged to more than a thousand by 1938.[46]

Growth fueled Gammage’s already expansive vision. More than six hundred respondents to a 1938 ASTC survey demanded baccalaureate degrees in the arts and sciences. Seventy-five percent of respondents admitted that they had matriculated because they “couldn’t afford to go anywhere else.” The president used these complaints to leverage more course offerings, especially

Figure 9. The main campus of Arizona State Teacher's College in the 1930s was unequipped to meet the demands of students who wanted more than a teaching degree. Arizona's reluctant, divided legislature forestalled expansion and forced president Grady Gammage to rely on boosters and outside investors to promote the institution's maturation into a research-focused university. Courtesy of the University Archives Photographs, Arizona State University Libraries.

in business, biological sciences, industrial arts, and agriculture during the war. Gammage also managed to persuade a *Republic* editor, also a state legislator, to sponsor a bill that ceased designating Flagstaff and Tempe institutions as teachers' colleges and allowed them to grant bachelor's degrees in nonteaching fields, critical steps in these schools evolving into four-year colleges. Tucson delegates buried the proposal with help from representatives of agriculture- and mining-dependent areas, Jeffersonian Democrats who opposed expansion. Their opposition reflected hostility from old-line investors, who had no interest in paying more taxes for an educational and research infrastructure unrelated to commodity production or transportation. These emperors of the colonial economy still had much power over a state struggling to demobilize. Southern Pacific Railroad executives, for example, forced a Casa Grande senator to oppose the proposal. "I personally favor your bill," another legislator confided to Tempe assemblymen. "But I was elected by Phelps Dodge (Mining Co.) and if I vote for it, my political career is finished."[47]

The education provisions within Ernest McFarland's G.I. Bill of Rights and the first wave of returning servicemen enabled Gammage to subvert such opposition. He drew public attention to Arizona's "extremely deficient" opportunities and, in the process, convinced Arizona Chambers, service clubs, veterans groups, and newspaper editors to support a new Phoenix-backed bill to meet postwar educational challenges. "The University of Arizona," *Republic* editors asserted, "isn't going to be able to meet the demands of the veterans in the post-war era." Tucson senators watered down the legislation, but the final act was more than a pyrrhic victory: the Tempe and Flagstaff schools were no longer designated just for teachers, and a new board of regents oversaw all three schools with the authority to decide if the colleges could grant bachelor's degrees. The interim board's composition reflected state population shifts: five seats went to Maricopa County, three went to Pima, and two represented other parts of Arizona. The body's inaugural 1945 meeting ended with an agreement to hire outside educational consultants, who quickly concluded that both state colleges should expand their degree and course offerings. The regents approved the recommendations, permitting the just-renamed Arizona State College at Tempe (ASC) to award education, liberal arts, and science degrees shortly thereafter.[48]

Grasstops support grew steadily. Thunderbirds embraced college athletics as a supplement to their large-scale tourism initiative. Their Sun Angel booster organization for the college picked the school's mascot, the Sun Devils, during preliminary meetings. But it was Gammage who saw the school's industrial potential. He, like other liberal Democrats, embraced growth, development, and prosperity as ingredients for general social democratic advancement. He said as much at a breakfast meeting in the fall of 1949, when he told rainmakers: "You need a great educational institution to make Phoenix great, and you have the makings of it right here at your doorstep." Of the summit, one financier recalled that "to men used to being wined and dined in the finest surroundings, this breakfast at Tempe was a pitiful little affair—some eggs and toast and juice served at tables in the old gymnasium," but Gammage "did the best he could. It worked." Walter Bimson was an early, important convert. He served on the regents' executive committee for the State College at Tempe and on the finance and educational relations committees. Yet the financier did not share Gammage's expansive vision for ASC. "I should not want to see established at Tempe a Law School, an Engineering School or a scientific, technical School of Agriculture," he explained to Gammage in 1952. Bimson had more practical desires: "I would not object to a continued expansion of the Business School, the Trade Schools covering machine shop practice, mechanical methods and practical building and architecture procedure."[49]

However, local high-tech executives and the branch managers of large corporations headquartered in the Steelbelt forced Bimson and other boosters to embrace ASC's evolution into ASU. These industrialists needed the kind of university Gammage envisioned. U of A, with its emphasis on agricultural sciences, was ill equipped and too distant to serve the Valley's high-tech investors. And by the mid-1950s unmet requirements for more highly educated workers turned into executive complaints about the small pool of trained engineers, scientists, and skilled laborers available in Phoenix. "Educational facilities for training technicians somewhat limited," one protested. Another demanded: "Improve educational facilities for advanced study." One wanted "expand[ed] education and campus laboratory facilities to better support the over-all requirements of industry, including contract services in research and development."[50]

Gammage had already reached out to new arrivals before the Chamber took note of this dissatisfaction. The president introduced himself to Daniel Noble in 1948, shortly after the engineer arrived to head Motorola's Phoenix operations. Labor and research needs converted Noble into a steadfast supporter of a science-based university. He helped convince Chamber men and Valley manufacturers to support Gammage with appeals to their bottom lines. "Either the industrialist becomes educated to the changing parameters of successful industry or," the executive predicted in 1961, "while he may not die, there is a good possibility that he will slowly fade away—accompanied by his corporation."[51]

But boosters and executives never embraced the philosophy embedded within Gammage's expansive vision. Both sets of businessmen sold higher education, like water and annexation, from within the confines of business climate doctrine. Businessmen shared an interest in increased educational opportunities, not democratizing higher education and bolstering all departments within the academy. They subsequently rooted their support in the Anglo, technocratic "cities of knowledge" ideal, which prioritized economic dynamism and innovation in pursuit of "brainpower." "The availability of engineers and scientists has failed to keep pace with the expanding demands of industry and the technology services," Noble cautioned months before the Soviets launched Sputnik. "This brainpower shortage endangers the economic health, as well as the national security of our country." "Rigorous selection of qualified students and training under the direction of a distinguished faculty," he predicted, "will save taxpayers money, . . . will bring . . . distinguished careers to the youth of Arizona; will not only support Arizona industry, but it will support the needs for national security." Noble often reiterated that *a* university was not enough. "We must have a truly high quality of graduate school in engineering and the physical sciences at ASU," he warned. "The industries can bring the brainpower to Phoenix, but they cannot keep [scientists and engineers] here in an intellectual vacuum."[52]

The grasstops provided Gammage the political backing to begin developing a research university. In 1947 legislative changes had given the Phoenix cohort a large voice on the board of regents. Eight regents, three from Maricopa County, served staggered eight-year terms, with ex-officio status conferred on the governor and state superintendent of education. By then, Walter Bimson and newsman Wes Knorpp were regents. The deck was thus somewhat stacked when Gammage approached the regents with a four-year plan to transform ASC into ASU. Unlike his industry-minded collaborators, he cast the undertaking as part of a national movement to assure increased access, more opportunity, and democratic advancement. His proposal divided the university into four colleges. ASC already offered education, liberal arts, and science education, but the university would now include applied sciences as well as business and public administration. The Chamber's support was critical when the regents put the initiative to a vote in 1954. Representatives from Maricopa County and Flagstaff favored the proposal, but the Tucson regents were bitterly opposed. The deadlock was broken only when Phoenix's own Governor Pyle cast the deciding vote on behalf of Gammage's scheme.[53]

City leaders, Chamber activists, and manufacturing executives expedited the establishment of ASU's highly regarded engineering program. Noble brokered a partnership between businesses and the state to ensure the department's maturation. He beseeched his peers to build a private foundation that earmarked contributions for the engineering faculty in order to quickly attract leading researchers. "Every dollar spent would come back to the community, not only in cash," he promised, "but in pride in the college accomplishment and standing, pride in the constructive community achievement, and pride in the sound growth not only of industry but of educational opportunities." Motorola's founder Paul Galvin personally set aside $150,000 (to be paid out over five years) to jumpstart the ASU Foundation in 1955. This association united education-dependent aerospace, high-tech, and electronics manufacturers. The association proclaimed their support for a general research university, but members nonetheless prioritized science and engineering above all else. Early achievements included raising $15,000 for a solar furnace as well as additional contributions from Valley firms to underwrite the equipment, lab space, and faculty hires needed for an engineering department. "Market demands for scientists and engineers are extremely high," Noble warned Valley Rotarians. "We cannot expect to attract and hold an adequate distinguished faculty unless the salaries offered meet the market." Noble's solution effectively circumvented state wage scales, reluctant legislators, and skeptical voters in order for the school to pay the "highest possible base salaries," with foundation funds "supplement[ing] the base." Members raised money for scholarships and fellowships and also acquired land around ASC for the proposed engineering program. GE gave the engineering school much needed equipment and ASC a computer to manage its administrative needs.[54]

Business also played an outsized role in the all-important name change from ASC to ASU. University lore lauds this rechristening as a grassroots movement of students, alumni, and Phoenicians, but the fifteen-year metamorphosis from teacher's college to research university was a business-driven initiative. A critical milestone was the year 1956. Representatives from the Phoenix Chamber and the new high-tech manufacturing community persuaded the regents to allow a new bachelor of science in engineering degree, which laid the groundwork for an engineering college able to grant master's degrees and doctorates. This essential step had only been possible because earlier private and public investment had provided the college with the characteristics of a research institute by the late 1950s. But regents and legislators still refused to designate the school a university. Tucson delegates forced a tabling of the discussion in 1954 and refused to allow the board to hear arguments in 1956. Tucson newsmen decried the effort to upgrade ASC as a waste that "obligates the state and every taxpayer in order to realize Maricopa's local ambitions." Tucson regents could not, however, prevent the matter from going on the ballot shortly thereafter. Institutional histories of the school laud two ASC alumni for leading the effort to make the issue into a ballot referendum to circumvent regents and legislators. Together with a number of undergraduates, the fable goes, these young businessmen, members of the Junior Chamber of Commerce no less, collected enough signatures to place the name change before voters in 1958. Pima, Santa Cruz, and Cochise County voters rejected the measure, but Proposition 200 still passed by two to one, a reflection of Maricopa County's rapid population growth and the mobilization on its behalf by so much of the city's civic and industrial elite.[55]

Boosters and industrialists remained closely involved with ASU in the ensuing years. Chamber general manager Lew Haas, for example, urged Gammage's successor, G. Homer Durham, to aim for a radical upgrading of the engineering program not in the proposed twenty years but in "a simple decade." "We can enlist the most powerful influences in the community to help you in any problems you might encounter," the Chamber executive promised in 1961. Motorola executives offered vital help in this period. They headed the ASU Foundation and its Industrial Advisory Committee. Membership included faculty from the school's science departments who often appeared on the payrolls of AiResearch, Sperry Rand, Reynolds Metals, and Kaiser Aircraft. These men collaborated to recruit faculty, improve the library, develop an "engineers in management" curriculum within the College of Business Administration, and integrate the humanities and social sciences "into a program in which industry would be interested." ASU also depended on the boosters in elected offices, especially Fannin. The governor enthusiastically supported more state "funds for the salaries and services of scientific minds as teachers in our institutions of higher learning and the expanded facilities and equipment in which they must work," a statement in sharp contrast with his concurrent warnings against federal education aid.[56]

Fannin's enthusiasm was hardly surprising: promoters were well aware that their Anglo, knowledge-based metropolis depended on the deeply interconnected ASU and Valley high-tech sector. More than 150 students enrolled between the time the school inaugurated graduate degree programs and the name change. Motorola and GE employed more than two-thirds of these advanced students. Many participated in a work-study program that ensured employment, a salary, and time to attend classes and study. An affiliated faculty plan also brought area specialists into classrooms, at ranks ranging from instructor to full professor, in order to better tailor courses to manufacturers' needs. Such collaborations thrilled Noble, who noted in 1963, "Motorola has had, at one time, more than five hundred members of its staff taking courses."[57]

ASU's metamorphosis, much like Phoenix's growth, was nonetheless a variation within the broader expansion of many research-intensive universities outside the industrial core, including the public schools anchoring North Carolina's Research Triangle. North Carolina governor Luther Hodges, like Phoenix boosters, only gradually embraced vocational schools, community colleges, and research universities as industrialization tools. Historians have noted his involvement with this famous region of knowledge but have still largely ignored his avid boosterism. Scholars instead singled him out as one of the South's education-oriented, racial moderates. Hodges did famously reject school closures and violent protests after the 1954 *Brown v. Board of Education* decision, even while he pursued limited desegregation policies. Yet he did so in the name of industrial recruitment, as he made clear in his 1962 autobiography, *Businessman in the Statehouse: Six Years as Governor of North Carolina*.[58]

Hodges was predisposed to favor both education and industry. The mill boy graduated from the University of North Carolina at Chapel Hill in 1919 and worked his way up from a textile plant's general manager to a New York–based vice president within Marshall Field and Company. The executive dedicated himself to politics and public service when he retired to North Carolina in 1950. He began his tenure as lieutenant governor in 1954, when the state ranked forty-fourth in per capita income. Low wages preoccupied him once he became governor after his predecessor's sudden 1954 death. Hodges considered inadequate pay indicative of meager individual opportunity and a paucity of outside investment. New tax codes, industrial-recruitment offices, and budgetary overhauls defined his early gubernatorial boosterism. And like the Phoenix Chamber men and so many other southern Democrats, Hodges had no interest in permitting trade unions to bargain for better working conditions or wages, either as a textile magnate or as governor. He strongly endorsed North Carolina's right-to-work law. In 1959 he famously sent state troopers and then the national guard to protect strikebreakers during the protracted and nationally reported strike that shut down a Henderson textile factory.[59]

Hodges had also been skeptical of higher education's industrial potential. He had initially feared that the rapid growth of North Carolina's colleges and universities would be an impediment to his definition of businessman's governance. He decried semi-autonomous administrators who "were presenting new programs for courses and degrees . . . without consulting anyone but their own trustees, who could not be expected to judge the worthiness of such programs objectively." "Unregulated proliferation," he predicted, "could result in a duplication of expensive teaching skills, libraries, laboratories, and other facilities that would wreck the entire system of state-supported higher education."[60]

Recruitment transformed Hodges into a higher-education advocate. "New or expanding industries asked about the quality as well as the quantity of the labor supply," Hodges recounted. "The answer we had to give was not satisfactory." He, like Fannin, used the governor's mansion to bolster public higher education. In 1955 Hodges persuaded assembly members to approve modest outlays for the state's four community colleges, arguing that adult education and technical training were cheap, accessible options that would relieve the fiscal pressure on senior colleges intended to train white-collar workers and professionals. Two years later he pushed the North Carolina General Assembly to approve an unprecedented $1 billion budget for the 1957–59 biennium, with more than a third earmarked for K–12 and higher education. His 1957 Community College Act included bonds and taxes to fund new schools and also incorporate existing small, private colleges into a state system, a plan akin to the relationship Balance Agriculture with Industry's architects had established between local communities and booster statesmen in Mississippi. North Carolina's Industrial Education Centers also relied on a similar policy structure. Hodges collaborated with the state Board of Education in 1958 to enable interested municipalities and local education boards to submit requests for state funds for equipment and instruction. Proposals included surveys of local job opportunities, labor pools, financial resources, and fundraising plans for buildings. The inaugural $2.3 million increased opportunities for more than eight thousand residents. Schools, Hodges enthused, trained "machine operators, craftsmen, technicians, and supervisors" through "courses in electrical code work, heat treating, precision measurement, and color television servicing." By 1960, more than twenty thousand Tar Heels had matriculated. Enrollment requirements still dictated that these opportunities were largely for whites, who had more access to the obligatory K–12 schooling and money for books and supplies.[61]

Hodges's scholastic about-face was most apparent in his enthusiasm for North Carolina State College and the University of North Carolina at Chapel Hill, two nodes in the vaunted Research Triangle. Ideas for a research park situated in the pastoral area between Raleigh, Durham, and Chapel Hill circulated among university members and boosters throughout the mid-1950s, but an Asheville construction magnate first approached Hodges in 1955. The governor welcomed the plan as a shared venture between state officials, school administrators, and industrialists, which he united under the Governor's Research Triangle Committee. Two years of surveys resulted in a 1957 work group directive to build and promote the Research Triangle Park, whose development relied on state funds, private investments, and public shareholders. Hodges considered the endeavor far from wasteful or redundant. It proved, he crowed, that "education is the chief business of the State of North Carolina" because policymakers were taking "a step further than most" to actively promote "greater interest in research in all areas of business, industry, and applied science." Initial recruitment nonetheless disappointed boosters. Before 1960, major investors included Astra, Inc., a Connecticut consulting firm specializing in atomic energy, the Atomic Energy Commission, and the Chemstrand Corporation. Dissatisfaction actually invigorated Hodges, who emerged as the area's key booster after 1965, the year he resigned from his position as U.S. secretary of commerce. The former governor utilized his contacts in the textile industry to recruit IBM, which led to a marked increase in corporate interest in the region. The Triangle soon emerged as a leader in medical technologies and research, a dominant sector in the lucrative post-1970 knowledge economy. Success was so great that Triangle administrators began to turn away manufacturing firms, a development that Hodges may well have anticipated in his farewell 1960 gubernatorial address, "The North Carolina Dream." He foresaw a future in which the "towers of colleges and universities" set the pace for this "enlightened land."[62]

Such ivory structures already existed in California, where the dynamic between educators, politicians, boosters, and investors differed sharply. The grasstops simply had less power within the Golden State. Yet the same bedfellows produced a revolution in mass higher education, embodied in the newly expanded University of California (UC) system. The San Diego campus, the country's most successful instantaneous postwar university, epitomized the overhaul of California higher education dictated under the 1960 Master Plan for Higher Education. Labor economist and UC president Clark Kerr had covertly infused this legislation with the promise of meritorious, democratic advancement for a postindustrial economy. The act established a three-tiered system of research universities, state colleges (now universities), and community colleges to ensure a tuition-free, low-fee education for every resident who wished to enroll. Kerr considered the California "multiversity" to be centuries removed from the early European "academic cloister . . . with its intellectual oligarchy." Kerr proved far more ambitious than Gammage. The Californian envisioned a multifaceted, expansive institution with "operations in more than a hundred locations, counting campuses, experiment stations, agricultural and urban extension centers, and projects abroad involving more than fifty countries." Kerr's UC would serve and absorb undergraduates, graduates, humanists, social scientists, engineers, professionals, administrators, farmers, industrialists, and politicians.[63]

The Santa Barbara campus's enlargement and the new Irvine, Santa Cruz, and San Diego branches stood out in this educational explosion. Kerr's expansionism partly relied on his capacity to win the cooperation of corporate executives and Golden State boosters, who swallowed their distaste for his liberalism. San Diego Chamber men, for example, had a decades-old education committee, which had assessed nursery, elementary, secondary, vocational, and postsecondary schooling. In the late 1940s, members advocated the larger body publicize both existing public and private higher education facilities to attract newcomers to their city. Much like their Phoenix counterparts, San Diego boosters did not foresee, until the early 1950s, that institutions of higher education might train professionals and entice investors. Promoters did have a working relationship with San Diego State College's (SDSC) leadership, who oversaw five thousand students studying business administration, nursing, education, art, music, and the liberal arts or pursuing premed or prelaw programs. The college's administrators often sought grasstops support for their school's expansion in this period. They beseeched local businessmen to back legislative proposals to allow the school to award a master of arts degree, to affiliate with the American Association of Universities and Colleges, and to offer new courses in the liberal arts rather than those merely designed for vocational degrees. As in Phoenix, branch plant managers proved themselves more eager than Chamber men to develop the college. Outside investors even put direct pressure on SDSC deans to set up extension classes for workers and to pursue advanced science and engineering degrees in the mid-1950s. Only these executives' complaints spurred Chamber men to prioritize science, engineering, technical, skilled trades, and professional education.[64]

San Diego boosters were thus primed to embrace Kerr's plan for another Southern California campus to serve the state's third-largest city. They organized a University of California subcommittee in 1955. The workgroup included bankers, newsmen, high-tech CEOs, and Naval Electronics Laboratory officials, who monitored relations with legislators and UC administrators, debated potential sites and necessary transportation improvements, undertook studies of how other science-focused institutions, such as Stanford and Caltech, facilitated industrialization and negotiated gift agreements between industrialists and university officials to quicken the campus's expansion. Local industrialists also lobbied legislators and educators. Like Motorola managers, Convair executives provided detailed reports to explain their needs and to emphasize a campus's usefulness to other investors. In 1956 General Dynamics provided $1 million to rapidly develop the physics, chemistry, mathematics, and engineering departments. As in Phoenix, this money was used to raise salaries and supply research funds to equip engineering and physics laboratories. General Dynamics CEOs joined local promoters in offering UC regents a 1955 proposal for a small university with the equipment and faculty needed to train the graduate students who were expected to fill openings in local defense and aviation firms. Only a thousand undergraduates would matriculate, receiving a thorough grounding in the natural sciences with "sufficient courses in the humanities and social sciences to insure . . . a well-rounded education experience."[65]

UC officials had much grander ambitions than the boosters and investors intent on a UC for San Diego. Kerr considered the branch a part of his ambitious master plan, but scientist Roger Revelle envisioned an educational acropolis, "the center to which all men turn to find the meaning of their lives and from which emanates . . . the light of understanding," The head of the UC's Scripps Institution of Oceanography was, as one journalist asserted, "in the forefront, arguing, explaining, bulldozing, pleading, and finally winning approval for . . . a university made up of twelve independent colleges." Revelle actually championed transforming his small oceanographic research station into a science-focused university, an expansion not out of line for a facility already functioning as a testing and research venue for naval submarine and sonar technologies and a graduate training facility offering degrees through an agreement with UCLA. In a manner more successful than the ASU Foundation, he built the University of California, San Diego (UCSD) on land surrounding Scripps "from the top down and not from the bottom up—from the inside out, not from the outside in" by headhunting at top schools with full professorships and above-scale wages. He also offered recruits promises of a grand, social-democratic adventure in modern science and education. By 1966, the faculty included two Nobel Prize winners and fifteen National Academy of Sciences members, and already supervised five hundred Ph.D. and nine hundred undergraduate students.[66]

Boosters and industrialists were thrilled. The Chamber's president lauded UCSD's 1960 founding as "probably the most important development in some time." "We'll be able to attract the kind of industry we need to broaden our industrial base," he enthused. "It's exactly what we wanted, a scientific and technical graduate school," a Convair executive celebrated. "It will encourage light industry to locate here."[67]

UCSD initially seemed more a technical school than a university. The arts, humanities, and social sciences languished until UCLA historian John Galbraith became chancellor in 1965. He endeavored to "build the most exciting intellectual environment in the States" through a great library and high-caliber hiring, notably that of philosopher Herbert Marcuse, who joined the UCSD faculty in 1965. But Galbraith needed businessmen to support the library and theater, warning: "The big question confronting us is whether the University of California will have two great campuses or three." "San Diego will be the third," he asserted. "We must see to it that the Legislature does not cut us off at the knees . . . and . . . we must . . . promote contributions from private sources." His ambitions ran afoul of a new era in California politics, when legislators and voters seemed less enthused with California liberals' mid-century social democratic statecraft, including the ambitious master plan. Kerr had found himself unable to boost faculty salaries in 1964 and subsequently hesitated to budget more book acquisitions for UCSD in 1965. Galbraith then threatened to delay his inauguration, which would have left the campus rudderless. He also publicly damned Kerr for keeping UCSD "one of the lesser campuses, or a science institute with a humanities tail." The tactic worked. The new repository helped remodel UCSD into a leading multiversity. Two decades later professors included eight Nobel laureates, sixty-four National Academy of Sciences members, two Pulitzer Prize winners, six National Medals of Science awardees, six MacArthur Foundation fellows, and more than a hundred Guggenheim recipients.[68]

The simultaneous development of UCSD, ASU, and Chapel Hill illuminates the complications arising from business-driven postsecondary expansion, the contradictions between corporate and social welfare states, and pragmatic policies supported by booster investors that redirected state power to serve industry without the oversight that unions, taxes, or regulations provided. Like elsewhere, private and public funding and support facilitated the maturation of Arizona's emergent educational infrastructure. State expenditures for education were high. Arizona eclipsed Colorado and New Mexico and matched California in per pupil spending in 1957, when Kerr had already begun expanding UC. The amount Arizonans directed to education remained far higher than national, southern, and Steelbelt averages in the 1960s, but California set the standard in these expansive years, a function of efforts to compete for investment and liberal initiatives to educate Baby Boomers. Californians received far more for the tax dollars spent on UC. Kerr's liberalism assumed that corporate capitalism could and should be transformed to build a social-democratic polity. Science and engineering still structured ASU, UC, and UNC, but Kerr held the social sciences and humanities to be vital to a master plan that would serve the academy and the citizenry. Hodges instead focused on Triangle schools and vocational institutions to better North Carolina's labor pool, whereas Phoenix boosters championed one university in the name of industrial recruitment, business innovation, and national defense. Neither sought a statewide university system to guarantee large-scale public access. ASU grew, of course, but without proper funding for the arts, humanities, and social sciences, much less a larger mission to improve educational opportunities around the state. Indeed, in his effort to expand the Tempe school, Noble often mentioned the citizens of Arizona as a mere afterthought in a manner analogous to grass-tops assurances that increasing personal property taxes would eventually pay dividends back to the citizenry.[69]

The Recreational Climate

ASU did far more than just train the Valley's workforce; the school also provided the sporting events, concerts, and theater productions that high-tech industrialists and boosters considered vital to the business climate. As with Phoenix's educational initiatives, a pleasure infrastructure had been a part of the New Dealers' prescriptions for wholesale reclamation. National Resources Planning Board officials, for example, had envisioned the Southwest industrializing under "a coordinated pattern of land use, transit and transportation, recreation development, water supplies, sanitary systems, and other essential facilities throughout the entire urban area." "The desirable urban environment," researchers concluded, had to have "homes, playgrounds, and schools separated from commercial and industrial districts," with "plenty of light and air and open green spaces throughout business and residential grounds."[70]

The grasstops also considered the arts and recreation vital to industrial recruitment. "Why should business support art?" a Marietta-Atlanta booster asked a Knoxville audience in 1966. "To draw and hold technicians, scientists. . . . Art makes the complete city. People want to live in complete, not incomplete cities." Well-trained engineers, scientists, and technicians were in short supply, which gave them increased power to dictate their own career paths. Many of these newly minted scientists and engineers embraced the rapidly developing suburban culture. They were, arguably, among the earliest suburbanites because they inhabited those communities that sprang up around the often remote national defense labs and industrial R&D facilities. After the war, and until the early 1960s, most enrollees in graduate engineering and physical sciences came from the white middle class. These new professionals, often family men, had less concern for pure research and more interest in lucrative industrial opportunities. California-based Douglas Aircraft Company courted this new cohort in ads that included images of suburban houses and luxury automobiles as well as men in pursuit of a litany of upper-middle-class leisure activities, including golfing and sailing. "Will your income and location allow you to live in a home like this . . . spend your leisure time like this?" asked a *Physics Today* ad. "They can," copywriters promised, "if you start your career now at Douglas!"[71]

The Chamber employed similar recruitment techniques to prove that Phoenix's physical climate would fulfill suburban fantasies. Promoters offered a thoroughly modern yet romantic West. The advertising committee, one historian asserted, employed the term "outdoor living" to emphasize the opportunity for year-round alfresco recreation and an escape from the rigid, fast-paced East Coast. Advertisements included pictures of backyard pools, trumpeted air conditioning, and promised well-kept parks, golf courses, campsites, and tennis courts. Recruitment literature increasingly celebrated the city's arts scene to complement the barrage of materials on Arizona's physical climate. "In the past we have been dwelling on the concept of Phoenix and Arizona being a wild and wooly West," one member of the advertising committee admitted in 1965. "Now we are trying to reach the cosmopolitan New Yorker . . . and picture to him the possibility of his coming to Phoenix and not having to leave any of the refinements."[72]

Chamber men pursued these opportunities for their own pleasure as well. Rainmakers had a genuine commitment to the arts. Walter Bimson owned one of the preeminent collections of Western art, which he showcased in every Valley National Bank branch. Barry Goldwater had a fondness for kachina "dolls," Hopi Indian religious figures. This avid sportsman also wanted well-manicured driving ranges and pristine wide-open spaces. His childhood friend Harry Rosenzweig gave generously to the Phoenix Symphony, Little Theatre, and Art Museum. These and other high-powered members of the Chamber and CGC also served as board members and fundraisers for each of these institutions. For example, Bimson and Snell rotated in and out of the leadership of the Phoenix Fine Arts Association. The pair helped create the core collections of European and neoclassical works in the Phoenix Art Museum through their connections with other aficionados eager to fund purchases or willing to donate pieces. One Valley artist noted at the museum's 1959 opening, "I'm astonished to see paintings here that it normally takes a museum ten years to collect." Haas considered this money well spent: "The Phoenix Little Theater is providing us with something that will definitely sell Phoenix as a Western cultural mecca." "A community needs cultural activities to attract the type of people that Phoenix wants," one CGC mayor declared in the 1960s, "electronics people. They'll support these institutions." "No industry is interested in a community that does not provide pleasant things," another promoter concurred. "Aesthetics are economical."[73]

City coffers also directly underwrote this relaxation infrastructure. Councillors first endorsed public money for professional sports. Several major league baseball teams, the nascent "cactus league," trained in the Valley. The Phoenix Municipal Stadium, where the New York Giants practiced and the city's minor league team also played, was privately owned until the proprietor threatened to sell in the early 1950s. City leaders, who relished the tourist dollars and industrial-recruitment advantages that baseball provided, paid a lot to keep the sport in the city: teams demanded expensive improvements up front and later insisted on a million-dollar stadium, which opened in 1965. The council also funded the arts. Bimson, then president of the art association, lobbied for a bond initiative to build the Phoenix Art Museum in 1950. "Are we content to make rapid strides in population and industrial growth," he asked, "but to permit our cultural development to lag embarrassingly behind?" City leaders initially balked, so Bimson personally raised $400,000 for a small facility, which opened in 1959. The collections soon overwhelmed the space, which prompted councillors to endorse a $500,000 bond to put toward expansion and followed up with contributions to the institution's annual budget.[74]

CGC approval signaled that boosters were now fully attuned to the arts' industrial potential. But investors demanded more than just galleries by the late 1950s. They wanted a fiscal, regulatory, and physical infrastructure in place to provide water, power, land, and labor. Boosters were hardly in a position to object: they were effectively at war with other promoters to secure new investments. Competition, moreover, seemed to work. Dollars, jobs, and people were flooding into a nascent Sunbelt, whose metropolitan districts seemed a century removed from a region once starved of credit, manufacturing, and opportunity. Hundreds of firms had already relocated or began operations in the Valley by 1960, which made this once colonial outpost an unquestionable epicenter of high-tech engineering and production.

PART III

Sprawl

Chapter 8

Industrial Phoenix

"Arizona's whole way of life and way of living is changing," *Business Week* reporters enthused in 1956. "The muscle and endurance that marshaled cattle in blistering sun is giving way to the quiet probing of a research engineer with a computer." True enough in Phoenix's case: between 1948 and 1964 alone, more than seven hundred firms relocated to, opened branch plants in, or started up in the Phoenix Valley. Power and persistence figured heavily in this postwar economic miracle. Members of the Chamber's Industrial Development Committee and the Thunderbirds put visitors up in lavish hotels, offered nightly cocktail hours to discuss the area's virtues, and hammered out company-specific agreements to craft and pass new laws, ordinances, or tax breaks.[1]

Such aggressive boosterism was a regional rule, not a local exception. Phoenix nonetheless sprawled atypically and archetypically, for rainmakers were promotional innovators. CEOs and experts grew to expect the deferential, red-carpet treatment perfected in the desert. Soon, rival cities sought to procure the weapons found in Phoenix's recruitment arsenal, but acquirement proved challenging. Few city-oriented business associations had as much in the way of local political power, economic resources, or national connections as the Phoenix Chamber. Phoenicians still did not prevail in every skirmish for investment, but these losses were really setbacks that increased promoters' resolve to fortify their desert armory.

Capital's Flight South and West

Industrialists had been moving into business-friendly environs like Maricopa County well before the academy turned its attention to the Rustbelt, the

Sunbelt, or globalization. Business began a substantial internal migration that superseded the limited prewar investment in the South and West and prefaced the major, late twentieth-century exportation of manufacturing outside the United States. World War II reconversion policies were partly responsible for the Steelbelt's subsequent hemorrhaging. Cost-plus guarantees, generous cancellation agreements, below-value surplus factory and inventory sales, and large tax breaks for retooling plants and equipment generated record profits for the country's largest businesses, those outfits best equipped to serve wartime needs, expand into larger conglomerates with vast product lines, and send their established and new operations into the interior.[2]

Capital fled early but seldom instantaneously. Few businesses could move their entire headquarters or cease production in older factories before or immediately after opening a new plant or announcing a division's relocation. For example, the Radio Corporation of America (RCA) began its operations in Camden, New Jersey, in 1919, opened a plant in Bloomington, Indiana, in 1940, built a factory dedicated solely to its television products in Memphis, Tennessee, in 1965, and started a facility originally dedicated just to the labor-intensive wiring for specific parts of its television sets in Ciudad Juarez, Mexico, in 1968. Executives ended Camden and Bloomington operations gradually by reducing the number of employees in the older sites as production increased in the newer facilities. RCA only announced their actual closure years later.[3]

The Steelbelt thus rusted while the South and West blossomed, providing more services and producing an astounding variety of goods as early as the mid-1950s. In 1954, employment in manufacturing in the South was just over half that in the Northeast; by 1970, it was almost three-quarters. But the largest trade, service, and government employment surges occurred in the West. California, Texas, and other arid states were responsible for 30.5, 15.9, and 14.2 percent, respectively, of the nation's overall increases in these fields between 1939 and 1954, effectively transcending their colonial past before southern states did. The West's percentage gains in nonagricultural employment, manufacturing jobs, manufacturing revenue, and per capita personal income also far surpassed the South's. Overall Mountain State employment rose 86 percent but only increased 4.5 percent in mining (with agriculture work plummeting by 31 percent). These changes bespoke the region's declining reliance on exporting raw materials and importing finished goods. The West's service economy expanded right alongside production output. Mountain State personal, business, and leisure sector hiring rose 135 percent between 1940 and 1960, far surpassing the national 27 percent uptick in these categories. High-tech electronics and aerospace firms also moved west, not south, first. Defense contracts alone funneled billions into the region. In the early 1960s, the West received half of all defense department R&D contracts, two-thirds of the missile awards, and 48 percent of National Aeronautics and Space Administration (NASA) expenditures. Together, investment for military and civilian needs gave the western portion of the developing Sunbelt a higher initial population upsurge and an earlier wage-scale elevation. Moreover, the South's per capital disposable income in 1960 had hardly caught up to what the Southwest had achieved a decade earlier.[4]

The blanket state-level spending statistics offered in many national and regional surveys failed to capture how spotty and transitory investment was. Lucrative enterprises tended to move to cities because urban areas had needed roads, utilities, and workers. Even firms more tied to commodities often came to towns first and then dispersed operations as costs escalated. For example, food, wood, and cotton production sectors first expanded in Chattanooga, Memphis, Nashville, and Knoxville during the 1950s and then moved outside Tennessee's urban centers during the 1960s, a relocation reflected in a dramatic drop in the percentage of the state's industrial workforce present in and manufacturing output emanating from these cities. Federal records were also misleading because statisticians often catalogued disbursements based on where contractors were headquartered, even though many often spent the money in new or established branch plants elsewhere. For example, Utah's largest defense contractor, Thiokol Chemical Corporation, invested north of Ogden to cut costs for missile and rocket fuel production in the early 1950s. Roughly a decade later, executives outsourced 86 percent of award moneys to plants in states with more industrial advantages. The government, however, still listed these funds as being spent in the Beehive State. Thus, Sunbelt industrialization was, as a rule, uneven. This irregular quality was a function of the hypercompetitive recruitment strategies responsible for colonial outposts becoming imperial metropolises with hinterlands stretching far outside their city limits.[5]

Phoenix's Industrialization

The Valley stood out among postwar boomtowns. Arizona's industrial employment jumped 466 percent between 1939 and 1959, twice the rate of all other states, save neighboring New Mexico, Nevada, and California. This figure includes metallurgy, printing, publishing, and food processing, but aircraft, electronics, machinery, and missiles fields still generated most of this groundswell. Such investment went primarily to Phoenix and represented not only a few large employers but also a litany of smaller machine shops and commercial outfits. In 1960 manufacturing displaced agriculture as the city's moneymaker and second-largest job source. Only the service sector employed more Phoenicians because investment-fueled population increases and business climate policies demanded more urban and suburban services. These industries expanded faster than the increase in total employment, especially in the construction, government, finance, insurance, real estate, communication, and utilities fields, during the 1940s and 1950s.[6]

Phoenix mushroomed over three distinct investment periods. New Deal spending, war production, and pre-Charter Government Committee (CGC) reconversion created six thousand new jobs, one-third within metallurgy. Hiring also increased in the food, printing, publishing, and evaporative cooling industries, which generally served local markets. Growth was extremely rapid between 1950 and 1958, when local firms added sixteen thousand new jobs. Metals continued to expand, but the electronics and aerospace industries provided the bulk of these opportunities, with the latter creating one-third of new openings and both serving a clientele beyond Maricopa County and the greater Southwest. Employment soared even higher between 1958 and 1964, when manufacturers created nineteen thousand new employment possibilities, mostly in electronics, computing, and aerospace (70 percent). These firms served national, not local or regional, markets, which signaled Phoenix's metamorphosis from import-reliant frontier into industrial-export metropole. The majority of the jobs created in the 1950s came from firms that established themselves in Phoenix during that decade. Post-1958 expansion resulted, by and large, from these same companies, which increased the scope of their operations in the city.[7]

High-tech industrialization created a ripple effect across different economic sectors, but opportunities were limited for women and minorities. A handful of firms in low-skill or labor-intensive sectors, such as garment or metal fabrication, reported having a minority-majority workforce. Investors in Nogales, for example, eagerly tapped the surplus pool of Mexican Americans. "The manufacturing of saxophones requires much skillful handiwork, which can't be automated," an owner reported. He echoed a century of racialized, engendered managerial assumptions about skill and labor costs: "The unskilled Mexican workers (both men and women) that I hired had the innate skill and artistic ability."[8]

Above all else, electrical, aerospace, and computing investment attracted and benefited skilled, educated, or professional Anglo men, the technocratic labor pool whom the grasstops favored over the Steelbelt's immigrant, white-ethnic, and minority workforce. Almost 80 percent of Arizona factories had a mostly or completely Anglo staff in the early 1960s. Aircraft and missile plants employed many engineers, machinists, researchers, and managers, who, given the limited access to higher education in this era, were almost guaranteed to be white men. Cherry-picking investors thus represented another aspect of Sunbelt racial moderation because booster strategies attracted and guaranteed a white population influx without overt racial demagoguery. Such solicitations brought "city of knowledge" workers to the Valley, the innovators who, as historical economist Gavin Wright emphasized, were absent from the pre–World War II South, much as they had been from the Southwest. Only twelve aeronautical and fifty-six industrial engineers resided in the state in 1950, but in just a decade their numbers swelled past four hundred. Technician ranks also ballooned. The number of highly skilled electrical workers increased from thirty-six in 1950 to 964 in 1960. Almost thirty-five hundred aeronautical, architectural, chemical, civil, electrical, geological, mechanical, metallurgical, chemical, mining, or structural engineers lived in the desert by the early 1960s.[9]

This electronics mecca still trailed behind western industrial giants Los Angeles and San Francisco. In 1962, Los Angeles had almost $2 billion in yearly sales, 595 plants, and 137,000 persons employed in the industry. San Francisco was a distant second with $739 million in sales, 180 plants, and 47,000 workers. Phoenix and San Diego tied for third place. Both had $185 million in sales and roughly the same number of engineers and production facilities. But only half the firms in Phoenix, unlike defense-dependent San Diego, produced products for the military. Valley output included a range of high-tech products: airplanes, aircraft parts, aluminum products, chemicals, gases, electronics components, gears, controls, scientific instruments, metal parts, missiles, rockets, plastics, tools, and dies. Light electronic output included sensors, small power sources, environment control systems, and tracking devices.[10]

Western rivals struggled to keep pace with California and Arizona's aggressive boosters. Prewar, less arid Colorado, for example, had seemed far more likely than laggard Arizona to develop significant manufacturing: Denver was already a major, bicoastal transportation hub. The mile-high grasstops stood in sharp relief to Valley rainmakers. They were not young, industry-minded boosters but graying figures proud that they had "turned sagebrush into sugar beets." A liberal mayor and a few energetic entrepreneurs undertook campaigns for wartime investment in Denver, including lobbying for a bombing range and factories for ships, planes, and munitions. High postwar unemployment and investment opportunities nonetheless failed to spur more activism. Local bankers, unlike the Bimsons, would not finance new initiatives, and industrialist Henry Kaiser reported returning to California "covered in hoarfroast" after scouting the area for a new installation. A younger, investment-focused cohort took charge in the 1950s and brought substantial manufacturing to the state. Economists still hesitated to deem the mid-1950s "a new era . . . that might be termed the era of industrialization." Even Boulder, a city renowned for its place in space-age technology and research, developed its science economy more slowly. The Western States Cutlery Company was the area's major preconflict manufacturer. By decade's end, boosters desirous of economic diversification had convinced Esquire-Coronet Magazine Subscription Service executives to establish their new headquarters in Boulder. Yet businessmen dithered in the aggressive pursuit of high-tech industries, only partnering with University of Colorado officials a decade later to capitalize on the town's open skies, proximity to Denver, and university. Shortly thereafter Ball Brothers moved its three-thousand person Aerospace and Research Division; the International Business Machines Corporation (IBM) arrived with work for five thousand in 1965.[11]

Even these sluggish arid-state boosters had more success than southern promoters in attracting lucrative manufacturing investment. Low-wage, low-growth manufacturing first displaced southern agriculture. Several electrical machinery plants opened in Tennessee between 1954 and 1963, for example, but manufacturing employment was highest in apparel and related products. Even the Atlanta–Cobb County area, the South's industrial juggernaut, trailed behind southwestern metropolises. Atlanta businessmen of course crowed when the U.S. Department of Commerce noted that between 1945 and 1955 "Georgia surpassed the national average rate of advancement in 23 out of 28 major fields of business and economic activity." "Expenditures for new plants and equipment," boosters highlighted, "increased . . . 133 per cent against 37 per cent for the nation." These sound bites were more impressive than the actual investments. The Georgia Division of Lockheed at Marietta, which began operations in the Bell Bomber plant in 1951, never developed the spin-off industries to complement the facility. Moreover, the high-skill, higher-wage work endemic to electronics never took place in this mammoth enterprise. The city still swelled to more than thirty thousand by 1976, but Lockheed's workforce of more than three thousand was an aberration. Only eight other firms, out of a total 102, employed between one hundred and five hundred residents. These businesses included paper, shoe, conveyer, lock, and lumber manufacturers as well as a Coca-Cola bottling facility, the local newspaper, and a poultry production plant. In contrast, aircraft, missiles, electronics, nonelectrical machinery, and fabricated metals drove Phoenix's initial postwar growth. Phoenix Chamber men, unlike their Marietta contemporaries, had even needed a separate, fifty-page directory of R&D support services, testing labs, and consultants for science-oriented industries in 1970.[12]

Phoenix-Style Industrial Recruitment

Yet corporate-welfare guarantees never completely ensured investment. Deals hinged on industrial-recruitment techniques that expanded state planning bureaucracies or established business-focused agencies, which buttressed the shift from "buying payroll" to building competitive "business climates." Phoenix Chamber men, like their competitors, both vied with and sought cooperation from neighboring boosters to compete. But it was largely Phoenix's rainmakers who oversaw Valley boosterism: their educational backgrounds, professional memberships, and business networks placed them midway between the desert's petit capitalists and the country's leading tycoons, providing them with early entrée into faraway executive boardrooms. The association also had a locational edge: none of the smaller towns in the area had a chamber, which attracted Mesa, Glendale, and Tempe businessmen to Phoenix's network of professionals and storeowners during the 1930s and 1940s. These cities grew as Phoenix industrialized, but the chambers founded in the postwar period did not contribute equally to central Arizona's development. The rainmakers, for example, bypassed the Tempe Chamber when working out deals for Arizona State University's (ASU) development and General Electric's (GE) investment. Tempeians only learned of the firm's plans after the Phoenix Chamber had finished negotiations.

Scottsdale's Chamber, in contrast, wanted the city to be a bedroom community, "not actively interested in *industrial* development." "We are not equipped to do a good job," a leading member explained. "Some of the inquiries are handled here; many are referred to the Phoenix Chamber."[13]

Phoenix boosters actively sought to partner with promoters to vie for investment. General Manager Lew Haas, for example, pressured Arizona Chambers to unite in lobbying for the Air Force Academy. "The big thing is to land it for the state," he explained to Goldwater, who served on the 1954 site selection team. Business leaders from Tucson, Douglas, Safford, Winslow, Prescott, Mesa, Yuma, and Phoenix eventually agreed to propose Prescott for the state's bid, which failed. Haas's efforts to forge a sustained alliance also floundered: he could not persuade Tucson businessmen during the bidding process to establish a small Washington office for the state's broad development. "Carl Bimson and I took off for Tucson," Haas confided to Goldwater, "couldn't get a flicker of interest . . . in helping finance such representation." "Phoenix firms," Haas continued, "decided they should not . . . defray the entire cost [because] . . . representation was for Arizona and not Phoenix alone."[14]

Phoenix Chamber men still proved themselves fierce and effective competitors. Their combined war chest, national standing, and local political power enabled them to pioneer, ape, and reshape a multitude of mid-century industrial-recruitment techniques to complement their multifaceted business climate. The Chamber's Industrial Development Program began in March 1948, which inaugurated a cohesive, systematic investment effort that improved earlier, piecemeal mobilization and reconversion campaigns. Leading members worked on the Industrial Development Committee (IDC), including Goldwater and air-conditioning executive Oscar Palmer. Division heads prioritized manpower and immediately sought fifty additional men to fill out their ranks and lead subgroups devoted to compiling statistics, advertising and publicity, industrial outreach, coordination with other Arizona business organizations, and fundraising for recruitment campaigns. Separate committees, such as the advertising work group, attributed to the overall campaign.[15]

Boosters justified their activism by pointing to the growth generated. Monthly investment reports always listed stark total payroll calculations to celebrate the Chamber's efforts. Such appraisals increasingly included the number of new jobs and expected returns to Phoenix retailers and service providers as the business climate ideal took hold in the mid-1950s. "A plant investment of $100,000," one member rejoiced, would produce: "An annual payroll of $200,000. The support of 1,000 people. A dozen retail stores. A ten-room school building. Sales and service for 200 cars. New revenue of $60,000 a year for railroads. A taxable valuation of $1,000,000. Markets for $300,000 worth of farm products annually. Opportunity for a dozen professional men. Annual trade expenditures of $1,000,000." Members also employed the CGC's language of selfless businessman's rule to explain their hard work. "The least of the banker's functions in industrial development is to lend money," Valley National Bank's (VNB) manager of economic development explained. "The banker must be willing, for the good of the community, to give all his skills to any interested business or industry, whether his institution makes loans or not." "We seek no publicity," he continued. "Our first job is to protect the economic health of the community" and to "keep Arizona in the lead of all states in growth rate of manufacturing employment."[16]

This worldview informed top promoters' plans for modern Phoenix. The first IDC members proclaimed the Valley's well-being dependent on a "well-balanced" or "well-rounded" economy that included industrial agriculture, tourism, wholesaling, distribution, and manufacturing. Boosters nonetheless prioritized electronics production, aerospace manufacturing, and R&D and thus sought to demonstrate that Phoenix could service the high-tech markets outside the Southwest and coastal California. Phoenicians focused on these industries because they correctly predicted that these sectors would rebound from their Depression era decline and prove a major force in postwar economic growth. These firms also seemed suited for the desert because they would not require as much water as agriculture or heavy industry. The Chamber "did not want dirty industries," lawyer Frank Snell recalled. "There was talk of a refinery in this area. We did our best to kill it." High-tech investment also helped ensure that industrial Phoenix would be Anglo and technocratic. This sector, Snell explained, was "inclined to bring . . . engineers and people who had somewhat higher income than you might otherwise have." In fact, the Chamber's board of directors would only entertain the oil company's offer if the factory was more than thirty miles outside the city limits. Still, the supposedly "clean industries," as Snell defined them, proved just as thirsty and toxic as heavy manufacturing. Semiconductor production, which Motorola first introduced into company product lines in the 1950s, required much water and yielded toxic by-products that Motorola and its Valley-based competitors simply dumped, often near residential water supplies.[17]

The Chamber vied for such investment with techniques that reshaped nationwide approaches. The IDC supplemented mass mailings, trips to the coasts, and feting of individual visiting executives in November 1958 when they sponsored a five-day tour of the Valley for relocation advisers. Visitors looked over area industrial sites and enjoyed local recreational opportunities. This event was the first of its kind and cost approximately $20,000. Boosters streamlined industrial recruitment further throughout the 1960s. In the late 1960s the manager of the Economic Development Department (formerly the IDC) made at least three trips a year to the Boston–New York, the Minneapolis-Detroit-Chicago, and the San Francisco–Los Angeles industrial zones. He met with executives who had contacted the Chamber or with those whose businesses the association's researchers had identified as "likely to be interested in Phoenix in the future." Those involved considered these preemptive calls imperative: "If this isn't done, the location for a new facility may be determined before we even hear about the company looking for a new area." Members also compiled a lengthy resource guide for high-tech firms, one of the first such catalogs for a city. The "1970 Directory of Scientific Resource in the Phoenix Area" showcased the multifaceted business climate, including "our unique and stimulating intellectual/cultural environment—and the vital contribution it makes in recruiting and keeping top scientific and management talent," "the low cost of housing in Metro Phoenix, schools, churches, hospitals," and a complete list of all R&D companies, nonprofit research organizations, government facilities, testing laboratories, computer centers, and professional associations.[18]

Financiers helped pay for such materials and much more. First National's William Coerver asserted, "Banks have probably done a better job than the Chamber of Commerce. By far." For good reason: the association simply did not collect enough in dues to compete effectively. It could not, for example, afford the 1948 Industrial Development Plan. The expansive initiative included an exhaustive survey of the area's resources, increased focus on publicizing the Valley's potential as a distribution point and manufacturing center, and a concerted effort to court and negotiate with firms in concert with civic groups and city leaders. In 1948, the IDC's chairman requested $15,000 in seed money, which did not cover expensive trips, recruitment packages, or publicity campaigns. It thus fell to VNB and First National to supply cash, personnel, and leaders (their vice presidents chaired the advertising and research subcommittees). Such contributions only increased as the escalating second conflict between the states necessitated the enlargement of the Chamber's fulltime staff.[19]

VNB also launched in-house efforts, which were thoroughly intertwined with the Chamber's. The firm's research department, for example, promoted Phoenix through two publications. Both began in the mid-1940s and went out on the firm's large, national mailing list, which included Chambers of Commerce, business research organizations, local politicians, state officials, congressional representatives, and business owners. The *Arizona Statistical Review* was, as the editor explained, "an encyclopedia on Arizona, but it consisted entirely of figures and no conversation." In contrast, the monthly *Arizona Progress* offered more than three thousand recipients, two-thirds of whom resided outside Arizona, colorful reports on the state's industrialization. Editor Herbert Leggett even began each issue with a humorous comment on politics, philosophy, or economics that spoke to the Chamber leadership's business-first vision.[20]

Financiers also staffed the Chamber, which relied on influential Phoenicians to travel and meet with executives. VNB executive Patrick Downey served as an official "promoter" during the 1950s. The Chamber initially bought his time from the bank, but VNB eventually assumed these costs so the Chamber could direct its resources elsewhere. Downey's tactics defined streamlined, professional business climate recruitment. He visited headquarters with a dossier that detailed why Phoenix was "especially conducive to technical and industrial growth." These reports included information on the city's weather, tax code, and labor market. He often started informal negotiations during these meetings by pressing for a company's specific needs or demands. Downey then returned to present a firm's requests to Haas. The general manager approved whatever deals he deemed necessary, dispatched a representative to make an offer to the company, and eventually alerted the city council to the terms and conditions that the Chamber had presented to CEOs.[21]

Bankers worked alongside nationally prominent rainmakers, like Eugene Pulliam. He vigorously sold Phoenix to his business contacts and connected boosters with other major publishers. He also collaborated with Chamber leaders, including the Bimson brothers, Haas, and Governor Howard Pyle to give the heads of newspaper advertising departments "an opportunity to see what Arizona has" and "to make missionaries out of you." He also feted pressmen from New York, Chicago, Detroit, and Los Angeles at a

January 1953 Westward Ho Hotel luncheon, where Pyle, Carl Bimson and other representatives from VNB and First National, and some transplanted CEOs spread the word that Arizona was devoted to free enterprise. "I am very happy to be here," a relocated AiResearch manager declared. The need to disperse operations, he revealed, had forced his reassignment, but he considered Phoenix an easy choice because of its dual climates. Other panelists emphasized the Valley's unlimited possibilities. "We have everything here but deep-sea fishing," a VNB executive asserted. "We don't build battleships either, but we do build quite a lot of other ships believe it or not . . . you can outfit the entire Pacific Fleet with fighter planes from Litchfield within a few hours time."[22]

In-house promotional materials also emphasized Phoenix's investment advantages, particularly the area's anti-union, low-tax, investment-focused ethos. For example, a Chamber brochure emphasized that all wage rates were "10 to 25 per cent lower in Arizona than in larger industrial areas" and that "the per man hour production is 10 to 25 per cent higher in Arizona." "A majority of the firms in Arizona are not unionized," IDC members boasted, before adding: "The firms that are unionized receive excellent cooperation from union management within the state." Manufacturers would find "no inventory tax on raw materials, parts, or finished products," and they would also benefit from cheap land, top schools, a leading research university, and "an abundance of water so far as domestic and industrial uses are concerned." Phoenix banks were guaranteed to be "industrial-minded and anxious to cooperate in every way possible." The entire city, the Chamber declared, "welcomes new industries."[23]

Rainmakers also devoted substantial resources to attract the educated, affluent whites whom the Phoenix elite welcomed into their neighborhoods and the high-tech manufacturers needed in their facilities. During the 1946–1947 fiscal year, Snell directed the National Advertising Committee to promote the Phoenix Valley in *Holiday Magazine* "to create a new interest in this area as a playground," *National Geographic* "to create a . . . desire to see and explore, the unique geographic features of our area," *Better Homes and Gardens* "to cause wealthy people to investigate advantages of living here, with the objective of purchasing a home," and *Fortune Magazine* "to cause wealthy men who represent management and industry to decide to investigate or consider this area as a good place to invest." Chamber men also targeted Easterners with promises of mild winters. Snell formulated three goals for this campaign: "1. . . . to extend season for arrival of wealthy tourists.

Figure 10. Boosters promised "Water's Fine!" in this 1950s Chamber advertisement showcasing two Arizona State coeds who "enjoy swimming in Phoenix all winter long." The publicity department often waited to release such copy and pictures until they heard of severe winter weather in the Northeast. Courtesy of the Arizona Historical Foundation, Subject Photograph Collection, folder 7, box 48.

2. To cause dissatisfaction with winter climate of home town and with the condition of being deprived of healthful sunshine and outdoor life. 3. To create a new interest in Valley as a resort area." Carl Bimson proudly recounted how he later commissioned ads with women in bathing suits by a pool or in shorts on a golf course with a proclamation about how warm and sunny Arizona was. But the Chamber's publicity department asked eastern editors to sit on these promotions until staffers learned of low temperatures or large snowstorms. Boosters then called papers and demanded, in Bimson's words, "Run that ad today!"[24]

Rainmakers also promoted Phoenix through *Arizona Highways* magazine, the world-renowned glossy replete with beautiful photographs and stories devoted to the state's landscape, culture, art, and history. The 1925 legislature had ordered production of a no-frills catalog of the state's roadways, which became a dazzling serial that sometimes included Goldwater's well-known photographs. Chamber men never controlled the magazine's publication or listed themselves as board members on the masthead. They nonetheless developed a mutually beneficial relationship with the publishers. The editor provided the association with color negatives for brochures and printed these expensive booklets at a reduced cost in the IDC's early years. The small but growing work group would not have been able to produce such quality promotional literature at the time. As the Chamber's resources increased, boosters began to offset the magazine's production costs. The association, for example, contributed the 150 color photographs for the March 1957 issue on Phoenix. Their overall investment in *Arizona Highways* paid dividends: members distributed up to seventy-five thousand copies of the monthly because, as one VNB executive noted, "It beats chain letters and give-away programs."[25]

Magazine editors mostly covered Arizona vistas but still devoted pages to modern Phoenix, the Chamber, and the business environment. Journalist Tim Kelly lionized Phoenix as the exemplification of an industrial "New West," where "no ugly smokestacks insult the Arizona sky, no growl of monotonous machines harshly stamp their audible imprint." "The plants," Kelly assured readers, "are . . . neat, attractive, quiet; models in many cases of laudable architectural design." He credited an "ultra-modern" association dedicated to "creating an average of 5,000 industrial jobs a year" for the Valley's transformation. Other journalists heaped praise on the Bimsons and VNB, "one of the great banks of America," editor Raymond Carlson proclaimed, "[that] create[d] a modern economic empire from a western frontier." Joseph Stocker deemed the brothers "quite selfless" for sending representatives to speak with other bankers across the country, disseminating pricey advertisements and brochures about Phoenix, aiding in efforts to repeal state tax laws so Arizona would be more competitive, and maintaining "an industrial department armed with elaborate data on labor pools, water, land values, transportation facilities, potential markets, tax laws and anything else of interest to business firms." John Herbert included more overt celebrations of the Phoenix business climate, including "realistic, moderate tax laws," the "Open Port Law," and the "Right-to-Work Law . . . that . . . maintain[ed] a proper balance with regard to the rights of individuals, organized labor, and plant management." "We are determined to maintain our favorable business climate," the essayist promised, "yielding an ever better life for its people and contributing importantly to the economy of the nation."[26]

White, suburban, residential ideals shaped how the grasstops fashioned and sold their city. Phoenix builders, often Chamber members, constructed Valley neighborhoods, and the city's idealized image as a western suburban metropolis in a kind of sociocultural example of assimilating Steelbelt standards and maintaining regional distinctiveness. The National Association of Home Builders' local chapter, the Arizona Home Builders Association (AHBA, later the Phoenix Association of Home Builders), carefully negotiated these conflicting desires. The umbrella organization sponsored a yearly National Home Week that included a Home Show and a "Queen" who presided over the expo. The Phoenix chapter remade the event to fit the Chamber's vision for a romantic, urban, Anglo metropolis in 1953. Showcased homes were distinctly suburban and southwestern, key components of the popular image of the West as the land of the new metropolitan cowboy conservative. Contractors promoted these dwellings in AHBA's *Arizona Homes.* East Coast recipients flipped through the pages, finding promises of the mild winter needed for a "Year 'round color garden" alongside pictures of lush lawns, wide driveways, and well-paved sidewalks and roads. Editors also highlighted such amenities as built-in ovens and ranges, garbage disposals, bathroom ventilating fans, washer-dryer combinations, mahogany kitchen cupboards, frost-free refrigerators, built-in electric clocks, leaded windows, mercury light switches, and walls with washable plastic paint. Some models even had air conditioning. These designs clearly belonged to the tamed West, where a family needed the popular ranch-style house with an "extra wide overhang [that] wards off the sun" but where "outdoor-indoor

Figure 11. Wide boulevards, protective carports, lush lawns, and a few yards with desert landscaping defined Scottsdale's 1960s Cox Heights development as a modern suburb even as the rugged red mountains in the background placed it firmly in the American West. Courtesy of the Arizona Historical Foundation, Subject Photograph Collection, folder 7, box 30.

living is achieved with Arcadia sliding glass doors in the breakfast nook." Some developers named their models without a hint of this western influence. Yet Chestley Manor, Cavalier Campus, Dennis Manor, and Westwood Heights stood alongside homes, such as Del Ray Estates, Siesta Homes, and Kachina Estates, that mixed eastern suburbia with the rugged West.[27]

AHBA also crowned a woman "Mrs. Arizona Home Owner" to reign over these enclaves. The national organization anointed celebrities, but boosters needed a winner, who embodied the romantic, residential Southwest, providing the feminine counterpart to their imagined cowboy conservative. Promoters expected their "Queen" to promote Phoenix, which led nominators to select competitors with at least some experience in modeling, singing, or dancing (one 1955 entrant was the 1949 Miss Junior America). Each subcontractors' association submitted one contestant, who, per the AHBA manager's guidelines, would "typify other young Arizona couples who own their own home and are enthusiastic about the opportunities for comfortable living offered by home builders here." A contestant earned up to thirty points for "beauty—face and figure," twenty for "personality and graciousness," thirty for "successful homemaker ability[,] Home life[,] Church and civic activities in the community," and a final twenty for "ability to meet people, express herself comfortably in public, radio, TV, etc."[28]

The pageant, winner, and prize all served the residential dimension of the local business climate. All competitors in the 1954 contest, held at the Westward Ho, were Anglo and wore a frock that cinched at the waist and flared out past the knee but well above the ankle, a "squaw dress creation" provided by the Arizona Fashion Council. Each of these 1950s-style housedresses had trim, fringe, and beadwork around the waists, hems, and bustlines in order to invoke a stylized vision of Native American clothing. The 1954 winner, Mrs. H. L. Thompson, was married to a police officer and had a boy and a girl, both under seven years old. "The Thompsons moved to Phoenix three years ago from Denver," the *Republic* reported, "live in a subdivision with a large back yard, where they hope to install a swimming pool." The grand prize was a trip to New York for an appearance on the popular television show "Queen for a Day," a treat for Thompson but also an opportunity to introduce this new western woman and her hometown to a national audience.[29]

Chamber men also incorporated nods to their maturing cowboy-conservative image when they entertained visiting CEOs and scouts. The Thunderbirds wined and dined visiting executives, who often stayed at the posh Westward Ho. Atop the high-rise sat the private Kiva Club, which the *Saturday Evening Post*'s Harold Martin called "a pleasant, glass-enclosed hideaway." The Thunderbirds ran the venue and brought CEOs up at dusk to show them the dynamic sunset over the "the wonders that have been accomplished here." A Thunderbird, Martin reported, "sheds his coat and drapes himself in a high-necked jacket of blue velvet. Around his neck he hangs a strand of silver beads from which dangles a large, fierce-looking bird, fashioned of turquoise and hammered silver. At his waist he cinches a heavy belt, also of silver, curiously wrought." "Attired like a Hopi medicine man getting ready to pray for rain," Martin continued, "he proceeds to his evening's labor, which consists of greeting strangers and telling them . . . how it has come to pass that Phoenix has grown so fast."[30]

Figure 12. Barry Goldwater appeared before this 1968 gathering of Republican Women at Scottsdale's Mountain Shadows Resort to show off his renowned collection of kachina figures (often called dolls) in the attire that the Royal Order of the Thunderbirds wore to entertain visiting scouts and executives. Courtesy of the Arizona Historical Foundation, Personal and Political Papers of Senator Barry M. Goldwater, folder 2, box 735.

The stylized, Old West iconography running throughout this industrial courtship distinguished Phoenix and the greater Southwest's industrialization from the South's development. Southerners struggled to convince potential transplants and investors that the region had overcome its peculiar past. Firms that required a skilled workforce, who tended to demand better cultural, recreational, and educational opportunities for themselves and their families, hesitated to move to the Southeast, particularly at the height of the southern civil rights movement. Massive resistance, particularly in the form of school closures and scattered racial violence, proved a heavy, embarrassing burden to southern boosters. In 1964, Bell Bomber general manager and Atlanta-Marietta booster James Carmichael had to openly stress "the Nation's Economic Problem No. 1 has become the Nation's Economic Opportunity No. 1." But promoters often complained that the modernizing South went unnoticed. When Luther Hodges led a 1959 recruitment initiative in Western Europe, the Tar Heel found that few realized his state's industrial potential. "I wanted to do my homework last night because . . . I knew nothing whatsoever about North Carolina," the chairman of West Germany's foreign trade committee confided to the governor. "In the only encyclopedia where I could find any reference . . . , I found just two items, namely the area in square miles and the percentage of Negroes in the state." Hodges often blamed this lack of information on the press: "Negroes entered the Greensboro schools without any trouble or disorder, and the next morning the *New York Times* carried the report of it on page thirty-four." "A Charlotte truck driver's wife taunted some young people and asked them to throw some icicles . . . at the Negro pupils as they went by," he fumed. "This incident was carried on page one."[31]

Journalists, for their part, tended not to identify the urban South as dynamic until it had seemed to become culturally indistinguishable from dynamic northeastern cities. In the late 1980s, when Charlotte was unquestionably a national center of banking and finance, reporters deemed it "the city without a past," "overwhelmingly . . . average," and "a fine, rich, upstanding city. It just isn't much of a fine, rich, upstanding Southern city. It has all of the quaint Southern appeal of Des Moines."[32]

Charlotte boosters would have chafed at comparisons with small midwestern towns or the once formidable Detroit, Buffalo, or Indianapolis. These cities labored to keep and attract new investment because CEOs often considered Steelbelt mines and smokestacks incompatible with pristine, knowledge-based metropolises. Indeed, widespread assumptions of systemic urban conflict, economic decline, and environmental degradation hindered Rustbelt rejuvenation. “Sure, we still make steel,” Pittsburgh promoters had asserted in the 1970s, “we still mine some coal. But the old stereotypes are ashes from the past.” The city was reborn as a millennial leader in robotic, software, and health sciences but was still not widely regarded as a genuine postindustrial oasis until the 1990s. One businessman complained to local reporters that “the only thing that hasn’t changed much is our image. . . . We’re well into our second renaissance, yet many sophisticated businessmen are only vaguely aware of our first, which began a quarter of a century ago.”[33]

In contrast, southwestern boosters used history to their advantage. Racism and legally enforced segregation shaped the entire nation, but the grasstops transformed the Southwest’s multiracial and multicultural past into an asset. The squaw dresses, kachina dolls, tacos, rodeos, and turquoise jewelry, which were prevalent throughout investment campaigns, negotiations, and cocktail hours, signified that this arid land had little in common with the Rustbelt and the South. The Southwest, Phoenix in particular, had an ethos that was rooted in an exciting past but was still unthreatening and modern. Anglo, elite, suburban-cowboy businessmen ruled this enchanted land and ensured that the area was a present-day oasis capable of supporting executives fleeing the Northeast and California.[34]

Recruitment still varied far more in style than in substance. All boosters prioritized expanding organizations dedicated to competition. Balance Agriculture with Industry’s 1944 revival, for example, had expanded the development program by adding committees and enlarging the full-time staff, which included “bird dogs,” who spent their time promoting Mississippi outside the state. The program’s overhaul inspired other southern boosters. Tennessee State Planning Commission officials advocated the legalization of subsidized investment bonds because hamlets had unconstitutionally floated thrice Mississippi’s total between 1935 and 1945. Planners then steered industrialization by hiring scouts, undertaking surveys of area business climates, and advising communities on how to utilize state laws to attract firms. Hodges, for his part, replaced old-timers serving in the Department of Conservation and Development’s Commerce and Industry Division. A close college friend and fellow retired textile magnate took over the entire agency, which gave new hires a leg up in making contacts with leading manufacturers.[35]

Steelbelt states often struggled to empower such bureaus. Ohio’s development department completed a systematic review of the state’s Appalachian region in the mid-1960s and included twenty-year plans for a new

Figure 13. Frank Snell (far right) gives Arizona State College president Grady Gammage a pat on the back during a 1954 Tempe plant opening, where Senator Carl Hayden (not pictured), executives Bill Moriarty and Walt Lucking, and other invited guests dined on staples of Anglo Western cuisine: hearty breads, baked beans, and grilled meats. Courtesy of the Arizona Historical Foundation, Subject Photograph Collection, folder 1, box 14.

regional development council, enlargement of transportation, leisure, and educational infrastructures, and an initiative to start county Community Improvement Corporations in the name of economic diversification through knowledge, recreation, and high-tech investment. The legislature proved uncooperative. The state department's staff remained small and unable to serve declining communities effectively.[36]

Not all tactics, as in Phoenix, relied on public policies or funds. Local, voluntary involvement helped establish a community's business-first attitude. Booster groups often organized phone banks and sent local delegations to visit CEOs. Amsterdam, New York, residents courted General Foods executives through the mail in 1962. Denizens included box tops and labels in their three thousand letters in order to prove that they already bought what they hoped to produce. Competition also led chambers to establish outposts in headquarter cities, such as Phoenix's hoped-for offices in D.C., in order to get the jump on new leads. Atlanta's association opened a branch office in New York City, an investment for "prospects from Boston to Baltimore" that coincided with a 1977 million-dollar public relations campaign to "sell metropolitan Atlanta as a location for business expansion and relocation." "To recruit industry," the president explained, "you must make yourself known."[37]

Heightened competition also fostered the kind of statewide or regional partnerships that Haas had wanted. The Atlanta grasstops united boosters under the Georgia State Chamber of Commerce in 1947 for "industrial, commercial and agricultural expansion" to mimic South Carolina, Florida, and Alabama groups. Atlantans dominated the membership, pledging coordination for the "progress, prosperity, and welfare of your state and your business." Mid-1950s cooperation for the "furtherance of a conservative business climate" took the form of advertising, data collection, negotiating with investors, and seminars with recruitment experts. The governmental department also sponsored off-the-record discussions of federal and state legislation, endorsed political candidates, updated members on legislative activity, and sponsored "Eggs and Issues" breakfasts for representatives and boosters. During the 1950s, the Memphis Chamber headquartered the Mid-South Progress Council, which included industrial development committees in 102 counties within east Arkansas, north Mississippi, west Tennessee, southeast Missouri, and northwest Alabama. Memphis boosters stockpiled recruitment brochures for each municipality, offered "professional industrial development representatives" to "determine . . . advantages that each town might offer," "assistance in procuring . . . area goods and services necessary for . . . operation," and "conferences with local . . . manufacturers . . . in regard to productivity of workers, availability of goods and services, and discussions of wage and fringe benefits."[38]

These promotional arsenals were invaluable, but few industrialists actually cited them when they explained their investment decisions. Phoenix investors, for example, referred to the multidimensional business climate. A Goodyear Aerospace Corporation's manager asserted that the company's decision to begin operating in Phoenix during World War II was out of necessity, but, he noted, the corporation returned after the war because of "ideal living conditions, space to expand and opportunities for the cultural and educational advancement of our personnel." "Basic economic reasons influenced the choice," Cannon Electric Company's Phoenix general manager explained, "availability of land and labor; suitable subcontractors and suppliers to support our type of manufacture; good housing and climate, an inducement to the recruitment of employees." "We needed a location fairly remote, yet near a major city," the president of Rocket Power, Inc., remarked. "We needed a dry climate and we needed a ready source of manpower." "I wanted a location that would help attract good men primarily," a Motorola vice president elaborated. "Phoenix offers good weather, with lots of sunshine and year-round outdoor activities." A vice president of National Castings Company, Capitol Foundry Division, regarded Phoenix as "ideal due to the climate, the availability of skilled and unskilled personnel, the fine transportation facilities and the availability of utilities and service facilities." "Of no less importance," he noted, "is nearby Arizona State University, which affords a reservoir of new talent as well as the means for continuing training and development." One executive, who had considered a move to Miami, revealed that "the whole matter that decided the location of the plant was business planning or community attitude."[39]

Chamber men nonetheless routinely lost investors and failed to close deals. Causes varied widely, especially as more cities and states began to compete more effectively for industry and, in the process, expand business-friendly expectations. CGC rule was just not satisfactory to some CEOs. "My main complaint about Phoenix is local government harassment[,] . . . restrictions, inspections, red tape, the changeable nature of political appointees, and lots of other things." Personal preference, especially as rivalry reduced distinct locational advantages, also made a difference. A DuPont executive was appalled that boosters refrained from promoting religion as a part of their business climate. He had attended Paul Fannin's Sunday luncheon for visiting CEOs and left astounded that grace had not been said before the meal. The magnate also complained that the governor's account of Arizona's growth "did not give some credit to the churches which have played such a tremendous part in the past and are now helping to mold a better moral fiber in your state." "I enjoyed my stay," he admitted but "will look for a town with good, strong churches which exert their influence."[40]

Backroom politics, not prayers, delivered NASA's Manned Space Craft Center to Houston, not Phoenix, in 1961. Administrators wanted transportation options, telecommunications, federal contractors, skilled labor pools, postsecondary schools, empty land tracks, and recreational opportunities in place. Phoenix boosters turned to Fannin to help prepare a proposal, which included raw statistics on Arizona's competitive educational infrastructure, vast surrounding territory, existing high-tech investment, skilled labor pool, and satisfied investor class. Brown and Root's Texas executives, who considered space exploration advantageous to their oil business, led Houston's campaign. George Brown had close ties with congressmen and chaired Rice University's board of trustees, which enabled him to work out complicated land deals between local tycoons and school administrators for the research nexus that NASA appointees desired. LBJ had also pressured Kennedy to let him chair the agency, which enabled the vice president to broker deals between boosters, politicians, and federal officials with whom he was well acquainted. LBJ even anointed Brown a civilian consultant on space policy.[41]

Motorola

These and other defeats did not prevent Phoenicians from upstaging most rivals, especially after Motorola, GE, and Sperry Rand settled in the Valley. These large outfits guided the area's overall industrialization. The head of Motorola's Missile and Space Instrumentation Section noted that between 1957 and 1962 more than a third of the company's $94 million in material purchases were ordered in Arizona. Some $7 million went to more than four hundred desert-based companies. GE and Sperry Rand had similar supply chains. These businesses had produced significant demand for, as one manager described, "small companies in Phoenix which are based on the high technical skill of a small number of persons." In contrast to Georgia, where technically advanced machine shops had not grown alongside Marietta's giant airplane factory, spin-off firms proved vital for plant expansions and new high-tech investment because Arizona-based suppliers reduced a firm's overhead dramatically.[42]

Motorola stimulated much of the Valley's early diversification. It was one of the few firms that ventured into Phoenix before the Chamber created the IDC or controlled the council. War-production and reconversion policies had transformed the Galvin brothers' radio company into a large corporation. Their embrace of Daniel Noble's FM technology to build two-way transceivers had led to lucrative contracts to produce sophisticated communications and radar equipment for the military. Wartime agreements, demobilization giveaways, and Cold War contracts then gave executives the market and capital to expand product lines and divide operations between civilian and defense needs.[43]

Boosterism and material advantages brought a small R&D facility to Phoenix in the late 1940s. Executives often cited fears of a bombing raid to explain their initial 1948 decision to send operations outside the Chicago area. Motorola nonetheless made its choice based on geography, market, and climate. Dispersal commenced with a lab devoted to military electronics, a venture suitable to the vast, remote, less populous Southwest, already home to military bases and government labs like Los Alamos. Plans stipulated a close working relationship between headquarters, where manufacturing occurred, and a remote site with the resources to engage in full-scale production in case, as executives explained to reporters, of a Soviet bombing raid. These limited needs did not demand the kind of infrastructure, workforce, and regulatory or tax guarantees that the IDC or CGC would later ensure. Grasstops activism still clinched the deal because Chamber men had already collaborated with liberals to make the city a regional hub between defense-dependent New Mexico and industry-rich California. Goods and personnel could reach either Albuquerque or Los Angeles in one and a half hours by air. Santa Fe, in contrast, lacked the rail and air services that connected Phoenix to Southern California and Chicago (through nonstop, six-hour flights). VNB banker Patrick Downey had spent the previous five years pressuring Motorola executives to come west. Yet 1948 discussions at the rainmaker-owned Camelback Inn actually revolved around the weather. Downey convinced industrialists that year-round sunshine for outdoor activities made Phoenix an ideal location for young engineers with families. Noble was predisposed to believe him: the engineer had lived in Arizona for health reasons as a young man and often reflected fondly on his days spent with an old mountaineer tracking mountain lions.[44]

Weather may have been a linchpin in 1948, but Phoenix's two climates enticed Motorola executives to increase the company's presence steadily. Noble deemed the physical environment an invaluable lure when hunting for top scientists from the armed services and elite universities, including Harvard: "Efforts to recruit professional help for assignment in Phoenix yielded responses 10-to-1, and sometimes as high as 25-to-1, over our recruiting efforts for other areas." "They became," Noble reported, "'Phoenix addicts' and the most extraordinary efforts to take them away from us have failed. Our turnover has been very low." Phoenix also appealed to these industrialists' business sense. "Government attitude . . . has been excellent," the Motorola president expounded in 1962. "The people that make the practical decision to determine whether or not this is a good business climate, have proven worthy partners with us." He shared the grasstops' embrace of state power to promote industrialization, not through redistribution, regulation, or union security, but via "this enlightened Government business atmosphere," which encouraged industry and ensured it played "its important role of providing stimulus to the economy."[45]

Motorola expanded along with the Valley. Five full-time employees worked in the thirty-six-hundred-square-foot lab in the International Life Insurance Building. Researchers initially complained that "Noble's Folly" had only a few contracts and tenuous links to Chicago factories. But Noble aggressively pursued new work for the facility. Agreements in 1949 with Sandia National Lab and the Atomic Energy Commission for new radar fuses and improved radar systems for nuclear weapons energized and expanded the team. CEOs announced that the entire Military Electronics Division would relocate to Phoenix in 1957. Motorola's foray into semiconductors also unfolded in Phoenix, not Chicago. In the mid-1950s, executives secured one of the few licensing agreements to use this cheap, compact, efficient technology in transistors and built a $1 million, fifty-seven-thousand-square-foot plant to house the Semiconductor Products Division. The sector grew exponentially: managers invested in a 230,000-square-foot facility in 1966. Noble crowed that the firm's choice had not been unwise. "Annual sales of the Division are the second largest in the world," he declared. "The Division has also gained world-wide recognition as a leader in the field of integrated circuit research, development and technology." The firm's entire Phoenix operations prospered. Goods and services had a $35 million market value, and payroll exceeded $17 million in 1960.[46]

General Electric

The business climate also brought GE to Phoenix. CEOs partly spread operations as a function of their postwar efforts to transform the company into a vast conglomerate. This "multipurpose engineering" firm, one historian recounted, "mov[ed] into nuclear power, computers, and plastics, . . . turning out millions of televisions, clothes dryers, and air conditioners," to complement defense-product divisions. GE had begun as an East Coast manufacturer: 92 percent of its domestically produced goods in 1929 came out of urban Steelbelt plants. Directors spent $500 million between 1946 and 1955 to buy abandoned war-production sites and build facilities abroad, in the developing Sunbelt, and also in the rural Northeast, Midwest, and Mid-Atlantic regions. There were immediate effects: Steelbelt installations accounted for only 83.5 percent of domestic production in 1947. Employment plummeted alongside continued diffusion: the Bridgeport staff dropped from 6,500 to 2,888 between 1947 and 1955, and the Schenectady workforce plunged from twenty thousand to eighty-five hundred over the next decade.[47]

Dispersal had grown out of an internal managerial revolution. Militant electrical workers transformed the company's employment practices from welfare capitalist to militantly anti-union. Executives perfected postwar policies that weakened solidarity, built alliances between employees and supervisors, and dispersed operations to reduce union density and power. CEOs also directly sought to shape the business climate ideal in their search for new corporate oases. For example, GE distributed a 1958 *Guide to Making a Business Climate Appraisal*, which prioritized "honest and efficient government, supported by a safe majority of alert, intelligent voters"; "an absence of unwarranted strikes and slowdowns"; "an adequate supply of people . . . , who have a good work attitude, who are properly educated, . . . and who have a good understanding of how our business system operates"; wage scales that "provide an opportunity for employers to operate profitably"; "community services and facilities . . . needed in operating businesses"; "a social and cultural atmosphere that will attract and hold good employees"; and "business citizenship . . . and courageous leadership in civic and political affairs."[48]

GE hence arrived in Phoenix to launch its new computing scheme, continue its manufacturing diaspora, and escape unions and high taxes. A lucrative 1956 contract to produce machines to handle Bank of America's daily business dealings inaugurated GE's fifteen-year computing foray. Management promised a device able to process fifty-five thousand transactions per day, provide rapid updates to customer accounts, track branches' daily balances, and route checks properly and efficiently. The Electronics Division's head, Vice President "Doc" Baker, predicted that this agreement would enlarge the just-founded, two-person Industrial Computer Section, transform the division into a leader in data processing, and make GE a rival to the established computing giants.[49]

The production facility's location divided GE administrators. The subdivision's manager, Barney Oldfield, considered the short-term contract a first step toward more fruitful possibilities but realized that this initial deal might not generate the revenue to make up for the expense of building a new branch plant. He thus deemed California's budding Silicon Valley the logical choice. After all, GE's Stanford Industrial Park staffers had developed the prototype that clinched the deal. Oldfield reasoned that at least R&D should remain in the Bay Area. GE could lease the necessary space, save the capital for building or renovating new facilities, and then abandon it or give the staff a new project after filling the first contract. He emphasized that competitors, including Hewlett-Packard, thrived in Northern California because, at the time, high-tech manufacturing costs were relatively lower than consumer-durable production. Oldfield also speculated that dollars-and-cents calculations did not capture Palo Alto's competitive advantages. He thought temperate California, with its large existing skilled labor pool, had an immeasurable asset: "It was a bitter cold day in November when we left the Syracuse airport and I still recall the thrill of basking in the warm sunshine when we reached the Stanford campus." "I made a rough calculation of the added cost of fulfilling the . . . contract if the headquarters and manufacturing facility were remote from the development engineering group," Oldfield recounted. "The estimate turned out to be several million dollars. I thought this would tip the scale."[50]

But President Ralph Cordiner, a visible hand in the burgeoning conservative movement, hated the Golden State's business climate. Progressively taxed, well-organized, and well-regulated California rankled his anti-union, free-enterprise politics, which had deepened during battles with the radical United Electrical Workers and continued during negotiations with the International Union of Electrical Workers. Material and ideological concerns informed his and other executives' resistance to expanding Bay Area operations. Bank of America managers wanted GE to manufacture the machines outside California to save an estimated $1.2 million in sales taxes. Schenectady-based site selection experts deemed start-up costs outside California "minimal compared with long term labor savings" based on estimates of operating costs and wage scales. "They were anxious to locate the Computer Department in Nashville, Tennessee because of the low labor costs, the favorable tax rate, and the accessibility to railroad transportation," Oldfield recalled. "We were able to shoot that down on the issue of lack of attractiveness to high grade professional people."[51]

Phoenix represented a compromise. The city was just eight hours by car from Los Angeles and a quick plane ride to San Francisco, a far shorter commute than the long sojourn between the Palo Alto lab and a Tennessee facility. Oldfield deemed the Valley's "way of life . . . generally attractive to professional people, though hardly on a level with the San Francisco Bay Area." Phoenix's business climate satisfied directors. GE's vice president for employee and public relations, Lemuel Ricketts Boulware, stated frankly to Chamber men in 1958: "My Company has chosen Phoenix as the location where the current good business climate can still be improved in a way that will help us make here the important expansion we expect our exciting new Computer Department to undergo in pursuing its obviously great technological and volume potential."[52]

The 1956 decision seemed promising. The Chamber arranged for front-office staff to settle in the downtown building that housed local radio and television stations and helped lease space in Arizona State College's (ASC) new engineering department, which, unlike more established programs elsewhere, had half-empty laboratories and offices. GE had to pour money into these temporary accommodations because the school lacked basic resources. Managers entered into an unwritten agreement to install a state-of-the-art computer, the IBM 704, which also served as the campus's computing center. This deal seemed advantageous to ASC administrators' goals to achieve university status and to GE executives' need for adequate facilities. Engineering faculty and students used the device in the classroom and shared space with students from the business college who took courses on data processing, machine accounting, and business systems analysis. GE used the IBM 704 for its operations but also offered services to area businesses that needed help with bookkeeping yet were unable or uninterested in purchasing their own computers.[53]

GE's investment proved a disaster. Scattershot, piecemeal work did not recoup the outlays for ASC's computing center. A bank paid just $100 for three amortization tables covering twenty years of transactions. School administrators also grew unhappy with the arrangement. University officials had traded space, power, and security for 10 percent of the computer's operating time but calculated that they only took up 1 percent and reported company personnel unwilling, possibly unable, to help with ASC's organizational tasks, such as admissions. Tensions mounted because parties had a gentlemen's agreement, which turned mediation into squabbling over contradictory recollections of past "non-official verbal discussions." Problems continued when GE replaced the IBM 704 with the GE 304 in the early 1960s. Professors considered the device excellent for accounting purposes

Figure 14. The 1956 deal to bring GE's Computing Department to the Phoenix Valley partially hinged on the installation and use of this computer, the IBM 704, at Arizona State College. The gentleman's agreement to share the IBM 704 between professors, administrators, and GE employees, who used empty offices and labs in the recently completed engineering department, broke down in the early 1960s. Courtesy of the University Archives Photographs, Arizona State University Libraries.

but unsuitable for scientific research. Also, computer courses had to be reformulated. Arizona State University (ASU) administrators accepted oral assurances that GE researchers would write new programs and provide training for faculty members, who, a dean reported, "were refused help in programming and in some cases even refused machine time." The deal unraveled after a series of acrimonious summer meetings in 1962. GE left campus offices, removed their computer, and relocated all operations to their manufacturing plant in the Valley. Executives did offer the university a research-suitable GE machine at below cost. ASU could not afford it and instead entered into a written agreement with AiResearch in order to replace the equipment. The firm paid $200,000 a month and guaranteed the university sixty hours of use per month.[54]

GE management considered the move a costly mistake. The venture had seemed promising: the firm fulfilled the first contract's terms with a machine that set the standard for banking technology for roughly forty years. Leaders even invested $3 million into a five-hundred-person Black Canyon Highway plant in 1958. GE secured a few more orders and seemed to be an emerging force in the computer sector just three years later. A director even proclaimed in the mid-1960s: "We like our relationship with Phoenix very much." But GE never became a computing giant. The division, isolated from the sector's Bay Area epicenter, was limited in scope and scale and increasingly served only the firm's accounting needs. A transplanted senior project member blamed this lag on the local labor pool, who lacked "the faintest idea how to use a computer to design another computer, and were too busy doing it by hand to find out." Few Palo Alto technicians had wanted to leave California to pick up the slack. "The staff were not enamored with Phoenix either as a place to visit or work," recalled the Industrial Electronics Division's head. One replant returned to his previous job with IBM within a year. GE abandoned computing after selling operations to the Honeywell Corporation in the early 1970s. "I have tried to imagine what would have happened," Oldfield later reflected, "if the company . . . had permitted us to locate astride what later became Silicon Valley, the home of Apple, Intel, Hewlett-Packard (HP), Beckman Instruments, Sygnetics, and the rest."[55]

Still, GE's arrival had represented a coup for the Phoenix Chamber. This prestigious investment and its early expansion had bolstered the Chamber's business-first ethos. The division's failure illustrates that aggressive recruitment, an expansive corporate-welfare state, and an enticing business climate attracted industrialists, but it also underscores that calculations that privileged profit margins and hard-line political-economic doctrines did not guarantee long-term success.

Sperry Rand

Victory, however, could be assured in the short term through political influence. Politics, for example, figured highly in the 1955 agreement to move the Sperry Rand Corporation's aviation electronics division to Phoenix. Scouts had evaluated potential sites nationwide for a year and narrowed the choice to five. Phoenix may have had an advantage because Snell knew the executives involved. Regardless, boosters labored for months to reach a deal, with negotiations taking place mainly between the Chamber and the corporation. Both the city and the association made formal proposals, after which Sperry CEOs sent their demands to both parties. The list included: elongation of a local airport's runways to accommodate the B-47s Sperry used to transport its products, financial backing for a manufacturing facility, and a repeal of the sales tax on products made in Arizona but sold to the federal government. The Bimsons directed the formal lobbying efforts. A VNB attorney delivered the pitch to the legislature. Carl, then serving as the Chamber's president, persuaded the Arizona Bankers Association to send a lawyer to speak to the legislature and convinced several other financiers to lobby on the bill's behalf during committee meetings. Rainmakers also fundraised among themselves, raising $650,000 in the seventy-two hours preceding vice president Percy Halpert's September site visit. Blue-jacketed, silver-adorned Thunderbirds feted Halpert at the Camelback Inn, where he learned firsthand why Phoenix would satisfy his personnel: he could golf, ride horses, and sunbathe. All the while, his chaperones assured him that the legislature would pass the bill to repeal the sales tax.[56]

Three months later, Sperry executives announced their unanimous decision from their company's New York headquarters. The news came just one day after the legislature approved the changes to Arizona's tax codes. Sperry Phoenix's operations manager enumerated seven key considerations: "Ready availability of land suitable for industrial development and production"; "enthusiastic and cooperative spirit displayed by the community and its leaders"; "excellent residential areas in all economic levels with attractive cultural-recreational facilities"; "growing opportunities for higher education in the physical sciences, electrical engineering and other technical fields"; "proximity to many major aerospace equipment markets, including several key military test areas and the West Coast complex of prime manufacturers"; "availability at reasonable cost of electric power, water, transportation, and other essentials to an electronics research, development, and production activity"; and "availability of adequate electronics-oriented small businesses to permit efficient subcontracting."[57]

The company prospered after operations began in 1957. It completed three plant expansions in just six years, employing about sixteen hundred people by 1963. An executive reported enthusiastically, "The commercial and military aspects of our business have done well here." He was also pleased that Sperry, like Motorola, had been able to recruit "many scientific and engineering people who [have] a definite preference for a Southwest location. . . . The attrition rate has proven to be remarkably low." Expansions, Halpert reassured boosters, were "evidence of our optimistic outlook for the future and of our basic satisfaction with the choice of Phoenix as the center of our aeronautical operations."[58]

Yet the Chamber had struggled to settle the initial arrangement. The rainmakers had comparatively more power over local governance than their proto-Sunbelt counterparts but relatively less influence over the state government. The Arizona GOP's growth had not yet yielded sustained control of the executive branch, nor a legislative majority dedicated to corporate welfare. Republicans' most substantial gains were in urban Tucson and Phoenix, also home to the state's most liberal Democrats, who spent the mid-1950s pursuing new members while purging Jeffersonian Democrats. Representatives from rural areas, which had not yet embraced hyperindustrialization, also had enough votes to stymie booster efforts. The sales-tax change had thus deadlocked the assembly.[59]

Chamber men used all the publicity tools at their disposal to rescind this toll. They begged Arizonans to "make your voices and wishes heard . . . so action will be taken soon to establish the kind of industrial climate which will attract more and more firms." Pulliam editorialists warned, "Arizona's entire economic future may well depend on repeal," and they published subscriber letters that deemed the tax a "vicious" "scheme to have other states' citizens pay our taxes." Newsmen also drew attention to AiResearch and Douglas Aircraft executives, who seemed prepared to call off planned expansions. An eight-hundred-signature CIO petition to repeal the levy was also well covered.[60]

But only liberal governor Ernest McFarland could call the legislature back for a special December 1955 session to settle the issue. The man who had ousted Pyle in 1954 still embraced industrialization but also remained skeptical of, if not hostile to, additional tax cuts for manufacturers and openly opposed additional revenue losses. He still demanded that lawmakers reconsider the proposal: "One large company which contemplates locating in Arizona has indicated it must know by approximately December 15 whether this tax is to be eliminated." "This company," the governor warned, "is of the opinion that it cannot compete with companies in other states where there is no such tax." He was in a quandary: "Our population is growing by leaps and bounds, and we must have additional and new employment," but "real property tax payers should not be required to carry this burden alone." He urged compromise in the form of a use tax, "an equalization of taxes," which "serve[d] a double purpose: the protection of industry in our state and the raising of revenue to take the place of that lost by the repeal of the tax on sales to the federal government."[61]

Gubernatorial Industrial Recruitment

Passage proved politically significant. McFarland's trade-off continued the political pragmatism that had led Carl Hayden to reverse his votes on the right-to-work controversy earlier in the decade. Such concessions paved the way for the next generation of Arizona-based national Democratic Party figures, including Governor Raul Castro (whom Johnson, Nixon, and Carter appointed to various embassies) and Governor Bruce Babbitt (Bill Clinton's secretary of the interior). Both Arizonans embraced the tenets of the business climate economic doctrine and focused their energies on civil rights, environmental, or social policies that did not substantially interfere with business decision making.[62]

The 1955 compromise also intensified boosters' efforts to control the executive branch. Accordingly, Fannin's 1958 gubernatorial campaign was a watershed moment for Arizona's brand of neoliberalism. His win, along with Goldwater's and Rhodes's reelections, inaugurated not a two-party system but the dominance of an enterprise-focused GOP. This southern-born, Phoenix-reared Chamber man had, like his childhood friend Goldwater, repudiated his family's Democratic allegiance. Fannin, however, embraced schooling. He returned to Phoenix after earning a degree in business administration from Stanford in 1930 and made a fortune through the expansion of a propane distribution company. The southwestern gas magnate blended business with politics. As the IDC's first chairman, he championed professional, efficient recruitment, especially through a policy of preemptively buying land for future investors. He also helped refashion the GOP, ran for Goldwater's Senate seat in 1964, and retained his business-first politics once in the Senate.[63]

Fannin championed "American risk capitalism" throughout his political career. He celebrated "the most efficient and democratic economic system man has to live under. Anyone can tell that our economic system is a better one than that of communism, socialism, fascism or any other system once he understands it." Liberals, he warned, had extended and enlarged federal authority "far beyond the limits originally set in the Constitution." His solution: "Take Government out of business by putting business into government." "If businessmen do not take a part in government," Fannin warned in 1964, "government will take business apart." Yet he also considered the state vital for his chief administrative goal, industrialization. "Government," he declared, "should provide a good climate for business and industry since government depends on business revenue for survival."[64]

Like North Carolina's Luther Hodges and Mississippi's Hugh White, Fannin sought to harness executive power in the name of statewide industrialization. He emphasized employment and payroll to sell the citizenry on industry-first diversification. "If we are to continue to grow and prosper," he warned legislators early in his first term, "ways must be found to provide an increasing number of new jobs for our expanding work force." Like Hodges, Fannin rejected the colonial economy: "The most promising field for employment lies in the establishment of new plants and factories compatible with Arizona's unique climate and scenic advantages." Hence education appeared high on the Arizonan's agenda, both to bolster ASU and start a state system of vocational schools and community colleges. Fannin, like Pyle before him, also wanted to streamline and redirect the state's energies to foster investment but, by the late 1950s, he needed to make Arizona competitive with recruitment-focused states that already had booster-controlled bureaucracies. He faced an uncooperative assembly in the late 1950s, when Hodges had already won over North Carolina assemblymen for this cause. Fannin entered office with just one Republican in the twenty-eight-seat Senate and twenty-five in the eighty-seat House. "I soon learned it was impossible to do anything without the support and cooperation of the legislature," Fannin recounted. "If the issue had any partisan overtones, it was like running into a stone wall."[65]

State constitutional appointment provisions also restricted Fannin's power over economic policy. The legislature had created an industrialization department, the Arizona Development Board (ADB), in 1954. The bureau, unlike the aggressive Mississippi, Tennessee, and North Carolina departments, could only create promotions and disseminate statistics. ADB spent just $30,000 on ads in national magazines and eastern newspapers, such as *Newsweek* and the *Wall Street Journal* (Florida dedicated $796,000; North Carolina earmarked $442,000). Each Arizona county nominated three candidates, but the governor chose the representative and the Senate confirmed the appointment. The fourteen members served staggered five-year terms on the board of directors. Even more vexing was Arizona's Industrial Commission (IC). McFarland's four-year tenure had placed several liberals in this venerable division, which since statehood had heard workmen's compensation grievances and generally had acted more on behalf of labor than of corporations. Officeholders' staggered multiyear appointments ensured that Fannin would not be able to appoint a new majority in his first two-year stint. His early attempt to create a separate labor department in order to reorient the IC's aims also failed.[66]

Fannin subsequently fought to increase his gubernatorial authority. He asserted that his personal staff was "too small and too lacking in both variety and extent of experience" for the proper "review and evaluation of existing state programs, the development of new ideas, the study and research necessary for intelligent action, and the initiation of new policies and programs." He complained that policy was left up to "the willingness of various executive and ministerial officers to be supervised." "There is no enforcible [*sic*] requirement," he railed. "They give particular attention to the policy goals of the appointive authority and they may in fact completely ignore such goals." He managed to establish two advisory groups to bring high-tech manufacturers into the statehouse. The Governor's Committee for Industrial Arizona included "40 industrialists many of whom retired from the leading corporations in the country, who act as Ambassadors for Arizona." Fannin named "experts at the executive level" and "industrial development specialists from several . . . banks, utilities and transportation companies" to the Arizona Community Development Advisory Committee (ACDAC). A VNB executive guided these businessmen, who concerned themselves with industrialization through outside capital investment. These consultants forged a new relationship between boosters, manufacturers, and state officials: Governor's Committee members promoted Arizona alongside paid investment scouts, while ACDAC advisers formulated plans to better attract and anchor wealth-producing electronics, computing, and aerospace industries.[67]

Fannin also increased spending in the name of recruitment. Money went to advertising and a detailed report of Arizona's advantages, limitations, and prospects, formulated by the same consultants who advised the Chamber and CGC. But Fannin also earmarked funds for an assistant for industrial development, who did not answer to legislators or agency appointees. Boyd Gibbons Jr. was a logical choice: he was a dedicated, card-carrying Phoenix Chamber man, who privileged "a good business climate and more particularly a receptive community attitude." He reported to Fannin, which generated complaints but nonetheless bypassed opposition from liberals serving in the legislature or in established executive agencies. Gibbons's responsibilities included acting as the secretary to Fannin's advisory groups, selling Arizona communities on the state's modernization program, and traveling the country to recruit industry, in much the same manner as VNB, First National, and Phoenix Chamber representatives and other states' bird dogs. Gibbons spent his five-year stint in dogged pursuit of investment: "Over a hundred thousand miles of travel outside the state and an estimated equal number of miles traveled within the state has brought us in direct contact with new industry prospects, displaying literature, selling our business climate advantages and showing communities in our state that might be potential areas of new plant location." He spent his early months in office meeting with the other sixty-three Arizona chambers to convince members to embrace diversification and overhaul their organizations, as Phoenicians had done in the 1940s to better compete for investment. Gibbons's executive authority proved more efficacious than Haas's voluntarist pleas to foster a more widespread interest in investment. Rural Arizona boosters even considered Gibbons an ally. "Merchants have been rather complacent," the Greenlee Chamber's president vented. "They seem to feel that since our economy depends entirely on the Phelps Dodge Corporation, that the corporation is expected to solve all of the problems. . . . They do not want to offend the corporation," he continued, "so perhaps we could discuss this further after your arrival."[68]

Eagerness helped Gibbons transform the Bisbee association. The former "Queen of the Copper Camps" had rebounded from the Depression after the federal government demanded more ore for the war effort and had survived the postwar slowdown in American copper mining because its deposits of low-grade copper were plentiful and Phelps Dodge had found and extracted lead and zinc in the area. Yet Bisbee had hardly thrived. Phelps Dodge deemed deposits depleted in 1967 and ceased all operations by 1974. Hence Bisbee boosters were receptive to Gibbons's arguments for diversification. The Chamber's general manager assured Gibbons, "Our community is not asleep. We are vitally concerned with what the '60s hold for us and are working toward developing our community facilities and advantages to the utmost so that we have a product that is salable and competitive with other communities in Arizona and the nation." The governor's aide was nonetheless dismayed at the local business association's general disorganization. He recommended that members start a monthly newsletter that included the names of the group's board of directors and utilize the same type of paper, font, and masthead in each issue. Gibbons also advised Bisbee boosters to enlarge their mailing list, create a membership manual, collect data on the community's economy, and publish a brochure to send out to corporations. The general manager thanked Gibbons profusely for his counsel and help. "For the first time in our community's history," he declared in 1960, "we now have a rather complete file of information covering our community which is available to all."[69]

Gibbons's travels outside Arizona were equally important. His first 1959 trip to Los Angeles underscored the limitations of Phoenix's program, no matter how ambitious in scale and scope, and emphasized the need for a larger, statewide initiative. His meeting with a Telecomputing Corporation vice president revealed that Arizona's business climate, while competitive, was not well known. "He sincerely bemoaned," Gibbons reported, "that only recently they had purchased high-priced land in nearby Reseda, California, to build a large plant wherein they were going to consolidate three plants under one roof as an economy move. . . . If he had known the full story of Arizona three months previous to my visit, he intimated that they might have put this operation in Arizona." This experience invigorated Gibbons, who returned with plans for increased promotional spending and more extensive trips. He first headed east in spring 1960 to meet with firms that already supplied Phoenix manufacturers. Fannin considered the expedition a success. Only two of the sixty companies that Gibbons courted eventually established Arizona operations, but he had, nonetheless, been able to widely promote Phoenix and the rest of Arizona.[70]

Unidynamics

Such aggressive recruitment and state assistance for booster organizations brought a Unidynamics branch plant, a division of the Universal Match Company (UMC), to central Arizona. Gibbons used his initial 1959 meeting with the Avondale–Goodyear–Litchfield Park Chamber to promote a carefully managed industrial campaign and introduce himself to receptive local businessmen. He sent numerous follow-up letters beseeching members to create an organization "that will devote its entire activities toward attracting and inviting new businesses." He offered them, on the governor's behalf, "any assistance to you in regard to a new industrial concern." "There are many frustrations and disappointments in work of this kind," he warned, before promising that "eventually one or two new plants will be established, and in your area there is no question about many new industries becoming established." The Chamber's president, after two years of careful consideration of the three communities' ability to attract and sustain investment, requested that Gibbons present a development plan to the rest of the membership. The Chamber man asked pointed questions that fell right in line with the rainmakers' long-held aims, including: "How does one go about securing a diversified industry? What are the proper steps to be taken in order to attract industry to our three Westside Communities[?] How can we Cahmber [*sic*] of Commerce best participate in an Industrial Development Program?"[71]

Gibbons's 1960 trip had also been vital: he had contacted UMC executives in Ferguson, Missouri. Two years later, a CEO called the governor personally to ask him to meet with an industrial scout, whom he identified as "Ben 'X'" of the "'X' Company." The scout was set to arrive in Phoenix that evening. The next morning, the visitor, per Gibbons's notes, had a two-hour breakfast meeting with the aide during which Gibbons gave the firm's representative "a detailed report on the availability of labor, the Arizona State University engineering graduate school program and a summary of economic advantages that Arizona could offer to this particular company. Immediately thereafter, he was given a 3-hour tour of four potential sites; spent two hours at [ASU] interviewing the Dean of the Engineering College and met with President [G. Homer] Durham of the University."[72]

The deal came together rapidly. "Five days later," Gibbons recorded, "a team of three men, all unidentified except for first names, came to Phoenix and specifically surveyed in detail the original four sites and spent several hours with [Gibbons's colleague] concerning recruitment of skilled labor and other facts involved with employment. Ten days later, Mr. [Carl] Gottlieb himself appeared on the scene and a tentative decision was made to narrow down the site selections to two." "At this time, in a meeting with the Governor," Gibbons noted, "Gottlieb identified himself and his company and asked that this be maintained in strictest confidence until a meeting could be held with their board of directors which he hoped would be within the next 90 days, at which time a decision might be made." In the interim, Fannin met with Unidynamics executives and board members. This hands-on approach was a success: six months after the preliminary meeting, UMC announced its Unidynamics division would establish a plant in Litchfield.[73]

Executives credited their decision to Arizona's expansive business climate. The manager of the firm's Phoenix operations stated unequivocally in private correspondence with Fannin, "Our decision to locate in the Valley was primarily based on the vigorous business influence existing in a growing metropolitan area. It is obvious that major companies such as General Electric, Motorola, and others have enjoyed a high degree of success here as a result of the spirit of unity and teamwork which exists among industries." ASU's engineering department was also important to the firm: "These institutions of higher learning have accomplished outstanding academic achievement. We find that a great percentage of college graduates are eager to remain in Arizona, and that climatic conditions and cultural advantages are conducive to attracting scientific and professionally trained personnel to this area." Gibbons's notes also indicate that ASU was a key selling point: "[Visitors] were particularly impressed with the University and its ability to offer graduate courses to the company's 100 engineers expected to be moved to Arizona."[74]

Fannin considered UMC a coup. The deal bolstered boosters' image of Arizona as a "BRAIN-POWER," which further removed the state from its colonial past and also distinguished it from decaying, working-class, smog-filled steel states. Fannin's plant dedication speech celebrated the investment as symbolic of businessmen's governance, which depended on the kind of partnerships that Chamber men had created during Phoenix's rapid industrialization and those collaborations that he, and other industry-minded Sunbelt governors, had sought to foster. Investment, he proclaimed, "was achieved by the management team of a fine national company, in cooperation with the officials of our state, county, and several city governments, augmented by the untiring efforts of many local private citizens involved in architecture, construction, finance, and services." Fannin was "proud of the record that Arizona is making as a frontier state in the West, experiencing the rebirth of capitalism within the framework of constitutional provisions that literally guarantee industry against discriminatory state taxes." He added that "In Arizona we have found a way for government—Federal,

State, and Local—to cooperate and associate with profit motive enterprise, without *dominating* it nor deterring from its main purpose of ever-expanding growth and providing the resultant jobs for our people." This balance was imperative because "state and local governments have a duty to impress upon our citizens that the United States is a business nation and that only private enterprise and profit motive can truly supply productive jobs for the people."[75]

Yet Fannin's words belied the resistance that he had encountered. Like Phoenix-focused boosters, the governor and his aide did not reach a deal with every potential investor. Fierce competition, for example, frustrated Gibbon's ability to lure a pants manufacturer, already in negotiations with Utah promoters, to Flagstaff. The governor also struggled to gain control over executive bureaucracies, like the IC but also the Arizona State Tax Commission and Arizona Corporation Commission, throughout his years in office. His machinations and personal advisers rankled liberal legislators and previous appointees, who in turn alarmed small businessmen. One entrepreneur worried that unionists and liberals could retake the executive branch and wanted assurances that "a czardom, with whomever [*sic*] is governor as czar, will not be thrust on the economy of Arizona" because "all of these agencies are formed in effect to protect the general public." He also denounced "the great bulk" of Fannin's agencies as "individually the creation and the well-loved children of particular industries and areas of free enterprise." Fannin staffers were dismissive of these protests: "Who in hell wants to believe that the half-baked [Junior Chamber] organization is absolutely right[?]"[76]

Despite these annoyances, Gibbons and Fannin still looked back on their tenure with pride. The administration counted itself responsible for roughly 275 new investments, more than half of which went to Maricopa County. The most notable among the fifteen largest plant openings were Unidynamics, the Emerson Electric Manufacturing Company, the Henry Winston Minerals Company, the Safford Manufacturing Company, a division of Form Mills, Yolande of New York, and the Henry I. Siegel Company. Fannin subsequently declared his terms as governor a success when he left office because Arizona's "business-minded" citizens, its moratoriums on "discriminatory State taxes" against industry, labor codes, and its advanced educational programs were "assurances that industry in our State is WELCOME, WANTED AND NEEDED." Accordingly, he continued, "This rapidly growing, pioneering frontier Western State is setting an example for other states and governments to follow."[77]

The Office Space Initiative

Phoenix in fact continued to be a leader when services and finance replaced manufacturing as the national economy's largest and most dynamic sectors. Such industries were largely responsible for the Southwest's postindustrial dynamism and the South's full transformation. Even the celebrated Atlanta–Cobb County area never became a diversified juggernaut until the metropolitan region became an epicenter of the postmanufacturing economy in the 1980s. Decades after the airplane factory reopened, the list of Cobb County's largest employers included just thirty manufacturers. High-tech investment had come to the area: most of the area's ninety-six firms, which included aerospace, computing, electronics, energy, health, instrumentation, pharmaceuticals, software, and telecommunications, employed far fewer than 150 workers each and generated less than $50 million in revenue. Cobb's biggest electronics producer, computing giant Hewlett-Packard, was the exception. The company employed more than four hundred workers, had more than $50 million in sales, and relied on more than forty small software spin-offs, together representing by far the largest high-tech investment subgroup. But Marietta was really a service center: 112 major employers belonged to the nonmanufacturing sectors, including retail, distribution, food, leisure, health, and public services; employment at the Six Flags over Georgia amusement park dwarfed all but Lockheed-Martin's roster. Marietta also won lucrative headquarters' deals, including a shared main office and service-training center for Volkswagen of America and Porsche Audi in the early 1980s.[78]

Phoenix too became a service city. The "headquarters city of the Southwest" emerged from the same kind of business climate and aggressive corporate relocation campaigns that had already industrialized the area. Service sector investment fitted within the Chamber's broad diversification scheme. Front offices did not represent a real challenge to Phoenix's arid environment because these businesses did not strain water supplies any more than new subdivisions did. High-rise office buildings also matched the Chamber's vision of Phoenix as an up-and-coming metropolis. This workspace initiative allowed boosters to pursue heavy manufacturers because their

CEOs kept their smokestacks and factories out of the Valley, which left the landscape relatively pristine and at the time ensured that only a firm's well-off, educated, largely Anglo managerial workforce would come to central Arizona. Members of the Chamber would even rely on the oft-repeated themes of trickle-down investment to justify prioritizing the higher-wage service sector: "Every additional 100 square feet of office space leased means another wage earner paying taxes, buying goods and services and generally contributing to our Valley's economy."[79]

The decision by U-Haul executives to move from Nevada to Arizona in 1967 spurred the Chamber to court similar ventures. The 750 workers in the new Phoenix offices managed more than ten thousand rental sites and more than 275,000 trucks and trailers, which have displayed Arizona license plates ever since. Two other smaller regional corporations finalized deals within the year, which inspired the Chamber's leadership to form the Office Building Committee. Old veterans from wartime reorganization and postwar recruitment campaigns jumpstarted this task force. Their aims were just as high: "(a) fill any space that is vacant and (b) create a need for new space." Boosters continued to rely on researching needs, refashioning the law, and aggressively pursuing investment. Committee members inventoried Phoenix's office space and generated reports on availability, cost, and location for interested firms. The Chamber appraisals included contact information for different properties as well as a list of already established headquarters in the Phoenix area. Members also monitored what other cities had done to attract such firms and doggedly pursued investors. The task force then investigated the necessary revisions to commercial real estate taxes, zoning ordnances, and regulations that would transform Phoenix's climate into one suitable for corporate headquarters.[80]

Boosters employed the same recruitment techniques. Banking and utility representatives feted Greyhound Corporation executives and lobbied the legislature to ensure that the firm's specific needs were met. The deal hinged on a revision to the state income tax law that exempted dividends from out-of-state subsidiaries paid to a parent corporation in Arizona. This bill, like the one that clinched the Sperry deal, represented a significant savings for Greyhound, which had grown in the 1960s from a small bus company with just two subsidiaries into one of the nation's thirty largest industrial firms with almost 150 divisions in transportation, food, finance, and other service fields. The firm had nearly seventy thousand employees and more than $3 billion in sales in the 1969–1970 fiscal year. The Chamber's subgroup concerned with legislation, then called the Business and Government Division, pressured state legislators to introduce the bill and spent the first session of 1971 lobbying for passage. The Chamber's work continued after legislative approval. Fourteen members spent the spring in Chicago to help employees and their families with relocation. A total of six hundred families—1,167 adults and 880 children—moved to Phoenix.[81]

This deal represented a major victory for the Chamber's new corporate headquarters' initiative. Boosters estimated that Greyhound would bring an additional $15 to $20 million to the Phoenix Valley in new home sales alone. Executives were also pleased. "Chicago is a good business city," a CEO explained in a 1971 relocation announcement, "but Phoenix offers us a substantial reduction in expenses—wages, rentals, communications." Management moved to Phoenix the Greyhound Corporation (its largest subsidiary), Armour and Company, Greyhound Bus Lines, Greyhound Leasing and Finance Corporation, and all but the service center personnel in the Greyhound Computer Corporation. Staff occupied almost all of a new $10 million, twenty-story downtown office building.[82]

Chamber men nurtured this postindustrial Phoenix. They settled agreements with American Express and Prudential Life Insurance roughly a year after U-Haul moved. Real growth came in the 1970s and 1980s. In 1975, 31,900 Maricopa County residents worked in fewer than two thousand finance, real estate, or insurance businesses. Another 81,900 worked in the private service sector, which encompassed almost sixty-five hundred different establishments. By June 1989, 73,400 people worked in nearly six thousand finance, real estate, and insurance firms. More than 250,000 worked in the private service sector in more than eighteen thousand individual businesses. Employment statistics underscored the Valley's next diversification phase. The state of Arizona still employed the most residents in 1989 (twenty-three thousand) but Motorola was a close second with twenty-one thousand employees. The city, county, and federal governments also appeared on the list of top employers, alongside Allied-Signal Aerospace Company, McDonnell Douglas Helicopter Company, Honeywell, and Intel. A number of firms headquartered in the Valley rounded out the list, including: Smitty's Super Valu Incorporated (5,980), American Express Travel (5,900), America West Airlines (5,762), AT&T (4,375), the Circle K Corporation (3,000), and the Marriott Corporation (2,950).[83]

Chamber men had thus created an industrial and service metropole out of a colonial outpost. Collaboration with local and state governments enabled Phoenix businessmen to deploy a remarkable amount of money, time, and political influence to draw industries into the Valley. Their success hinged on a sizable degree of public funds and private reserves to disseminate publications and dispatch recruiters across the country. Efforts to retain Motorola, land the Sperry deal, convince GE to stage its computer operations in Phoenix, develop the Arizona hinterland, and transfer large portions of Greyhound to the Valley show that much more than air conditioning went into making this desert miracle. The city's growth had not simply happened but was a part of a systematic effort to remake the region and the national economy, and to reorient American politics toward an underlying principle that the government and the citizenry should be working in the interest of business profitability, mobility, and expansion.

Chapter 9

The Conspicuous Grasstops

"Arizonans have been denying their paternity," radical journalist Andrew Kopkind asserted in 1965. "According to the dominant myth, Phoenix rose from the desert by a mystical exercise of frontier spirit and Christian capitalism, unhindered by government." But "Phoenix is no paradise," he emphasized to *New Republic* readers. "The contrast between the Southside and the affluent new Phoenix on the other side (literally) of the tracks . . . is wide. *Apartheid* is complete." "Phoenix finds that it does not have the tools," Kopkind continued, "in terms of attitudes and instruments—to deal with its affairs. It is at the mercy of its own myths."[1]

Kopkind's account was tailor-made for the weekly's liberal subscribers, the type of readers horrified by Barry Goldwater's presidential run just one year before. But many Americans had already encountered a very different story about modern Phoenix. Numerous journalists, particularly in business periodicals, waxed rhapsodically about the Valley of the Sun's development, leadership, and politics. They offered laudatory accounts of grasstops' reclamation of agricultural fields, shop floors, and local governments across the South and Southwest. In fact, celebrations of business climate industrialization permeated print culture, largely through announcements for new plant openings, articles on industrial growth, and Chamber advertisements for new investments. This material, moreover, drew attention to the partnerships between high-ranking business conservatives and regional economic elites, whose ever-strengthening ties to top industrialists transformed them into supporters of, spokesmen for, and leaders of the growing conservative movement. This good press, in turn, promoted capital flight, boosterism, and sprawl—but also the ability of these businessmen to dismantle the New Deal order.

The Phoenix Chamber's increasing prestige exemplified the critical, discernible role of such peripheral boosters to the fundamental transformation of American capitalism. Growth propelled the city and its rainmakers into the national spotlight. Journalists extolled the city's virtues, marveled at its development, and spotlighted the more colorful Chamber men throughout the 1950s. Rainmakers carefully shaped their public image as cowboy conservatives, who tamed the desert with free-enterprise values yet also wrapped themselves in the mantle of individual entrepreneurship, even as large conglomerates generally underwrote the Valley's metamorphosis. Few writers questioned boosters' assertions or policies, which in effect gave the Chamber elite a pulpit to help redefine the entire West as a frontier for rugged individuals who challenged the liberal establishment, not a land of great inequality where radicals, laborites, and New Dealers had once forged a tenuous Popular Front. This renown reinforced rainmaker connections with the cohort of national businessmen at the helm of the conservative movement, who now touted Phoenix outside Arizona to increase pressure on other municipalities desperate to attract or keep industry. Phoenix, in short, became a model metropolis, the envy of investment-hungry civic leaders across the country and a gateway for a remarkable number of Arizonans, who moved into leading roles in national business circles and political networks.

This arid incubator of neoliberalism thus complicates much of the recent scholarship on the modern Right. Much of the literature on 1970s conservatism lavishes attention on free-market, antigovernment ideology of that decade. These histories too often downplay or ignore the rich history of this worldview that can be found in the developing Sunbelt. Moreover, the discourse of economic development, urban boosterism, and good governance that evolved out of discussions in this region's business associations proved as vibrant and influential as the tax policy innovations and regulatory reforms that scholars such David Harvey, Geoffrey Hodgson, and Kim Phillips-Fein have identified as the distinctive product of postwar think tanks, faculty clubs, and Gotham's corporate headquarters.[2]

Scholars and journalists have also misidentified the South as the preeminent crucible of modern conservatism. The Northeast certainly had its share of right-wing firebrands, as did the West. But the arid states have largely been ignored as the breeding grounds for antiliberal insurgencies. True, the South had far more representatives in Congress and votes in the Electoral College than the Southwest. Moreover, as many books and newspapers stress, Democrats tried to keep their party together by balancing presidential tickets with Southerners in the postwar period. Yet few have noted that Republicans also struggled to paper over the prominent territorial divides in their fractured GOP, evidenced in part by the Sunbelt Westerners filling out the party's slates. Two, Goldwater and John McCain, even called Phoenix home.[3]

Such grasstops candidates indicate that regional transformation and national political change had their origins in urban areas, not the rural South. Political scientists have calculated that a southern congressional veto certainly limited liberalism between 1933 and 1952, but agrarian representatives nonetheless voted for much of the New Deal's original labor and welfare provisions because this legislation did not unduly intrude upon the southern economic order or protect agricultural and domestic workers. Southern support for economic liberalism faltered during World War II, when unions seemed poised to upset the regional status quo. New research on the South in these formative years and after have shown that the territory's urban boosters, like their Phoenix counterparts, challenged liberal regulatory doctrine before, during, and after the planter caste's about-face. The most sustained, successful assaults on the New Deal state occurred in the postwar period, when investment-focused promoters, industry-tied urbanites from the manufacturing core, and even some commodity-beholden agrarians aggressively pursued conservative business climate policies. These intraregional allies did not so much guarantee a continued disparity between production strongholds and emergent metropolises but instead spawned a transregional, observable, competitive ethos, which made insecurity, instability, and inequality the national rule, not a sectional exception. The resultant investment in the South and Southwest and divestment in the Steelbelt and along the urban Pacific Coast thus wrought the suburban growth, white flight, and metropolitan conflict over schools, housing, and taxation, fights that underlay the Right's post-1968 suburban maturation.[4]

Phoenix Spotlighted

Phoenix and its southwestern sister cities had in fact outshone their southern competitors even before Kevin Phillips published *The Emerging Republican Majority*. Charlotte, North Carolina, for example, could never quite shake a reputation for southern provincialism despite its rapid growth in the postwar decades. Boosters described their city as the "Industrial Center of the Carolinas" during World War II and later deemed it "one of the great trading centers of the Southeast" and "a cosmopolitan society which enjoys a healthy balance between time-honored traditionalism and modern progressivism." *Business Week* profiles in 1949 and 1951 highlighted the town's economic diversification, particularly the move away from textiles. Journalists all but repeated the association's proclamation that Charlotte was "unsouthern, untypical" because the new white-collar residents had "dilut[ed] southern provincialism with cosmopolitan flavor." Nevertheless, reporters still noted that Charlotte lacked a "decent auditorium," a "really good" eatery, and noteworthy nightlife. Backhanded compliments plagued the Queen City for decades, even as journalists celebrated Phoenix and other western Sunbelt cities as being at the frontier of advanced manufacturing and urban sophistication. Charlotte finally emerged as a nationally respected center of banking and distribution in the 1980s and 1990s, decades after the city's rapid growth had begun.[5]

Phoenix, in contrast, had basked in celebratory coverage since the 1940s. Milton MacKaye called it "Palm Beach, Red Gap and Mr. Babbitt's Zenith all rolled into one" in a 1947 *Saturday Evening Post* report. Though he lavished praise on agricultural harvests, rugged mesas, and breathtaking deserts, rapid urbanization impressed him the most: once "this townsite had on it only one building, a crude one-story adobe," now "Phoenix has modern department stores and fashionable shops. . . . In merchandising and in prices, Phoenix is hard to distinguish from New York, Miami and Los Angeles."[6]

George Henhoeffer, *Business Week*'s Phoenix-based correspondent, reported dynamism emblematic of modern Phoenix five years later. He pinpointed the 1881 O.K. Corral shoot-out as the end of Arizona's "gun-slinging, hell-for-leather adolescence. . . . Wyatt Earp opened the trail for new men with visions of building powerful economic empires that were to become instrumental in the blossoming of the nation's youngest state." Henhoeffer went on to laud Phoenix boosters, not marshals, for attracting 120 new investors, adding ten thousand new job opportunities, and enlarging the annual payroll by more than $30 million in just four years. The journalist also congratulated voters for doing everything possible "to turn their sandy ranges into green fields for the out-of-state manufacturer."[7]

The venerable *Wall Street Journal* took note of Phoenix and the state's rapid transformation in its March 1953 "Arizona Survey." Staffers dedicated more than two pages to dude ranches, mines, cotton fields, saddle shops, and squaw dress designers but still emphasized the growing aircraft industry, the expanding readership of *Arizona Highways*, and Valley National Bank's (VNB) impressive reserves. Nascent sectors, including the fashion industry, also impressed writers. "Take one authentic Indian squaw dress. Redesign it to give it fullness and flair," one reporter gushed, "and you've got the frock that single-handedly pushed resort wear into Arizona's industrial big time." Seven hundred and fifty workers employed in forty firms produced about $4 million worth of clothes, which, the journalist explained, "aren't exact copies of actual Indian clothes." "We've redesigned the squaw dress," a clothier expounded. "[Indian women] just cut a hole in a piece of cloth and sew it up along the sides like a sack. On them it looks good, but American women insist on dresses that fit." The manufacturing present nonetheless dominated the spread. A reporter posited that industrial workers best represented modern Phoenix but still lavished the most attention on CEOs, who went on the record to proclaim Arizona's two climates boons to themselves and their workforces.[8]

Phoenix's prominence only increased. "Phoenix has the sun in the morning and the moon at night. And it's oh, so easy to love," *Good Housekeeping* told readers. *Holiday Magazine* called it the "sunniest city in the U.S.A. . . . Perfect for whatever outdoor activity a family wants." The tamed, air-conditioned desert fascinated others. "Arizona by and large has none of its past to bury," *Business Week* claimed in 1956. "It doesn't have a rank of slum apartments and lofts. It doesn't even have much of a legacy of race feeling." The *Saturday Evening Post*'s Harold Martin celebrated the neighborhoods that Kopkind later found so repulsive. "In all directions sprawl the mushrooming suburbs," Martin enthused in 1961. "Beyond the great hump of Camelback Mountain sits . . . a fabulous spa set down in the middle of the desert." "Less spectacular to the eye, but as productive of great wealth, is the steel fabricating plant," he raved, "manufacturing a new type of cotton-harvesting machine, and the fine new factory . . . build[ing] $15,000,000 worth of air conditioners every year." He quoted VNB's Herbert Leggett to extol the conquered Valley's virtues: "I awaken in my air-conditioned home in the morning. I take a dip in my swimming pool. I dress and get into my air-conditioned automobile and drive to the air-conditioned garage in the basement of this building. I work in an air-conditioned office, eat in an air-conditioned restaurant and perhaps go to an air-conditioned theater."[9]

Phoenix boosters and their Sunbelt rivals often touted cooling systems to reporters even though such comforts remained scarcer than their words suggested. Central air was just too expensive, and window unit prices had only dropped in the 1940s. In the 1950s, then, central air was rarely found outside high-tech plants, lucrative enterprises, and expensive new homes. Usage increased after the Federal Housing Authority (FHA) began to cover the cost in new homes in 1957 (though many Phoenix builders relied on ineffective box units when constructing less affluent subdivisions). But only two-thirds of Arizona homes had any kind of climate control device, and only one-third had sought-after central-air systems by 1970.[10]

Indeed, air conditioning had actually comforted few who moved into the urbanizing South and Southwest in the postwar period (much less those who stayed in or relocated to the more rural parts). There had been a noticeable increase in some kind climate control in homes and factories during the 1950s. Use increased in the 1960s. Yet a decade later the presence of any type of climate control device ranged from 75 percent in metropolitan California to 47 percent in urban and suburban Georgia. Far fewer residents had the celebrated air systems that many journalists and scholars credited with the growth of these cities. Less than a third of households in the urban Sunbelt had this amenity. Even in metro Georgia, Florida, and North Carolina fewer than 25 percent of homes had central air.[11]

Journalists also took boosters at their word when promoters credited their success to a modern form of rugged western individualism. "I'm not riding on anyone's coattails," David Prouty told *Better Homes and Gardens.* "If I do something, it's my triumph. If I fail, it's my failure. I'm a lot more of an *individual*. . . . I work about twice as hard in Arizona because I want to," he continued: "back in the East, everything is defined for you. Here the whole place is growing, expanding, and there's no limit." Likewise, the *Saturday Evening Post*'s Martin considered Phoenix emblematic of entrepreneurial possibility, not white-collar, bureaucratic corporate investment. He reported that none of the city's newly arrived millionaires "had any resources except their wits" and seemed to embody the modern promise of western opportunity. "The migration that began just after the war was something different," he proclaimed. "They were young and strong and broke and restless, and fired with the same westering spirit that had sent the covered wagons across the plains a hundred years ago, . . . not moving in little frog-hops from a city apartment to a house in the suburbs . . . [but moving] across a continent, tearing up old deep-grown roots, abandoning the social and economic patterns of the older settled areas to make a new life for themselves . . . in a vast empty land where it didn't matter who a man's family was, or how much money he had, or what school he'd gone to—or whether he'd gone to school at all."[12]

Rainmakers greatly influenced these admiring accounts of the city and its business climate. Boosters put up or, at the very least, feted visiting journalists, which often paid off handsomely. A *Holiday* reporter spent a month in Phoenix with an area freelance photographer, the *Arizona Republic* staff, and the Chamber's leadership. The celebratory six-page 1953 spread would have cost $40,000 as an ad. Boosters likewise arranged three weeks of meetings with CEOs, bankers, and policymakers for *Wall Street Journal* writers. *Business Week* gave Henhoeffer no authorial credit for his profile on Phoenix, but the Chamber men did in the pages of *Phoenix Action!* The writer had relied on interviews with promoters and the organization's picture file for his piece. The association was more than delighted to report that members had received a dozen inquiries from interested businesses, including a large commercial refrigeration and cold storage firm, after Henhoeffer's article appeared.[13]

Phoenix's well-crafted image proved the envy of other Sunbelt boosters. In 1956, *Abilene Reporter News* editors urged Texans to model themselves after the Phoenicians: "You could search the earth without finding a spot less suited for the building of a city and the development of industrial and commercial interests of great power and scope than Phoenix." "The human factor," not air conditioning, Abilene writers asserted, "started the wheels turning and has kept them spinning. . . . Abilene has every advantage that Phoenix has and in more abundance. See to it that our leaders seize on the vision and never let it wane."[14]

Such coverage influenced rivals' desire to mimic the Phoenix Chamber's programs. "El Paso does nothing to get new industries," a booster lamented in the early 1960s. "Instead of luring them with special tax deals, we're likely to push them away by throwing all kinds of problems at them. Zoning, water, things like that. Problems that could be easily overcome if we wanted them to." He envied Valley counterparts who could introduce industrial scouts to the Goldwater family, promise them land, and guarantee them support because they had an "electorate willing to approve $209 million in business-backed bond issues in two years." He complained that "El Paso has already lost its spot as the number-one city in the Southwest. Unless we start hustling after new industry, we're going to wind up in serious trouble." "I hate to express it publicly," an El Paso bank president confided, "but it's true that our leadership has been sort of mediocre. We didn't have the influx of well-educated people in the industrial and commercial world. Phoenix did." Another El Pasoan admitted, "We haven't always done a selling job of what we've got. Phoenix has done a better job."[15]

California Chamber men also envied their Phoenix counterparts. The Golden State stood for everything that many business owners and executives, such as General Electric's (GE) Ralph Cordiner, despised about doing business in modern America. California continued to prosper, but neighboring states, and Phoenix in particular, had lured a significant share of California's existing and potential industry away. Eighty thousand jobs in metropolitan Los Angeles's once robust aircraft industry evaporated between 1957 and 1963, leaving the unemployed to seek work elsewhere or move into the burgeoning missile sector. Business organizations viewed such figures as proof that their interwar competitive edge was lost. Golden State associations subsequently sought advice from their Arizona rivals. The industrial commercial coordinator for San Bernardino asked to meet with Boyd Gibbons personally in 1963: "California does not have the best business climate desired by industry. We would consider this trip very beneficial and at some later date maybe legislation could be introduced at our own State Capitol."[16]

San Diego Chamber men proved especially reactive. Their city depended on defense, with such work often reaching 70 percent of the county's manufacturing employment between 1950 and 1963. Job growth had increased 276 percent during this period, with the largest gains in electrical machinery (733 percent) and aircraft parts (418 percent). This success bred complacency. By the mid-1950s, the Chamber's Industrial Development Committee's roster had declined substantially from its earlier 130-person contingent, a figure then in line with the promoter totals for the aggressive Los Angeles and San Francisco associations. The aerospace industry's slow disappearance alarmed San Diego businessmen. In a 1957 program of action, boosters decried their being "subject to the fortunes of the aircraft industry and shifting sands of government defense spending." Two years later, they undertook a systematic, five-year initiative because aircraft production and total manufacturing employment had continued to decline. Industrial diversification into consumer products and various service sectors underwrote their plans to improve investor assistance, "sell all of San Diego County," "establish closer working relationships with existing industries," and "support city and county general planning" because "future industrial growth and planning cannot be divorced." They initially resisted "'give-away' concessions" but found themselves "continually pressed for increased promotional effort, more positive community support and businesslike handling of the needs of new industry." To compete, the Steering Committee created the Traveling Industrial Drummers in 1961 (an itinerant, well-trained contingent similar to Mississippi "bird dogs"), pursued building an industrial development corporation in 1962 (an enterprise analogous to Philadelphia's public-private investment-focused organization), and later created the "Key Men," who, like the Phoenix Thunderbirds, feted visiting scouts. The San Diego grass-tops also visited Philadelphia, Atlanta, and Phoenix Chambers to observe their initiatives. "The businessman's approach to economic development," the head of the San Diego group's Industrial Department remarked after his 1963 trip to Phoenix, "is surely one to be commended. We were thoroughly impressed with what you gave us and everyone we talked with the rest of the day was also impressed with this businessman's approach in [*sic*] attracting industry to the State of Arizona."[17]

Spotlighted Phoenicians

Phoenix Chamber men also frequently received individual recognition. Journalists and financiers, for example, regarded Walter Bimson as a maverick. He had earned their admiration: VNB was the nation's 557th-largest firm in 1933. When Bank of America's Amadeo Peter Giannini died in 1949, VNB was the Rocky Mountain West's most substantial institution and the country's seventy-sixth-biggest bank. Expansion resulted from Bimson's "people's bank" philosophy, which allowed pragmatic acceptance of federal moneys to underwrite what Bimson deemed "the instruments of democratic process," including small checking accounts, consumer credit lines, and installment loans for home improvements, used cars, and other relatively small purchases. VNB's prominence increased as these initiatives and its booster policies became standard. Texas financiers even lauded the firm's newsletter as "one of the better monthly reviews," which "has been quite influential in attracting new businesses to the area." Bimson's postwar influence expanded with his firm. He directed the Los Angeles branch of the Federal Reserve Bank of San Francisco, served on the American Bankers Association's Small Business Commission, and joined the Department of Commerce's Business Advisory Committee.[18]

These positions enabled him to better attack financial regulation. His continued opposition separated him from Giannini and Marriner Eccles. Bimson, in contrast to the western bankers who had influenced the New Deal, publicly defamed liberalism with rhetoric honed while he boosted for Phoenix. He had no "patience whatsoever with those who would discard a proven and successful system and attempt to make America over along lines that have failed again and again." He downplayed reconversion statecraft, instead congratulating "the American businessman," who "constructed new plants, re-equipped his factories with new machines, built millions of new homes, poured out an endless stream of cars, radios, [and] refrigerators." New living standards, he asserted in the nascent language at the heart of the mid-century conservative movement, resulted from the "system of democratic capitalism and individual freedom."[19]

Bimson's Phoenix-based struggle against taxes and redistribution informed his later national crusades. He demanded that Congress end levies on dividends and limit the federal personal income tax to at most 50 percent. He also campaigned against federal aid and subsidies for small business in the late 1940s. Bimson, despite his efforts to lure large manufacturers to Phoenix, considered modest enterprises vital to economic diversification, upward mobility, and political stability. He observed that financiers were not providing sufficient funds for small businesses, which Bimson predicted would necessitate federal intervention, thus endangering his brand of capitalism. He maintained the general spirit of his early experiments for a private New Deal by championing private capital to start and buoy small firms. He wanted local banks to make federally guaranteed loans without government supervision because he theorized that local oversight would reduce paperwork, limit the references needed, and circumvent drawn-out, expensive long-distance communications.[20]

Bimson found few supporters among the nation's elite banking circles. He first touted his plan while serving in the secretary of commerce's twenty-four-person advisory group to the Senate Committee on Banking and Currency. Appointees disagreed on the scheme's finer points yet shared Bimson's commitment to small business. Their proposal ended taxes on corporate dividends to spur investment and created an agency that guaranteed loans without utilizing federal funds. Bimson personally lobbied Philadelphia, Chicago, and New York capitalists for a $10-million start-up fund in order to demonstrate the proposal's feasibility. All refused to participate. They agreed in principle but nonetheless considered their existing expenditures sufficient. Rejection compelled Bimson to ask the Treasury Department, Federal Reserve Board, Federal Deposit Insurance Corporation, and FHA for a loan with interest. He also appeared before the Senate Committee on Banking and Currency to lobby for the legislation and assure concerned members that the plan did not represent a step toward socialism. The measure never appeared before the full Senate. Moreover, the actual Small Business Administration (SBA), established under the 1953 Small Business Act, contradicted Bimson's preferred program. SBA acted as a direct lender, not an inert backer. Officials could advance $150,000 in individual loans and $100 million to bid on federal contracts, which they could subcontract out to smaller firms.[21]

This failure did not slow Bimson's ascent into American banking's upper echelon. Entrepreneurs, financiers, and executives came to champion his ideas just twenty years after his Harris Trust employers had ridiculed his plans for a people's bank. One banker thanked him "for going ahead in the face of criticism" and "ma[king] a substantial contribution, not only to banking, but to the economy by your thoughts." Bimson's invitations to speak also increased. American Airlines executives heard Bimson call well-informed businessmen a powerful deterrent against another depression in 1957. A "brilliant business genius" could not "take off into the wild blue yonder," Bimson warned Alaskan bankers that same year, because successful ventures "involve[d] lawyers, accountants, tax experts, business engineers, market research." He advocated that the assembled financiers follow his example and "be the leader of every worthy community project."[22]

The younger Bimson's reputation likewise increased. Carl ceased promoting FHA Title I loans but remained active with local groups, such as the Phoenix Chamber and the Arizona Bankers Association, published celebratory accounts of VNB, and spoke before business groups. He often promoted easier consumer credit as sound business, exemplary boosterism, and good politics. He, for example, conflated the firm's installment loan program with Phoenix's recovery in a 1945 issue of *The Burroughs Clearing House*. The *Christian Science Monitor* published his 1956 "Formula for Frontier Financing," in which he recounted how Walter had transformed VNB into a "public service" for development, which ensured that "Arizona offers [industry] a rare combination of skilled labor, dry climate, many tax free advantages, plenty of working space and the utmost of cooperation from banks and public officials." He also pushed local financiers to "muster the economic power of his business behind causes, activities, and organizations designed to improve the efficiency of government and the climate of business." He even offered the inside story of the lobbying efforts behind the Sperry tax deal to stress, as he did to the Ohio Bankers Association in 1960, that businessmen represented "the best hope for stopping the present political drift toward a government-controlled economy."[23]

Prominence gave Walter new leadership opportunities. He directed the National Retail Credit Men's Association in the mid-1940s, held high-ranking positions in the Financial Public Relations Association throughout the 1950s, and served on the U.S. Chamber of Commerce's Finance Committee (and chaired its Sub-committee on Credit Unions) in the late 1950s. The American Bankers Association's president requested Bimson to head its Installment Credit Commission in 1955, which made him a member of the Executive Council and Credit Policy Committee. Five years later, ABA convention delegates elected him president.[24]

Top managers represented the Bimsons in person when travel and membership obligations prevented them from appearing before interested audiences. Employees went west to California and east to the South, Northeast, and Midwest. Vice president James Patrick traveled, in the late 1960s alone, to San Francisco, Houston, Dallas, St. Louis, Atlanta, Chicago, and Shelbyville, Indiana, where he urged his hometown's boosters to emulate the Phoenix Chamber.[25]

The Bimsons' gospel also appeared in their employees' writings. VNB's Research Department head, Herbert Leggett, the self-styled 1943 "refugee from Wall Street" who had waxed rhapsodic about central air to reporters, wrote and edited most of the widely circulated *Arizona Progress* during its first sixteen years of publication. "New industries create new jobs, new taxable wealth and new sources of local income," he enthused. Charts depicting rising taxes appeared alongside endorsements of reduced manufacturing levies and warnings that "voters (as well as non-voters) have only themselves to blame" for higher duties. Leggett also kept tabs on GOP affairs, celebrated the steady rise in Republican registration, and openly criticized liberal Democrats.[26]

The local and national prominence of VNB and Walter Bimson generated journalistic interest in both. Through interviews Bimson was able to craft an image of himself as a bold rule breaker and to establish VNB's reputation as an agent for free-enterprise politics. For example, Keith Monroe's 1940 celebratory profile in *American Magazine*, "Bank Knight in Arizona," praised Bimson for "sen[ding] emissaries all over the country to bring new businesses, army bases, flying schools, branch factories, government housing, and other wealth-producing operations into the desert . . . [and for] laying vast, finely detailed plans to make Arizona bloom in the postwar period as never before." "All of which is unorthodox banking," Monroe observed, "but profitable." He also extolled "people's bank" credit policies even though other financiers deemed these loans "undignified," "unprofitable," and "immoral." "Immoral to show a couple how they can afford to have a baby?" Bimson asked Monroe during questioning. "Immoral to get a man started in a business of his own? Nonsense."[27]

Bimson later styled himself as a kind of metropolitan cowboy, one very much at home in the reclaimed frontier that fellow Chamber men offered in promotional literature. The *Saturday Evening Post*'s Neil Clark, for example, let Bimson speak for himself in a 1954 profile that offered readers a populist banker dedicated to individual opportunity, not corporate investment. "People must always have the chance to go freely into business for themselves, to succeed or fail, and if they fail, to try again," the financier explained. "I like to see mobs of people around tellers' cages and officers' desks, not just depositing dribbles so we can send gobs to millionaires, but making use, themselves[,] of every banking service." The increasingly famous financier even described himself and his 1933 move to Phoenix as simply "brash," a word well within the Phoenix Chamber's lexicon to describe themselves, their industrialization initiatives, and their political campaigns.[28]

Visible Partnerships

Such publicity strengthened the reciprocal alliances between city businessmen, like the Bimsons, and outside executives to ease capital migration, advance the conservative movement within the GOP, and further dismantle the New Deal order. These partnerships had an obvious impact at the local level. GE chairman Ralph Cordiner campaigned for Congressman John Rhodes in 1956 and decried the labor movement's attempt to repeal the right-to-work law. He stated bluntly that GE would never invest in a state without restrictions on union security.[29]

Such collaboration provided executives with financial and political dividends. GE's vice president for employee and public relations, Lemuel Ricketts Boulware, tested his particular brand of business conservatism in Phoenix. He had already perfected a labor relations technique that crippled unions and hired Ronald Reagan as a spokesman for GE's brand of antiliberal, antilabor, free-enterprise conservatism before his firm initiated its Valley computing venture. Just a few years later, Boulware launched his political career with a speech before the Phoenix Chamber. Like the assembled grasstops insurgents, Boulware lamented that business leaders had failed "to have business and our economic system understood. . . . We businessmen have become the whipping boys for opponents." Complacency had allowed unionists to become "overly prominent . . . in community chest and civic affairs," which accounted for voters supporting "fresh mistakes" in regard to "spending, inflation, taxes, productivity, and freedom." "We businessmen cannot look elsewhere for citizens to blame," he admitted. "We have long had the opportunity and responsibility to do our considerable part." His solution: "Not only money—and lots of it—but lots of volunteer *leg-work* and *mental sweat*."[30]

Phoenix boosters and GE executives used their influence to draw attention to Boulware's address, "Politics . . . The Businessman's Biggest Job in 1958," an influential rallying cry for mid-century conservatives. The *Republic* excerpted large portions of the address under the heading, "Politics Called 'Business of All.'" GE printed more than two hundred thousand copies. Senators and representatives included it in the *Congressional Record*, and *American Business*'s editors reprinted the piece in its entirety. A National Association of Manufacturers' board member cribbed Boulware's text for his lectures, and other businessmen asked for copies to distribute among their peers.[31]

Phoenix was also a staging ground for Reagan's political career. The veteran Hollywood actor, former Screen Actors Guild president, and self-described New Deal Democrat found work hosting General Electric Theater in the mid-1950s. He also toured GE facilities to deliver the anti-union messages at the core of Boulware's management philosophy. Phoenix thus served as but one stop in Reagan's postwar political pilgrimage. In these years, the wayfarer vacationed at his in-laws' Valley vacation house, near the Goldwaters, who were friendly with the Davises (the parents of his second wife, Nancy). Reagan found Senator Goldwater "a very pleasing fellow to be with." "I was on the mashed potato circuit," he remembered, "doing my own speeches and my own research and everything. I was getting further and further away from the Democratic philosophy until I became a Republican, but 'The Conscience of a Conservative' was a very great factor in all of that in helping me make up my mind." Reagan's 1961 speech before the Phoenix Chamber highlighted this reconsideration. Liberals, he cautioned, "appeal[ed] not to the worst, but the best in our nature, they have used our sense of fair play . . . and have perfected a technique of 'foot in the door' legislation . . . , always aiming at the ultimate goal—a government that will someday be a big brother to us all." Reagan demanded businessmen lead the fight against fifth-column socialism: "Wars end in victory or defeat . . . by 1970 the world will be all slave or all free."[32]

Reagan and Goldwater's political odysseys forged a deep, friendly alliance between Boulware and Goldwater. Boulware's retirement enabled him to spend time and money on Goldwater's presidential campaign and his later senatorial runs. Goldwater, in turn, bent Boulware's ear about up-and-coming Republicans elsewhere and beseeched him to work on their behalf. Each considered the other vital to the conservative movement. "I can remember very well," Goldwater reflected in the early 1980s, "the great inspiration that you provided for me as you so stubbornly, rightly, and forcefully fought with the union that was trying to take over your company [in the 1950s]." The Arizonan freely admitted: "I wish we had more like you around. The woods are full of softies today, not many tough ones left." He declared that "Lem Boulware is going to go down as one of the men we should have had more of as we progressed through these years." Boulware responded: "It is to *you* we all owe the bringing of sensible conservatism out into the open, raising it to recognized importance and respectability, and seeing that it became such compelling 'news' that the biased media, educators, clergy and politicians of both parties could no longer dare ignore it." Boulware celebrated, "You may have lost the one battle along the way, but *you are now winning the war.*"[33]

Grasstops Washingtonians

Goldwater and Boulware had reason to consider themselves vindicated in the early years of the Reagan administration. Phoenicians and their grasstops counterparts had struggled on and over Capitol Hill for decades. Grasstops congressmen were unquestionably rooted in and identified with their regions yet rose to national prominence because of their replantation in Washington. Strom Thurmond stood out among the Southerners. His infamous civil rights record overshadowed his multifaceted massive resistance to mid-century liberalism. South Carolina's governor had considered his 1948 presidential bid under the States Rights Democratic Party a national crusade against New Deal era excesses and bristled when Southerners pronounced themselves Dixiecrats. The term invoked images of populist, white demagoguery, not the organization's cadre of lawyers, businessmen, and industrialists hell-bent on elite reclamation. Thurmond's counterparts remained in Congress after his 1948 loss. They actually eased capital mobility by voting with northeastern Republicans who represented business conservatives, not GOP moderates. Two Steelbelt Republicans, for example, introduced Taft-Hartley, but 80 percent of southern Democrats voted for the bill, which affirmed states' ability to restrict union security after Arkansans, Floridians, and Arizonans had already passed right-to-work referenda. This industry-focused coalition, which Thurmond joined when he arrived in the Senate in 1954, blocked liberal efforts to remove tax exemptions on municipal bonds, equalize employee benefits at New York state levels, and repeal section 14(b) throughout the 1950s and 1960s. Thus, this alliance effectively insured at the federal level that boosters could attract investment without eroding the union, oversight, and tax differential between the industrial core and its periphery.[34]

Federal bureaucracies were as important to protecting regressive business climates as congressional chambers. Luther Hodges, for example, used agencies as venues to devise, reshape, and implement policies that redirected investment, spread the business climate gospel, and established the foundations for the low-wage, high-turnover, postindustrial Nueva South. Textiles, Rotary International, and big-city business had transformed the mill boy into a rural plant manager and then into a leading businessman, who remained a public servant dedicated to North Carolina, industry, and the Democratic Party. Roosevelt officials tapped the Manhattan-based Marshall Field executive to serve in the Office of Price Administration in 1944 to replace just-ousted liberals. Hodges's service impressed Truman appointee Clinton Anderson. The New Mexico Democrat subsequently asked Hodges to serve under him in the Department of Agriculture. Hodges declined the position but acted as a short-term consultant to Anderson and to army officials in Germany, which enabled him to send his former employers information on federal initiatives to revive German textiles. He later retired from Marshall Field's in order to head the Economic Cooperation Administration's industry division in West Germany. He spent two years traveling around Western Europe. His new high-ranking job and long-standing Rotary membership wrought professional and personal relationships with industrialists who shared his aversion to state-protected taxation, regulation, and unionization. Hodges introduced these European contacts to Marshall Field's executives eager to venture into Continental recovery and then called on the Europeans when he launched an international investment initiative from North Carolina's statehouse in the late 1950s.[35]

Competition had spurred this transatlantic quest. Hodges had run a statewide campaign for lieutenant governor in 1952, a victory that relied less on the grassroots support that he would later celebrate and more on his business connections with other grasstops North Carolinians. His victory had upset the state's agricultural elite, who continued to eye Hodges with suspicion after his predecessor's sudden 1954 death opened up the governor's mansion to Hodges. Hodges's boosterism thrilled the citizens who hoped for better jobs and schools. Their support secured his 1956 gubernatorial bid and enabled him to scout for industry first in New York, which recruiters often trolled, and then in Western Europe, where few had hunted after World War II. Hodges enticed English, French, German, and Swiss industrialists with the same business climate that had tempted domestic businessmen: an advantageous tax code, freedom from state regulation, and a cheap workforce, trained in public vocational schools and colleges—not at managerial expense.[36]

Regional and national recognition for this drive followed. Hodges's fame, success, and party loyalty made him JFK's pick for commerce secretary, an office the North Carolinian used to promote the kind of business politics that had inspired him to run for office. Hodges's commitment to industrialization remained when he retired in 1965. He returned to North Carolina to oversee the Research Triangle Park's development, which required him to draw on his extensive corporate connections and to travel overseas to hunt for the businesses that remade the area into an epicenter of the lucrative knowledge economy, multifaceted service industry, and global neoliberal manufacturing belt.[37]

City-based western Republicans, whether elected or named to office, also played a pivotal role in making regional politics into national policies. Orme Lewis, for example, had long been active in the Phoenix Chamber and the Arizona GOP. He never sympathized with New Deal statecraft. ("Skeptical is putting it mildly," he later scoffed.) He thus eagerly joined Goldwater and Rhodes in Washington as assistant secretary of the interior after Eisenhower's first election. Lewis oversaw Public Lands Management until 1955, when he resigned to resume his lucrative Phoenix law practice. The *Saturday Evening Post* published his impressions of the job, the federal bureaucracy, and state power that same year. The Anglo elite masculinity embedded within the Chamber's broad counterrevolution structured his account. Lewis described himself as "the caretaker for all our human and all our national resources"; "a kind of Lord High Executioner . . . for the conservationists, duck hunters, fisherman, miners, oil drillers and the private concessionaires in all our national parks"; and "the Great White Father to a total of nearly 4,000,000 Polynesians, Micronesians, Guamanians, Hawaiians, Eskimos, Indians, Virgin Islanders and Puerto Ricans." Lewis listed a litany of "comic, incredible, exotic and exasperating incidents" that left him terrified of sprawling, entrenched federal bureaucracies. Readers, especially those in business, praised Lewis for his fearless account. "We have too much government, too much land and resources in Federal ownership, and too much dependence on Washington," a forest economist with the National Lumber Manufacturers Association complained.[38]

Goldwater nonetheless stood out among the Phoenicians on Capitol Hill. He spent much of his first term traveling the country to deliver speeches for the Republican Senate Campaign Committee. He advanced a Phoenix, rather than a Dwight Eisenhower, Republicanism. The retailer's attacks traversed party lines: he defamed anyone still promoting the expansion, no matter how limited, of the welfare state. When he did speak before the Senate, he preached the developing business climate gospel that boosters and executives continued to negotiate across the emerging Sunbelt. "Our problem is not in Europe. It is not on the shores of Asia. It is wrapped up in the Treasury of the United States and the budget of the United States," Goldwater declared during a 1953 Senate floor debate over the federal debt limit. "It's obvious that the Administration has succumbed to the principle that we owe some sort of living, including all types of care to the citizens of this country," he confided to friends. "I am beginning to wonder if we haven't gone a lot farther than many of us think on this road we happily call socialism."[39]

Goldwater staked out his most distinctive and politically consequential positions when he challenged both Eisenhower moderates and Democratic Party liberals on issues of trade unionism. He, for example, clashed publicly with supporters of the Eisenhower administration's labor policy. He sponsored a 1954 amendment to the 1947 Taft-Hartley Act that would give much of the federal government's power over industrial relations to the states. He argued that, with these proposed revisions, states could conceivably pass laws that would require 95 percent, not just a majority, of the work force to support a union before certification. One liberal senator later told reporters that Goldwater's proposals "are determined . . . to drive a blow at organized labor that will send it rolling and rocking for weeks and months and years to come."[40]

Increasing public concern over labor's power actually gave Goldwater a chance to make himself a household name and spread the labor politics central to the Sunbelt's creation. The U.S. Senate created a Select Committee on Improper Activities in the Labor or Management Field (also known as the McClellan or Rackets Committee) in 1957 after headline-grabbing scandals, especially those involving the Teamsters and Jimmy Hoffa, seemed to tie the labor movement to a vast network of organized crime interests. Goldwater and other Republicans on the Rackets Committee criticized Teamster leaders but targeted Walter Reuther, the ambitious, visionary United Auto Workers (UAW) president. Goldwater ignored Reuther's earlier radical political affiliations and grilled him about union contributions to and influence on state and national Democratic Party leaders, the aggressive and sometimes violent nature of UAW organizing efforts, and Reuther's larger ideological and political ambitions.[41]

Reuther embodied Goldwater's profound fear of increased trade union power both on the shop floor and in politics. The senator disliked Reuther's "bold statements on matters of domestic, foreign, and political policy which have only a most obscure bearing on the interests and welfare of labor union members." He pushed Republicans to ask, "Do these statements of Walter Reuther constitute a proper function of his responsibility to the members of these unions?" Goldwater also chastised Detroit's Economic Club, well marbled with executives from the Big Three automakers, for their unwillingness to curb UAW economic or political ambitions. His 1958 reprimand, reminiscent of the complaints he lodged against timid businessmen in his Depression era editorials, included a declaration that Reuther was "more dangerous to our country than Sputnik or anything Soviet Russia might do." The antagonism between both men reached its zenith during a well-noted exchange at Reuther's three-day interrogation before the Senate Rackets Committee, when Goldwater told the UAW president that he would "rather have Hoffa stealing my money than Reuther stealing my freedom."[42]

This public conflict generated broad interest in Arizona's junior senator. Goldwater received support from college-age conservatives, members of the lower middle class, small-business owners, a smattering of corporate executives, and a gaggle of unionists. "We of organized labor's rank and file should show to him our thanks and appreciation for his exposure of the use, theft and private control of our dues money by our own leaders," a Californian asserted. A Kansas machinist wanted Goldwater to "do something about the union shop, before a 'REAL MEAN MAN' [*sic*] like Hitler, Hoffa, Stalin or Beck comes to power." A UAW Local 719 member "hope[d] and pray[ed] that your investigation will some day force Mr. Reuther to represent the workers that pay for representation, and stop using them as pawns in his unholy fight for power."[43]

Arizonans too admired their junior senator, reelecting him to a second term that made headlines in 1958. Pundits considered this and other Arizona GOP victories, such as Fannin's gubernatorial win, evidence of a profound shift in Arizona's political character. Goldwater also received more national respect and acclaim: he had triumphed in a mid-term election cycle that Democrats had dominated. Major news outlets, notably *Time* and the *Saturday Evening Post*, took notice of this rugged Westerner and devoted pages to him as a modern cowboy whose conservatism placed him at odds with laborites and liberals. Republican senator Everett Dirksen also praised Goldwater openly for his "courage, your singleness of purpose and your determination to get a job done in a field of endeavor which has frightened so many in public life because they were afraid of reprisal." Richard Nixon even asked Goldwater to help revitalize the badly beaten GOP. When Goldwater accepted the chairmanship of the Republican Senate Campaign Committee, he announced that he was "proud of being a conservative" and demanded "the party quit copying the New Deal."[44]

The "Draft Goldwater" effort grew out of this electoral coup. Disaffected Eisenhower supporter Clarence Manion began a search for a presidential nominee to challenge the northeastern Republicans shortly after Goldwater's victory. Manion hosted a well-known weekly radio show, which featured a phalanx of individuals hostile to mid-century liberalism, including Goldwater, who also appeared in a 1957 *Manion Forum*. Manion fully embraced the Arizonan as a conservative frontrunner after Goldwater won over a meeting of South Carolina Republicans with a declaration that the 1954 *Brown v. Board of Education* decision was unconstitutional. Manion subsequently contacted the senator to pen a manifesto for the coalescing conservative movement and also hired William Buckley's brother-in-law, Brent Bozell, to pen Goldwater's *Conscience of a Conservative*. The book represented a kind of fusionist manifesto, in line with Buckley's and Frank Meyer's *National Review.* The volume offered numerous complaints against modern liberalism, which ranged from the balance between states' rights and civil rights, the increase in taxes and farm subsidies, and the expansion of the labor movement and the welfare state. The Freedom for Labor chapter, states' rights section, and material on Arizona's refusal of Federal Aid to Education courted Goldwater's wing of the broad conservative movement. The injection of Christian rhetoric was an obvious nod to Buckley's crowd. Bozell even included Ayn Rand's bifurcated language of collectivism versus freedom when he described how welfare threatened free enterprise.[45]

The book only increased Goldwater's standing. He took losing the 1960 GOP nomination in stride, urging his supporters to "grow up" and channel their enthusiasm for him into a general election win for Nixon. Many interpreted his words as a challenge to prepare for 1964. Leading businessmen began to organize a pro-Goldwater coalition within the GOP as early as the summer of 1961. CEOs donated thousands, including the du Pont and Eli Lilly families as well as Walt Disney, Walter Knott, Charles Edison, and Boulware. Leading economists, such as Milton Friedman, embraced the senator's views, while Manion's audience of largely midwestern mid-sized business owners, members of the Young Americans for Freedom and the Young Republicans, and readers of the *National Review* maintained their support throughout Kennedy's term. White suburbanites joined this base. Wives went door to door, and their daughters dressed as cowgirls for the Arizonan's campaign. These "Goldwater Girls" and the senator's delegates, predominately white men under fifty, dominated coverage of the GOP's 1964 convention. Supporters drank carbonated Gold Water, wore clear-plastic water-drop-shaped jewelry with gold flakes inside, and plastered their cars with "AuH_2O" bumper stickers at the San Francisco "Woodstock for Conservatives."[46]

Goldwater's nomination provoked fear and frustration. He shocked liberals when he declared in his acceptance speech, "Extremism in the defense of liberty is no vice!" and "Moderation in the pursuit of justice is no virtue!" But Republican apparatchiks found themselves at loggerheads with his handlers, namely, Dean Burch, Richard Kleindeinst, Dennison Kitchel, and long-time manager Stephen Shadegg, who formed a tight-knit group of self-described cowboys and showed little interest in following party precedent. Outsiders deemed them the Arizona Mafia and looked askance at the money (more than $500,000) that Harry Rosenzweig had insisted on raising from his Phoenix offices, not the GOP's Washington headquarters.[47]

Johnson forced Goldwater to stray from his bread-and-butter politics. The president solicited corporate support and coffers through summits, pledges to make specific cuts in the federal budget, and assurances of his support for Kennedy's tax cuts for businesses. CEOs, for their part, backed and funded LBJ because many who may have agreed with Goldwater politically feared wasting their vote on the obvious loser and thus sacrificing their influence. Losing this constituency pushed handlers to abandon the battle over economic policy in favor of a war over culture, what staffer Clifton White called "the moral crisis" when he privately urged Goldwater to approve the documentary *Choice*. Over shots of a topless dancer, dancing teenagers, arrested black protestors, the narrator announced, "There are two Americas." Citizens for Goldwater groups received the film, but NBC refused to air the graphic production. Goldwater vetoed any mass showings. "I'm not going to be made out to be a racist," he declared after a viewing. But even though he bristled at comparisons to those he considered backwards segregationists, he nonetheless issued statements that fell in line with their politics and demands. He decried drug abuse and urban violence and called busing an infringement on individual liberty and local control. His sputtering campaign ended in a dramatic defeat. He carried only Arizona, Alabama, Louisiana, Georgia, Mississippi, and South Carolina. He spent election night in an Arizona Biltmore suite, where he received the news that LBJ had won more than 60 percent of the popular vote and Democrats had secured sixty-eight-seat and 295-seat majorities in the Senate and the House, respectively.[48]

Yet Goldwater, not LBJ, emerged as the celebrated elder statesman after 1964. The senator prevailed because he remained committed to his business-first policy perspective. Hypergrowth, anti-union, low-tax, deregulatory peripheral politics became mainstream orthodoxy, which, in turn, increased attention to political fights over individual rights. Goldwater's career then took a twist: he became the seemingly unlikely champion of liberal causes divorced from economic justice because he continued to oppose the federal government's intrusion into the personal lives of its citizens. He, for example, famously championed abortion rights. He had privately facilitated his daughter's safe, medical abortion in Mexico in the mid-1940s and remained steadfast on this issue. He only equivocated publicly when he needed the endorsement of Arizona's growing pro-life contingent for his 1980 reelection campaign. His support for individual liberties then hardened after his 1989 retirement. Goldwater railed against a 1992 Arizona proposition to ban abortions unless needed to save the mother's life, and he supported a Phoenix ordinance that prohibited discrimination against gays and lesbians in employment, housing, and public accommodation. At the end of his life, he once again made national news when he lambasted the ban on gays in the military and dismissed Clinton's "don't ask, don't tell" compromise as a farce in 1993.[49]

Arizonans on the High Court

Goldwater's continued political influence depended partially on his ability to place supporters in positions of power. Nixon gave many of Goldwater's disciples (including those who were not from Arizona) important positions within his administration, including Dean Burch, who chaired the Federal Communications Commission, Richard Kleindienst, William Rehnquist, and Richard Burke, who all served in the Department of Justice. Goldwater, for his part, very much prided himself on Rehnquist's and Sandra Day O'Connor's Supreme Court nominations. "I think of all the things I have done in my life," Goldwater crowed, "this one topped them all because [O'Connor] is not only a complete woman, but a dear friend and an Arizonan of whom I will always be proud."[50]

Both jurists did much to enshrine the fundamentals of Sunbelt booster economic and governance policies in federal statecraft. Recent assessments show that the Rehnquist Court did not fundamentally advance the conservative movement's social agenda but still furthered its economic and governmental philosophy. Social issues unquestionably divided the post-1991 conservative bloc, yet O'Connor, Rehnquist, Antonin Scalia, Anthony Kennedy, Clarence Thomas, and, until the mid-1990s, David Souter consistently agreed to devolve more power onto the states except in cases where these governments attempted to regulate business. Rehnquist and O'Connor voted almost identically on these issues, both of which were at the crux of both grasstops industrialization and neoliberal jurisprudence.[51]

Neither Rehnquist nor O'Connor was a part of the Chamber's wartime rebirth. These transplants' judicial philosophies had instead been nurtured by families averse to mid-century liberalism. Phoenix nonetheless served as an incubator for their careers and rulings: they joined natives and recent arrivals eager to be a part of a prominent, vanguard state GOP, do business in the well-publicized last frontier of free enterprise, or take part in the construction and preservation of the area's renowned business climate.

Rehnquist had grown up in affluent Shorewood, Wisconsin, far from the arid Valley. His father, the child of Swedish immigrants, never attended college and sold paper wholesale to support his wife, a University of Wisconsin graduate, who spoke five languages, freelanced as a translator, and eagerly participated in civic affairs. Rehnquist's parents discussed politics openly in their small brick home, where they celebrated Wendell Willkie, Herbert Hoover, and Robert Taft. Rehnquist spent a year at Kenyon College after graduating from high school. He left for the Army Air Corps in 1943 and spent much time in North Africa, where hostilities had largely ended. The Midwesterner appreciated the climate. "I wanted to find someplace like North Africa to go to school," he later recounted. The G.I. Bill provided the money, but the Southwest lacked the educational infrastructure that he craved. So he went farther west. He graduated Phi Beta Kappa at Stanford in 1948, went on to earn master's degrees at both Stanford and Harvard, and later enrolled in Stanford Law School, graduating first in his class and then clerking for Supreme Court Justice Robert Jackson.[52]

Rehnquist left Washington for Phoenix in 1953. Some biographers assert that he wanted an arid environment and just flipped a coin to decide between Albuquerque and Phoenix. Rehnquist later credited his move to his admiration for "the lost frontier here in America. . . . Not just free enterprise in the sense of a right to make a buck," he clarified, "but the right to manage your own affairs as free as possible from the interference of government." He blended his professional career with his political interests. He, for example, openly opposed civil rights legislation in 1964 hearings over a Phoenix Public Accommodations Ordinance. He called its passage a "mistake" in letters to the *Republic* because it "does away with the historic right of the owner of a drug store, lunch counter, or theater to choose his own customers." The founders, Rehnquist asserted, "thought of it as the 'land of the free' just as surely as they thought of it as the 'land of the equal.'" His stance separated him somewhat from the Charter Government Committee's architects, who had long practiced accommodation and tokenism in their efforts to appear racially progressive and substantiate claims of differences between de facto and de jure segregation.[53]

Involvement with efforts to keep African Americans from voting dogged Rehnquist's career even more than these public statements. The Arizona

NAACP charged that Rehnquist, as early as 1958, had joined Anglo lawyers who stopped African Americans at polling places. "Voters were being challenged in several precincts in South Phoenix," the head of the Maricopa County Democratic Headquarters later testified. "I was told it was William 'Bill' Rehnquist . . . asking people . . . to read printing on a white card[.] People were leaving the lines and were not voting. . . . A precinct committeeman[,] a black woman, said her people were frightened and afraid to vote." The Democratic activist considered politics the motivation. "We had a big Registration drive that year and a lot of the people were voting for the first time after the challenging started we no longer had people waiting," she explained. "I tried to get the precinct people to go door to door to get out the vote but word was out they were afraid to vote."[54]

The controversy did not keep Rehnquist out of the Arizona GOP's inner circle. He played a vital role in Goldwater's presidential bid. Rehnquist wrote speeches, counseled the senator on his vote against the 1964 Civil Rights Act, and provided him with the legal argument for his opposition. Rehnquist also worked with political scientist Harry Jaffa to draft Goldwater's later justifications. Goldwater recited their arguments to court voters even though he had supported the Phoenix ordinance.[55]

Rehnquist's activism earned him a place in the Nixon administration. Then deputy attorney general Kleindienst hired the transplant as the head of the Office of Legal Counsel to help in efforts to "unpack" the Warren Court and overturn liberal activist jurisprudence, which required, in John Dean's words, appointing "strict constructionist" judges, who would "interpret the Constitution rather than amend it by judicial fiat." Lawyers in the attorney general's office pressured liberal jurists, most notably LBJ appointee Abe Fortas, to leave the bench. Rehnquist, for his part, studied decisions to identify nominees, made recommendations to Attorney General John Mitchell, and conducted subsequent interviews. Candidates, Rehnquist outlined in an internal memo, "will generally not be favorably inclined toward claims of either criminal defendants or civil rights plaintiffs—the latter two groups having been the principal beneficiaries of the Supreme Court's 'broad constructionist' reading of the Constitution."[56]

Rehnquist met this requirement, yet serendipity defined his eventual nomination. Justices Hugo Black and John Marshall Harlan's 1971 resignations surprised the administration, and neither Rehnquist nor Virginian Lewis Powell appeared on the initial shortlist. "I'm not from the South, I'm not a woman, and I'm not mediocre," Rehnquist quipped when reporters asked if he would be named. Nixon championed Virginia congressman Richard Poff, Californian William French Smith, or Philadelphia prosecutor Arlen Specter, but only after aides reminded him that he had not appointed a Jew. "He's strong on law enforcement, and the rest," Nixon responded. "I might consider him, if we went to play the Jews." The president also resisted pressure to select a woman: "I don't think a woman should be in any government job whatever. I mean, I really don't. The reason why I do is mainly because they are erratic. And emotional. Men are erratic and emotional too, but the point is a woman is more likely to be." Dean later credited himself for Rehnquist's candidacy. "The president has a perfect candidate right under his nose," Dean reportedly confided to a Nixon adviser. "Rehnquist makes Barry Goldwater look like a liberal." Goldwater told Nixon that Rehnquist was "probably the greatest authority on the Constitution in the country today." The president nonetheless equivocated until the American Bar Association rejected his nomination list and Nixon learned that Rehnquist had been Justice Jackson's clerk.[57]

Rehnquist's quick confirmation to the Court and to the position of chief justice generated tremendous controversy. Judiciary Committee Democrats feared Rehnquist's and Poff's ascension. Senators Birch Bayh, Gary Hart, Sam Ervin, and Edward Kennedy spent the first day grilling Rehnquist about overturning past precedent and limiting congressional powers. Bayh admitted that Democrats feared that "the President has thought that the whole purpose for these nominations is to turn around the Court and thus turn around the series of interpretations that have been put on the laws over the past 20 years."[58]

Rehnquist faced tough questions in regard to his antidesegregationist views and political activities. In 1971 and 1986, Committee members discussed his public opposition to the Phoenix Public Accommodations Ordinance, the integration of Phoenix public high schools, and involvement with voter intimidation efforts. The nominee fell back on denial and backtracking to answer these queries. In 1971, Rehnquist stipulated that he no longer opposed the accommodations act, continued to consider busing "artificial," and asserted that his polling "responsibilities, as I recall them, were never those of challenger, but as one of a group of lawyers working for the Republican Party in Maricopa County who attempted to supply legal advice to persons who were challengers." These attorneys did not target minority voters, he testified, but focused on "areas in which heavy Democratic pluralities were voting together, with some reason to believe that tombstones were being

Figure 15. William Rehnquist poses with a 1971 *Arizona Republic* editorial cartoon celebrating his appointment to the Supreme Court. Phoenix cartoonist Reg Manning placed Rehnquist at the top of his list of "Arizonans in High Appointive Jobs in Washington" that "Kind of Makes Our Buttons Pop." Manning also listed Dean Burch (who served as chairman of the Federal Communications Commission and the Republican National Committee), Richard Kleindienst (who served as Nixon's attorney general), Isabel Burgess (whom Nixon appointed to the National Transportation Safety Board), and Robert Mardian (brother of Phoenix mayor Samuel Mardian and a member of Nixon's Department of Health, Education, and Welfare, the Attorney General's Office, and the Committee to Re-Elect the President). Courtesy of the Arizona Historical Foundation, Isabel Burgess Collection, folder 11, box 21.

voted at the same time." Controversy erupted after a short memo with Rehnquist's initials surfaced from Justice Jackson's old files. "A Random Thought on the Segregation Cases" maintained: "It is an unpopular and unhumanitarian position, for which I have been excoriated by liberal colleagues, but I think *Plessey v. Ferguson* was right and should be reaffirmed." Disagreement ensued, and continues, over whether the missive represented Rehnquist's opinion and an attempt to sway the justice or a position Jackson asked his clerk to draft in preparation for a vote. Rehnquist first disavowed the one-and-a-half page, single-spaced piece and only reluctantly identified it as a "bald, simplistic conclusion, which was not an accurate statement of my views at the time."[59]

During the 1971 hearings, Rehnquist received much support from Phoenicians, including O'Connor. Mainstream reporters' attacks on the state senator's former classmate led her to beseech friends and colleagues to lobby lawyers, legislators, and church officials across the country to support Rehnquist. She also asked newsman Eugene Pulliam, one of her close associates, to publish editorials favoring Rehnquist in Indiana, home to Bayh, one of Rehnquist's biggest Senate critics. Upon confirmation, Rehnquist wrote O'Connor personally to thank her.[60]

Their friendship belied their radically different backgrounds. O'Connor was a native Arizonan who lived with her grandparents in El Paso during the school year and returned to the remote Lazy B ranch, situated on the Arizona–New Mexico border, every summer. Her father, Henry Day, shaped her politics. He built one of the largest western cattle operations and accepted federal subsidies when the Depression ravaged his outfit, yet opposed the New Deal and liberal programs. A native Californian, he also pushed his academically gifted daughter to attend Stanford. She enrolled in 1946, completed her economics degree in 1949, and finished her law degree just two years later. Rehnquist, whom O'Connor had dated briefly, finished first and O'Connor third, but law firms only offered her employment as a legal secretary. She subsequently follow her husband, John Jay O'Connor, to Frankfurt, Germany, where he worked for the Judge Advocate General Corps, and then to Phoenix when a top partnership hired him. "John and I felt," she later explained, "we would have an opportunity to be more actively involved with our community than might be the case if we were to return to California." She could still not secure a position, though she had scholastically outshone her husband, and only later started a practice with a local lawyer. "Other people who had offices in the same shopping mall repaired TVs, cleaned clothes, or loaned money," she remembered. "It was not a high-rent district. I got walk-in business. People came in to see me about grocery bills they couldn't collect, landlord-tenant problems, family members and other everyday things."[61]

O'Connor dedicated herself to civic and political causes. She served, like other wives and mothers, on many boards and committees, including the Heard Museum's board of trustees and Arizona State University law school's board of visitors. She hence bridged the divide between her contemporaries, who remained dedicated electoral shock troops throughout their lives, and her successors, who ran for office. In 1965 O'Connor began work in the state attorney general's office. "I persisted," she remembered, "and got a temporary job and quickly rose all the way to the bottom of the totem pole in that office. As was normal for a beginner, I got the least desirable assignments." Her hard work paid off: she was appointed to a vacant seat in the state Senate in 1969, won reelection twice, and served as the majority leader in the legislature, the first woman to hold the office in the United States. She exhibited a more pragmatic interpretation of post-1964 conservatism: she fought spending increases but also supported a state Medicaid program, the repeal of a law barring women from working more than eight hours a day, which had kept many out of high-paying professional jobs, and a measure to make public meetings accessible to citizens. Her popularity helped her win a spot on the Maricopa County Superior Court in 1974. Five years later, Governor Bruce Babbitt appointed O'Connor to the Arizona Court of Appeals.[62]

Her place among the Chamber elite buoyed her aspirations. The O'Connors spent time with powerful Arizona Republicans, including Goldwater, Pulliam, Rosenzweig, and Rehnquist. She actively campaigned for Goldwater in 1958 and 1964. He, in turn, became her political mentor. These connections helped her land the job in the attorney general's office. Goldwater even wanted her to run for governor in 1978, but she declined this "draft," citing a familial commitment.[63]

O'Connor did allow Reagan and his staffers to name her to the Supreme Court three years later. The president had promised to nominate a woman during the campaign, if only to assuage voters who feared his aggressive military rhetoric. Reagan met with her for just forty-fine minutes in July 1981. He reportedly kept their conversation to their mutual acquaintances, fondness for horses, and love of the West, which reflected his confidence in staffers' vetting procedures.[64]

O'Connor's nomination polarized the Right. At her confirmation hearings, Thurmond encapsulated the views of many Republicans, who thought her appointment would signal a new chapter in American federalism. Her experience in state governance, he explained in his opening remarks, "gives us hope that she will bring to the Court, if confirmed, a greater appreciation of the division of powers between the Federal Government and the governments of the representative States." But her refusal to answer questions about her personal political beliefs and her opinions on past court decisions, especially *Roe v. Wade* (1973), enraged social conservatives. Jerry Falwell denounced her publicly, and antiabortion advocates lambasted her on the Senate floor. Goldwater defended her. "Every good Christian ought to kick Falwell right in the ass," the senator declared. "I don't like getting kicked around by people who call themselves conservatives on a non-conservative matter. It is a question of who is best for the Court. If there is going to be a fight in the Senate, you are going to find 'Old Goldy' fighting like hell."[65]

Such colorful ripostes overshadowed senatorial inquiry into O'Connor's conception of federalism and liberal judicial activism, subjects less discussed in newspaper articles and historical accounts. O'Connor boldly proclaimed in her opening statement that she had a great "appreciation of the disparate and distinct roles of the three branches of government at both the State and the Federal levels" and regarded "the proper role of the judiciary is one of interpreting and applying the law, not making it." Yet she equivocated somewhat when senators further probed her views on judicial power. She defined the *Brown* ruling "as an accepted holding of the Court" and an agreement between jurists "that the previous understanding of the 14th amendment was a flawed understanding" after Democratic Senators Patrick Leahy and Joseph Biden asked her about the ruling. "I do not know that the Court believed it was engaged in judicial activism," she responded. "I did not participate in the debate, and the hearings, and the arguments; and I cannot tell you all that went into the making of that decision."[66]

O'Connor's confirmation was a watershed moment. She and Rehnquist formed the core of a bloc that, in the words of one legal scholar, eventually transformed the meaning of the First Amendment from protecting "Eugene V. Debs and Martin Luther King, Jr., rebels and rabble rousers" to shielding "Lorillard Tobacco and Ted Turner: money and marketing." Rehnquist dedicated his tenure to countering more than thirty years of liberal, activist jurisprudence and to protecting free enterprise. "I came to the court sensing," he explained in a rare interview, "there were some excesses in terms of constitutional adjudication during the era of the so-called Warren Court." "The boat was kind of keeling over in one direction," he elaborated, "my job was, where those sort of situations arose, to kind of lean the other way."[67]

Justices did call Rehnquist the "lone dissenter" until the landmark 1976 *National League of Cities v. Usery* decision. The Court had ruled that state and local governments had to follow the federal minimum wage law in 1975. Rehnquist wrote and signed the only dissent, which argued that the ruling violated the protections the Tenth Amendment provided the states. The five-to-four *Usery* vote reversed the decision. Rehnquist convinced four judges that lawmakers had violated the states' rights clause in the Bill of Rights. He rejected congressional authority to force state and local governments to follow federal minimum wage and maximum hours laws in the majority opinion. Congress had the right to "exercis[e] its express powers to tax and regulate commerce," he submitted, but these laws threatened the "separate and independence existence" of the states. The Court had not invoked the Tenth Amendment since *West Coast Hotel Co. v. Parrish*, the 1937 "switch in time that saved nine." Scholarly reassessments in the years since *Usery* was overturned (and then in some respects reaffirmed) now interpret the 1976 decision as the first signal that the Court would begin to dismantle the governmental framework that had not only underpinned the New Deal but also enabled the enactment of other mid-century liberal reforms.[68]

O'Connor's ascension five years later provided an important vote for Rehnquist's agenda. Her stance on women's issues has dominated studies of her opinions, yet research on other aspects of her legal thought suggests that she consistently protected states' rights while serving on the Rehnquist Court. Her vote proved vital in shifting the Court's tenor even before Reagan and George H. W. Bush were able to appoint additional jurists to the bench. For example, only Powell, Rehnquist, and O'Connor dissented when the 1985 *Garcia v. San Antonio Metropolitan Transit Authority* decision reversed *Usery*. Each wrote a separate dissent, but all three expressed concern that the majority had ignored the protections the Bill of Rights had afforded to the states. She remained a consistent negative vote when jurists considered state laws that imposed new regulations on industry at the state level. The post-1991 conservative bloc did not side with the states or protect their power to police commerce but instead ruled in favor of corporations that opposed these regulations. Legal scholars have therefore argued that these decisions indicate that the new majority, including O'Connor, had more concern for commerce than federalism. She voted with the post-1991 conservative bloc on more than 80 percent of cases involving states' rights and the regulation of industry. Such rulings, in effect, further repealed mid-century governmental limitations on business, reoriented the state toward protecting and promoting industry, and helped guarantee that regional industrialization would erode, not improve, national living and work standards.[69]

The mainstream press and the academy had discovered the Sunbelt just as Rehnquist's dissents laid the groundwork for American jurisprudence's transformation. Long before Phillips described the Sunbelt in *The Emerging Republican Majority*, the grasstops had already weakened support for the liberal regulatory state through an expansive antiliberal growth agenda fought out in those trading outposts that would become sprawling, industrial juggernauts. By then, the South and Southwest's industrialization had clearly not advanced a grassroots liberalism as New Dealers had predicted. Boosters, executives, experts, and journalists had instead reclaimed these backwoods territories and in the process so eroded living, working, and regulatory standards in the rest of the country that the cost and profit differential between doing business in the Sunbelt and operating in the Rustbelt had effectively evaporated.

Chapter 10

"A Frankenstein's Monster"

Desert politics began to attract attention, much of it critical, as sprawling Phoenix basked in the accolades from leading business periodicals and grasstops men and women began to make their presence felt in the highest levels of national affairs. For example, veteran *Washington Post* correspondent Chalmers Roberts took a break from the diplomatic beat to report on the "Thunder on the Right." His 1961 reports warned of a "reactionary right," namely, its chief spokesman Barry Goldwater, its financial backers ("the newly rich in Texas and Arizona" and California's "big and little donors"), and its news sources. Phoenix loomed large in his reportage: Eugene Pulliam's dailies were "jammed with the words of the ultra right," and local "Democrats, conservative as well as liberal," were quick to blame "ultra rightists" for "transforming Phoenix's claim to be 'the valley of the sun' into what some of them call 'the valley of fear.'"[1]

Yet Andrew Kopkind uncovered just a few years later that even Goldwater's compatriots in the Chamber were afraid of "a Frankenstein's monster which no longer does their bidding." An unnamed banker confided: "our state and our city are suffering from an excessive orientation toward conservatism." Even Phoenix mayor Milton Graham thought something amiss. "In some areas," he told the *New Republic*'s reporter, "we've been blindly conservative (and I consider myself a conservative)." The "sad qualification was necessary," Kopkind opined, because "'conservatism' is so much a part of the credo that anyone who dares criticize must do so in its name." Phoenix "is no longer a frontier town," he surmised, "but rather a huge, unplanned urban complex having more in common with, say, Detroit than with Dodge City."[2]

Like the Motor City and other American metropolises in the 1960s and 1970s, the Phoenix Valley was in crisis. Race and class resentments had already pushed middle-income whites farther out into the suburbs and infuriated the white working class. But grasstops growth had also incubated a metropolitan political paralysis that pitted Sunbelt investors and boosters against a horde of critics, some of them radicals, others moderates, or liberals, but also those residents whom boosters considered their base: white homeowners. Accordingly, the business elite's opponents held a range of philosophical and party allegiances. Indeed, they tended to fight with each other while they assailed business rule as having abandoned its own self-proclaimed principles: individual advancement, minimal governance, and low taxation.[3]

Skirmishes erupted over revenue collection and state authority, but the larger war was over rightful representation and rule. In fact, grassroots rebellions had a reciprocal relationship with national movements that reshaped American expectations for and definitions of representative democracy in the 1960s and 1970s. Frustration with malapportionment traversed party lines, political movements, and philosophical divides. In this period, prominent liberal Democrats, civil rights organizations, League of Women Voters chapters, insurgent southern Republicans, and other metropolitan residents all hotly debated and then rejected the checks and balances, present in most state constitutions, against mass democracy. Supreme Court justices ultimately provided the legal justification to empower urban and suburban districts by redefining genuine enfranchisement as "one man, one vote." These rulings had a direct impact on those who waged local struggles for representation, empowerment, and change. Enforcement enfranchised suburban voters, transformed state legislatures, and later fused metropolitan coalitions to rewrite good-government charters. Such reforms ultimately left Sunbelt cities, states, and political parties rife with the same conflicts that divided cities and states in the Northeast and Midwest and on the Pacific Coast.[4]

These clashes also drove the popular redefinition of liberalism and conservatism. A phalanx of critics laid claim to the business elite's language of freedom, democracy, and free enterprise in order to demand ward voting, compliance with federal legislation, and tax relief. This popular repurposing of such potent political rhetoric was a vital part of many urban insurgencies, including those of the white suburban rebels who benefited the most from reapportionment. These homeowners shared the sales-tax burden with working-class minorities but still bore much of the property-tax load because they were also the target of city annexation programs designed to maintain white metropolitan voting majorities. These suburbanites subsequently decried public welfare programs to help minorities while also assailing city planners and Chamber officials as agents of a creeping atheistic socialism that endangered the Republic. Aroused residents often justified their fervor as a function of their work ethic and piety. Yet the sacred often mixed with the secular within this broad, late twentieth-century populism. After all, knee-jerk bigotry, historians have noted, ran throughout this rebellion.[5]

The "paranoid style" in American politics that Richard Hofstadter famously outlined still does not explain this and other racist, sexist, religious, and secular expressions of late twentieth-century white populism. Homeowning heretics were in fact rejecting business governance, which seemed incompatible with the free-enterprise conservatism that boosters and CEOs had trumpeted during capitalism's intraregional migration. Voters had observed levies rise, governments expand, and central cities usurp neighborhoods despite booster promises to reduce taxation, limit government, and stop corruption. To be sure, many petit-bourgeois insurgents invoked religion to justify their rage but all largely framed their critique of business rule in the same language as that of their grasstops and investor-class opponents, including the anti-Communist antistatism that had long infused Sunbelt campaign rhetoric. In the process these dissenters redefined themselves as the true conservatives, the guardians of democracy, capitalism, and, for the devoted, Protestantism, in order to situate themselves against both liberals and economic elites.[6]

Containment

Populist campaigns against personal property taxes represented one dimension of a building popular protest against taxation, underrepresentation, and elite governance. These tax revolts reflected homeowner rage not only against liberals and minorities but also against boosters and their investors. The latter opposed grassroots initiatives to reduce such levies because business climate infrastructure required revenue. But the steady increase in sales and personal-property taxes generated friction between businessmen and voters, which became a general hostility toward business influence and even growth. Boosters thus constantly strove to win voter support for business climate policies, while resisting civil rights advocates' demands that they follow federal and state laws, appeased voters opposed to sprawl, and countered criticism that good-government charters were undemocratic. Long-standing resentment eventually begat electoral challenges. Most promoter machines lasted through the 1950s; few survived the 1970s intact.[7]

Proactive countermeasures had in fact always been a part of industrialization regimes because businessmen feared residents did not support local boosterism, much less understand American capitalism. For example, a leading Marietta-Atlanta Chamber man warned in 1946 that those reared during the New Deal "accept statism, collectivism and government control . . . as the perfectly natural order of life. . . . Where in our education process can a young man learn what it is [to] manage and to own?" he asked. Pressure to school residents on business-first principles came from local elites and national leaders. U.S. Chamber of Commerce officials suggested affiliates hold a "Business-Education Day" in 1949. The official guidebook deemed the plan, modeled after existing Michigan initiatives, an effort "to foster better understanding between businessmen and teachers."[8]

Peripheral chambers embraced this program, either by sponsoring Business-Education Days or comparable initiatives. Seventy-two Atlanta manufacturing, wholesaling, distribution, retail, food production, banking, insurance, and service establishments, all Chamber members, hosted twenty-three hundred area public school teachers in 1950. "Visiting teachers spent the entire day at their respective establishments," leading promoters reported, "a behind-the-scenes view of American business to equip them to present a clearer picture of business to their pupils." San Diego boosters inaugurated their Business-Education Day in 1956. Materials emphasized the importance of "witnessing enterprise in action—private enterprise by a free people." "You play a key part in our system of enterprise," coordinators emphasized in 1957: "You will receive information first hand from businessmen about business methods and policies . . . and get ideas for new courses to prepare students for business." Attendance was of course vital: "The future of our country depends as much on our system of education as it does on the strength of the family. Through your part in enterprise we all gain benefits."[9]

Boosters also turned to school boards or legislatures to influence public instruction. "Custodians of our entire American heritage," Paul Fannin told legislators considering a 1962 elementary and secondary school bill, must offer "a continuous program of American history and courses comparing American free enterprise with Socialism and Communism." State representatives mandated more focused guidance in 1971: students needed a semester-length course in "the essentials and benefits of the free enterprise system" to graduate. "State universities are certainly not hot beds of conservative thought," the bill's sponsor explained. This Phoenix-based, Republican real estate appraiser accordingly considered the class "some foundation to stand on when [a student] does come up against professors that are collectivists or Socialists." Arizona teachers presented pupils with such arguments through materials that the state superintendent of public instruction produced himself or ordered from the Foundation for Economic Education, a postwar clearinghouse for antiliberal screeds. These instructional aids reiterated the claims that ran throughout the modern conservative movement and business climate zeitgeist, including "Minimum wage laws always contribute to unemployment," "The Free Market encourages free and responsible individualism," and "Collectivism as a way of life is a manifestation of the abyss into which men sink when not motivated by the pursuit of truth and justice." "When you read this stuff," an educator commented in a 1973 *Nation* report, "you laugh out loud. It's a comic book." Yet twenty states followed Arizona's lead before decade's end.[10]

Metropolitan Phoenix Politics

But Arizona's free-enterprise education requirements still failed to stop the Charter Government Committee's (CGC) collapse. Generational changes partly influenced the organization's waning influence and the Phoenix charter's third revision. Leaders had feared the coming turnover for a decade. Executive officers, for example, contacted the old guard in 1965 to identify "young men . . . as a first step towards building them into leadership positions." Stalwarts had little faith in their replacements. "You don't have any really great personalities like we had," Pyle lamented in 1976. Expanding membership rolls had also slowly transformed the association. Most members were still area businessmen, but corporate officers increasingly held top positions in the growing organization, not the close-knit grasstops. Motorola, Merrill Lynch, AiResearch, Price Waterhouse, Western Savings and Loan, Transamerica Title Insurance, and General Electric (GE) managers held more seats than local business operators on the Chamber's

1967–1968 board of directors. They tended to be based in but not bound to Phoenix. The president abruptly resigned in October 1962, when American Airlines reassigned him to Fort Worth. Moreover, he and other executives often had important responsibilities to their home offices and were not as invested in Phoenix politics as Goldwater's generation. But the entire membership also had different plans for the Chamber and metro Phoenix. "Individual freedom," "opportunity for all," and "preserve and strengthen competitive free enterprise" were long-term objectives for the 1972–1973 fiscal year, but so were the environment, law and order, education, a "sound and healthy economy," and "coordinated long-range planning." Leaders elaborated that these goals depended on attracting tourists and corporate headquarters, not manufacturers. Indeed, industrial recruitment appeared nowhere on this agenda.[11]

External pressures also hastened the end of business rule. Anglo suburbanites and small businessmen unaffiliated with the Chamber bedeviled the CGC. These self-identified conservatives had increasingly borne the burden of funding corporate welfare: Arizona ranked seventeenth in per capita levies ($208.35) in 1960 and eleventh in regard to taxes as a percentage of personal income (10.36 percent to sixteenth-placed California's 10.14 percent). And the frustrated did complain. Spotty and inefficient public services in residential areas provoked some outcries. But these and other complaints were really about taxing and spending. Some Phoenicians said as much: "My taxes were increased from $155 a year ago," a resident fumed to *Republic* editors in 1953, "to $254.20. . . . I am willing to pay my fair share, but don't intend being a sucker."[12]

Booster Republicans considered religiously devout transplants among the most vexing homeowners. Migrants from the South and Midwest poured into Phoenix. Many of them were evangelicals and fundamentalists, who brought their faith and values with them. Many Christians went to the Golden State of course but thousands also moved to other parts of the maturing Sunbelt, Arizona included (some transplants were even a part of the California backwash that would continue as more Pacific Coast executives shifted aerospace and electronics production to neighboring states where business taxes were lower, anti-union statutes more stringent, and recruitment giveaways more generous). New arrivals zealously built communities with a firm commitment to spreading a stridently anti-Communist Christianity. Their convictions aligned with the secular rhetoric not the actual practice of Sunbelt boosterism and governance. Suburban evangelicals prized local communities governed by democratic ideals that would not restrict individual entrepreneurship, civic participation, economic opportunity, or an individual's relationship with God. Top Phoenix Republicans, whether in local, state, or national office, also roundly condemned federal intervention as a threat to free enterprise, democracy, and individual advancement. Yet their business conservatism consciously relied on the state to protect the elite's self-ascribed right to rule, not empower the citizenry. And even the most religious Chamber men rarely publicized their faith or openly articulated their belief that liberalism was economically and spiritually profane.[13]

Devoted suburbanites would publicly decry booster rule as an abomination but they would also stand beside their more secular neighbors when they rebelled against a business rule that they considered an affront to democratic capitalism. Indeed, the most outspoken metropolitan renegades attacked grasstops statecraft in the Chamber's own language of efficient, corruption-free, free-enterprise governance. This rhetoric, for example, robbed Phoenix of federal funds for urban renewal. CGC mayors had, for their part, unequivocally supported downtown revitalization in the 1950s, yet had chafed at the national guidelines and codes needed for federal support. "The city can regenerate itself," Mayor Jack Williams proclaimed, "[just] as the Phoenix bird regenerated itself from the ashes." But expensive growth policies prompted his successor, builder Samuel Mardian, to declare that nationally funded urban renewal represented "the only practical way to rehabilitate blighted areas." Application, however, required minor changes to the housing code in 1959, such as a ban on outhouses and a requirement that sinks run hot and cold water.[14]

But a 1960 amendment triggered a grassroots' repeal effort. The change had merely clarified when officials could enter properties and outlined how residents could appeal to stop an inspection. Nonetheless, Phoenicians insistent on pay-as-you-go, limited governance decried the change in the boosters' own business-first rhetoric. Baptist minister Aubrey Moore called it "the kind of inroad that has led countries down the road to socialism." He and other protestors swarmed a January 1961 public hearing. "The philosophy behind these laws is that of communism," one charged. Another asked, "Who's the city to tell me I have to have a hot water heater? I have a right to bathe in cold water if I want to." A rental property owner balked at paying for private baths because she felt that neither she nor her tenants needed or could afford them: "We have a nice clean community toilet." Pulliam newspapers also denounced the code and urban renewal plan. Editorials called downtown regeneration "federalized property management" and warned that acceptance of these dollars would give the "combined federal bureaucracy the right to condemn and tear down homes, stores, office buildings and the like, moving the owners out bodily and acquiring title to their property."[15]

These issues bedeviled the Phoenix establishment facing an election. Chamber men agreed to "assume full leadership," but decades of good-government, investment-focused rhetoric hamstrung those staffing the campaign and speakers' bureaus. Mardian openly derided "militant minions" that were "out to destroy trust and faith in our civic leadership. . . . The fact is that the housing codes strengthen our Constitutional property rights," he asserted. "The housing code is as American as the Constitution itself. The . . . code guards the sanctity of our homes and makes a house worthy of being called a home." Officials also attempted to rewrite the proposal, but federal mandates constrained amendments, and small revisions failed to satisfy challengers. A contemporaneous CGC electoral victory then bolstered Mardian's confidence that voters sided with him. Hostility nonetheless continued. Another 1963 proposal sparked a small January protest, which the council ignored when it approved the code in February. Opponents then gathered enough signatures to place the issue before Phoenicians. Voters repealed the entire code by a wide margin in May, the CGC's first major defeat.[16]

Phoenix sprawled without a housing code for more than five years. Nixonian New Federalism partly inspired city officials' next foray into residential regulation. HUD block grants gave local governments more control over federal funds, which balanced the fiscal needs of cities against protections for state and local autonomy. The administration had a vested interest in preserving the authority of local governments: they had been responsible for nurturing much of the GOP's grasstops vanguard and creating the business climates in step with the conservative movement's economic philosophy. This national policy change also fitted well with the rainmakers' worldview because local control had represented a bulwark against liberalism more than an outright rejection of state or centralized power. Desperate Phoenix policymakers subsequently drafted changes to codes for *new* housing in order to apply for these much needed funds. Rules nonetheless included provisions that *all* housing have, for example, a kitchen, indoor plumbing, and a minimum ceiling height. "It's not a housing code," a city official stated. "It's making the building code applicable to the maintenance of existing dwellings." And no protests arose after the council approved these amendments in 1970.[17]

The Charter Government Committee's Collapse

But these rebellions had also coincided with electoral challenges to the Chamber's political representatives. Since the CGC's 1953 victory, oppositional slates had tended to campaign on reduced individual taxes and more public services, had failed to mount an effective challenge, and had not generated voter interest. Phoenicians, moreover, did not go to polls in record numbers to support the Stay America Committee (SAC) in 1961, the "ultras" whom Chalmers Roberts covered for the *Washington Post*.[18]

Yet SAC, which arose out of the zoning protests, did spark a local debate about basic definitions of democracy, freedom, and conservatism. This genuinely diffuse, grassroots campaign relied on housewives ringing doorbells and making phone calls. "We don't really have an organization," a candidate explained. CGC governance and the business climate united nominees and supporters, who considered the status quo an insidious plot against democratic capitalism. The outspoken clergyman from the housing code hearings represented the faithful alongside the Reverend Wesley Darby, a thirty-three-year-old Valley native who had previously balanced his ecclesiastical duties with work as Greenlee County's deputy assessor. Their slate included Ted MacDonald, a college-educated, forty-seven-year-old insurance agency owner, who had started in the industry while living in Texas. MacDonald had moved to Arizona to establish his own firm, just like thirty-two-year-old SAC candidate Thomas Davis, who applied his business administration and economics coursework from Los Angeles State College to manage his accounting outfit. Mayoral candidate W. Buckner Hanner was among the servicemen who had flocked to Phoenix. He was a class apart from John Rhodes and William Rehnquist. The Seattle native had worked in radio before graduating from high school, joined the Marines during World War II, and used the G.I. Bill to pay for his business administration degree. The University of Southern California alumnus balanced his job at an accounting firm with membership in the John Birch Society, enlistment in the Marine Corps Reserves, and a commitment to his family, who, as boosters had intended, delighted in their environs: "We (the family) love all outdoor activities."[19]

Hanner and his running mates' rhetoric, background, and appeal established them as part of an evolution in the American populist tradition. Ordinary Americans increasingly embraced such white grassroots renegades in the 1960s and 1970s, including those on the extreme Right. Indeed, Phoenix insurgents had much in common with the better known George Wallace. This perennial presidential candidate packaged his racism within a mantle that celebrated the hard working everyman, decried liberal disregard for the common folk, called on the God-fearing to lead, and promised freedom from government interference in schools, churches, and police forces, while guaranteeing authoritarian state policies designed to apply the law and restore order.[20]

SAC's populist platform very much reflected the growing multifaceted critiques of and solutions to business-first governance. The slate supported direct elections for the police chief and city finance director, championed ward voting, advocated firing the city manager in order to give elected officials, not appointees, more power over day-to-day affairs, and urged a ballot referendum to repeal and revise the charter. SAC candidates mixed their general fight for representative, responsive government with individual concerns. Darby passed around "girlie magazines," which he emphasized were easily obtained and thus evidence of "a growing moral decay." MacDonald decried road conditions because narrow gauges and missing left-turn arrows endangered the citizenry. Hanner demanded pay increases for police officers and firefighters, which reflected SAC complaints that CGC fiscal policies were irresponsible and burdensome and an implicit acknowledgment that investment had not yielded universal economic advancement. Candidates also found booster rhetoric and politics incongruous, particularly increasing property taxes and doubling water rates.[21]

SAC considered the increased rates and taxes evidence of a Communist conspiracy, not a booster-built corporate welfare state. Hanner deemed CGC members, including Goldwater, dupes who did not realize that the housing code had been an attempt to give the International City Managers Association control over Phoenix. Hanner held that the National Municipal League, the organization that had given Phoenix multiple All-American City awards, controlled urban America through "itinerant experts," such as Kansas City native Ray Wilson. The CGC's city manager seemed to be one of those "experts . . . planning to plan us out of our freedom." Hanner even alleged that Wilson could unseat elected representatives, tangible proof of an imminent "Metro plot" by "Socialistic planners" "to erase all city, county and state boundaries for easier political control" in order to commandeer American power sources, like the Colorado River dams, and destroy state capitals.[22]

Such far-fetched accusations reflected the extent to which booster containment strategies, such as the widespread education initiatives, had constrained mainstream political rhetoric. Anti-Communist, free-enterprise politics had never utilized a nuanced vocabulary to explain the critical role of governance to national and grasstops business conservatism. The uncertain and the opposed only had such terms as "socialism" and "Communism" to describe the state's expansion, articulate how annexation did in fact disenfranchise homeowners, and complain that voters had little power over the unelected bureaucrats who oversaw day-to-day governance.

CGC enthusiasts subsequently struggled to use their established political lexicon to deflect these accusations. A former CGC councilman publicly fumed that the opposition was "making irresponsible and malicious statements under the guise of superpatriotism [*sic*], which does violence to the anti-Communist cause." Others complained that the "militant group" ran a "quiet type of whispering campaign" because members lacked "the intestinal fortitude to tell us to our faces the blubberings we've been hearing." But Mardian struggled to defend himself: "I am not a dupe of the Communist conspiracy. I do not take orders from a super-governmental agency in Chicago. . . . The City Manager of Phoenix cannot fire me. I do not approve of vice or pornography. I am not dedicated to the elimination of our traditional political subdivisions or to the creation of a municipal dictatorship. I have no desire to make your life uncomfortable."[23]

CGC defenders' difficulties reflected how their good-government, investment-first, conservative governance was at odds with the mass democracy ideals fueling campaigns for civil rights, reapportionment, and tax relief. Pulliam-press editorialists, for example, had considered the housing code an affront to limited governance but still defended the all-powerful city manager and at-large voting in the 1961 election. "The old days of intolerable interference in running the government" would return, newsmen warned, if SAC was able to fire the city manager, institute district voting, and give department heads "direct access to council members in conducting the business of government." No less than the definition of conservatism, liberalism, and radicalism was at stake in this contest. "Here is one of the most responsible, progressive yet stable groups ever to hold municipal office," the first CGC mayor commented. "To claim it has leftist tendencies is to depart from the real situation altogether and begin pulling up fantasies." "Candidates are attacking the Arizona and Phoenix brand of conservatism," *Republic* reporters warned. "Arizonans . . . don't want government to do for people what people can do for themselves. They distrust central bureaucracies. They object to socialism and statism." "These principles are held and practiced by the Charter Government," CGC staffers emphasized. "Vote for them . . . if you want your state to continue the fight to make conservatism respectable across the nation."[24]

SAC was a tangible menace. Insurgents had already frustrated urban renewal efforts, but now national attention to "ultra-conservatives," as *New York Times* staffers deemed upstarts, threatened the Chamber's carefully constructed business climate. Even conservative syndicated columnist Victor Riesel disliked these "ultra groups," who "scare the suspender buttons right off such veteran anti-Communists as myself." The SAC campaign also instigated open discussion of Phoenix politics among the electorate. Some regarded these rebels as dangerous and delusional. Methodist clergyman Paul Alexander told churchgoers that East Coast, far-right extremists had founded the slate. "At least one," he recounted, "is reliably reported to be a member of the John Birch Society. Two of them are openly anti-Semitic[,] . . . who offer nothing but hate and suspicion and innuendo as their stock in trade." Others fretted that leaders would later court "these 'fire in the belly' radical rightists," as part of "the drudgery that wins elections." Yet some, who had observed quick, quiet suburban annexations, had shouldered tax increases, and had paid higher utility bills, defended SAC and defamed the CGC: "An extreme right-wing type of government is what was created for us by our founding fathers, not the New Frontier monstrosity of today which is strangling freedom to an ever increasing degree."[25]

A SAC victory proved a pipedream, not a nightmare, in 1961. Only 29 percent of eligible voters bothered to go to the polls. Thirty-two thousand out of forty-five thousand endorsed the CGC in the primary, results that preempted a general election. Candidates did carry some precincts, five in the south side and two in the north side. "I've spoken to about 45,000 people on communism and Americanism," Hanner declared. "Nobody can say I did nothing about the Communist threat."[26]

This Anglo discontent coexisted with liberal and minority discontent with CGC rule. Investment had not yielded substantive dividends in working-class Anglo and non-Anglo neighborhoods. In the mid-1960s, African Americans had a disproportionately small presence in all employment sectors except domestic service, entertainment, and recreation. Few had skilled, professional, or managerial positions. Black entrepreneurs did own businesses on the south side, mostly service or retail establishments. A few operated banks, insurance companies, or real estate firms. Mexican Americans also had limited opportunities, which did not stop them and undocumented Mexican workers from moving into booming Maricopa County in the 1950s. Low estimates showed that their numbers surged along with those of Anglos, jumping from roughly sixteen thousand to 61,460 as Phoenix neared the half-million mark in 1960. Few enjoyed the fruits of the Valley's industrialization. Only 33.5 percent had a high school diploma, much less the training for the most lucrative work in the Valley. A small number headed taverns, markets, or other service-oriented firms. Twenty-one percent lived below the poverty line, more than double the percentage of Anglos. At-large elections and literacy tests thus only added to the general civic disenfranchisement of Valley minorities.[27]

Campaigns for racial progress had continued during this period, well after Phoenix's fledgling Popular Front collapsed. The subsequent civil rights campaigns did not directly challenge the CGC until the early 1960s because leaders came from professional and proprietor stock, who stood by interwar voluntarist solutions. Friendly House directors, who still largely resided on the north side, continued to advocate for Americanization after World War II. Many board members also deemed federal social services unnecessary and intrusive. Great Society programs divided the leadership, who would only make a proposal after contentious debates and backdoor maneuvering. Federal officials would then deny the request because staffers uniformly ignored African Americans' requests for help finding employment, a violation of the just-passed 1964 Civil Rights Act.[28]

Postwar social justice initiatives thus had much in common with moderate desegregation campaigns elsewhere in the nation. For example, the largely middle-class Greater Phoenix Council for Civic Unity (GPCCU), Arizona Council for Civic Unity (ACCU), local affiliate of the National Association for the Advancement of Colored People (NAACP), and area chapter for the Urban League, whose membership rolls often overlapped with other Arizona- and Phoenix-based civil rights organizations, all backed a late 1940s effort to end school segregation. Leaders Lincoln and Eleanor

Ragsdale also received support from the Anglo business elite, who pressured legislators to pass a bill that allowed individual school boards to desegregate voluntarily, a position in line with racially moderate southern solutions. African American activists and local white attorneys then filed suit on the behalf of three students to force the Phoenix board to integrate schools. GPCCU, NAACP, and ACCU paid the lawyers appearing before the Arizona Supreme Court, which declared segregated schools unconstitutional a year before the 1954 *Brown v. Board of Education* decision. The ruling had little immediate impact. Few minorities lived in Phoenix Union High School's district, and only a handful were reshuffled within the Valley's public schools. Small changes nonetheless pleased the GPCCU members who preferred incrementalism in order to keep the peace and protect their children.[29]

Action displaced maneuvering in the early 1960s. Mexican Americans' boycotts of downtown bargain department stores, like Sears, where Mexican Americans did much of their shopping, improved hiring practices. Well-planned campaigns also gave African Americans a foothold in the city's largest, most prominent firms. In the fall of 1962, two of the city's most prominent and affluent African American civil rights activists, Lincoln Ragsdale and George Brooks, conferred privately with Valley National Bank (VNB) executive James Patrick to demand an end to discriminatory hiring practices. Ragsdale purposely goaded Patrick, calling him "a bigot, a Hitler, a hater," as activists filed into the building. They asked tellers for "seventy-five pennies as partial change for a dollar," while those in line behind them sang "We Shall Overcome." The demonstration was effective. VNB hired its first African American cashier within a month.[30]

Ragsdale and other NAACP members also organized hundreds to apply for work at GE, Sperry Rand, and Motorola. Carpools brought jobseekers directly to personnel offices. "Cordial but firm" managers, Brooks remembered, asserted: "'We are not going to hire any black folks here. We must give these jobs to parents of white engineers we want to recruit.'" Employers did not buckle until 1962, when a Maricopa County Welfare Department employee turned over a memo which stated that a major manufacturer wanted "a young woman on welfare, eighteen years of age, with a high school diploma, who must be white." The NAACP investigated the matter and used the document to provide the state attorney general with a verifiable case of racial discrimination. Brooks then publicly accused county officials of "being in collusion with firms to deny black people jobs." Press coverage embarrassed both the Welfare Department and Motorola, which immediately placed the first African American on the manufacturing line.[31]

Young protestors also played a pivotal role in ending booster governance. Upstarts from outside south Phoenix's small proprietor or professional ranks were less interested in middle-class business concerns, questioned the basic definitions of representation, access, and justice, and hence challenged both south-side and city hall leadership. To this end, many leading Mexican American activists were inspired more by unionists in the mines and fields outside Phoenix than by the stewards of Friendly House. These Chicanos were often the sons and daughters of laborers, whose organizational acumen and militancy inspired them to use leafleting, picketing, and policy to reclaim the Valley for the grassroots. Such politics certainly inspired Mildred Brown, the bilingual Chicana social worker from a small southern Arizona town who assumed Friendly House's directorship in 1965. She openly opposed Americanization and the funneling of residents into unskilled, temporary day-labor work, a practice that assumed jobseekers did not speak English or have higher aspirations. She also offered services to all those interested, regardless of race or national descent. Moreover, the organization's new, professional social work department matched services and employment opportunities to local needs and desires. These programs and directives alienated the old leadership, who abandoned the organization early in Brown's tenure.[32]

Young Mexican Americans also emphasized community and activism, alongside advancement, when they established Chicanos por la Causa (CPLC). Key activists, including Gustavo Gutierrez, Arturo Rosales, Joe Eddie López, and Rosie López, had all been involved in the United Farm Workers' attempts to unionize Arizona laborers in the 1960s, which predated the famous grape boycott that drew national attention to field hands protesting peonage in California. These Arizonans also took their crusade for justice to Arizona State University (ASU), demanding equitable access and hiring along with courses in Chicano history and literature. But these renegades wanted to transform the entire Valley, not just its university and surrounding farmland. Money from the Southwest Council of La Raza (later the National Council of La Raza), the Ford Foundation, and the U.S. Department of Housing and Urban Development funded their radical critique of the rural and urban status quo. "The people of this country must come to realize that the genocide of the Indian and the brutal colonization of the Chi-

Figure 16. Daniel Ortega addressed a 1970s Chicanos por la Causa meeting with the organization's former president Eddie López seated on his left. Members dedicated themselves to activism, empowerment, and enfranchisement, which contrasted sharply with the longtime leaders of Phoenix's Friendly House, an organization that had emphasized Americanization and voluntarism. Courtesy of the Where Worlds Meet Collection, Chicano Research Collection, Arizona State University Libraries.

cano, is as much an expression of America's cancer—*racism*—as is the ugly history of slavery and oppression of the Black man," CPLC president Joe Eddie Lopez asserted in the group's mission statement.[33]

Denunciations and initiatives centered on representation, access, and power. "The leadership of this city has made no real commitment to solving the problems of poverty," a neighborhood organizer railed. This empowerment ethos ran throughout programs to register and educate voters, to facilitate economic advancement, train community leaders, and aid rural Chicanos. Grassroots, not middlebrow, democratic ideals also permeated campaigns, especially Phoenix-area education initiatives. Organizers helped parents improve schools by explaining existing policies, turning out voters for board elections, and demanding that administrators hire Chicano teachers and counselors. Success was tangible: all schools soon had faculty committees on "human relations" as well as student and parent advisory groups.[34]

But these older associations struggled to attract younger African Americans. Student Non-Violent Coordinating Committee, Congress of Racial Equality, and Black Panther Party chapters appealed to these younger residents, who found themselves at odds with the Anglo business elite and the middle-class NAACP leadership. Some upstarts even rejected pleas to practice nonviolence. Rioters threw stones, fired weapons, looted stores, and destroyed property on the south side in late July 1967. The mayor attempted to install a curfew and quell the mayhem with increased police presence. His efforts only worsened the conflict. Protestors burned a house and several police cruisers. Law enforcement officials made almost three hundred arrests. Radicals then met with the mayor and a long-time NAACP activist after the five-day conflict ended. They demanded more community services, but mayoral assurances for improved race relations proved hollow. Phoenicians instead received less support and more police presence.[35]

Civil Rights activists had already challenged booster rule before the 1967 uprising. In the 1963 three-way city council race, the Action Citizens' Ticket (ACT) represented the politically reengaged south side and the generational shift within the business elite. Lincoln Ragsdale, Anglo liberal Democrat Richard Harless, teacher Madelene Van Arsdell, businessman Manuel Peña, and educator Charles Farrell included Ed Korrick on their slate. As the son of retailer Charles Korrick, whose department store competed with Goldwater's, the younger Korrick stood somewhat outside the Phoenix Chamber of Commerce, whose leadership corporate executives and branch plant managers now dominated. "I did not have any argument of principle with Charter Committee in the past," he later explained, "but felt that it should democratize and broaden its base. . . . What has started as dedication to the reform movement," he emphasized, "has ended in dedication to 'the establishment.'" ACT's platform did challenge the status quo. Candidates attacked the CGC for spending money on golf courses, not pools, parks, or youth centers. They promised to fight discrimination, raise city employee salaries, subsidize residential water bills, pave south-side neighborhood roads, and apply for federal aid. "Many millions," one candidate asserted, "have been lost through inaction and lack of leadership." Their politics impressed the Phoenix Central Labor Council, who gave support after a long absence from local affairs.[36]

ACT squared off against the CGC and another set of free-enterprise-attuned suburbanites. Candidates on the new Honesty, Economy, and Representation ticket (HEAR) jettisoned SAC's anti-Communist warnings, not its basic criticisms of CGC rule and desires for residential services and empowerment. "We don't know what's going on in City Hall is our platform," the mayoral candidate explained. Neither the "liberal" ACT and the "conservative liberal" CGC, he explained, "has the capacity to adequately represent the best interests of all the people." In contrast, the self-described "nonpartisan and conservative" HEAR advocated increased spending, lower taxation, and better representation through a reduction of the duties on food and medicine, reinstating the office of tax assessor to equalize assessments, and improving public neighborhood infrastructure. Candidates also opposed a 3 percent room tax to pay for a civic auditorium, wanted to limit annexations, and denounced "dictatorial" planning and zoning policies, all elements of business climate statecraft.[37]

The two fronts forced the CGC to hire a full-time public relations agency, which managed a campaign anchored in promises of expansion, efficiency, and thrift and in old attacks on labor, liberalism, and bossism. CGC defenders called the HEAR slate "ultra-conservatives," whose opposition to expansion would yield independent satellite communities that would choke the city with unplanned, revenue-draining, environmentally damaging suburbs. Reporters called ACT candidates "a combination of liberal politicians (who see the Phoenix City Hall as a way station to the state capital building) and well-heeled labor leaders (who have tried unsuccessfully to organize city hall with union members)." "Liberal-labor bosses," a contender remarked, "want to take over the entire city, returning to the patronage-ridden system. . . . Improvements in various parts of the city," he warned, "would be dependent upon the favor of the bosses." Charter candidates argued that ACT's platform and policies were also an unnecessary extension of government power. "You simply can't do what these people propose," a candidate warned, "without doubling taxes, relying on federal aid and spending the taxpayers into oblivion."[38]

The CGC had a close call in 1963, just two years after SAC's defeat. More than 53 percent of registered voters participated in the primary, more than in any city election since 1949. Participants overwhelmingly endorsed the CGC's mayoral pick, but HEAR council candidates did well in northwest suburbs, and ACT nominees received at least twenty-five thousand votes, which necessitated a general election. Turnout remained high in December: 43.4 percent of registered voters returned to their polling places, still higher than in any contest since 1951. ACT endorsees each received between twenty-six thousand and thirty-five thousand votes. They even benefited from HEAR's endorsement, a populist concession to Phoenix liberals who stood a chance of defeating the CGC. "We didn't win," an ACT contender admitted, "but we did shake up city hall!" Ragsdale was particularly proud of minority involvement: "We rallied this community like it had never been rallied before."[39]

ACT and the HEAR ticket had provoked the electorate. "In the beginning of the Charter Government, I worked for them," James DeWitt lamented. "They have been in office too long. They are thinking in the past and doing nothing to solve the problems of today." Some mixed their annoyance at the CGC with a desire for better representation. One *Republic* reader even denounced newsmen for ignoring this democratic ideal. "You further erred in reporting as fact that 'the Charter Government represents all elements and groups,'" the Phoenician fumed. "In truth, no six people could." Yet critics did not necessarily profess faith in rival slates. "ACT candidates have shown me nothing in the way of a definite program," DeWitt asserted, and "HEAR guys . . . are worse. . . . I can find only one thing that they stand for," he lamented, "tax equalization, which I have advocated for so long, as executive secretary of the Arizona Homeowners Association. But this is only appealing to the ignorance of voters. Only a fool would think that the city council has anything to do with equalization."[40]

Grassroots insurrections plagued the CGC. Adaptation proved difficult. Leaders expanded the selection committee and created a new subgroup to increase membership. They campaigned earlier, brought more members into election efforts, prepared material on the CGC's history for voters, and worked out methods to improve candidate selection. The nominating committee also selected Dr. Morrison Warren, an African American teacher, and Frank Benites, the Mexican American chair of the Phoenix Labor Council, for the 1965 ticket. Both lived on the south side and won. Then in 1969 the CGC nominated Calvin Goode, a young African American activist who had headed Phoenix's Community Action Program (Leadership and Education for the Advancement of Phoenix).[41]

Goode won in a watershed election year when the CGC seemed to be publicly unraveling. Three-term mayor Milton Graham had wanted an unprecedented fourth term, but only a select few had ever been allowed a third. The selection committee refused to back him and the rest of the incumbent council. They ran anyway. Though CGC picks won a plurality together, voters had split their ballots, opening the door for the popular Korrick (who had run as an independent). CGC higher-ups ushered him into the fold for the 1971 election, but this stopgap did not prevent Gary Peter Klahr from winning a seat as an independent in 1973. The Bronx-born lawyer defined himself as a rebel. He had registered as a Republican to spurn his New Deal Democrat parents, sued the Arizona board of regents to stop mandatory Reserved Officers' Training Corps (ROTC) training, filed the claim that triggered Arizona's reapportionment, and switched his party affiliation after he started taking high-profile American Civil Liberty Union cases. During his 1971 campaign, Klahr criticized the charter as undemocratic. He remained a critic in office: advocating an end to at-large elections, lambasting CGC "rent a minority" policy as illusionary representation, and assailing the Pulliam press for brainwashing voters into thinking that only the CGC could "keep us from having rats in the street and prostitution." This renegade worried stalwarts: "Nobody in town knows who Charter is." "We really don't know what the people want," the mayor fretted.[42]

But the CGC ultimately imploded. Two-term councilwoman Margaret Hance broke with the group when the selection committee refused to endorse her 1975 mayoral run. The TV producer joined a packed field of thirty-three candidates, twenty independent of a slate, vying for seven seats. Though hopefuls declared themselves unconnected to the "self-appointed political machine which calls itself Charter Government," they were hardly united. Representation issues, such as ward voting and city-manager power, divided these candidates.[43]

CGC stalwarts dismissed challengers in the language of professionalism, order, and clean governance that had first brought them to power.

Figure 17. The Charter Government Committee's control of the city council ended in 1975, when voters elected just two members of the slate. The victors, pictured here after their swearing in, included new faces and voices, who may have protested grasstops control but did not immediately amend Phoenix's charter. Courtesy of the University Archives Photographs, Arizona State University Libraries.

"Most of the candidates are inexperienced and they just can't deal with issues," a strategist warned. District-voting supporters, the mayor proclaimed, would place "city government . . . into the hands of private political interests." He also lauded the ticket tradition: "There is such confusion on who is running." CGC nominees also continued to proclaim themselves community-minded volunteers. "We are not politicians," one announced, "we have no desire to make a career out of public office."[44]

Yet the electorate was divided. "I will not vote against a system that has proven its success time after time," Sandra Mara proclaimed. Opponents, in contrast, often conflated their distaste for the CGC's power with their resentment toward at-large voting and city fiscal policies. ASU student Mark Stearns lambasted *Republic* editorialists for "childish mudslinging" assertions that independents "are for a 'puppet' manager and a costly manipulated ward system." Robert Ehrlich questioned the "growth mania" that underlay CGC politics and the business climate ideal: "I . . . would like to ask the mayor . . . how many dollars we are going to save in services we won't have to provide for those who didn't move here." He had little concern for investment. "Too bad about the business interests who wax fat on growth," he declared. "Let them go elsewhere."[45]

Election results bespoke building discontent with booster rule. Seventy-seven percent of voters picked independents in the November primary. Hance secured the mayorship, and twelve candidates, with six forming a loose alliance against CGC picks, vied for council positions. Four unaffiliated contestants won in December. Two, Rosendo Gutierrez and Calvin Goode, had been CGC incumbents whom the selection committee refused to renominate.[46]

Hance's six-year tenure was still not a fundamental break with CGC governance. She never pretended otherwise. "While I am not the Charter Committ's [*sic*] candidate for mayor," she told voters, "I support the strong council-manager form of government. It has guided the city very well for the past twenty-five years." She also lauded "business-minded government" policies that "recogniz[ed] the needs of business to profit, have not been overly restrictive and have seen that business can also be good corporate citizens interested in the same goals for the same reasons as is government." She thus conducted "the business of building a great City" by utilizing the CGC council's arsenal of incentives in a "regulatory relief program" to "make Phoenix attractive for commercial and industrial location, eliminate barriers to growth, and preserve the community's esthetic values and appearance." Her administration did adapt to the new metropolitan politics. City bonds, not higher individual or business taxes, paid for city infrastructure projects and services which business owners demanded and Phoenix's 25 percent increase in size and population required.[47]

CGC founders nonetheless considered Hance's run an affront. "We don't like the fact that we're criticized[,] and you know we are unmercifully," CGC founder Margaret Kober complained in a 1976 interview. "A little group of people get in a closed room (smoke-filled, usually; designated as such) and select a handful of people and they put them up," she continued. "But I don't know any better way." Her frustrations pinpointed why the CGC no longer served as a kingmaker: Sunbelt urban management was anathema to local and national concerns for transparent governance and civic participation. The committee, for example, endorsed several candidates in 1977, but many now considered such support a hindrance to their campaign. Some Charter stalwarts later regrouped as the Phoenix 40, whose leaders, including lawyer Frank Snell, came from the CGC's long-standing inner circle of successful businessmen. Members publicly pledged not to undermine the Chamber or council's power. Their influence still proved negligible. Critics wrote them off as a "white-collared executive group of crime stoppers."[48]

This municipal realignment had occurred alongside a movement to overhaul the city's charter. Klahr had offered a tepid retreat from midcentury metropolitan politics before his later reregistration with the Democratic Party. He and other businessmen in the Representative Citizen's Association drafted and campaigned for a district system and an eight-member council. The proposal did not fundamentally challenge booster governance: districts gave Republicans distinct advantages in all but two areas. Voter registration, not population, set these precincts and thus would have left non-Anglo neighborhoods in the south section underrepresented and marginalized, while privileging grasstops neighborhoods as well as the enclaves where white populist insurgents resided. The Chamber and CGC subsequently dedicated their resources to defeating the 1967 referendum.[49]

But the issue continued to resurface. A 1973 initiative, which proposed to balance the council with five ward representatives and three at-large members, forced the old guard to recycle warnings incongruous to the redefinition of democratic governance. Pulliam editorialists dismissed malapportionment claims ("Thanks to the support of the Charter Government Committee, the minorities have been well represented down through the years") and raised the specter of the raging New York City fiscal crisis ("No one wants to see ward politics do to Phoenix what it has done to New York"). Advocates, in contrast, rooted their support in the increasingly predominate one-man-one-vote ideal. "It is unreasonable to think of an at-large Congress . . . or legislature," Joseph Pegnato asserted. "At large . . . government . . . is not responding to the needs of all the people." "Just because a black, chicano or an anglo [*sic*] is 'hand picked,'" Sandra Wilks fumed, "does not make he or she representative of a particular minority or majority." "Let democracy work! Let the people in their local areas decide who shall represent them." The measure still failed by more than thirty-two thousand votes, with just fewer than fifty thousand residents in support.[50]

An overhaul finally came in the 1980s. An October 1981 *Phoenix Gazette* poll revealed that 65 percent of respondents wanted a district system. Reformers then circulated petitions to expand the city council to eight members, institute a ward system for council seats, and retain an at-large vote for the mayorship in June 1982. Proposition 200 combined all of these planks. The December 1982 special election was still hotly contested. Opponents from the city's elite business circles outspent supporters by a margin of three to one. "I think we're going straight into ward politics," a former mayor warned. "Barry Goldwater feels the same." High-ranking Chamber members predicted inefficient backdoor dealing and corruption, which would "undercut the council-manager form of city government because individual council members go directly to department heads to resolve problems." The association's support helped, not hindered, their opposition. "A small group of self-appointed manipulators control who is elected to the City council," one supporter charged, "operat[ing] under the assumption that they . . . alone know what is best for the city." Such accusations resonated with voters. One Phoenician supported the revisions because "the *Arizona Republic* is against it." Nonetheless, the initiative nearly failed.[51]

Grassroots Insurgencies

But similar challenges had already toppled booster regimes elsewhere in the Sunbelt. San Diegans, for example, had already grown weary of growth, taxation, and business rule by 1961 when Chamber men launched their Build Industrial Growth (BIG) program. Boosters sent denizens a request for $1 and a postage-paid return envelope in order to build community support and financial reserves. Reaction was, unlike in years past, decidedly mixed. A few respondents sent coordinators thank-you notes with their contributions. Others gave happily but wanted less outside investment: "Imagine the publicity and daily interest that could be generated in the community, if BIG essentially assisted a brand new, 'home grown' company to get started." Some offered advice in lieu of a donation: "Let's attract tourists and retired middle class citizens who come here with money to spend for homes, autos, services, and merchandise." A contingent rejected growth and business climate statecraft outright. "You people sure have unlimited guts, flooding the countryside with this BIG krap [*sic*] asking the citizens to wreck the city further," a San Diegan raged. "I hope the lot of you rot in *hell*." A transplanted Phoenician even dismissed the good-governance guarantee embedded within Sunbelt boosterism: "S.D. should first rid itself of the rotten city government and make this a decent place for the people who are already living here. . . . For our taxes we get less return than any other city." Others wanted lower residential duties, implicitly or explicitly asking why they never enjoyed the promised reductions or saw free-enterprise principles in action. "Every time the population increases," another commented, "TAXES go up instead of down. In a well run Business [*sic*] the greater the volume the lower the cost of the product to the consumer. Evidentially this doesn't apply to services rendered by the City."[52]

As in Phoenix, such frustrations fed the multifaceted campaigns to end grasstops governance. Across the Southwest, civil rights proponents, liberals, and suburbanites frustrated revenue initiatives, staged popular protests and launched numerous oppositional slates. Charges of undemocratic corruption, like those the business elite had lobbed at petit-capitalist politicians a generation before, permeated this next era in municipal reform. Progressive Dallas residents, who ran on promises of better public health and housing policies, defined themselves against the "status quo, to closed meetings, closed doors, and . . . the 'father knows best' approach." In San Jose white homeowners led the first successful charge against the local Chamber's political machine. And in Austin an array of challengers unified against the city's aging businessmen, though insurgents were unable to build any kind of unified majority council in the 1960s.[53]

Upstarts gained ground throughout the 1960s and 1970s. Grasstops politicians, like CGC representatives, relied on the same rhetoric of good-government reform that promised to protect residents from ward bosses and "Eastern-style" politics, anachronistic warnings in a period when residents from a range of backgrounds and devoted to a multitude of causes demanded equal representation. The grasstops also staved off challengers by diversifying slates, fulfilling constituents' demands, making first-ever campaign stops in non-Anglo and Anglo working-class neighborhoods, and undertaking limited reform, such as adding new council seats and overhauling nominating systems. But voters ultimately dismantled the electoral rules that insulated booster machines. Many of the mid-century charters were redrafted either wholesale or piecemeal through referenda by 1980. Albuquerque, Dallas, San Antonio, and San Jose abandoned at-large elections in the 1970s, whereas San Diego's at-large provisions remained in effect until 1988, six years after Phoenicians amended their charter.[54]

Southern Chamber regimes also collapsed in this period. These machines had always depended on an unequal, tenuous alliance with African American elites, who, in turn, had some influence on the white business establishment. As in Phoenix, 1960s student radicalism and federal voting and civil rights guarantees proved potent challenges to grasstops governance. Protestors filed suit against at-large election clauses in city charters and defeated white businessmen politicians in city council and mayoral contests throughout the 1960s. White suburbanites were also a part of this general challenge to southern businessmen's rule, especially as conflict between central cities and suburbs escalated over taxation and desegregation.[55]

Such uprisings influenced William Hartsfield's retirement from the Atlanta mayor's office in 1961. His twenty-three-year tenure had relied on a coalition of white business advisers and African American elites, who delivered electoral support. The alliance splintered in the 1960s when Atlanta became an epicenter of the southern civil rights movement. Black Atlanta college students instigated the transformation of Atlanta politics when they purchased space in the *Constitution* for their "Appeal for Human Rights." The missive, appearing just a month after the 1960 Greensboro sit-ins, promised legal, nonviolent methods "to secure full citizenship rights as members of this great Democracy." "We cannot tolerate," the activists proclaimed, "the discriminatory conditions under which the Negro is living today in Atlanta, . . . supposedly one of the most progressive cities in the South." The proclamation alone strained the Hartsfield regime. But the ensuing sit-ins led to intergenerational fights between black Atlantans, conflicts between business owners and elected officials, and dramatic protests and counter-demonstrations throughout the central business district.[56]

Court-ordered desegregation and moderate compliance also created a wedge between Atlanta's grasstops and white working-class voters. The latter, unlike wealthy whites, depended on public transportation, recreation, and education, the services integrated throughout the 1950s and 1960s. Suburbanites offered staunch resistance, abandoned just-desegregated spaces, and moved to free themselves from city levies. These municipal duties were a key issue: working-class whites considered their taxes payment for the public amenities they needed and were, in their minds, losing to black Atlantans. Free-enterprise, anticommunist rhetoric thus colored segregationist literature conflating racial antagonism with taxation. "SHALL YOU CONTINUE TO PAY FOR THEIR PLEASURE?" read one broadside. "While they sit in the shade and spoon in the moon light, multiplying like rats, we continue to bleed ourselves with heavy taxes to carry the socialistic burden of feeding and clothing them. They do not remain as slaves and therefore are certainly not your wards."[57]

Frustrated white Atlantans found a champion in Lester Maddox, who owned the Pickrick Restaurant, a cafeteria-style greasy spoon popular with Georgia Tech students and area laborers. Like ACT and HEAR candidates in Phoenix, Maddox belonged to the petit-capitalist class, who had ceased filtering through city hall during Hartsfield's reign. Maddox and his supporters had borne much of the tax burden required to build Atlanta's business climate. This southern municipal renegade was as long on folksy charm, fury at white elites, and dedication to individual rights as George Wallace. These principles shaped Maddox's values-inflected segregationist politics and his electoral campaigns. And Atlantans knew his views. A decade of "Pickrick Says" advertisements in the Sunday paper touted the restaurant and decried integration.[58]

Fame propelled Maddox's 1957 mayoral run from a joke to a threat. An informal poll indicated that the late entrant led in six of Atlanta's eight wards. The mayor then fervently campaigned to forestall "another Little Rock" with a $50,000 war chest, which city businessmen raised in two days. He subsequently won by more than seventeen thousand votes. Maddox nonetheless did well among the white working class and even among the middle class and affluent.[59]

Losing failed to dissuade Maddox. He organized Georgians Unwilling to Surrender (GUTS) in the face of the 1960 Atlanta boycotts that had at least partly inspired Hartsfield's retirement. Maddox borrowed heavily from the grasstops' political playbook: he demanded businessmen refuse to surrender, delighted that counterboycotts had made "the slowdown of the blacks look like child's play," and directed broad class-based appeals to the sanctity of private property and individual rights. He also denounced his elite opponents for jeopardizing the free market. "Atlanta businessmen who believe in our system of free enterprise and freedom of choice," he asserted, "should speak up and be heard, before Atlanta is falsely recognized as being controlled by 'so-called' liberals."[60]

Popular support fueled Maddox's 1961 mayoral bid against Ivan Allen Jr., the Chamber's president. Economic progress through gradual desegregation and token integration defined Allen's campaign, whereas Maddox assailed such policies as a part of a general assault on the American principles that the business elite had once made touchstones of their reform efforts. At issue, one of his ads read, "is whether we will return to sensible constitutional government BY and FOR YOU, the people, or if we will continue to compromise, surrender, and place ourselves under the control of those who would harm our families, destroy our property values, take our jobs, direct our businesses, tell us where to work, who to hire, where to live and what to think." The Atlanta primary, unlike the simultaneous Phoenix contest, ended in a near tie. Allen did prevail in the later runoff, with African Americans casting the votes that offset Maddox's inroads among all segments of white Atlantans, including the business elite.[61]

Victory did not quell the building white working-class revolt. Atlantans stunned city leaders when residents turned out in record numbers to reject a 1962 bond of $80 million to pay for the kind of city infrastructure and improvements integral to the business climate. Middle- and working-class whites conflated taxation, spending, and integration to explain their opposition: "Taxpayers are tired of paying hard-earned money for things that they will not be able to enjoy because of the prospect of forced integration, which means that the facilities would be used almost entirely by Negroes." Opposition continued when Allen backed a less expansive 1963 initiative. Objectors then alleged that civil rights groups controlled the mayor. "Don't give the 'CAPTIVE MAYOR' of the Minority Bloc a blank check to use against the OTHER voters and tax-payers of Atlanta," a leaflet proclaimed. "VOTE AGAINST BONDS!" Allen eked out a narrow victory this time around, but only by spending $25,000 to court black Atlantans and affluent whites.[62]

Realigning the Sunbelt

Such bitter fights over Sunbelt city governance also informed a larger evolution within state and party politics. White suburbanites played a pivotal role in southern postwar realignment and reapportionment. These residents had supported Eisenhower, filed suits for better representation, and voted Republicans into office. Atlanta fitted within this regional trend: a metropolitan majority sent two conservative Republicans to Congress in 1966, the same year Maddox's gubernatorial victory signaled a sea change in Georgia politics. The dark horse had triumphed in the primary after the frontrunner withdrew and others tried to finesse their frustrations with LBJ, the 1964 Civil Rights Act, and the national Democratic Party. "He's a folk hero," one supporter said of Maddox. "People look at him and understand exactly what he stands for and it's what they stand for." Allen, for his part, decried this constituency as "the rabble of prejudice, extremism, buffoonery, and incompetency."[63]

But Maddox's primary victory did not ensure a general election win. He faced a moderate write-in and a formidable Republican, Howard "Bo" Callaway, a textile heir and Georgia's first GOP congressman since Reconstruction. Callaway's allegiance to "God, the individual, and free enterprise" had appealed to white suburbanites in 1964 and also made him politically indistinguishable from Maddox. Yet Callaway was, as a fellow delegate described, "slicker,": "He uses code names such as 'property rights,' which means 'we ain't gonna serve no niggers.'" The three-way race ended with Callaway in a three-thousand-vote lead. Georgia law required the assembly to decide the winner when contests did not yield a clear majority. Legislators overwhelmingly sided with Maddox, the Democrat. But the 1967 vote nevertheless foreshadowed the Republican revolution: GOP legislative ranks steadily increased (especially after redistricting gave Atlantans more seats), and metropolitan Georgia later elected some of the country's foremost post-Reagan conservatives, including Bob Barr and Newt Gingrich.[64]

Similar populist, free-enterprise, individual-focused, religiously-inflected politics bedeviled the Phoenix GOP establishment. In the early postwar period, leaders had shown little tolerance for party members as openly devout to God as they were to free enterprise. John Conlan included. Unlike SAC candidates, the Illinois native had seemed well suited to grasstops conservatism: he had a chemistry degree from Northwestern, a law degree from Harvard, had studied international trade and investment on a Fulbright scholarship to the University of Cologne, and then worked overseas in the Army's Judge Advocate General core. He had also left the military a firm believer "in a limited government with balance" and emphasized this principle throughout the political science courses that he offered at ASU in the 1960s.[65]

But Conlan put his faith on display. He considered himself ostracized from the "'in' group in the Republican party," despite recruiting "thousands of people" and helping to challenge South Phoenix voters (Conlan maintained that Rehnquist "wasn't involved in the precincts. He was our attorney at our headquarters.") Conlan's feelings were justified: Paul Fannin had fired the transplant from his 1958 gubernatorial campaign for "selling Bibles instead of the work he was supposed to be doing." But Scottsdale suburbanites would elect him to the State senate in 1965, just after Klahr's reapportionment suit fully enfranchised these white suburbanites, many as devoted to the free market, local control, and God as Conlan. During his seven years in office, he supported lower taxes, tougher drug laws, and free enterprise course requirements.[66]

His political and religious perseverance was fully realized after additional population growth created Arizona's fourth congressional district. Both the Arizona Christian Conference on Adult and Youth Programs and the Executive Committee of Billy Graham's Arizona Crusade supported his 1972 campaign to bring "constitutional government" and "individual freedom" to the House. Once in Washington, Conlan won the favor of top Christian conservatives, including strategist Richard Viguerie and Nixon aide Charles Colson, who floated his name in the press as a future presidential contender. Arizona Senators Fannin and Goldwater could no longer sideline Conlan or make wholly secular appeals to his supporters. "Conlan has a personal relationship with Jesus Christ," a voter noted in a letter asking Goldwater if he had been saved, "Why don't you get him to tell you about it? Ask him what Christ means to him. You'll be glad you did." Goldwater had had little problem with Shadegg's proselytizing but this conservative constituent's convictions puzzled Goldwater, who admitted in 1980: "I can't really make out what [evangelicals] want."[67]

Goldwater's generation had come to see themselves as on the defensive by the 1970s and 1980s. They encountered what Orme Lewis described as "real primary contests," like Stephen Shadegg's surprising loss to Evan Mecham in 1962. But rainmakers fought to maintain their power. Lewis, for example, joined others in the "Early Birds" in the 1970s, an "elite corps" of three hundred Republicans dedicated to the "survival of our American Heritage and the philosophy of our Republican Party." Such initiatives still failed to stymie the populist redefinition of conservatism or keep the old guard at the GOP's helm. "I am afraid the party we helped to build has fallen on bad times," Shadegg lamented in the 1980s. "In the olden days," he remembered, "candidates emerged from the party ranks, usually progressing from minor office to major." Shadegg much preferred to draft candidates and disliked those entrants like "John McCain, who barely met the residential qualifications, with no roots in the Republican Party, spent almost a million dollars to win the race for Congress in a safe Republican district."[68]

Phoenix Republicanism had inadvertently helped dethrone its own patriarchs. The same free-enterprise, individual-minded populist politics that had weakened the CGC installed Mecham in the governor's mansion. He triumphed in 1986, just twenty years after Maddox had upset Georgia politics, a year after Arizona GOP registration surpassed Democratic membership rolls, and during the same election that Goldwater endorsed McCain to fill his Senate seat. Mecham had been a fixture in state politics since his 1962

Senate run. His particular brand of conservatism had been influenced by boosters, nurtured by business climate governance, and then proven ripe for insurgent campaigns. Few establishment Republicans supported his perennial campaigning. In 1962, the stridently anti-Communist Catholic banker Frank Brophy had tried to mentor Mecham, urging him to soften his public attacks on Republican leaders. But Brophy grew increasingly nonplussed with the nominee's politics, admitting in 1973, just a few years before the financier's death, that Mecham's loss to Hayden had been a blessing: "he didn't turn out to be the brightest man I've ever known."[69]

Little could deter the Glendale Mormon. Mecham ran for the GOP's 1964 gubernatorial nomination by accusing governor and Senate hopeful Fannin of waste, extravagance, immorality, and bossism. Defeat did not dissuade Mecham from mounting five later bids. Another loss seemed imminent in the 1986 primary contest between Burton Barr and Mecham. The influential state Senate majority leader, also the Phoenix 40's pick, represented everything the perennial candidate "despised about Arizona politics. He'd wielded his authority in the state legislature to enrich himself and his friends, while giving lip service to the needs of the state." Mecham's 54 percent primary victory shocked Arizonans. Polls had indicated that he would only receive 5 percent of the vote. "It's not socially acceptable in some circles to admit you're voting for Evan Mecham," an aide explained. The nominee then triumphed in the three-way general election against a Democrat (a Phoenix 40 endorsee and the former state superintendent of public instruction) and a third-party candidate (a wealthy real estate developer).[70]

Mecham, like Maddox, embodied late twentieth-century white populism. The self-described "Constiutionalist" had appealed to the common folk by promising to limit spending, pledging to reduce the sales tax, and vowing to revoke state observance of the federal Martin Luther King Jr. holiday. A local newscaster credited the outcome to "a huge reservoir of people who feel anger toward the system, who think government does things to them, not for them." But supporters portrayed Mecham's base differently. "Mecham had everything against him except that he opposed the higher taxes all of his establishment rivals favored," an independent Flagstaff city councilwoman explained. "For every sushi bar in the state, I counted 40 bowling alleys," the coordinator of his southern Arizona campaign elaborated, "Working classes saw Mecham as the enemy of BMW owners who exploit them." "The Mechamites," a staffer reiterated, "include many non-religious blue-collar workers, farmers and small business owners," "raucous,

Figure 18. Evan Mecham's 1962 primary victory had shocked Phoenix booster Republicans, who disdained him and his increasingly potent brand of white populism. GOP leaders offered the nominee little help in the general election, though his Senate campaign materials, here at Republican headquarters for Districts 36 and 37, appeared alongside placards for Chamber stalwarts, such as John J. Rhodes, seeking reelection. In later years, Republicans outside the party establishment would pose more primary challenges to grasstops Phoenicians who found themselves on the defensive at home and in Washington. Arizona State Library, Archives and Public Records, History and Archives Division, Phoenix #01-4052.

anti-establishment beer bar crowds," and those who "accept that the Bible is the literal word of God and that the United States Constitution was divinely inspired."[71]

Arizonans largely considered Mecham's short tenure disastrous. His first sixty-seven-page budget transferred legislative power to executive-branch appointees, cut $300 million in expenditures, and demanded the repeal of a once temporary 1 percent sales-tax increase that had become permanent. Legislators balked and only agreed to consider the decrease if Mecham's "War on Waste" investigation could prove the levy unnecessary. The governor's crusade for "fiscal and social responsibility" fitted within his 1962 pledge for free-enterprise solutions to meet "the needs of our people." Like other populists, Mecham was preoccupied with pocketbook politics. "Our income tax rates are near the national average," he noted in a 1988 address, "our sales tax ranks among the top ten in the nation, and Arizona was 14th in the nation in state taxes as a percentage of personal income." Yet Mecham, like many grassroots rebels, also invoked the free-enterprise rhetoric behind the mid-century business tax revolt: "To attract new industries and create new jobs for Arizonans, we must hold the line on taxes." His expenditure proposals reflected this reinterpretation of booster growth politics: he wanted to slash university budgets and dedicate an additional $1 million for a rural job and investment initiative.[72]

His racial politics generated far more controversy than his economic ideas. *New York Times*, *Wall Street Journal*, *Washington Post*, and *Time* journalists took note of Mecham when he ended state recognition of Martin Luther King Jr. Day. Ten thousand protesters gathered in Phoenix on January 20, 1987. U2 and Stevie Wonder boycotted the state, and the National Football League canceled plans to hold the 1993 Super Bowl in Arizona. State officials calculated that the decision had cost $500 million in lost tourism revenue. National and local disgust and mockery, analogous to the response Maddox had received, increased after Mecham complained of too many African American National Basketball Association athletes, objected to civil rights for gays and lesbians, asserted working women were responsible for rising divorce rates, told members of a Jewish audience that they lived in a "Christian nation," made racist remarks against Asian visitors, and defended creationism in the classroom ("the teacher doesn't have the right to try to prove otherwise").[73]

Recall demands turned into an actual movement 180 days after Mecham's inauguration, the legal time requirement for such an effort. Some Arizonans stood by their governor. A critic complained, "My relatives are convinced that Mecham has a divine mandate." Others were eager to get him out of the governor's mansion. A Phoenix developer bemoaned, "He's had a really adverse effect on the business climate." "This state has had enough," a GOP state representative told reporters. A gay Phoenix businessman collected 350,000 signatures, twice the support needed, in just a few months. Noted Arizona Democrats Morris Udall and Bruce Babbitt signed the petitions, and Goldwater publicly asked for Mecham's resignation. Mecham lampooned the effort in the salty tongue that Maddox and other populist candidates favored: "If a band of homosexuals and a few dissident

Democrats can get me out of office, why heavens, the state deserves what else they can get."[74]

Citizens never went to the polls to decide the matter. Arizona Supreme Court jurists canceled the May 1988 recall election after Mecham was impeached on charges of concealing a $350,000 campaign contribution, loaning $80,000 in public funds to support his car dealership, and obstructing justice. After Mecham won an acquittal on all counts, he announced his sixth gubernatorial bid for a "kindler, gentler" Arizona a year later. Defeated in the 1990 GOP primary, he also lost a Senate gambit two years later.[75]

Yet Goldwater and his generation were not chastened by either the Mecham challenge or the demise of CGC rule. The Chamber's Depression era pioneers actually expressed a tremendous sense of accomplishment even as their influence in local and state politics declined. Goldwater thanked Walter Bimson on the occasion of his 1970 retirement for "your forward looking, modern banking technique [that] opened up funds for the young businessmen." Years after Pulliam's death, Goldwater told a biographer that the newspaperman was "one of the greatest men who ever lived" and credited him with "creating a two party system in Arizona" and "making a success of the efforts to change our city government." Goldwater's peers were equally proud of their senator's efforts to bring Phoenix's brand of Republican politics to Washington. "I have treasured your friendship through the many years," Bimson wrote to Goldwater, "and have felt a feeling of confidence in the future of our State and our Nation because you were in a position to influence public opinion in a direction that I have always supported." "You have made a great contribution towards saving this country," Brophy wrote in the late 1970s. "I regard you as one of the group comprising Senators Taft, McCarthy, Jenner, McCarran; Generals McArthur, Chenualt and Patton; Robert Welch, Westbrook Pegler, Whitaker Chambers and numerous other who have been uncompromising in their loyalty to God and country."[76]

Epilogue

Whither Phoenix?

Decades after the Chamber published the inaugural edition of *Whither Phoenix?* and years after the Charter Government Committee collapsed, both critics and celebrants considered Arizona a crucible of American conservatism. Armed "Minutemen" policed the state's border with Mexico, the legislature passed one of the most restrictive anti-immigration laws, state officials drastically cut social welfare programs, and Sheriff Joe Arpaio made the national news when he swept neighborhoods to find illegal immigrants, whom he detained in a veritable city of surplus military tents, put to work on chain gangs, and forced to wear pink underwear. Americans were nevertheless shocked when Jared Lee Loughner opened fire on Congresswoman Gabrielle Giffords and thirteen others in Tucson on January 9, 2011. Loughner was a schizophrenic who acted without political motivation. Still, many initially assumed his assassination attempt was symptomatic of escalating hostility toward Democrats. Someone had already shattered a window in Giffords's Tucson office after she voted for health care reform, and more than a few Republicans had attended a fundraiser where they had a chance to "shoot a fully automatic M16 with Jesse Kelly" in order to "help remove Gabrielle Giffords from office."[1]

Economic decline framed this effervescence of right-wing sentiment. High-tech industries had begun to pull out of metropolitan Phoenix during the 1970s, which left the Valley, as *Barron's* reporter Jonathan Laing noted in 1988, "as much a one-industry town as Houston or Denver. . . . The industry isn't oil, of course. It's growth," which "creates the illusion of prosperity." As a consequence, services increasingly dominated Maricopa's economy, exacerbating the insecurity endemic to business climate industrialization. Residents of "a twenty-first century Detroit in the making," scholar Andrew Ross surmised, now competed with each other for less-plentiful, -skilled, and -remunerated work. Reliance on home construction also made postindustrial Phoenix an epicenter of the housing crisis that preceded the Great Recession. Prices dropped 50 percent between 2006 and 2008. Foreclosure signs were thus already ubiquitous when Honeywell executives, who had made their firm a top employer by buying and consolidating high-tech outfits (including GE's computing division), announced that seven hundred jobs would go to Mexico and the Czech Republic to ensure the company was "globally competitive."[2]

A new generation of boosters has come to the fore to court investors from around the world. Yet their recruitment drive has more in common with desperate efforts to buy payroll than postwar initiatives to build a business climate. "The Chinese should feel that Phoenix is the most welcome place in the US for their industry and for their people," the Greater Phoenix Economic Council's president explained after Asian entrepreneurs were offered incentives to manufacture solar panels in Central Arizona. "We have to put a million working class Hispanics to work," he continued. "Fifty percent of these children speak English as a second language . . . and they are not all going to be at Google. Our preference has been to think of manufacturing in aerospace and semiconductor, but a big part of it is going to be in simpler operations like solar panel assembly."[3]

The grasstops' successors, including John McCain, thus inherited a political and economic imbroglio. The celebrated POW married heiress Cindy Hensley in May 1980. Her family had deep roots in the Valley's business community and the state GOP. Her father, Jim, did not belong to the Phoenix 40, but he was nonetheless one of the richest Arizonans. The San Antonio native had graduated from Phoenix Union High School in 1936—just when Chamber men began to publicly denounce the New Deal. Hensley served overseas during the organization's wartime rebirth but eventually became a force within the group. Although he was jailed for flouting postwar price controls on liquor, this encounter with the liberal state did not prove a setback. In 1955 he founded Hensley and Co., which soon became an exclusive distributor for Anheuser-Busch.[4]

Hensley's good fortune later provided the wealth necessary to jumpstart McCain's political career. As Hensley and Co.'s new vice president of public relations, McCain established a home in John Rhodes's district after the congressman announced his retirement in 1981. McCain won the GOP primary the next year but initially struggled to win the confidence of a skeptical Goldwater. McCain's diligence eventually impressed the elder statesman. "John is going [*sic*] a superb job," Goldwater told a friend after McCain's 1984 reelection. "I coach him all I can; I work him into everything I can; he comes to meeting after meeting that has absolutely nothing to do with his district."[5]

McCain secured Goldwater's endorsement and won his Senate seat in 1986 yet still faced opposition from a band of critics, not unlike those who had bedeviled the Chamber and CGC. Like his predecessor, McCain was a more secular conservative who held moderate views on immigration reform and many of the "culture war" issues that animated so many within the GOP. He ran to the "left" of George W. Bush when he sought the 2000 Republican presidential nomination. In 2008, he finally won the top spot on the GOP ticket, but many within his party, and in Arizona, considered him insufficiently committed to their brand of social conservatism. Still, he secured a respectable 54 percent of the vote in Arizona, where libertarian Bob Barr polled better than Ralph Nader, the perennial left-wing protest-vote presidential favorite. McCain then faced a tough reelection campaign. Tea Party candidate J. D. Hayworth, a former representative and conservative radio personality, forced McCain to spend $20 million in the 2010 primary and to align himself with the kind of right-wing social and immigration agenda against which he had used the "maverick" moniker to define himself throughout his just-completed presidential run.[6]

McCain's electoral difficulties demonstrated that the political currents that had brought Evan Mecham into, and then carried him swiftly out of, the governor's mansion in the late 1980s had continued to course through Arizona. Republicans devoted to limiting abortions, protecting gun rights, and deporting illegal immigrants detested McCain's uncomfortable attempt to court them. "People would be calling in to headquarters every week, absolutely enraged, threatening to leave the party because of some comments McCain made," a Republican leader reported.[7]

The sons and grandsons of Phoenix booster Republicans have faced similar electoral challenges. Stephen Shadegg's son John, for example, faced vigorous opposition to his reelection as a stalwart House Republican in 2008 despite the fact that his district remained one of the few where voters still identified strongly with the mid-century Chamber's growth politics. His retirement in 2010 opened the door for another grasstops descendant, Ben Quayle, Eugene Pulliam's great-grandson and former vice president

Dan Quayle's son. The younger Quayle faced a crowded primary, little voter interest, and a small scandal over his past contributions to *Dirty Scottsdale*, a web site reporting on Valley club culture. The Republican nonetheless won his primary and trounced his conservative Democratic opponent by a twelve-point margin in 2010.[8]

But Quayle and Shadegg also faced opposition from their left flank, particularly from the state's nascent liberal-labor-ethnic political coalition. Republican Party numbers had been declining slowly but steadily even before 2008, though most defectors reregistered as independents. "The economy is a huge reason," a Valley nurse explained. Arizona trade unions enrolled little more than 6 percent of all working residents, putting the state on par with the Deep South. But organized labor was making its presence felt in the health care and tourist industries. Unions also tended to be staunch proponents of a much more liberal policy when discussion turned to immigration reform. Not unexpectedly, the growing Latino population within Arizona, nearly one-third of all state residents, became increasingly alienated by the anti-immigrant policies of the state and national GOP. Phoenix businessman Elias Bermudez, for example, had joined the GOP because it "believed more in family, morality and the ability of the individual to succeed by pulling himself up by his own straps." But Republicans lost his vote because of initiatives that he thought denied immigrants basic human rights and privileged the Minutemen agenda.[9]

Yet these millennial political, demographic, economic developments merely underscore how unexceptional Phoenix and the rest of the Sunbelt had become. Islands of economic dynamism remain—such as that capital of the Nueva Global South, North Carolina's Research Triangle Park. Nevertheless, home foreclosures, bankruptcies, and layoffs were national norms, not regional trends. Some European companies had even come to see the United States as an investment opportunity because its wage standards and workplace regulations put it, from the perspective of many foreign executives, on par with Mexico. And when it came to business taxes, the federal government had continued the precedent set in the Sunbelt: by the end of the first decade of the twenty-first century, 55 percent of U.S. companies had not paid federal income taxes since 2000. A tide of northeastern and midwestern conservative politicians, in Congress and in numerous statehouses, even sought to build upon an earlier set of business tax cuts, regulatory restrictions, and state-directed industrialization initiatives. They, for example, sought passage of right-to-work laws and limits on public employee unionism, the kind of antilabor legislation that trade unionists and liberals had kept out of the Steelbelt. A majority of Americans polled also sided with the most regressive components of Arizona's anti-immigrant statutes.[10]

Yet progressive alliances, similar to those in Arizona, fought these recent policy initiatives and previous neoliberal reforms. A majority of Americans supported congressional efforts to repeal tax cuts for top wage earners, and many expressed support for making businesses pay their fair share of the tax burden. In 2011 Wisconsin public employee unionists occupied their capitol to stop a draconian antilabor bill, an uprising that garnered national and international support. Immigrants' rights groups, often with cooperation from business owners, lawmakers, and unionists, have quashed state bills that sought to mimic Arizona immigration restrictions and have also led dramatic protests and boycotts to pressure Arizona businesses to use their power to repeal these provisions. Organized labor has vigorously sought to empower workers, mount legal challenges to punitive union legislation, and enter into coalitions with environmental groups to make sure that new jobs will be good and green.[11]

Small groundswells and large protests indicate that Phoenix, and the rest of the nation, may once again unchain itself from an unsustainable political-economic past. Perhaps Phoenicians will embark on a wholesale reimaging, rebuilding, reclamation of their city and region into the kind of modern, dynamic, socially democratic oasis that had taken shape in the 1940s. Another Phoenix was possible then, another America is possible now.

Abbreviations

An asterisk denotes collections that were unprocessed or in the process of being organized when research was conducted.

ABB	*Arizona Business Bulletin*
AH	*Arizona Highways*
AHBC	Arizona Home Builders Collection, Arizona Historical Society, Tempe
AHF-Goldwater*	Personal and Political Papers of Senator Barry M. Goldwater, Arizona Historical Foundation, Tempe
ALJ	*Arizona Labor Journal*
AN	*Arizona News*
AP	*Arizona Progress*
AR	*Arizona Republic*
AT	*Arizona Times*
ASU-Ephemera	Ephemera Collection, Department of Archives and Special Collections, Arizona State University, Tempe
ASU-Oral-Histories	Oral History Collection, Department of Archives and Special Collections, Arizona State University, Tempe
AZ-AFL-CIO*	Arizona AFL-CIO Records, Department of Archives and Special Collections, Arizona State University, Tempe
AZ-Bar	Arizona Bar Foundation Oral History Project, Arizona Historical Society, Tucson

Board-Records	Board of Directors Records, Greater Phoenix Chamber of Commerce, Phoenix
Boulware	Lemuel Ricketts Boulware Papers, Rare Book and Manuscript Library, University of Pennsylvania, Philadelphia
BW	*Business Week*
Candler	Asa Griggs Candler Papers, Manuscript, Archives, and Rare Book Library, Emory University
Carmichael	James V. Carmichael Papers, Manuscript, Archives, and Rare Book Library, Emory University
Chamber-Binder*	Chamber History Binder, Greater Phoenix Chamber of Commerce, Phoenix
Chamber-Interviews*	Chamber Centennial Oral History Interviews [audiotapes], Greater Phoenix Chamber of Commerce, Phoenix
Chamber-Oral-History-Binder*	Chamber Centennial Oral History Interviews Binder, Greater Phoenix Chamber of Commerce, Phoenix
DP	*Dynamic Phoenix*
Fannin	Paul Fannin Papers, Arizona State Library, Archives, and Public Records, Phoenix
GB	*Gold Bond*
Goldberg*	Robert Goldberg Collection, Arizona Historical Foundation, Tempe
Governor-Files	Governor's Files, Arizona State Library, Archives, and Public Records, Phoenix
Governor-Subject-Files	Governor's Office Subject Files, Arizona State Library, Archives, and Public Records, Phoenix
Hance	Margaret Hance Papers, Department of Archives and Special Collections, Arizona State University, Tempe

Hayden	Carl Hayden Papers, Department of Archives and Special Collections, Arizona State University, Tempe
Hodges	Luther Hartwell Hodges Papers, Southern Historical Collection, Louis Round Wilson Special Collections Library, University of North Carolina, Chapel Hill
Hunter	Floyd Hunter Papers, Manuscript, Archives, and Rare Book Library, Emory University
Kantz	William Kantz Collection, Arizona Historical Foundation, Tempe
Kober	Margaret B. Kober Collection, Arizona Historical Foundation, Tempe
LAT	*Los Angeles Times*
Legislative-Files	Legislative Files, Arizona State Library, Archives and Public Records, Phoenix
Lewis	Orme Lewis Collection, Arizona Historical Foundation, Tempe
Lewis-Roca	Orme Lewis and Paul M. Roca and Phoenix Chamber of Commerce Collection, Arizona Historical Society, Tempe
Lopez	Rose Marie and Joe Eddie Lopez Papers, Department of Archives and Special Collections, Arizona State University, Tempe
Mardian	Samuel J. Mardian Jr. Collection, Department of Archives and Special Collections, Arizona State University, Tempe
McFarland	Public and Personal Papers of Ernest McFarland, McFarland Historic State Park, Florence, Arizona
Mecham*	Evan Mecham Collection, Arizona State University Archives and Special Collections, Tempe

Miami	Miami Chamber of Commerce Papers, Charles W. Tebeau Library, Historical Association of Miami, Florida
OPR	Office of the President Records, Department of Archives and Special Collections, Arizona State University, Tempe
PA	*Phoenix Action!*
Palmer	Charles Forrest Palmer Papers, Manuscript, Archives, and Rare Book Library, Emory University
PAM	Phoenix Art Museum Collection, Arizona Historical Foundation, Tempe
PCGR	Phoenix City Government Records, Arizona Historical Society, Tempe
PG	*Phoenix Gazette*
PGB	*Phoenix Gold Bond*
Phoenix-Records	City Clerk Official Records, Phoenix City Hall, Phoenix
PHP	Phoenix History Project, Arizona Historical Society, Tempe
Pyle	Howard Pyle Collection, Department of Archives and Special Collections, Arizona State University, Tempe
Rosenberg-Scrapbook*	Allen Rosenberg "Phoenix Chamber of Commerce 1964–1965" Scrapbook, Greater Phoenix Chamber of Commerce, Phoenix
Rosenzweig*	Newton Rosenzweig Collection, Arizona Historical Foundation, Tempe
Saufley*	William Saufley Collection, Arizona Historical Foundation, Tempe
SD	San Diego Chamber of Commerce Records, Special Collections and University Archives, San Diego State University, San Diego
SEP	*Saturday Evening Post*

Shadegg*	Stephen C. Shadegg Collection, Arizona Historical Foundation, Tempe
Sibley	John A. Sibley Papers, Manuscript, Archives, and Rare Book Library, Emory University
Snell	Frank Snell Papers, Arizona Historical Foundation, Tempe
Stuart	Stuart Family Papers, Department of Archives and Special Collections, Arizona State University, Tempe
UT-Goldwater	Stephen Shadegg/Barry Goldwater Collection, Center for American History, University of Texas, Austin, Austin
VF	Vertical Files, Marietta Public Library, Marietta, Georgia
VFRPC*	Valley Field Riding and Polo Club Collection, Arizona Historical Foundation, Tempe
VNB	Valley National Bank Collection, Arizona Historical Society, Tempe
WP	*Whither Phoenix?*
WPost	*Washington Post*
WSJ	*Wall Street Journal*

Notes

Introduction

Note to epigraph: Kevin Phillips, *The Emerging Republican Majority*, 2nd ed. (Garden City, N.Y.: Anchor Books, 1970), 442.

1. Ibid., 24 (quoted from the preface), 437, 438.

2. Peter Wiley and Robert Gottlieb, *Empires in the Sun: The Rise of the New American West* (New York: G. P. Putnam's Sons, 1982), 165; Bradford Luckingham, *The Urban Southwest: A Profile History of Albuquerque, El Paso, Phoenix, and Tucson* (El Paso: Texas Western Press, 1982), 52, 109; Bradford Luckingham, *Phoenix: The History of a Southwestern Metropolis* (Tucson: University of Arizona Press, 1989), 221–68; William Collins, *The Emerging Metropolis: Phoenix, 1944–1973* (Phoenix: Arizona State Parks Board, 2005); United States Census Bureau, "Table 1: Annual Estimates of the Population of Metropolitan and Micropolitan Statistical Areas: April 1, 2000 to July 1, 2006 (CBSA-EST2006-01)"; United States Census Bureau, "Population Estimates for the 25 Largest Cities"; Daniel González, "With New Immigration Law and Arizona's Slow Economy, Laborers See Work Drying Up," *AR*, August 9, 2010, http://www.azcentral.com/news/articles/2010/08/09/20100809day-laborers-no-work-immigration-law.html.

3. Philip Selznick, *TVA and the Grass Roots: A Study in the Sociology of Formal Organization* (Berkeley: University of California Press, 1949).

4. Pierre Bourdieu, "The Essence of Neoliberalism," *Le Monde Diplomatique* (December 1998), http://mondediplo.com/1998/12/08bourdiu; Susan George, "A Short History of Neoliberalism: Twenty Years of Elite Economics and Emerging Opportunities for Structural Change," in Walden Bellow, Nicola Bullard, and Kamal Malhotra (eds.), *Global Finance: New Thinking on Regulating Capital Markets* (London: Zed Books, 2000), 27–35; Gerard Levy and Dominique Levy, *Capital Resurgent: Roots of the Neoliberal Revolution*, trans. Derek Jeffers (Cambridge: Harvard University Press, 2004); Marion Fourcade-Gourinchas and Sarah Babb, "The Rebirth of the Liberal Creed: Paths to Neoliberalism in Four Countries," *American Journal of Sociology* 108 (November 2002), 533–79; David Harvey, *A Brief History of Neoliberalism* (Oxford: Oxford University Press, 2005).

5. For accounts of the Right's rise and politics see: Lisa McGirr, *Suburban Warriors: The Origins of the New American Right* (Princeton: Princeton University Press, 2002); Thomas Sugrue, *Origins of the Urban Crisis: Race and Inequality in Postwar Detroit* (Princeton: Princeton University Press, 1996); Becky Nicolaides, *My Blue Heaven: Life and Politics in the Working-Class Suburbs of Los Angeles* (Chicago: University of Chicago Press, 2002).

6. Little work on business conservatism questions this label's use (Kim Phillips Fein is the exception, *Invisible Hands: The Businessmen's Crusade Against the New Deal* (New York: W. W. Norton, 2009), 321–22) but others have documented how "conservative" became an umbrella term for those opposed to liberalism and radicalism see: George Nash, *The Conservative Intellectual Movement in America, Since 1945* (Wilmington, DE: Intercollegiate Studies Institute, 1998), 131–53; Jennifer Burns, "Godless Capitalism: Ayn Rand and the Conservative Movement," in Nelson Lichtenstein (ed.), *American Capitalism: Social Thought and Political Economy in the Twentieth Century* (Philadelphia: University of Pennsylvania Press, 2006), 271–90; Jennifer Burns, "Liberalism in the Conservative Imagination," in Neil Jumonville and Kevin Mattson (eds.), *Liberalism for a New Century* (Berkeley: University of California Press, 2007), 58–74. For examples of the business elite's frustrations with the new definition of liberalism see: [Herbert Leggett], "Liberalism," *AP*, October 1952, 1; Elizabeth Tandy Shermer, "Origins of the Conservative Ascendancy: Barry Goldwater's Early Senate Career and the De-legitimization of Organized Labor," *Journal of American History* 95 (December 2008), 678–709, esp. 690–97.

7. William Cronon, *Nature's Metropolis: Chicago and the Great West* (New York: W. W. Norton, 1991); Gerald Nash, *The Federal Landscape: An Economic History of the Twentieth-Century West* (Tucson: University of Arizona Press, 1999), 3–54; C. Vann Woodward, *Origins of the New South* (Baton Rouge: Louisiana State University Press, 1951); Sheldon Hackney, "Origins of the New South in Retrospect," *Journal of Southern History* 38 (1972), 191–216.

8. Bruce Schulman, *From Cotton Belt to Sunbelt: Federal Policy, Economic Development, and the Transformation of the South, 1938–1980* (New York: Oxford University Press, 1991), 3–38, quoted 3; Richard Lowitt, *The New Deal and the West* (Bloomington: Indiana University Press, 1984); Gavin Wright, "The New Deal and the Modernization of the South," *Federal History* 2 (2010), 58–73.

9. Scholars have hotly debated the momentous sea change described here. Many have asserted that the Sunbelt was riddled with contradictions, which, taken together, defy Phillips's description of monolithic metropolitan incubators of free enterprise and conservatism. "States tilt from liberal to conservative," Carl Abbott asserted, "or mix the two in odd local brews, on the basis of internal dynamics of personality, party organization, and parochial issues." Leading scholars, notably Amy Bridges, have also maintained that the Sunbelt did not stretch much past the continental divide because the postwar South did not exhibit the same overall jump in population, investment, and metropolitan development. The Sunbelt moniker, Abbott contended, "allowed the

South to escape its own history and to transform instantly from a 'backward' to a 'forward' region" even as these states continued to lag behind. Relatedly, Richard Bernard, Ronald Bayor, and Elliott Barkan have shown that the Sunbelt was not uniformly vibrant: rural decline and inner-city poverty accompanied the rapid growth of affluent, white suburbs in even the sunniest of areas. Deindustrialization was likewise spotty, which has inspired Andrew Needham and Allen Dieterich-Ward to claim that the Sunbelt had much in common with the Rustbelt. For good reason, millennial America's dynamic postindustrial metropolises (cities including Boston, Chicago, Raleigh-Durham, and Las Vegas) had far more in common with each other than with the struggling communities in their hinterlands. To this end, the pioneers of the new suburban history, Joseph Crespino, Kevin Kruse, and Matthew Lassiter, have uncovered clear parallels between the political allegiances of and protests by the South's affluent racial moderates, the West's environmentally attuned cowboy conservatives, and the Northeast's devotees to law and order. See Carl Abbott, *The New Urban America: Growth and Politics in Sunbelt Cities* (Chapel Hill: University of North Carolina Press, 1981), 8; Blaine Brownell, "Introduction," in Raymond Mohl (ed.), *Searching for the Sunbelt: Historical Perspectives on a Region* (Knoxville: University of Tennessee Press), 3; Richard Bernard and Bradley Rice, *Sunbelt Cities: Politics and Growth Since World War II* (Austin: University of Texas Press, 1984); Carl Abbott, "New West, New South, New Region: The Discovery of the Sunbelt," in Mohl, *Searching for the Sunbelt*, 7–24, esp. 16; Amy Bridges, "Politics and Growth in Sunbelt Cities," in Mohl, *Searching for the Sunbelt*, 85–104; James Cobb, *Industrialization and Southern Society, 1877–1984* (Lexington: University Press of Kentucky, 1984), 27–51; Cobb, *The Selling of the South: The Southern Crusade for Industrial Development, 1936–1990* (Urbana: University of Illinois, 1993); Jeff Roche, "Cowboy Conservatism," in David Farber and Jeff Roche (eds.), *The Conservative Sixties* (New York: Peter Lang, 2003), 79–92; McGirr, *Suburban Warriors*; James Gregory, *American Exodus: The Dust Bowl Migration and Okie Culture in California* (Oxford: Oxford University Press, 1989); Brian Allen Drake, "The Unnatural State: Conservatives, Libertarians, and the Postwar American Environmental Movement" (Ph.D. diss., University of Kansas, 2006); Matthew Lassiter, *The Silent Majority: Suburban Politics in the Sunbelt South* (Princeton: Princeton University Press, 2006); Kevin Kruse, *White Flight: Atlanta and the Making of Modern Conservatism* (Princeton: Princeton University Press, 2005); Joseph Crespino, *In Search of Another Country: Mississippi and the Conservative Counterrevolution* (Princeton: Princeton University Press, 2007); Tami Friedman, "Communities in Competition: Capital Migration and Plant Relocation in the U.S. Carpet Industry, 1929–1975" (Ph.D. diss., Columbia University, 2001); Guian McKee, *The Problem of Jobs: Liberalism, Race, and Deindustrialization in Philadelphia* (Chicago: University of Chicago Press, 2008); Miriam Greenberg, *Branding New York: How a City in Crisis Was Sold to the World* (New York: Routledge, 2008); Sean Safford, *Why the Garden Club Couldn't Save Youngstown: The Transformation of the Rustbelt* (Cambridge: Harvard University Press, 2006); Andrew Needham and Allen Dietrich-Ward,

"Beyond the Metropolis: Metropolitan Growth and Regional Transformation in Postwar America," *Journal of Urban History* 35 (2009), 943–69; Howard Gillette Jr., *Camden after the Fall: Decline and Renewal in a Post-Industrial City* (Philadelphia: University of Pennsylvania Press, 2005); Jefferson Cowie, *Capital Moves: RCA's 70-Year Quest for Cheap Labor* (New York: New Press, 2001); James L. Peacock, Harry L. Watson, and Carrie B. Matthews (eds.), *The American South in a Global World* (Chapel Hill: University of North Carolina Press, 2005).

10. Quoted in Robert Dreyfuss, "Grover Norquist: 'Field Marshall' of the Bush Plan," *Nation*, April 26, 2001, http://www.thenation.com/doc/20010514/dreyfuss. For discussion of works that assume this antistatism stands for all those on Right, leading to arguments that the expansion of the state under conservatives is hypocritical, see: Julian Zelizer, "Rethinking the History of American Conservatism," *Reviews in American History* 38 (June 2010), 367–92.

11. Richard Parker, "If We're All Keynesians (Again), Just What Sort of Keynesians Are We?" Paper delivered at the "Capitalism in Question (Because It Is)" symposium, Pitzer College, Los Angeles, May 3, 2010; Sven Beckert, "Emancipation and Empire: Reconstructing the Worldwide Web of Cotton Production in the Age of the American Civil War," *American Historical Review* 109 (2004), 1405–38; Mary O. Furner, "New Liberalism: Policy Knowledge," in Neil J. Smelser and Paul B. Baltes, *International Encyclopedia of the Social and Behavioral Sciences* (Amsterdam: Elsevier, 2002), 1159–99; David Vogel, "Why Businessmen Distrust Their State: The Political Consciousness of American Corporate Executives," *British Journal of Political Science* 8 (January 1978), 45–78.

12. On think tanks and economics departments importance: Harvey, *A Brief History of Neoliberalism*, 19–31; Juan Gabriel Valdez, *Pinochet's Economists: The Chicago School in Chile* (New York: Cambridge University Press, 1995); Daniel Yergin and Joseph Stanislaw, *The Commanding Heights: The Battle for the World Economy* (New York: Simon and Schuster, 1999). For arguments for neoliberalism's American origins in the New York fiscal crisis and the postwar South's industrialization see: Greenberg, *Branding New York*; Kim Moody, *From Welfare State to Real Estate: Regime Change in New York City, 1974 to the Present* (New York: New Press, 2007); Joshua Freeman, *Working Class New York: Life and Labor Since World War II* (New York: New Press, 2000), 256–87; Nancy MacLean, "Southern Dominance in Borrowed Language: The Regional Origins of American Neoliberalism," in Jane L. Collins (ed.), *New Landscapes of Inequality: Neoliberalism and the Erosion of Democracy in America* (Santa Fe: School for Advanced Research Press, 2009), 21–38; Bethany Moreton, "The Soul of Neoliberalism," *Social Text* 25 (Fall 2007), 103–23.

Chapter 1. Colonial Prologue

1. George Leonard interview by Karin Ullman, June 17, 1976, transcript, 1, PHP.

2. William Cronon, *Nature's Metropolis: Chicago and the Great West* (New York: W. W. Norton, 1991), 41–45, 265–78, esp. 278.

3. C. Vann Woodward, *Origins of the New South* (Baton Rouge: Louisiana State University Press, 1951); Woodward, "New South Fraud Is Papered by Old South Myth," *WPost*, July 9, 1961, 3; Mancur Olson, "The South Will Fall Again: The South as Leader and Laggard in Economic Growth," *Southern Economic Journal* 49 (1983), 917–32; Sheldon Hackney, "Origins of the New South in Retrospect," *Journal of Southern History* 38 (1972), 191–216; Bruce Schulman, *From Cotton Belt to Sunbelt: Federal Policy, Economic Development, and the Transformation of the South, 1938–1980* (New York: Oxford University Press, 1991), 3–38; Gerald Nash, *The Federal Landscape: An Economic History of the Twentieth-Century West* (Tucson: University of Arizona Press, 1999), 3–54, esp. 20; Donald Worster, *Rivers of Empire: Water, Aridity, and the Growth of the American West* (New York: Pantheon Books, 1986); Richard Lowitt, *The New Deal and the West* (Bloomington: Indiana University Press, 1984).

4. Gavin Wright, *Old South, New South: Revolutions in the Southern Economy Since the Civil War* (New York: Basic Books, 1986), vii–viii, 13–15, 61–64, 156–57, esp. 14 and 270.

5. Martin Sklar, *The Corporate Reconstruction of American Capitalism, 1890–1916: The Market, the Law, and Politics* (New York: Cambridge University Press 1988); On the South see: Pete Daniel, *The Shadow of Slavery: Peonage in the South, 1901–1969* (Urbana: University of Illinois Press, 1972); Pete Daniel, *Breaking the Land: The Transformation of Cotton, Tobacco, and Rice Cultures Since 1880* (Urbana: University of Illinois Press, 1985); John Dollard, *Caste and Class in a Southern Town* (Garden City, NY: Doubleday, 1957); Glenda Elizabeth Gilmore, *Gender and Jim Crow* (Chapel Hill: University of North Carolina Press, 1996); Nancy McLean, *Behind the Mask of Chivalry: The Making of the Second Ku Klux Klan* (Oxford University Press, 1995); Wright, *Old South, New South*; Cindy Hahamovitch, *The Fruits of Their Labor: Atlantic Coast Farmworkers and the Making of Migrant Poverty, 1870–1945* (Chapel Hill: University of North Carolina Press, 1997). On the West see: James W. Byrkit, *Forging the Copper Collar: Arizona's Labor Management War of 1901–1921* (Tucson: University of Arizona Press, 1982); Nash, *The Federal Landscape*, 3–41; Tomas Almaguer, *Racial Fault Lines: The Historical Origins of White Supremacy in California* (Berkeley: University of California Press, 1994); Gordon Morris Bakken and Brenda Farringson (eds.), *Racial Encounters in the Multi-Cultural West* (New York: Garland, 2000); William Francis Deverrell, *Whitewashed Adobe: The Rise of Los Angeles and the Remaking of Its Mexican Past* (Berkeley: University of California Press, 2004); Neil Foley, *The White Scourge: Mexicans, Blacks, and Poor Whites in Texas Cotton Culture* (Berkeley: University of California, 1997); Nayan Shah, *Contagious Divides: Epidemics and Race in San Francisco's Chinatown* (Berkeley: University of California, 2001); Katherine Benton-Cohen, *Borderline Americans: Racial Division and Labor War in the Arizona Borderlands* (Cambridge, MA: Harvard University Press, 2009). For systemic malapportionment see: Douglas Smith, "Into the Political Thicket: Reapportionment and the Rise of Suburban Power" in Matthew D. Lassiter and Joseph Crespino (eds.), *The Myth of Southern Exceptionalism* (New York: Oxford University Press), 263–285.

6. Earl Pomeroy, *The American Far West in the Twentieth Century* (New Haven: Yale University Press, 2008), 92–98; James Byrkit, *Forging the Copper Collar: Arizona's Labor-Management War of 1901–1921* (Tucson: University of Arizona Press, 1982), xiv; Luckingham, *Urban Southwest,* 52–86.

7. Pomeroy, *American Far West in the Twentieth Century,* 92–98; Byrkit, *Forging the Copper Collar*; Peter Dimas, "Progress and a Mexican American Community's Struggle for Existence: Phoenix's Golden Gate Barrio" (Ph.D. diss., Arizona State University, 1991), 49–53.

8. Padraic Mawn, "Phoenix, Arizona: Central City of the Southwest, 1870–1920" (Ph.D. diss., Arizona State University, 1979), 219–50; John Gunther, *Inside U.S.A.* (New York: Harper and Brothers, 1947), 901; Workers of the Writers' Program of the Works Projects Administration in the State of Arizona, *Arizona: A State Guide* (New York: Hastings House, 1976), 79–80; Larry Schweikart, *A History of Banking in Arizona* (Tucson: University of Arizona Press, 1982); Ernest Jerome Hopkins, *Financing the Frontier: A Fifty Year History of the Valley National Bank* (Phoenix: Valley National Bank, 1950); Jacqueline Dowd Hall et al., *Like a Family: The Making of a Southern Cotton Mill World* (Chapel Hill: University of North Carolina, 1987).

9. Philip VanderMeer, *Desert Visions and the Making of Phoenix, 1860–2009* (Albuquerque, University of New Mexico Press, 2010), 38–39; Luckingham, *Urban Southwest,* 52–86.

10. Bradford Luckingham, *Phoenix: The History of a Southwestern Metropolis* (Tucson: University of Arizona Press, 1989), 84–86, quoted 85.

11. Ibid., 84–87.

12. Mawn, "Phoenix, Arizona," 470–75; quoted Luckingham, *Phoenix*, 76.

13. Robert Autobee, *The Salt River Project* (Denver: Bureau of Reclamation History Program, 1993), quoted 26; Mawn, "Phoenix, Arizona," 219–50.

14. Mawn, "Phoenix, Arizona," 470–95.

15. Quoted VanderMeer, *Desert Visions and the Making of Phoenix*, 97.

16. Michael J. Kotlanger, "Phoenix, Arizona, 1920–1940" (Ph.D. diss., Arizona State University, 1983), 57–61, esp. 57.

17. Luckingham, *Phoenix*, 76; Kotlanger, "Phoenix, Arizona," 60–71.

18. Dimas, "Progress and a Mexican American Community's Struggle for Existence," 49–53; Herbert Peterson, "A Twentieth Century Journey to Cibola: Tragedy of the *Bracero* in Maricopa County, Arizona, 1917–21" (Ph.D. diss., Arizona State University, 1975); Raymond Rodríguez, *Decade of Betrayal: Mexican Repatriation in the 1930s* (Albuquerque: University of New Mexico Press, 1995); Camille Guerin-Gonzales, *Mexican Workers and the American Dream: Immigration, Repatriation, and California Farm Labor, 1900–1939* (New Brunswick, NJ: Rutgers University Press, 1994).

19. Hahamovitch, *Fruits of Their Labor.*

20. Arthur G. Horton, *An Economic, Political, and Social Survey of Phoenix and the Valley of the Sun* (Tempe, AZ: Southside Progress, 1941), 153–54.

21. Ibid.

22. Ibid.

23. Mawn, "Phoenix, Arizona," 220–91, esp. 289; Judith Anne Jacobson, "The Phoenix Chamber of Commerce: A Case Study of Economic Development in Central Arizona" (master's thesis, Arizona State University, 1992), 6–11, esp. 10; Luckingham, *Phoenix*, 80.

24. Dimas, "Progress and a Mexican American Community's Struggle for Existence," 71–73, esp. 72.

25. Ibid., 71–73; Kotlanger, "Phoenix, Arizona," 333–39, quoted on 333; quoted in Luckingham, *Phoenix*, 85, 86; *The Phoenix Gold Bond* had become *The Gold Bond* by 1929. Phoenix Chamber of Commerce, *PGB* (Phoenix: Phoenix Chamber of Commerce, 1925); Phoenix Chamber of Commerce, *PGB* (Phoenix: Phoenix Chamber of Commerce, 1926); Phoenix Chamber of Commerce, *GB* (Phoenix: Phoenix Chamber of Commerce, 1929) [all copies found in "1920's" section, Chamber-Binder]).

26. Mawn, "Phoenix, Arizona," 220–91, esp. 289; Jacobson, "Phoenix Chamber of Commerce," 6–11, esp. 10; Luckingham, *Phoenix*, 80; Tim Kelly, "The Changing Face of Phoenix," *Arizona Highways* 40 (March 1964), 2–23, esp. 10, quoted 10.

27. Booker T. Washington, "The Race Problem in Arizona," *Independent*, October 26, 1911, 909–13, esp. 909, 912–13.

28. Quoted Dimas, "Progress and a Mexican American Community's Struggle for Existence," 52; quoted Kotlanger, "Phoenix, Arizona," 430; G. Wesley Johnson Jr., "Directing Elites: Catalysts for Social Change," 13–32, esp. 14–26, in G. Wesley Johnson Jr., *Phoenix in the Twentieth Century: Essays in Community History* (Norman: University of Oklahoma Press, 1993).

29. VanderMeer, *Desert Visions and the Making of Phoenix*, 60–64; "Statement of the Case for the Phoenix Art Museum," n.p., folder 1, box 3, PAM.

30. Mary Ruth Titcomb, "Americanization and Mexicans in the Southwest: A History of Phoenix's Friendly House, 1920–1983" (master's thesis, University of California, Santa Barbara, 1984), 37–44, 52, esp. 37–38, esp. 71.

31. Matthew Whitaker, *Race Work: The Rise of Civil Rights in the Urban West* (Lincoln: University of Nebraska Press, 2005), quoted 5; Michael Bernstein, "Geographical Perspective on Skid Row in Phoenix, Arizona" (master's thesis, Arizona State University, 1972); Kotlanger, "Phoenix, Arizona," 396–480.

32. Titcomb, "Americanization and Mexicans in the Southwest," 18–22. Dimas, "Progress and a Mexican American Community's Struggle for Existence," 49–51; Bernstein, "Geographical Perspective on Skid Row in Phoenix, Arizona," 3; Kotlanger, "Phoenix, Arizona," 427.

33. Kotlanger, "Phoenix, Arizona," 410–20; Susie Sato, "Before Pearl Harbor: Early Japanese Settlers in Arizona," *Journal of Arizona History* 14 (Winter 1977), 317–34, esp. 326–28; Viviana Wei Chiang, "The Chinese Community in Phoenix, Arizona: A Study of Acculturation and Assimilation" (master's thesis, Arizona State University, 1970), 21–52, esp. 41, 52.

34. Kotlanger, "Phoenix, Arizona," 400–409, quoted 407; Alexandra Harmon, *Indians in the Making: Ethnic Relations and Indian Identities Around Puget Sound* (Berkeley: University of California Press, 1998); David Wallace Adams, *Education for Extinction: American Indians and the Boarding School Experience, 1875–1928* (Lawrence: University Press of Kansas, 1995).

35. Alan Vernon Johnson, "Governor G. W. P. Hunt and Organized Labor" (master's thesis, University of Arizona, 1964); Benjamin Taylor, *Arizona Labor Relations Law* (Tempe: Bureau of Business Research Services, College of Business Administration, Arizona State University, 1967), 2–16, quoted on 12, 14; Micaela Ann Larkin, "Labor's Desert: Mexican Workers, Unions and Entrepreneurial Conservatism in Arizona, 1917–1972" (Ph.D. diss., University of Notre Dame, 2008), 12–70, esp. 20–36.

36. Larkin, "Labor's Desert," 12–106, esp. 83–86, quoted 83–84.

37. Earl Zarbin, *All the Time a Newspaper: The First 100 Years of the* Arizona Republic (Phoenix, *Arizona Republic*, 1990), 83–93; Nancy Anderson Guber, "The Development of Two-Party Competition in Arizona" (master's thesis, University of Illinois, 1961), 33–59.

38. Zarbin, *All the Time a Newspaper*, 83–93; Robert Alan Goldberg, *Barry Goldwater* (New Haven: Yale University, 1995), 12–25; Rick Perlstein, *Before the Storm: Barry Goldwater and the Unmaking of the American Consensus* (New York: Hill and Wang, 2001), 17.

39. Guber, "The Development of Two-Party Competition in Arizona," 33–59.

40. Sklar, *Corporate Reconstruction of American Capitalism*; Earl Black and Merle Black, *The Rise of the Southern Republicans* (Cambridge, MA: Harvard University Press, 2002); Pomeroy, *The American Far West in the Twentieth Century*, 300–337.

41. James C. Cobb, *Industrialization and Southern Society, 1877–1984* (Lexington: University Press of Kentucky, 1984), 5–50; Wright, *Old South, New South*, 12–197; Jonathan Wiener, *Social Origins of the New South* (Baton Rouge: Louisiana State University Press, 1978), 137–221, quoted 158, 173–75; Charles Martin, "Southern Labor Relations in Transition: Gadsden, Alabama, 1930–1943," *Journal of Southern History* 47 (November 1981), 545–68.

42. Thomas Hanchett, *Sorting Out the New South City: Race, Class, and Urban Development in Charlotte, 1875–1975* (Chapel Hill: University of North Carolina Press, 1998), 93–95; Atlanta Chamber of Commerce, *City Builder*, November 10, 1916, esp. 23, folder 8, box 3, Candler; Nathan Daniel Beau Connolly, "By Eminent Domain: Race and Capital in the Building of an American South Florida" (Ph.D. diss., University of Michigan, 2008), 40–94; "5,000 See Farming Begin in 'Glades; Seminoles Relinquish Sovereignity," *Miamian* 7, no. 10 (March 1927): 5; Sylvia Altman, "CC's Story—Through the Years," *Metropolitan Miamian* 49, no. 3 (April 1957), quoted 1.

43. Cobb, *Industrialization and Southern Society*, 5–50; Hanchett, *Sorting Out the New South City*, 93–95.

44. Amy Bridges, *Morning Glories: Municipal Reform in the Southwest* (Princeton: Princeton University Press, 1997), 100–101, n. 6; Luckingham, *The Urban Southwest*,

53–74; Roger Lotchin, *Fortress California, 1910–1961: From Warfare to Welfare* (New York: Oxford University Press, 1992).

45. Lotchin, *Fortress California*.

46. Lotchin, *Fortress California*, esp. 74–79; Departmental Reports of the San Diego Chamber of Commerce from Nov. 1, 1928, to October 31, 1929, folder 8, box 65, SD.

47. William Collins, *The New Deal in Arizona* (Phoenix: Arizona State Parks Board, 1999), 20–58; quoted in VanderMeer, *Desert Visions and the Making of Phoenix*, 117.

Chapter 2. Contested Recovery

1. Richard Lowitt and Maurine Beasley, *One Third of a Nation: Lorena Hickok Reports on the Great Depression* (Urbana: University of Illinois Press, 2000), 238, 240, 252, 253.

2. National Emergency Council, *Report on Economic Conditions of the South* (Washington, D.C.: Government Printing Office, 1938), 1.

3. Jason Scott Smith, *Building New Deal Liberalism: The Political Economy of Public Works, 1933–1956* (Cambridge: Cambridge University Press, 2006), 86–93; Jennifer Klein, *For All These Rights: Business, Labor, and the Shaping of America's Public-Private Welfare State* (Princeton: Princeton University Press, 2003); Nelson Lichtenstein, *State of the Union: A Century of American Labor* (Princeton: Princeton University Press, 2002), 122–52; Meg Jacobs, *Pocketbook Politics: Economic Citizenship in Twentieth-Century America* (Princeton: Princeton University Press, 2005), 179–262.

4. National Resources Planning Board, *Preliminary Statement, Regional Development Plan, Pacific Southwest, Region 8: Report to the National Resources Planning Board* (Washington, D.C.: U.S. Government Printing Office, 1941), 197, 210; David Lilienthal, *TVA: Democracy on the March* (New York: Harper and Brothers, 1944), xi (emphasis in original); National Resources Planning Board, *Regional Planning Part XI: The Southeast* (Washington, D.C.: Government Printing Office, 1942), 134.

5. Smith, *Building New Deal Liberalism*, 91–93.

6. Collins, *New Deal in Arizona*, 42–96; 237–95.

7. Robert Korstad and Nelson Lichtenstein, "Opportunities Found and Lost: Labor, Radicals, and the Early Civil Rights Movement," *Journal of American History* 75 (December 1988): 786–811; Patricia Sullivan, *Days of Hope: Race and Democracy in the New Deal Era* (Chapel Hill: University of North Carolina Press, 1996); Risa Goluboff, *The Lost Promise of Civil Rights* (Cambridge: Harvard University Press, 2007).

8. Jordon Schwarz, *The New Dealers: Power and Politics in the Age of Roosevelt* (New York: Alfred A. Knopf, 1993), 195–248, quoted 318.

9. Lilienthal, *TVA*, xii, 6, 9, 36–41, 107 (emphasis in original).

10. Lowitt, *New Deal and the West*, 81–99, 218–28, quoted 99.

11. Ibid., quoted 98; Mawn, "Phoenix, Arizona," 324–38; Schwarz, *New Dealers*, 233–37; Collins, *New Deal in Arizona* 22–23, 52, 107–41, 169–73, 192–93, 201–36.

12. Linda Gordon, "Dorothea Lange Photographs the Japanese American Internment," in Linda Gordon and Gary Y. Okihiro (eds.), *Impounded: Dorothea Lange and the Censored Images of Japanese American Internment* (New York: W. W. Norton, 2006), 5–46; Daniel Geary, "Carey McWilliams and Antifascism, 1934–1943," *Journal of American History* 90 (December 2003), 912–34, quoted 913.

13. Schwarz, *New Dealers*, 297–342, quoted 300.

14. Gerald Nash, *A. P. Giannini and the Bank of America* (Norman: University of Oklahoma Press, 1992); Marquis James and Bessie James, *The Story of Bank of America: Biography of a Bank* (New York: Harper and Brothers, 1954), quoted 375.

15. Sidney Hyman, *Marriner S. Eccles: Private Entrepreneur and Public Servant* (Palo Alto, Calif.: Graduate School of Business, Stanford University, 1976); David Kennedy, *Freedom from Fear: The American People in Depression and War* (Oxford: Oxford University Press, 1999), 67–69, 78, 323–81.

16. Schwarz, *New Dealers*, 59–95, quoted 61 [emphasis in original] and 78.

17. Ibid., 59–95; Char Miller and David Johnston, "The Rise of Urban Texas," in Char Miller and Heywood Sanders (eds.), *Urban Texas: Politics and Development* (College Station: Texas A&M University Press, 1990), 3–32.

18. James Patterson, *Congressional Conservatism and the New Deal: The Growth of the Conservative Coalition in Congress, 1933–1939* (Lexington: University of Kentucky, 1967), esp. vii, quoted 13–15.

19. Ira Katznelson, Kim Geiger, and Daniel Kryder, "Limiting Liberalism: The Southern Veto in Congress, 1933–1950," *Political Science Quarterly* 109 (Summer 1993), 283–306.

20. Schulman, *From Cotton Belt to Sunbelt*, 44; quoted Selznick, *TVA and the Grass Roots*, 62.

21. Schwarz, *New Dealers*, 233–35.

22. Colin Gordon, *New Deals: Business, Labor, and Politics in America, 1920–1935* (New York: Cambridge University Press, 1994); Sanford Jacoby, *Modern Manors: Welfare Capitalism Since the New Deal* (Princeton: Princeton University Press, 1997); Klein, *For All These Rights.*

23. Phillips-Fein, *Invisible Hands*, 3–26.

24. Guber, "The Development of Two-Party Competition in Arizona," 43; quoted VanderMeer, *Desert Visions and Making of Phoenix*, 80.

25. Jack August Jr., *Vision in the Desert: Carl Hayden and Hydropolitics in the American Southwest* (Fort Worth: Texas Christian University Press, 1999); quoted John Gunther, *Inside U.S.A.* (New York: Harper and Brothers, 1947), 899.

26. Ernest W. McFarland, *Mac: The Autobiography of Ernest W. McFarland* ([s.l.:] Ernest W. McFarland, 1979), 44–49; Barry Goldwater to Henry Ashurst, September 25, 1940, in James McMillan (ed.), *The Ernest W. McFarland Papers: The United States Senate Years, 1940–1952* (Prescott, AZ: Sharlot Hall Museum Press, 1995), 26; Ernest McFarland, [Speech], typescript, September 9, 1940, folder 8, box 131, subseries 1, series 10, subgroup I, McFarland; Ernest McFarland, [Speech], typescript, 1940, folder 8,

box 131, subseries 1, series 10, subgroup I, McFarland; Ernest McFarland, [Speech], typescript, August 7, 1940, folder 8, box 131, subseries 1, series 10, subgroup I, McFarland; "Radio Program in [*sic*] Behalf of Judge Ernest W. McFarland, candidate for United States Senator," August 28, 1940, typescript, folder 8, box 131, subseries 1, series 10, subgroup I, McFarland; "Speech [August 7, 1940, Casa Grande, Arizona]," in McMillan, *Ernest W. McFarland Papers*, 15–16

27. David Brinegar to Ernest McFarland, July 5, 1951, 1, folder 10, box 47, series 4, subgroup I, McFarland; Dennis Preisler, "Phoenix, Arizona During the 1940s: A Decade of Change" (master's thesis, Arizona State University, 1992), 40–42; Collins, *The Emerging Metropolis*, 36.

28. Collins, *New Deal in Arizona*, 107–41, 192–93; Ann Carey McFeatters, *Sandra Day O'Connor: Strategist on the Supreme Court* (Albuquerque: University of New Mexico Press, 2005), 22–46.

29. I had difficulty establishing exactly when boosters began discussing structural changes to the Chamber and the Valley's economic base because though newspapers and internal oral histories have survived, the Chamber's records from 1934 to 1944 have been lost (a fiscal year's records were organized chronologically in unpaginated, unindexed bound volumes). When I visited the Chamber offices in July 2007, no one had any memory of these years' books ever having been on the shelf. Board of Directors, Minutes of Meeting, April 6, 1933, Vol. "1932–1933," Board-Records; quoted in Kristine Minister, memo, "Potential Audio Segments for Annual Video," May 3, 1988, 1, Chamber-Oral-History-Binder; Orme Lewis interview by Kristina Minister, April 14, 1988, audiotape, side 1, tape 1, Chamber-Interviews.

30. Daniel Bell, "The Dispossessed," in Daniel Bell (ed.), *The Radical Right* (New Brunswick, N.J.: Transaction, 2002), 1–46; Richard Hofstadter, "The Psuedo-Conservative Revolt," in Bell, *The Radical Right*, 75–96.

31. Orme Lewis interview by Kristina Minister, April 14, 1988, audiotape, side 1, tape 1, Chamber-Interviews; Newton Rosenzweig interview by Kristina Minister, March 21, 1988, audiotape, side 2, tape 3, Chamber-Interviews; on cowboy conservatism/conservatives see: J. Craig Jenkins and Teri Shumate, "Cowboy Capitalists and the Rise of the 'New Right': An Analysis of Contributions to Conservative Policy Formation Organizations," *Social Problems* 33 (December 1985), 130–45; Jeff Roche, "Cowboy Conservatism" in David Farber and Jeff Roche (eds.), *The Conservative Sixties* (New York: Peter Lang, 2003), 79–92.

32. Frank Snell interview by Kristina Minister, April 26, 1988, audiotape, side 1, tape 10, and side 1, tape 11, Chamber-Interviews; Lewis interview by Minister, audiotape, side 1, tape 2; Harry Rosenzweig interview by Kristina Minister, March 27, 1988, audiotape, sides 1 and 2, tape 13, Chamber-Interviews.

33. Frank Snell interview by G. Wesley Johnson, September 22, 1977, transcript, 13–47, esp. 13, PHP; Denison Kitchel interview by Robert Goldberg, typescript, November 18, 1989, 6–7, Goldberg [unprocessed, unboxed collection].

34. "History of the Valley Field Riding and Polo Club," folder 5, box 17, VFRPC; "Minutes 1929–1959," folder 5, box 1, VFRPC; Charles Pulaski to Frank Clelland Jr. and Joseph Voorhees, March 21, 1990, folder 10, box 8, VFRPC; John Baldwin Jr. to Mr. and Mrs. Gilbert Bradley, December 12, 1979, folder 7, box 7, VFRPC. For membership restrictions see: Tim Brown to Charlie Pulaski, May 18, 1990, folder 10, box 8, VFRPC; "Article III Membership," undated, folder 6, box 7, VFRPC; Orme Lewis to Ed Bringhurst, June 27, 1961, folder 7, box 7, VFRPC. For postwar parties see: folder 2, box 8, VFRPC.

35. Collins, *Emerging Metropolis*, 214–19; Walter Bimson, "Current Economic Delusions," January 30, 1946, typescript, 2, 5, 8, folder 231, box 28, VNB.

36. Don Dedera, "Walter Reed Bimson: Arizona's Indispensable Man, Compleat Banker," *AH* (April 1973), 26–29, quoted 22; Hopkins, *Financing the Frontier*, 207–12.

37. Walter Bimson interview by G. Wesley Johnson, December 29, 1975, 1–2, PHP; Carl Bimson interview by Karin Ullman, July 22, 1976, transcript, 1–5, PHP; Hopkins, *Financing the Frontier*, 6–167; Collins, *New Deal in Arizona*, 34–36; quoted Dedera, "Walter Reed Bimson," 26.

38. Quoted Neil Clark, "The Brash Banker of Arizona," *SEP*, April 10, 1954, 22; quoted Joseph Stocker, "Valley National Bank: Financing America's Flourishing Frontier," *AH* 32 (November 1956), 5; Hopkins, *Financing the Frontier*, 212–54, quoted 212, 217–18, 250; quoted Schweikart, *A History of Banking in Arizona*, 107.

39. Hopkins, *Financing the Frontier*, 230–31, 237–48.

40. Ibid.; Carl Bimson interview by Kristina Minister, April 14, 1988, audiotape, side 1, tape 7, Chamber-Interviews; Collins, *New Deal in Arizona*, 345–50; Schweikart, *A History of Banking in Arizona*, 103–5.

41. Carl Bimson, "An Address Before the Miami Rotary Club," February 28, 1935, in Carl Bimson, *Addresses of Carl A. Bimson* (self-published, 1960), vol. 1, 1, deposited at Arizona Historical Foundation (Tempe); Carl Bimson, "Radio Talk on KTAR," March 29, 1936, in ibid., vol. 2, 7.

42. Bimson interview by Minister, side 1, tape 8.

43. Hopkins, *Financing the Frontier*, 230–35.

44. Quoted in ibid., 233; H. L. "Doc" Durham interview [by unnamed VNB employee], September 23, 1969, transcript, 3–5, folder 29 ("General Bank History, Executive Personnel Interview transcripts—H. L. Dunham, 1969"), box 2, VNB.

45. Hopkins, *Financing the Frontier*, 217–25.

46. Ibid.; Bimson interview by Minister, side 2, tape 7.

47. Hopkins, *Financing the Frontier*, 222–25; Larry Schweikart, "A Record of Revitalization: Financial Leadership in Phoenix," in Johnson, *Phoenix in the Twentieth Century*, 123–38, esp. 125–26; Michael Francis Konig, "Toward Metropolitan Status: Charter Government and the Rise of Phoenix, Arizona, 1945–1960" (Ph.D. diss., Arizona State University, 1983), 203–6.

48. Bridges, *Morning Glories*, 99–101, n. 6; Schwarz, *New Dealers*, 264–84.

49. Cobb, *Industrialization and Southern Society*, 27–50; Thomas Scott, "Winning World War II in an Atlanta Suburb: Local Boosters and the Recruitment of Bell Bomber," in Philip Scranton (ed.), *The Second Wave: Southern Industrialization from the 1940s to the 1970s* (Athens: University of Georgia Press, 2001), 1–23; Richard Combes, "Aircraft Manufacturing in Georgia: A Case Study of Federal Industrial Investment," in ibid., 24–42; Karen Ferguson, "The Politics of Exclusion: Wartime Industrialization, Civil Rights Mobilization, and Black Politics in Atlanta, 1942–1946," in Scranton, *The Second Wave*, 43–80; Jack Claiborne, *Crown of the Queen City: The Charlotte Chamber From 1877–1999* (Charlotte: KPC Custom Publishing, 1999), 53–68.

50. Cobb, *Industrialization and Southern Society*, 37–39; Ernest Jerome Hopkins, *Mississippi's BAWI Plan: An Experiment in Industrial Subsidization* (Atlanta: Department of Research and Statistics, Federal Reserve Bank of Atlanta, 1944), 11–15, quoted 19; Jack Prince, "History and Development of the Mississippi Balance Agriculture with Industry Program, 1936–1958" (Ph.D. diss., Ohio State University, 1961), 25–26, 57–59.

51. Hopkins, *Mississippi's BAWI Plan*, 1–26.

52. Ibid., esp. 15–23, quoted 15; Tami Friedman, "Communities in Competition: Capital Migration and Plant Relocation in the U.S. Carpet Industry, 1929–1975" (Ph.D. diss., Columbia University, 2001), 106–21, quoted 115.

53. Hopkins, *Mississippi's BAWI Plan*, esp. 16–18, quoted 31–32 and 40; Prince, "History and Development of the Mississippi Balance Agriculture with Industry Program," 88–90, 166–168.

54. Hopkins, *Mississippi's BAWI Plan*, esp. 20–41, quoted 20.

55. Ibid., iii–iv, 3–9, 30–52; Prince, "History and Development of the Mississippi Balance Agriculture with Industry Program," 25–26, 83–86, 114–26; James Cobb, *The Selling of the South: The Southern Crusade for Industrial Development, 1936–1990* (Urbana: University of Illinois Press, 1993), 5–63.

56. Frank Snell interview by G. Wesley Johnson, September 22, 1977, transcript, 109, PHP; Bill Beardsly interview by G. Wesley Johnson, October 11, 1978, transcript, 26–39, PHP; Bridges, *Morning Glories*, 100; Bradford Luckingham, *Urban Southwest*, 82–83; Harold Martin, "The New Millionaires of Phoenix," *SEP*, September 30, 1961, 25–31.

57. Rosenzweig interview by Minister, side 1, tape 4; Milton Sanders interview by Meredith Snapp, December 29, 1977, transcript, 11–37, PHP; "The Phoenix Thunderbirds," *Phoenix* 20 (June 1966), 4–10; quoted Michael Kotlanger, "Phoenix, Arizona, 1920–1940" (Ph.D. diss., Arizona State University, 1983), 382; Robert Goldwater interview by Dean Smith, November 5, 1984, transcript, 8–13, folder "Goldwater Family History—Oral Histories (by Dean Smith), 1981–1984," box 1, series 1, AHF-Goldwater; Frank Snell, "For Graduation American Institute for Foreign Trade," May 29, 1952, typescript, 10, folder 15, box 2, Snell.

58. Howard Pyle interview by G. W. Johnson, February 2, 1976, transcript, PHP, 33; Mark Wilmer interview by Zona Davis Lorig, September 8, 1994, transcript, PHP; Snell interview by Johnson, 1–30, esp. 13.

59. Snell interview by Johnson, 63–69, 73–74, 30–31, esp. 13; Frank Snell interview with Arizona Historical Society, Tucson, typescript, 22–30, esp. 1, AZ-Bar.

60. Frank Snell, "Government in Business," May 19, 1952, transcript, 1, 3, folder 14, box 2, Snell; Frank Snell, "The Case for Entrepreneur," *ABB* IX (March 1962), 1–4, esp. 4, folder 7, box 3, Snell; Frank Snell, "Economic Democracy," [1939], folder 8, box 1, Snell; Frank Snell, "Professional Men in Civic Life," November 25, 1939, folder 13, box 1, Snell; Frank Snell, "A Challenge," March 7, 1940, folder 14, box 1, Snell; Frank Snell, "Arizona," [1930s], folder 2, box 1, Snell; Frank Snell, "Doing Our Part," [1930s], folder 6, box 1, folder 8, box 1, Snell; Frank Snell, "What Is Wrong with Us?" October 1938, folder 21, box 1, Snell.

61. Frank Snell, "Program for the Chamber of Commerce," June 23, 1939, folder 10, box 1, Snell; Frank Snell, "President's Report for Fiscal Year May 1, 1939–May 1, 1940," April 26, 1940, folder 15, box 1, Snell.

62. Arthur Horton, *An Economic, Political, and Social Survey of Phoenix and the Valley of the Sun* (Tempe: Southside Progress, 1941), unpaginated "Aims and Acknowledgments" section.

63. Ibid., 65–77.

64. Ibid., 145–53, 189–91, esp, 189, quoted 145.

65. Ibid., 149–58, 189–91.

66. *Record of Commission*, vol. 18: Aug. 9, 1939–Feb. 12, 1941, 519–20, 535, Phoenix-Records.

Chapter 3. The Business of War

1. Quoted Horton, *An Economic, Political, and Social Survey of Phoenix and the Valley of the Sun*, 145, 197.

2. Paul Koistinen, *Arsenal of World War II: The Political Economy of American Warfare, 1940–1945* (Lawrence: University of Kansas Press, 2004), 52–54; Wright, "The New Deal and the Modernization of the South," 58–73, esp. 68–69; Jack Ballard, *The Shock of Peace: Military and Economic Demobilization after World War II* (Washington, D.C.: University Press of America, 1983), 32–51.

3. Ballard, *Shock of Peace*, 32–51; Koistinen, *Arsenal of World War II*; Abbott, *New Urban America*, 102–4.

4. Ballard, *Shock of Peace*, 130–39; Ronald W. Schatz, *The Electrical Workers: A History of Labor at General Electric and Westinghouse* (Urbana: University of Illinois Press, 1984), 8–10.

5. Andrew Workman, "Manufacturing Power: The Organizational Revival of the National Association of Manufacturers, 1941–1945," *Business History Review* 72 (Summer 1998), 279–317; David Witwer, "Westbrook Pegler and the Anti-Union Movement," *Journal of American History* 92 (September 2005), 527–552; Ballard, *Shock of*

Peace, 130–39; Norman Markowitz, *The Rise and Fall of the People's Century: Henry A. Wallace and American Liberalism, 1941–1948* (New York: Free Press, 1973).

6. VanderMeer, *Desert Visions and the Making of Modern Phoenix*, 96–98, quoted 98.

7. Quoted Preisler, "Phoenix, Arizona During the 1940," 69; Carl Hayden to George Todt, February 14, 1941, 2, folder 12, box 50 series 5, subgroup I, McFarland.

8. *Standard of California* 31 (Spring 1944); J. W. Studedaker to Ernest McFarland, January 7, 1943, folder 3, box 129, subseries 1, series 9, subgroup 1, McFarland; "Summary Report on the Arizona Program of Vocational Training for War Production Workers," [1943], folder 3, box 129, subseries 1, series 9, subgroup 1, McFarland; *Record of Commission*, vol. 18: Aug. 9, 1939–Feb. 12, 1941, 437–38, 541, 542–44, esp. 544, Phoenix-Records.

9. James McMillan, *Ernest W. McFarland: Majority Leader of the United States Senate, Governor, and Chief Justice of the State of Arizona* (Prescott, Ariz.: Sharlot Hall Museum Press, 2004), 97; Dean Smith, "Military Bases Everywhere," in Brad Melton and Dean Smith (eds.), *Arizona Goes to War: The Home Front and the Front Lines During World War II* (Tucson: University of Arizona Press, 2003), 88–107.

10. Mary Melcher, "The War on the Home Front," in Melton and Smith, *Arizona Goes to* War, 108–24, esp. 109–10; McMillian, *Ernest W. McFarland*, 96–97; quoted Luckingham, *Phoenix*, 140.

11. Quoted Matthew Gann McCoy, "Desert Metropolis: Image Building and the Growth of Phoenix, 1940–1965" (Ph.D. diss., Arizona State University, 2000), 42, 44; Luckingham, *Phoenix*, 107–47, quoted 141.

12. Luckingham, *Phoenix*, 107–147, quoted 141; quoted Charles Sargent, "Arizona's Urban Frontier: Myths and Realities," in Charles Sargent (ed.), *The Conflict Between Frontier Values and Land-Use Control in Greater Phoenix: Report on Conference Held at Arizona State University* (Phoenix: Arizona Council on the Humanities and Public Policy, 1976), 19; Dean Smith, "Military Bases Everywhere," in Melton and Smith, *Arizona Goes to War*, 88–107; George Henry Nicholas Luhrs interview by Charles Colley, transcript, June 1977, 111, ASU-Oral-History.

13. G. Wesley Johnson, "Directing Elites: Catalysts for Social Change" in Johnson, *Phoenix in the Twentieth Century*, 14–29, esp. 24–28; quoted Jacobson, "The Phoenix Chamber of Commerce," 26.

14. Jacobson, "Phoenix Chamber of Commerce," 6–26, quoted 25; McCoy, "Desert Metropolis," 99–100; Walter Martin, untitled report on reorganization, March 22, 1934, vol.: "1932–1933," Board-Records. For extent of activities see entire bound volume of Board of Directors' Meeting Minutes/Activities labeled "1932–1933," Board-Records. Expense and time dictated that the most important changes and the formal reorganization waited until January 1946, see: Board of Directors, Minutes of Meetings, April 16, 1945, May 7, 1945, June 18, 1945, July 16, 1945, July 18, 1945, August 13, 1945, November 15, 1945, Vol.: "1945–1946," Board-Records; Board of Directors, Minutes of Meeting, July 16, 1948, Vol.: "1948–1949," Board-Records.

15. "Valley of Sun's Ad Program is Settled," *WP* 1 (November 1945), 3; "All of Valley Is Covered in Chamber's Trade Directory," ibid., 1 (June 1946), 1; Hebert Askins, "Paper Will Mirror Arizona Growth, Prexy [*sic*] Askins Says," ibid., 1 (November 1945), 1.

16. Snell interview by Johnson, December 7, 1978, 3; Board of Directors, Minutes of Meeting, May 7, 1945, Vol.: "1945–1946," Board-Records; Elizabeth Haas interview by Meredith Snapp, January 5, 1978, transcript, 1–6, PHP; Tim Kelly, "The Changing Face of Phoenix," *AH* 40 (March 1964), 2–23, quoted 10.

17. Harry Rosenzweig interview by Kristina Minister, March 27, 1988, audiotape, side 1, tape 13, Chamber-Interviews; Allen Rosenberg interview by Kristina Minister, March 28, 1989, audiotape, side 1, tape 12, Chamber-Interviews.

18. Board of Directors, Minutes of Meeting, March 18, 1946, Vol.: "1945–1946," Board-Records; "Legislature Committee Created by Chamber," *WP* 1 (May 1946), 1–2; "Statewide Unity Cited As Main Achievement," ibid., 1 (June 1946), 4; "Gathering of Chamber Managers Set Feb. 1," ibid., 2 (December 1946), 4; Konig, "Toward Metropolis Status," 198–203; Collins, *Emerging Metropolis*, 18–20, quoted 19.

19. Minutes of Industrial Development Committee, July 8, 1942, vol. 2: 1941–1946, Miami; Publicity Committee Meeting, June 18, 1940, vol. 1: 1939–1941, Miami.

20. Minutes of the Special Committee on Negro Housing, November 18, 1941, typescript, 1, vol. 2: 1941–1946, Miami; Minutes of the Special Labor Study Committee, November 22, 1943, typescript, 2–4, vol. 2: 1941–1946, Miami.

21. Robert Fairbanks, "Dallas in the 1940s: The Challenges and Opportunities of Defense Mobilization," in Miller and Sanders, *Urban Texas*, 141–53.

22. Gregory Hooks, "Guns and Butter, North and South: The Federal Contribution to Manufacturing Growth, 1940–1990," in Scranton (ed.), *Second Wave*, 255–85; Thomas Scott, "Winning World War II in an Atlanta Suburb: Local Boosters and the Recruitment of Bell Bomber" in Scranton (ed.), *Second Wave*, 1–23; Richard Combes, "Aircraft Manufacturing in Georgia: A Case Study of Federal Industrial Investment" in in Scranton (ed.), *Second Wave*, 24–42; Karen Ferguson, "The Politics of Exclusion: Wartime Industrialization, Civil Rights Mobilization, and Black Politics in Atlanta, 1942–1946," in in Scranton (ed.), *Second Wave*, 43–80; "Cobb County Chamber of Commerce," undated, folder 199, VF; list of "Charter Members, Cobb County Chamber of Commerce, September, 1942 to September, 1943," undated, VF; "Rickenbacher Training School Is Dedicated," unattributed clipping, Carmichael; "Rickenbacher School Formally Opened," unattributed clipping, Carmichael.

23. Charles Palmer, Statement of Business Conditions, Southeast Section, before U.S. Chamber of Commerce, May 2, 1938, 1, folder 7, box 4, Palmer; L. P. Dickie to John Sibley, June 26, 1941, folder 4, box 16, Sibley.

24. Atlanta Chamber of Commerce, "1949 Report: Estimated Income and Expenses," folder 1, box 83, Sibley; letterhead example: Robert Jones Jr. to John Sibley, April 24, 1941, folder 4, box 16, Sibley.

25. Koistinen, *Arsenal of World War II*, 52–54; Abbot, *New Urban America*, 102–4; Schulman, *From Cotton Belt to Sunbelt*, 92–100, quoted 95; Nash, *American West in*

the Twentieth Century, 193–200; NRPB, *Regional Planning Part XI*, 34–46; Pomeroy, *The American Far West in the Twentieth Century*, 116–48.

26. Nelson Lichtenstein, *Labor's War at Home: The CIO in World War II* (Philadelphia: Temple University Press, 2003), 203–32.

27. Ballard, *Shock of Peace*, 32–51, 130–39; Robert Lewis, "World War II Manufacturing and the Postwar Southern Economy," *Journal of Southern History* 73 (2007), 837–66; Richard Pourade, *City of the Dream: The History of San Diego* (La Jolla, Calif.: Copley Books, 1984), 62–66; quoted in Stephen Leonard and Thomas Noel, *Denver: Mining Camp to Metropolis* (Niwot: University Press of Colorado, 1991), 234; Fairbanks, "Dallas in the 1940s," 150; "Army Keeps Bell Aircraft Georgia Plant as Reserve," *WSJ*, December 26, 1945, 8.

28. National Resources Planning Board, *Regional Planning Part XI*, 4–7, 30–36, 134, 170, 236–244; National Resources Planning Board, Region 8, *Preliminary Statement, Regional Development Plan, Pacific Southwest, Region 8: Report to the National Resources Planning Board* (Washington, D.C.: Government Printing Office, 1941), 193–219; Ballard, *Shock of Peace*, 32–34.

29. Louise Field, *Postwar Planning in the United States: An Organization Directory* (New York: Twentieth Century Fund, 1944), v; George Simons Jr. and Ernest Hopkins, *Directory of Postwar Planning Agencies and Their Activities in the Sixth Federal Reserve District* (Atlanta: Research and Statistics Department, Federal Reserve Bank of Atlanta, 1943), 1–13.

30. Field, *Postwar Planning in the United States*, 15–16, 71–72.

31. Robert Collins, *Business Response to Keynes, 1929–1964* (New York: Columbia University Press, 1981), 81–87, 129–41, quoted 81–82.

32. Quoted in ibid., 83.

33. Ibid., 81–87, 129–41; Simons and Hopkins, *Directory of Postwar Planning Agencies and Their Activities in the Sixth Federal Reserve District*, 1–8, 14–15, 40–50, quoted 41; Field, *Postwar Planning in the United States*, 18–25; A. L. Zachary to John Sibley, September 20, 1948, with "The Next Ten Years" enclosure, 10, folder 1, box 83, Sibley.

34. Fairbanks, "Dallas in the 1940s," 150.

35. Board of Directors, Minutes of Meeting, July 16, 1948, vol.: "1948–1949," Board-Records; Barry Goldwater to Norman Hull and Board of Directors [of the Phoenix Chamber of Commerce], December 26, 1946, 1–2, folder 1, box 4, series 4, SSG I, SG II, Saufley.

36. McFarland, *Mac*, 58–95, quoted 87, 95.

37. Ibid., 58–95; McMillan, *Ernest W. McFarland*, 73–95, quoted 95; Ernest McFarland, "Small Business, The Necessity for its Preservation, and its Relation to the Rehabilitation of Returning Servicemen," undated, 2, 5–6, folder 4, box 47, series 4, subgroup I, McFarland.

38. Sidney Osborn, "Wings Over Our Western States," November 19–20, 1945, 1, 2, 6, folder 9, box 77, Governor-Subject-Files.

39. *Record of Commission*, vol. 22: Jan. 2, 1946–Nov. 26, 1946, 90–291, Phoenix-Records.

40. Ibid., 289; *Record of Commission*, vol. 23: Dec. 2, 1946–June 27, 1947, 63, Phoenix-Records; *Record of Commission*, vol. 24: July 1, 1947–Jan. 20, 1948, 271–72, Phoenix-Records.

41. Collins, *Emerging Metropolis*, 4–24.

42. Ibid.; VanderMeer, *Desert Visions and the Making of Phoenix*, 115–16.

Chapter 4. The Right to Rule

1. Karen Smith, "Community Growth and Water Policy," in Johnson, *Phoenix in the Twentieth Century*, 155–66, esp. 160–61; Collins, *Emerging Metropolis*, 24–25, 118; Board of Directors, Minutes of Meetings, April 16, 1945, May 7, 1945, June 18, 1945, July 16, 1945, July 18, 1945, August 13, 1945, November 15, 1945, May 20, 1946, Vol.: "1945–1946," Board-Records; Board of Directors, Minutes of Meeting, February 17, 1947, Vol.: "1946–1947," Board-Records.

2. "Big Pay Roll Looms If Plant Released," *WP* 1 (November 1945), 2; Board of Directors, Minutes of Meetings, April 16, 1945, May 7, 1945, June 18, 1945, July 16, 1945, July 18, 1945, August 13, 1945, November 15, 1945, May 20, 1946, Vol.: "1945–1946," Board-Records; Board of Directors, Minutes of Meeting, February 17, 1947, Vol.: "1946–1947," Board-Records; Board of Directors, Minutes of Meeting, May 17, 1948, 4, Vol.: "1947–1948," Board-Records; C. E. Gollwitzer, "President's Annual Report, 1942–43," June 21, 1943, 4–5, and W. F. Asbury, "President's Annual Report, 1943–44," June 30, 1944, 3, in 1940s section, Chamber-Binder; citation for Chamber's involvement: "Phoenix Chamber Praised for Action in Reynolds Plant Strike Agreement," *PA!* 3 (October 1948), 1; Konig, "Toward Metropolis Status," 220–21; Collins, *Emerging Metropolis*, 24–25, 39, 118; Barry Goldwater to *Arizona Labor Journal* editor [1946], folder 1, S. 4, SSG I, SG II, AHF-Goldwater.

3. Lichtenstein, *State of the Union*, 1–9, 105–10, 178–211; on "racketeering": Andrew Wender Cohen, *The Racketeer's Progress: Chicago and the Struggle for the Modern American Economy*, 1900–1940 (Cambridge: Cambridge University Press, 2004), 233–95.

4. Elizabeth Fones-Wolf, *Selling Free Enterprise: The Business Assault on Labor and Liberalism, 1945–60* (Urbana: University of Illinois Press, 1994); Lawrence Richards Jr., "'Union Free and Proud': America's Anti-Union Culture and the Decline of Organized Labor" (Ph.D. diss., University of Virginia, 2004); Elizabeth Tandy Shermer, "Counter-Organizing the Sunbelt: Right-to-Work Campaigns and Anti-Union Conservatism, 1943–1958," *Pacific Historical Review* 78 (February 2009), 81–118, esp. 91–92. There is a fourth type of union security agreement, the agency or "fair-share" shop, under which nonmembers pay a percentage of union dues. This clause does not become pertinent until after the 1950s with the NRTWC pushing to overturn such agreements made in RTW states like Texas, which led to a 1963 U.S. Supreme Court

decision that stipulated that the agency shop was implicitly banned in states that had passed RTW laws.

5. Lizabeth Cohen, *Making a New Deal: Industrial Workers in Chicago, 1919–1939* (New York: Cambridge University Press, 1990); Lichtenstein, *Labor's War at Home*, 71–81.

6. Darryl Holter, "Labor Law and the Road to Taft-Hartley: Wisconsin's 'Little Wagner Act,' 1935–1945," *Labor Studies Journal* 15 (Summer 1990), 20–47; Shermer, "Counter-Organizing the Sunbelt," 93–94.

7. Shermer, "Counter-Organizing the Sunbelt."

8. Ibid., 92–93.

9. Ibid., 94.

10. Larkin, "Labor's Desert," 107–43, esp. 115–17, 131–35.

11. Collins, *Emerging Metropolis*, 39; Taylor, *Arizona Labor Relations Law*, 30; Leo Troy and Neil Sheflin, *U.S. Union Sourcebook: Membership, Finances, Structure, Directory* (West Orange, NJ: Industrial Relations Data Information Services, 1985), 7–3 and 7–4;

12. Shermer, "Origins of the Conservative Ascendancy," 683–85; Larkin, "Labor's Desert," 107–43; Walter J. Gershenfeld, "Unionization of Public Employees in Arizona," *ABB* 14 (March 1967), 53–61, esp. 57–58.

13. Horton, *An Economic, Political, and Social Survey of Phoenix and the Valley of the Sun*, 167–70; Bridges, *Morning Glories*, 107; Cohen, *Racketeer's Progress*.

14. Michael Wade, *The Bitter Issue: The Right to Work Law in Arizona* (Tucson: Arizona Historical Society, 1976), 36–41; Taylor, *Arizona Labor Relations Law*, 23–24; Charles Buxton Harrison, "The Development of the Arizona Labor Movement" (master's thesis, Arizona State College, 1954); "Strike-Bound Hotel Finds New Trouble," unattributed clipping, frame 142, City of Phoenix Scrapbook October 10–November 28, 1946, Scrapbook CD 2, AHF-Goldwater; "Mauling by Pickets Reported as Hotel Gets Non-Union Help," unattributed clipping, frame 122, City of Phoenix Scrapbook, October 10–November 28, 1946, Scrapbook CD 2, AHF-Goldwater; "Call Police to Westward Ho Strike," unattributed clipping, frame 121, City of Phoenix Scrapbook, October 10–November 28, 1946, Scrapbook CD 2, AHF-Goldwater; Collins, *Emerging Metropolis*, 40.

15. Larkin, "Labor's Desert," 107–43, esp. 107–8, 136–41, quoted 108, 138.

16. Robert Alan Goldberg, *Barry Goldwater* (New Haven: Yale University, 1995), 14–19, 47; "Employee Handbook 1954," 7, folder 1, S. 5, SSG I, SG II, Saufley; "As Pedro Sees It," June 2, 1951, vol. XIV, no. 6, 7, folder 2, Saufley.

17. Quoted in Shermer, "Origins of the Conservative Ascendancy," 685.

18. Sue Porter Benson, *Counter Cultures: Saleswomen, Managers, and Customers in American Department Stores, 1890–1940* (Urbana-Champaign: University of Illinois Press, 1988); quoted in Goldberg, *Barry Goldwater*, 89; "As Pedro Sees It," June 2, 1951, vol. XIV, no. 6, 4, 9, folder 2, Saufley.

19. Playbill: "The Death of a Customer: An Original Training Play in Three Acts," presented at the Phoenix College Auditorium, November 1, 1949, folder 3, Saufley; script: "The Death of a Customer," undated, folder 3, Saufley.

20. Quoted in Shermer, "Origins of the Conservative Ascendancy," 686.

21. Ibid.

22. Ibid, 686–87.

23. Barry Goldwater to Wade Church, July 5, 1946, folder 1, S. 4, SSG I, SG II, Saufley.

24. Quoted in Larkin, *Labor's Desert*, 141; Miller, "A History of the Enactment of the Arizona Right to Work Law," 10–17.

25. Miller, "A History of the Enactment of the Arizona Right to Work Law," 10–17, 30; "New Legislators' List," *Your Legislative Voice*, November 1952, 1, Other Chambers of Commerce, 1951–1952, box 67, Governor-Files; Paul Kelso, "The 1948 Elections in Arizona," *Western Political Quarterly* 2 (January 1949), 92–96, esp. 93–95.

26. Wade, *The Bitter Issue*, 36–41; Kelso, "The 1948 Elections in Arizona," 95; Joe Stocker interview by Robert Goldberg, typescript, October 26, 1990, 24, Goldberg.

27. Veterans Right to Work Committee, *Honest Factual Information About the "Right to Work" Measure* (Phoenix: Veterans Right to Work Committee, n.d.), 1, 3, WL-23, Ephemera Collection (Arizona State University Archives and Special Collections, Tempe); Larkin, "Labor's Desert, 186.

28. Quoted Shermer, "Counter-Organizing the Sunbelt," 99; "Reporter's Transcript of Hearing Before Senate Judiciary Committee on Senate Bills Nos. 6 and 61 and House Bill 25 (So-Called 'Right to Work' bills), Held Feb. 8, 1945," 23–25, 37, vol. 5, box 1, Legislative-Files.

29. "Reporter's Transcript," 113–15, 71, 46–47; quoted Shermer, "Counter-Organizing the Sunbelt," 103.

30. Quoted Shermer, "Counter-Organizing the Sunbelt," 104; quoted Shermer, "Origins of the Conservative Ascendancy," 698.

31. Stewart Udall, *A Veteran's Look at the "Right-to-Work" Bill* (Phoenix: Citizens Committee Against the Right to Starve, 1946), unpaginated; D. A. Baldwin to Sir and Brother, May 24, 1946, folder 12, box 226, AZ-AFL-CIO; "Resume of Minutes of State Committee Against Right to Starve," May 19, 1946, folder 12, box 226, AZ-AFL-CIO; "Minutes of Labor Defense Committee Meeting," May 12, 1946, folder 12, box 226, AZ-AFL-CIO; "Tucson Committee Against 'Right to Starve' Meeting," October 14, 1946, folder 12, box 226, AZ-AFL-CIO; *Who's Racketeering Now?: The True Story of Mr. Vance Muse and the Origin of the So-Called 'Right-to-Work' Bill* (Phoenix: Citizens Committee Against the Right to Starve [1946]), 4, WL-6, ASU-Ephemera.

32. "Reporter's Transcript," 39–41, 58, 61–62, 118–19; Udall, *A Veteran's Look at the "Right-to-Work" Bill*, unpaginated.

33. Shermer, "Counter-Organizing the Sunbelt," 108–9.

34. Orme interview by Minister; Collins, *Emerging Metropolis*, 40–42; Wade, *Bitter Issue*, 36–41; Shermer, "Origins of the Conservative Ascendancy," 686.

35. Konig, "Toward Metropolis Status," 169–70; Collins, *Emerging Metropolis*, 25, 39. Dennis Preisler, "Phoenix, Arizona During the 1940s," 76–77.

36. Shermer, "Counter-Organizing the Sunbelt," 108–9; Miller, "A History of the Enactment of the Arizona Right to Work Law," 1–2, 58; Taylor, *Arizona Labor Relations Law*, 23–36.

37. Shermer, "Counter-Organizing the Sunbelt," 94–97, quoted 94; quoted Cobb, *Selling of the South*, 108.

38. Shermer, "Counter-Organizing the Sunbelt," 89–90.

39. Ibid., 97–98.

40. Ibid., 101–3.

41. Ibid., 103–8, quoted 104.

42. Ibid., 108–9, esp. n. 40.

Chapter 5. Grasstops Democracy

1. Quoted Rolf Felstad, "All American Cities of 1950," *Minneapolis Sunday Tribune* (reprint), 1, 3, folder 4, box 1, MK-AHF.

2. Samuel Hays, "The Politics of Reform in Municipal Government in the Progressive Era" *Pacific Northwest Quarterly* 55 (October 1964), 157–169; Daniel Amsterdam, "The Roaring Metropolis: Business, Civic Welfare, and State Expansion in 1920s America" (Ph.D. diss., University of Pennsylvania, 2009).

3. Robert Johnston, *The Radical Middle Class: Populist Democracy and the Question of Capitalism in Progressive Era Portland, Oregon* (Princeton: Princeton University Press, 2003); Cohen, *Racketeer's Progress*, 1–59; Bridges, *Morning Glories*; Abbott, *New Urban America*, 141–45; Cobb, *Industrialization and Southern Society*, 99–120.

4. Mawn, "Phoenix, Arizona," 324–38, 420–46.

5. Ibid., 324–38, 420–30; Bridges, *Morning Glories*, 58–71, esp. 59, 60, 62; quoted Luckingham, *Phoenix*, 67.

6. Kotlanger, "Phoenix, Arizona," 481–82; Mawn, "Phoenix, Arizona," 426–46.

7. Mawn, "Phoenix, Arizona," 420–46; Luckingham, *Phoenix*, 66–67.

8. Mawn, "Phoenix, Arizona," 446; ; quoted Stephen Rockstroh, "An Analysis of Phoenix Municipal Administration, 1881–1952" (master's thesis, Arizona State College, 1952), 90; Luckingham, *Phoenix*, esp. 73.

9. Matthew Whitaker, *Race Work: The Rise of the Civil Rights in the Urban West* (Lincoln: University of Nebraska, 2005), 56, 101–2, esp. 92; Mary Melcher, "Blacks and Whites Together: Interracial Leadership in the Phoenix Civil Rights Leadership," *Journal of Arizona History* 32 (Summer 1991), 195–216, esp. 196–97; Kotlanger, "Phoenix, Arizona," 413–50; Gary Tipton, "Men out of China: Origins of the Chinese Colony in Phoenix," *Journal of Arizona History* 18 (Autumn 1977), 341–56; Chiang, "The Chinese Community in Phoenix, Arizona," 51–54; Kotlanger, "Phoenix, Arizona," 423; Titcomb, "Americanization and Mexicans in the Southwest," 22–71; Val Cordova interview by N. J. Coulter, July 7, 1976, transcript, 14–19, PHP.

10. Quoted in Luckingham, *Urban Southwest*, 72–73; Collins, *New Deal in Arizona*, 340–41.

11. Titcomb, "Americanization and Mexicans in the Southwest," 47; Cordova interview by Coulter, 14–19; *Record of Commission*, vol. 18: Aug. 9, 1939–Feb. 12, 1941, 12–15, esp. 13, 15, Phoenix-Records; Whitaker, *Race Work*, 93–101, quoted 15; Melcher, "Blacks and Whites Together," 196–97.

12. *Record of Commission*, vol. 18: Aug. 9, 1939–Feb. 12, 1941, 39–40, Phoenix-Records; Collins, *Emerging Metropolis*, 36.

13. Quoted in Whitaker, *Race Work*, 90–91; quoted in Collins, *Emerging Metropolis*, 36.

14. Kotlanger, "Phoenix, Arizona," 490–509; Collins, *New Deal in Arizona*, 340–41.

15. Quoted Luckingham, *Phoenix*, 143–45; quoted Bridges, *Morning Glories*, 107, n. 32.

16. Luckingham, *Phoenix*, 143–45; Roy Hislop interview by Karin Ullmann, August 25, 1976, transcript, 44–46, PHP.

17. *Record of Commission*, vol. 20: May 27, 1942–Mar. 14, 1944, 8–9, 145, Phoenix-Records; quoted in Luckingham, *Phoenix*, 144–46; Zarbin, *All the Time a Newspaper*, 170–72.

18. Frank Snell interview by Kristina Minister, April 26, 1988, audiotape, sides 1 and 2, tape 10, Chamber-Interviews; *Record of Commission*, vol. 20: May 27, 1942–Mar. 14, 1944, 145–46, Phoenix-Records.

19. Zarbin, *All the Time a Newspaper*, vii–viii, 170–75, 181; Wes [W. Knorpp] to Barry Goldwater, May 23, 1940, folder 1, box 1, Subseries: Writings, AHF-Goldwater; Charles Walters interview by Robert Goldberg, transcript, August 31, 1991, 10, Goldberg.

20. Snell interview by Minister, side 1, tape 10; Zarbin, *All the Time a Newspaper*, 170–75, quoted 170, 171, 175.

21. Quoted Luckingham, *Phoenix*, 146; quoted Zarbin, *All the Time a Newspaper*, 172.

22. Preisler, "Phoenix, Arizona During the 1940s," 27–46.

23. Ibid., 27–30; *Record of Commission*, vol. 20: May 27, 1942–Mar. 14, 1944, 197–99, Phoenix-Records; Luckingham, *Phoenix*, 145–47; quoted Bruce Zachary, "Effects of the Federal Public Housing Movement upon Phoenix Arizona, 1937–1949" (master's thesis, Arizona State University, 1997), 99–100; Zarbin, *All the Time a Newspaper*, 172.

24. Zarbin, *All the Time a Newspaper*, 172–75; quoted Luckingham, *Phoenix*, 146; *Record of Commission*, vol. 22: Jan. 2, 1946–Nov. 26, 1946, 175–76, Phoenix-Records; "Advertisers Are Named By C of C," *AT*, August 14, 1947, unattributed clipping, frame 17, City of Phoenix Scrapbook, August 5–December 2, 1947, Scrapbook CD 2, AHF-Goldwater; Preisler, "Phoenix, Arizona During the 1940s," 29–50; Collins, *Emerging Metropolis*, 46–50; Snell interview by Minister, sides 1 and 2, tape 10, side 1, tape 11.

25. C. E. Gollwitzer, President's Annual Report, 1942–43, June 21, 1943, 1–2, "1940's" section, Chamber-Binder; Snell interview by Minister, side 1, tape 10.

26. Ray Busey interview by Ann Goldberg, April 27, 1976, 45–46, PHP; *Record of Commission*, vol. 22: Jan. 2, 1946–Nov. 26, 1946, 179, Phoenix-Records; quoted John Dale Wenum, "Spatial Growth and the Central City: Problems, Potential, and the Case of Phoenix, Arizona" (Ph.D. diss., Northwestern University 1968), 111, n. 2; Preisler, "Phoenix, Arizona During the 1940s," 40–42; Collins, *Emerging Metropolis*, 6–14, 47–51, quoted 47.

27. Karen Smith, "Community Growth and Water Policy," in Johnson, *Phoenix in the Twentieth Century*, 155–166, esp. 160–61; Collins, *Emerging Metropolis*, 24–25, 118, 266–67; Board of Directors, Minutes of Meetings, April 16, 1945, May 7, 1945, June 18, 1945, July 16, 1945, July 18, 1945, August 13, 1945, November 15, 1945, May 20, 1946, vol.: "1945–1946," Board-Records; Board of Directors, Minutes of Meeting, February 17, 1947, Vol: "1946–1947," Board-Records; Preisler, "Phoenix, Arizona During the 1940s," 50; *Record of Commission*, Vol. 22: Jan. 2, 1946–Nov. 26, 1946, 310, Phoenix-Records; Whitaker, *Race Work*, 82–83

28. *Record of Commission*, vol. 22: Jan. 2, 1946–Nov. 26, 1946, 176, Phoenix-Records; *Record of Commission*, vol. 24: July 1, 1947–Jan. 20, 1948, 179–217, esp. 179, Phoenix-Records.

29. Collins, *Emerging Metropolis*, 86; Wenum, "Spatial Growth and the Central City," 92–144, esp. 127–28; Konig, "Toward Metropolis Status," 81–96, quoted 88.

30. *Record of Commission*, vol. 26: July 6, 1948–Feb. 23, 1949, 179, Phoenix-Records; *Record of Commission*, vol. 27: Mar. 1, 1949–Aug. 30, 1949, 435, Phoenix-Records.

31. Board of Directors, Minutes of Meetings, June 20, 1949, June 24, 1949, vol,: "1948–1949," Board-Records; Board of Directors, Minutes of Meetings, July 11, 1949, July 18, 1949, vol.: "1949–1950," Board-Records; *Record of Commission*, vol. 27: Mar. 1, 1949–Aug. 30, 1949, 354–55, 433–37, 500, Phoenix-Records.

32. *Record of Commission*, vol. 24: July 1, 1947–Jan. 20, 1948, 179–217, esp. 179, 200, 215, Phoenix-Records.

33. Ibid., 179–217; Preisler, "Phoenix, Arizona During the 1940s," 48–50; Collins, *Emerging Metropolis*, 50–52, 266–67; *Record of Commission*, vol. 25: Jan. 26, 1948–June 29, 1948, 179, 200, 215, 244, Phoenix-Records; Nicolaus [*sic*] Udall interview by N. Snapp, undated, transcript, 17–18, PHP.

34. Rosenzweig interview by Minister, side 2, tape 4; Brent Whiting Brown, "An Analysis of the Phoenix Charter Government Committee as a Political Entity" (master's thesis, Arizona State University, 1968), 96; *Record of Commission*, vol. 26: July 6, 1948–Feb. 23, 1949, 177, 183, Phoenix-Records; Ray Busey, untitled report [1961], folder 11, box 2, PCGR; "Charter Revision Committee [Roster]," October 24, 1947, folder 11, box 2, Phoenix-Records; Ray Busey interview by Ann Goldberg, April 27, 1976, 1–13, 5, 8, 10, PHP.

35. Brown, "An Analysis of the Phoenix Charter Government Committee as a Political Entity."

36. Collins, *Emerging Metropolis*, 58–69; *Record of Commission*, vol. 24: July 1, 1947–Jan. 20, 1948, 104–6, esp. 104, Phoenix-Records; *Record of Commission*, vol. 26: July 6, 1948–Feb. 23, 1949, 90–94, 118–19, Phoenix-Records; *Record of Commission*, vol. 26: July 6, 1948–Feb. 23, 1949, 56–60, 90–94, 118–19, 179–86, 196–200, 323–26, Phoenix-Records.

37. *Record of Commission*, vol. 26: July 6, 1948–Feb. 23, 1949, 12–15, 56–60, 179–86, 196–200, 323–26, Phoenix-Records; Zarbin, *All the Time a Newspaper*, 194–96.

38. Konig, "Toward Metropolis Status," 53; Dix Price interview by G. W. Johnson, October 18, 1978, 17–19, PHP; Eli Gorodezky interview by Karen Smith, June 28, 1978, transcript, 12–14, PHP; Brown, "An Analysis of the Phoenix Charter Government Committee as a Political Entity," 33–36, 99–117; Zarbin, *All the Time A Newspaper*, 195. The number involved in the first CGC race has always been contested, in part because the CGC kept no formal roster and coverage did not differentiate between the slate, the core group of activists (usually estimated at 29), and CGC members.

39. Denison Kitchel interview by Robert Goldberg, typescript, November 18, 1989, 7, Goldberg [unprocessed, unboxed collection]; Luckingham, *Phoenix*, 151; Goldberg, *Barry Goldwater*, 77–78; Konig, "Toward Metropolitan Status," 58; Collins, *Emerging Metropolis*, 221–23; Newton Rosenzweig interview by Kristina Minister, March 21, 1988, audiotape, side 2, tape 3, Chamber-Interviews; Harry Rosenzweig interview by Minister, side 1, tape 13.

40. Barry Goldwater to Willie [Saufley] and Bob [Goldwater], undated, folder "Saufley, William E. (Goldwater Store Manager), 1939–1958 (1 of 3)," box 7, AHF-Goldwater; Harry Rosenzweig interview, side 1, tape 13.

41. VanderMeer, *Desert Visions and the Making of Phoenix*, 131; Harry Rosenzweig interview, side 1, tape 13.

42. Harry Rosenzweig interview, side 1, tape 13; Newton Rosenzweig interview, side 2, tape 3; Brown, "An Analysis of the Phoenix Charter Government Committee as a Political Entity," 87, n. 1; Collins, *Emerging Metropolis*, 51; Walters interview, 3; Goldberg, *Barry Goldwater*, 77–78, quoted 77; Konig, "Toward Metropolis Status," 57–59. There exists much disagreement among the CGC's leadership on who organized the slate: Price interview, 19–20; Gorodezky interview, 14–18.

43. *Record of Commission*, vol. 26: July 6, 1948–Feb. 23, 1949, 55–60, 196–200, 323–26, Phoenix-Records; Udall interview by Snapp, 17–19; Collins, *Emerging Metropolis*, 53–60; Nicholas Udall interview by Dean Smith, typescript, November 2, 1990, unpaginated, ASU-Oral-Histories.

44. Collins, *Emerging Metropolis*, 58–59; Walters interview, 2, 7, 9; quoted Goldberg, *Barry Goldwater*, 76; Orren Beaty, "Ballot Due on Changes in Charter," *AR*, November 8, 1949, unattributed clipping, frame 12, Scrapbook CD 5, AHF-Goldwater.

45. "Only One Sure Way for the Voters," unattributed clipping, Scrapbook 2, Kober; "Deppe Through as Manager if CAG Wins City Election, Busey Says," *AR*, November 2, 1949, unattributed clipping, frame 6, Scrapbook CD 5, AHF-Goldwater;

" All Mayor, Most Council Candidates Are Active," *AR*, November 5, 1949, unattributed clipping, frame 10, Scrapbook CD 5, AHF-Goldwater.

46. Russ R. Pulliam, "Methodism Shaped Life View of Publisher Pulliam," *DePauw Alumnus*, July 1979, 34–35; Luckingham, *Urban Southwest*, 89, Zarbin, *All the Time a Newspaper*, 180–85, quoted 180, 181; Frederick Marquardt interview by G. W. Johnson, November 15, 1978, transcript, 4–7, PHP; Russell Pulliam, *Publisher Gene Pulliam, Last of the Newspaper Titans* (Ottawa, IL: Jameson Books, 1984), 134–36; "Fairness in Phoenix," *Time*, January 7, 1966, 41.

47. Fenwick Anderson, "Bricks Without Straw: The Mirage of Competition in the Desert of Phoenix Daily Journalism Since 1947" (Ph.D. diss., University of Illinois, Urbana-Champaign, 1980), 29–66.

48. Quoted Goldberg, *Barry Goldwater*, 78–79; "Boss Control of City Hall Raised as Major Issue at Campaign Rally," *AR*, October 27, 1949, unattributed clipping, frame 1, Scrapbook CD 5, AHF-Goldwater; "All Mayor, Most Council Candidates Are Active," *AR*, November 5, 1949, unattributed clipping, frame 10, Scrapbook CD 5, AHF-Goldwater.

49. Michael Konig, "The Election of 1949: Transformation of Municipal Government in Phoenix," in Johnson, *Phoenix in the Twentieth Century* 167–77; Walters interview, 6; Harry Rosenzweig interview, side 1, tape 13; quoted Goldberg, *Barry Goldwater*, 79, 80.

50. "The Smoke Screen," *AR*, November 6, 1949, unattributed clipping, frame 8, Scrapbook CD 5, AHF-Goldwater; "Ministers of City Back Charter Slate," *PG*, October 27, 1949, unattributed clipping, frame 5, Scrapbook CD 5, AHF-Goldwater; "Boss Control of City Hall Raised As Major Issue at Campaign Rally," *AR*, October 27, 1949, unattributed clipping, frame 1, Scrapbook CD 5, AHF-Goldwater.

51. "Deppe-Imler Claims—and the Truth," *PG*, October 27, 1949, unattributed clipping, frame 3, Scrapbook CD 5, AHF-Goldwater; "Be Sure You Vote in the City Primary Tomorrow" postcard, frame 15, Scrapbook CD 5, AHF-Goldwater; Kober; "Death Knell of City Hall Bossism," unattributed clipping, Scrapbook 2, Kober.

52. "Voters Will Rally Behind This Group,"unattributed clipping, Kober; "Death Knell of City Hall Bossism."

53. The Smoke Screen," *AR*, November 6, 1949, unattributed clipping, frame 8, Scrapbook CD 5, AHF-Goldwater "Budgets Prove Mr. Deppe Unqualified," "Yes, Mr. Deppe—You Asked for It," unattributed clipping, frame 8, Scrapbook CD 5, AHF-Goldwater.

54. Orren Beaty, "Ballot Due On Changes in Charter," *AR*, November 8, 1949, unattributed clipping, frame 12, Scrapbook CD 5, AHF-Goldwater.

55. Konig, "Toward Metropolis Status," 60, 202–3; Goldberg, *Barry Goldwater*, 79–80; quoted in McCoy, "Desert Metropolis," 113–14.

56. Quoted McCoy, "Desert Metropolis," 113; Board of Directors, Minutes of Meeting, October 17, 1949, 4, vol.: "1949–1950," Board-Records; "Ministers of City

Back Charter Slate," *PG*, October 27, 1949, unattributed clipping, frame 5, Scrapbook CD 5, AHF-Goldwater; Konig, "Toward Metropolis Status," 61.

57. *Record of Commission*, vol. 27: Mar. 1, 1949–Aug. 30, 1949, 354–57, 436–37, 500, Phoenix-Records; Collins, *Emerging Metropolis*, 87–88; Konig, "Toward Metropolis Status," 92–96, quoted 94; "Ministers of City Back Charter Slate," *PG*, October 27, 1949, unattributed clipping, frame 5, Scrapbook CD 5, AHF-Goldwater.

58. "Mayor Udall & Charter Ticket Win Sweeping Victory in City," *AN*, November 11, 1949, 1; Brown, "An Analysis of the Phoenix Charter Government Committee as a Political Entity," 47, 121–22; Goldberg, *Barry Goldwater*, 80; Orren Beaty, "Election Victors Plan Study of City Problems," *AR*, November 10, 1949, unattributed clipping, frame 16, Scrapbook CD 5, AHF-Goldwater; Orren Beaty, "Election Victors Plan Study of City Problems," *AR*, November 10, 1949, unattributed clipping, frame 16, AHF-Goldwater; "Present Phoenix Majority Group Swept Out of Office; Record Vote," *Nogales Daily Herald*, November 9, 1949, unattributed clipping, frame 20, Scrapbook CD 5, AHF-Goldwater.

59. Amsterdam, "Roaring Metropolis," 39–110.

60. Ibid.; Lizabeth Cohen, *Making A New Deal: Industrial Workers in Chicago, 1919–1939* (Cambridge: Cambridge University Press, 1990); Guian McKee, *The Problem of Jobs: Liberalism, Race, and Deindustrialization in Philadelphia* (Chicago: University of Chicago Press), 19–40.

61. "Communities in Competition," 20–105, quoted 73; Joshua B. Freeman, *Working-Class New York* (New York: New Press, 2001), 23–71; Lichtenstein, *State of the Union*, 54–140.

62. Kruse, *White Flight*, 19–42; Amsterdam, "Roaring Metropolis," 167–213.

63. Abbott, *New Urban America*, 123–25, 144–45; Kruse, *White Flight*, 25–29, quoted 28; Floyd Hunter, "Process Recording of Interview: Atlanta Power Structure," 3, folder 5, box 16, Hunter.

64. Richard Bernard, "Metropolitan Politics in the American Sunbelt," in Mohl, *Searching for the Sunbelt*, 69–84, quoted 72–73; Cobb, *Industrialization and Southern Society*, 99–120, quoted 102.

65. Kruse, *White Flight*, 19–41.

66. Bridges, *Morning Glories*, 52–174.

67. Ibid., 29–62, 125–50; Timothy Gilfoyle, "White Cities, Linguistic Turns, and Disneylands," *Reviews in American History* 26 (March 1998), 175–204; Jessica Trounstine, *Political Monopolies in American Cities: The Rise and Fall of Bosses and Reformers* (Chicago: University of Chicago Press, 2008), 42–60.

68. Adam Cohen and Elizabeth Taylor, *American Pharaoh: Mayor Richard J. Daley—His Battle for Chicago and the Nation* (Boston: Little, Brown, 2000).

Chapter 6. Forecasting the Business Climate

1. Frank Snell interview by Kristina Minister, April 26, 1988, audiotape, side 1, tape 10, Chamber-Interviews.

2. John D. Strasma, *State and Local Taxation of Industry: Some Comparisons* (Boston: Federal Reserve Bank of Boston, 1959), 13–16, esp. 16

3. Gerald Whitney Stone, "A Study of Business Tax Burdens in the Southwest" (master's thesis, Arizona State University, 1969), 1; John D. Strasma, "Taxation of Industry: Part II—Comparisons in Massachusetts," *New England Business Review* (March 1959), 1–4, quoted 4; John Due, "Studies of State-Local Tax Influences on Location of Industry," *National Tax Journal* 14 (June 1961), 163–73.

4. Quoted Strasma, *State and Local Taxation of Industry*, 22; Thomas Kenny, "Planning Tomorrow's Plants: New Light on Site Seeking," *Dun's Review and Modern Industry* 73 (March 1959), 90–91, 104–11, quoted 104, 106.

5. Strasma, *State and Local Taxation of Industry*, 14–22, A-4–A-11.

6. Ibid.; George Ellis, "Why New Manufacturing Establishments Located in New England: August 1945 to June 1948," *Monthly Review of the Federal Reserve Bank of Boston* 31 (April 1949), 1–12, esp. 9; Kenny, "Planning Tomorrow's Plants," 111.

7. Edmund Schmidt and James Whitman, *Plant Relocation: A Case History of a Move* (New York: American Management Association, 1966), 42–49.

8. John Tomb, "Should Industry Move South?" *Harvard Business Review* 31 (September–October 1953), 83–90; Blake Johnson to Boyd Gibbons Jr., June 28, 1963, folder "Chambers of Commerce Out-ofState [*sic*]—Misc.," box 315, Governor-Files; John Harter to Gibbons, November 21, 1963, folder "Chambers of Commerce Out-ofState [*sic*]—Misc.," box 315, Governor-Files; Lee G. Sanders, "Electric Boomlet in Santa Barbara Now a Boom," *Western Electric News* (June 1958), 9–11; McKee, "Problem of Jobs," 19–78; Gall, *Politics of Right to Work*.

9. Carl Bimson, "Remarks Before Membership Committee Meeting," September 17, 1952, in Carl Bimson, *Addresses of Carl A. Bimson*, vol. 2 (Self-published, 1960), unpaginated, deposited at Arizona Historical Foundation (Tempe).

10. Meeting Minutes enclosed with V. O. Allen to Gibbons, August 5, 1959, 2, folder 4, box 8, Fannin; Western Business Consultants, *Economic Analysis and Projection for Phoenix and Maricopa County* (Phoenix: Maricopa County Planning and Zoning Department, 1960), 1–75, esp. 2; Western Management Consultants, *The Economy of Maricopa County 1965 to 1980* (Phoenix: Western Management Consultants, 1965), 1–86, esp. 9.

11. Western Management Consultants, *The Economy of Maricopa County 1965 to 1980*, 113–26.

12. Ibid., 113–26, quoted 124; Western Business Consultants, *Economic Analysis and Projection for Phoenix and Maricopa County*, 72–75.

13. Board of Directors, Minutes of Meeting, October 20, 1947, vol.: "1947–1948," Board-Records.

14. Collins, *Emerging Metropolis*, 61–63, quoted 62–63; Margaret Kober [Radio Address], November 2, 1951, 2–4, folder 4, box 1, Kober.

15. Dix Price, "Statement by Dix Price at First Meeting of New Phoenix City Council on January 4, 1954," January 4, 1954, 1, folder 4, box 1, Korber; Collins,

Emerging Metropolis, 63–65, quoted 64; Luckingham, *Phoenix*, 172; Brown, "An Analysis of the Phoenix Charter Government Committee as a Political Entity," 44–68.

16. Adam Díaz interview by Karen Ullmann, April 16, 1976, transcript, 1–7, esp. 6, PHP; Adam Díaz interview by Reba Welss Grandrud, February 17, 1998, transcript, 18–36, esp. 33, PHP.

17. Anders Walker, *The Ghost of Jim Crow: How Southern Moderates Used Brown v. Board of Education to Stall Civil Rights* (Oxford: Oxford University Press, 2009); Kruse, *White Flight*, 19–41; Schwarz, *New Dealers*, 233–35.

18. "Chamber of Commerce Committees for 1946," undated, 2, folder 15, box 50, Carmichael; A. L. Zachary to John A. Sibley, September 20, 1948, typescript with "The Next Ten Years" enclosure, 1–3, 14, folder 1, box 83, Sibley; Atlanta Chamber of Commerce, Minutes of Board of Directors' Meeting, March 29, 1949, 3, folder 2, box 83, Sibley; Floyd Hunter, "Process Recording of Interview: Atlanta Power Structure," 9, folder 5, box 16, Hunter.

19. Industrial Development Steering Committee Minutes, October 23, 1956, folder 2, box 48, SD; see also the files on the San Diego Chamber's committees, goals, and meeting minutes (folder 7, box 42, folder 3, box 46, folder 7, box 69, SD) as well as similar records for the Phoenix Chamber, especially the volumes ranging from 1932 to 1964, Board-Records.

20. Walter Ong interview by Kristina Minister, April 13, 1988, audiotape, sides 1–2, tape 5, Chamber-Interviews; Collins, *Emerging Metropolis*, 239, 252–55, 337, 355; "'Women Power' List Released by Committee," *WP*, 3 (February 1948), 1; Howard Pyle interview by G. W. Johnson, February 2, 1976, transcript, 32, 75, PHP.

21. United States Commission on Civil Rights, *Hearings Before the United States Commission on Civil Rights, Phoenix, Arizona, February 3, 1962* (Washington, D.C.: Government Printing Office, 1962), esp. 10, 45, 49, 88.

22. Minutes of Industrial and Business Development Committee, May 9, 1968, 2, folder 4, box 46, SD; Minutes of the Industrial and Business Development Committee, June 13, 1968, 2, folder 4, box 46, SD; Minutes of the Meeting of the Education Committee, September 15, 1965, folder 10, box 30, SD.

23. Nicholas Udall interview by Dean Smith, typescript, November 2, 1990, unpaginated, ASU-Oral-Histories; Charles Walters interview by Robert Goldberg, transcript, August 31, 1991, 2, 3, 7, 9, Goldberg; Milton Sanders interview by Meredith Snapp, December 29, 1977, transcript, PHP; Newton Rosenzweig interview by Kristina Minister, March 21, 1988, audiotape, Chamber-Interviews; Phoenix Chamber of Commerce Publicity Department, Press Release, June 10, 1964, 1, Rosenberg-Scrapbook; Sam Mardian interview by Kristina Minister, March 13, 1988, audiotape, side 2, tape 6, Chamber-Interviews.

24. Eli Gorodezky interview by Karen Smith, June 28, 1978, transcript 14–18, 21–22, PHP; Newton Rosenzweig, Dick Smith, and Dorothy Theilkas to Friend of Charter Government, December 11, 1963, folder 13, box 2, PCGR. In the early years of the CGC's reign, there was an exception to the two-term limit. Kober served three terms

because most members from the 1951 ticket had decided not to seek reelection. Mrs. Leslie [Margaret] Kober interview by S. Laughlin, June 18, 1976, transcript, 12–13, PHP; Newton Rosenzweig interview by Minister, side 2, tape 4. A real discrepancy exists between the CGC founders' characterizations of their group. During its reign, all uniformly stood behind its arguments of nonpartisan good-government. In later interviews and especially within their private and public remembrances, many, such as Kober, Goldwater, Walters, and Carl Bimson, admitted that their critics' charges had some truth to them but remained unapologetic. A few, such as Newton Rosenzweig, never conceded any allegations of undemocratic elitism in later questioning. See Newton Rosenzweig to Darwin [Aycock], October 30, 1981, folder: Rosenzweig: Government & Public Policy, Charter Government Committee, 1981, box: unassigned, Rosenzweig.

25. Brown, "An Analysis of the Charter Government Committee as a Political Entity," 123–24; *Record of Commission*, vol. 35: January 1, 1956–December 31, 1956, 46–47, Phoenix-Records; G. Wesley Johnson Jr., "Directing Elites: Catalysts for Social Change," in Johnson, *Phoenix in the Twentieth Century*, 13–32, esp. 24–27.

26. "The Record for the First Two Months," *City Manger's News Bulletin*, March 4, 1950, 1–2; Collins, *Emerging Metropolis*, 60; Ray Wilson, "Phoenix—A City of Planned Progress," October 27, 1951, 2–3, folder 4, box 1, Kober.

27. Board of Directors, Minutes of Meeting, June 19, 1950, 3, vol.: "1949–1950," Board-Records.

28. *Record of Commission*, vols. 18–40, Phoenix-Records; for specific examples see: *Record of Commission*, vol. 27: March 1, 1949–August 30, 1949, 170, 377–78, Phoenix-Records; *Record of Commission*, vol. 35: January 1, 1956–December 31, 1956, 356–57, Phoenix-Records.

29. Burke Payne, "Tax and Budget [Committee Report]: Study of City Budget," *PA* 5 (June 1950), 6; John L. McAtee, "City Expansion [Committee Report]: One of Chief Chamber Aims," *PA*, 6 (June 1951), 5.

30. Boyd Gibbons, "Report to Governor Paul Fannin on 'Prospecting' Tour to Los Angeles, December 2–5, 1959," undated, 2, folder 11, box 11, Fannin; Board of Directors, Minutes of Meeting, October 20, 1947, 5–6, vol.: "1947–1948," Board-Records; C. E. Van Ness, "1948–49: A Great Year of Accomplishment," *PA* 4 (May 1949), 1–2; Barry Goldwater to Lewis Haas, June 30, 1954, Pdf 19, reel 30, CD 7, series VI, AHF-Goldwater; Lewis E. Haas to [Henry] Zipf, December 22, 1953, Pdf 19, reel 30, CD 7, series VI, AHF-Goldwater.

31. Barry Goldwater to Howard Pyle, May 1, 1954, folder 3, box 1, Pyle; William Saufley to Barry Goldwater, May 10, 1954, 1, folder "Saufley, William E. (Goldwater Store Manager), 1939–1958 (1 of 3)," box 7, AHF-Goldwater; Orme Lewis interview by Kristina Minister, April 14, 1988, audiotape, side 2, tape 2, Chamber-Interviews; quoted in Earl Zarbin, *All the Time a Newspaper*, 185; Guber, "Development of Two-Party Competition in Arizona," 33–34; Goldberg, *Barry Goldwater*, 14–19, quoted 47; Barry Goldwater to Jack Williams, June 5, 1968, 1, folder "Goldwater: Personal, Alpha

Files—Williams, Jack, 1 of 7, 1955–1968", box W, AHF-Goldwater; Howard Pyle, "Making History: Good, Bad, and Indifferent," March 6, 1985, typescript, 7, folder 6, box 12, ASU-Oral-Histories; Ruth Adams interview by G. Wesley Johnson, September 29, 1978, 19, PHP; Ross R. Rice, "The 1958 Election in Arizona," *Western Political Quarterly* 12 (January 1959), 266–75.

32. Adams interview by Johnson, 19; John J. Rhodes interview by Dean Smith, transcript, May 1, 1991, 8, 10, ASU-Oral-History; John J. Rhodes interview by Zona Davis Lorig, November 30, 1992, transcript, PHP.

33. Stephen Shadegg, *Arizona Politics: The Struggle to End One-Party Rule* (Tempe: Arizona State University Press, 1986), 7; Columbus Giragi to W. P. Stuart, August 28, 1935, folder 5, box 1, Stuart; Frank Brophy interview by Patricia Clark, undated, transcript, 2, ASU-Oral-History.

34. C. V. Gulley to Orme Lewis, October 26, 1945, folder 14, box 7, Lewis; Minutes of Meeting of Republican State Central Committee, November 3 and 4, 1945, 2, 8–9, folder 15, box 7, Lewis.

35. Goldberg, *Barry Goldwater*, 27; Quoted Goldwater, *Delightful Journey*, 112; Jason Crabtree LaBau, "Phoenix Rising: Arizona and the Origins of Modern Conservative Politics" (Ph.D. diss., University of Southern California, 2010), 25–35, 110–116, 122–128, quoted 28, 35, 112–112, 127; Brophy interview by Clark; Andrew Needham, "The Conscience of a Conservationist: Barry Goldwater and Environmental Change in Postwar Arizona" in Elizabeth Tandy Shermer (ed.), *Barry Goldwater and the Remaking of the American Political Landscape* (Tucson: University of Arizona Press, 2013).

36. Shermer, "Origins of the Conservative Ascendancy"; LaBau, "Phoenix Rising," 25–35, 110–116, 122–128, quoted 26, 35, 127.

37. Shadegg, *Arizona Politics*, 31–32; "Republican Party Platform—1948," 2, folder 4, box 7, Lewis; "Republican Party Platform 1959," 1, folder 13, box 7, Lewis.

38. O. D. Miller interview by Karin Ullmann, June 29, 1976, transcript, 28–30, esp. 29, PHP; Rhodes interview by Smith, 11–12; Royal D. Marks interview by Karin Ullman, June 25, 1976, transcript, 18–23, PHP; "Censorship and the Pulliam Press," *Arizona Frontiers* 2 (December 1961), 3–4.

39. Ruth Fitzgerald to Howard Pyle, October 9, 1950, 1, folder 1a, box 19, Pyle; [Unsigned] to Howard Pyle, June 20, 1950, folder 1a, box 19, 1, Pyle; Milton MacKaye, "The Cities of America: Phoenix," *SEP*, October 18, 1947, 93; Barry De Rose to Carl Hayden, August 23, 1960, folder 7, box 547, series I, Hayden.

40. Zarbin, *All the Time a Newspaper*, 183; "Pima County Volunteer Help" [1958], unpaginated, folder: "Volunteer Lists," box 3H489, UT-Goldwater; "Maricopa County Volunteer Help" [1958], unpaginated, folder: "Volunteer Lists," Box 3H489, UT-Goldwater; "Projects Accomplished by Republican State Committee in 1961" [1962], unpaginated, loose in box 68, Shadegg; Larkin, *Labor's Desert*, 234–38; Neil Clark, "The Amateur Governor of Arizona," *SEP*, June 16, 1951, 29+.

41. Catherine Rymph, *Republican Women: Feminism and Conservatism from Suffrage through the Rise of the New Right* (Chapel Hill: University of North Carolina Press, 2006); Michelle Nickerson, *Mothers of Conservatism: Women and the Postwar Right* (Princeton: Princeton University Press); "Maricopa County Volunteer Help" [1958], unpaginated, folder: "Volunteer Lists," Box 3H489, UT-Goldwater; Evelyn Mann to Barry Goldwater, August 22, 1958, folder: "Tucson Coffees," Box 3H489, UT-Goldwater; "[Guest list] Barry Goldwater Luncheon—August 24 at the home of Mr. and Mrs. Wm C. Schwab," August 24 [1958], folder: "Tucson Coffees," Box 3H489, UT-Goldwater; "Letter for those in attendance at the Badet home," September 3, 1958, folder: "Tucson Coffees," Box 3H489, UT-Goldwater; Velma Rudd Hoffman to Barry Goldwater, June 11, 1953, 1, 3, film file 16: Senator Goldwater Arizona Files, microdex 1: Republican Organizations, AHF-Goldwater; Elizabeth LaZear to Barry Goldwater, February 5, 1953, film file 16: Senator Goldwater Arizona Files, microdex 1: Republican Organizations, AHF-Goldwater; Jennie Tannenhill to Barry Goldwater, May 10, 1953, film file 16: Senator Goldwater Arizona Files, microdex 1: Republican Organizations, AHF-Goldwater.

42. Quoted in Shermer, "Origins of the Conservative Ascendancy," 690–92.

43. Ibid., 694; Wade, *Bitter Issue*, 38–41; Guber, "Development of Two-Party Competition in Arizona," 67–68, 108–23; Roy Elson, "Orchestrating Senator Carl Hayden's Last Campaign," *Journal of Arizona History* 41 (December 2000), 413–24, quoted 413.

44. Rice, "1958 Election in Arizona," 267; J. E. Woodley to Howard Pyle, October 9, 1950, folder 33 box 74, Pyle; Pyle, "Making History," 7.

45. Guber, "Development of Two-Party Competition in Arizona," 33–34, 53–55; Pyle, "Making History," 8–9; Shadegg, *Arizona Politics*, 107–46.

46. Guber, "Development of Two-Party Competition in Arizona," 33–34, 53–55; Pyle, "Making History," 8–9; Lawrence Mehren, "Water: Arizona's Critical Asset," 11 *ABB* (February 1964), 3–9, esp. 3, 5; Howard Pyle interview by Jack August, transcript, November 9, 1982, 1, 13–14, ASU-Oral-History; Carl Hayden to Ed Carranza, February 19, 1958, folder 11, box 34, Hayden; Carl Hayden to Paul S. McKusick, November, 1, 1956, folder 11, box 34, Hayden.

47. "Nonpolitical Politician," *Time*, March 26, 1951, 26; Shadegg, *Arizona Politics*, 32, 65–71.

48. Shadegg, *Arizona Politics*, 32, 65–71; Goldberg, *Barry Goldwater*, 32, 84–86, 94; Guber, "Development of Two-Party Competition in Arizona," 75–100; Howard Pyle, "Address by Governor Howard Pyle," October 30, 1952, typescript, 7–8, folder 1, box 34, Pyle; Pyle, untitled legislative address January 23, 1951, 4, folder 5, box 33, Pyle.

49. Ernest McFarland [campaign speech], undated, 2, 4, folder 19, box 186, series 8, subgroup II, McFarland; quoted in Rex Stanley, "Arizona Politics Hottest in 38 Years," *Denver Post*, October 24, 1950, unpaginated, folder 1, box 20, COPE; McMillan, *Ernest W. McFarland*, 288–89; McFarland, *Mac*, 227–34; Martha Sonntag Bradley, *Kidnapped*

from That Land: The Government Raids on the Short Creek Polygamists (Salt Lake City: University of Utah Press, 1993), 113–59; N. D. Houghton, "The 1954 Elections in Arizona," *Western Political Quarterly* 7 (December 1954), 594–96; Pulliam, *Publisher Gene Pulliam*, 169–70.

50. James Johnson, *Arizona Politicians: The Notable and the Notorious* (Tucson: University of Arizona Press, 2002), 101–10, 158–67; Shadegg, *Arizona Politics*, 197–99; Micaela Anne Larkin, "Southwestern Strategy: Mexican Americans and Republican Politics in the Arizona Borderlands" in Shermer, *Barry Goldwater and the Remaking of the American Political Landscape.*

51. Douglas Smith, "Into the Political Thicket: Reapportionment and the End of Southern Exceptionalism," in Matthew D. Lassiter and Joseph Crespino, *The Myth of Southern Exceptionalism* (Oxford: Oxford University Press, 2010), 263–85; Eugene Moehring, *Resort City in the Sunbelt: Las Vegas* (Reno: University of Nevada Press, 1989), 223–27.

52. Sylvia Altman, "CC's Story—Through the Years," *Metropolitan Miamian* 49 (April 1957), 7; Cobb, *Industrialization and Southern Society*, 102–4.

53. Gordon E. Baker, *The Reapportionment Revolution: Representation, Political Power, and the Supreme Court* (New York: Random House, 1966); Bernard Grofman, *Voting Rights, Voting Wrongs: The Legacy of Baker v. Carr* (New York: Priority Press, 1990); Smith, "Into the Political Thicket."

54. Ross R. Rice, "The 1966 Elections in Arizona," *Western Political Quarterly* 20 (June 1967), 529–34; Ben Avery, "All 28 State Senators Might Run at Large," *Arizona Republic*, June 16, 1964, February 3, 1964.

55. Ethan Rarick, *California Rising: The Life and Times of Pat Brown* (Berkeley: University of California Press, 2005).

56. Lassiter, *Silent Majority*, 228–32.

57. Earl Black and Merle Black, *The Vital South: How Presidents Are Elected* (Cambridge, MA: Harvard University Press, 1992), 141–49.

58. Alex Lichtenstein, "The End of Southern Liberalism: Race, Class and the Defeat of Claude Pepper in the 1950 Democratic Primary," unpublished article in author's possession, presented at the Center for the Study of Work, Labor, and Democracy's Speakers' series, University of California, Santa Barbara, September 26, 2008.

59. Earl Black and Merle Black, *Rise of the Southern Republicans* (Cambridge, MA: Harvard University Press, 2003), 72–138; Lassiter, *Silent Majority*, 228–32; Merle Black, "The Transformation of the Southern Democratic Party," *Journal of Politics* 66 (November, 2004), 1001–17; Kari Frederickson, *The Dixiecrat Revolt and the End of the Solid South, 1932–1968* (Chapel Hill: University of North Carolina, 2000).

60. Shermer, "Counter-Organizing the Sunbelt," 89.

61. Ibid., 114–118.

62. Ibid.; Charles Baird, "Right to Work Before and After 14(b)," 19 *Journal of Labor Research* (Summer 1998), 471–93.

63. Paul Kelso, "The 1952 Elections in Arizona," *Western Political Quarterly* 6 (March 1953), 100–102, quoted 100; Howard Pyle to Courtney Own, March 18, 1954, "Right to Work" enclosures, 1, folder 6A, box 9, Pyle; Collins, *Emerging Metropolis*, 41–43; Taylor, *Arizona Labor Relations Law*, 17–24, quoted 17–18.

64. Taylor, *Arizona Labor Relations Law*, 52–56; Walter R. Gershenfeld, "Unionization of Public Employees in Arizona," *ABB* 14 (March 1967), 53–61, quoted 58.

65. Shermer, "Counter-Organizing the Sunbelt," 90–91; Georgia State Chamber of Commerce, *1959 Industrial Survey of Georgia* (Atlanta: Georgia State Chamber of Commerce, 1959), 29, folder 7, box 187, Davis.

66. Luther Hodges, *Businessman in the Statehouse: Six Years as Governor of North Carolina* (Chapel Hill: University of North Carolina Press, 1962), 30–46, 157–60, esp. 30–31, 43, and 160.

67. Robert Spinney, "Municipal Government in Nashville, Tennessee, 1938–1951: World War II and the Growth of the Public Sector," 61 *Journal of Southern History* (February 1995), 77–112, esp. 103.

68. Advisory Commission on Intergovernmental Relations, *State-Local Taxation and Industrial Location: A Commission Report* (Washington, DC: Government Printing Office, 1967), 31.

69. Industrial and Business Development Committee, Tax Free Municipal Bonds Report, April 13, 1967, folder 2, box 43, SD; quoted Allen Dieterich-Ward, "Mines, Mills, and Malls: Regional Development in the Steel Valley" (Ph.D. diss., University of Michigan, 2006), 101.

70. Robert Cline et al., *Total State and Local Business Taxes: 50-State Estimates for Fiscal 2006* (Washington, DC: Ernst and Young for the Council on State Taxation, 2008).

71. Western Business Consultants, *Economic Analysis and Projection for Phoenix and Maricopa County*, 72–75; Western Management Consultants, *The Economy of Maricopa County, 1965 to 1980*, 110–120, quoted 120; "Inventory Tax Cut," *PA* VIII (January 1953), 1.

72. Carl Bimson interview by Kristina Minister, April 14, 1988, audiotape, side 2, tape 7, Chamber-Interviews; Board of Directors, Minutes of Meeting, February 20, 1950, March 20, 1950, vol.: "1949–1950," Board-Records; Board of Directors, Minutes of Meetings, January 17, 1949, and May 16, 1949, vol.: "1948–1949," Board-Records; Floyd Rains to Howard Pyle, September 4, 1952, f11, box 67, Governor-Subject-Files.

73. Stone, "A Study of Business Tax Burdens in the Southwest," 1–2, 36–50.

74. Ibid., 1–2; Advisory Commission on Intergovernmental Relations, *State-Local Taxation and Industrial Location*, 31–48.

Chapter 7. "Second War Between the States"

1. "Second War Between the States," *BW*, May 17, 1976, 92–98+; L. Langway, "War Between the States," *Newsweek*, May 5, 1975, 65+; "New War Between the States: Tax

Subsidies for Industry," *U.S. News and World Report*, November 25, 1963, 117–18; Phoenix Chamber of Commerce, *What Phoenix and Arizona Have to Offer the Textile Industry* (Phoenix: Phoenix Chamber of Commerce, 1960).

2. Board of Directors, Minutes of Meeting, March 31, 1952, vol.: "1951–1952," Board-Records; Board of Directors, Minutes of Meeting, July 21, 1947, vol.: "1947–1948," Board-Records; Smith, "Community Growth and Water Policy"; Collins, *Emerging Metropolis*, 117–19.

3. Smith, "Community Growth and Water Policy"; Collins, *Emerging Metropolis*, 117–19.

4. Collins, *Emerging Metropolis*, 117–19.

5. Ibid., Smith, "Community Growth and Water Policy"; Board of Directors, Minutes of Meeting, March 31, 1952, 2–3, vol.: "1951–1952," Board-Records.

6. "Project Should Pay Taxes," *AR*, October 21, 1958, folder 1 of three labeled Salt River Project v. Arizona Public Service Company "Operation Project Survival," box unassigned, Shadegg; untitled speaking points document, undated, 4–6, folder 1 of three labeled Salt River Project v. Arizona Public Service Company "Operation Project Survival," box unassigned, Shadegg.

7. R. J. McMullin, "Top Secret Conference Re: APS Attack on SRP," November 21, 1962, folder 1 of three labeled Salt River Project v. Arizona Public Service Company "Operation Project Survival," box unassigned, Shadegg; "The Salt River Project Does Help!" *AR*, unattributed clipping, Shadegg.; "Here's the Complete Story About the Salt River Project's Importance to YOU," *AR*, Shadegg; E. K. Carpenter to V. A. Pierce, Memo: Operation Project Survival, December 12, 1962, Shadegg; R. J. McMullin, "Salt River Project Manager Challenges Editorial's View," *AR*, December 27, 1962, folder 2 of three labeled Salt River Project v. Arizona Public Service Company "Operation Project Survival," box unassigned, Shadegg.

8. Stephen Shadegg, "It Was Never Nothing," unpublished memoir, undated, 251–58, folder Shadegg Writings "It Was Never Nothing," box unassigned, Shadegg. A different interpretation of these tax issues was published just prior to this book's completion: Andrew Needham, "The End of Public Power: The Politics of Place and the Postwar Electric Utility Industry" in Zelizer and Phillips-Fein (eds.), *What's Good for Business*, 157–176.

9. August, *Vision in the Desert*.

10. Goldberg, *Barry Goldwater*, 71–74, quoted 73; Barry Goldwater, *Delightful Journey: Down the Green and Colorado Rivers* (Tempe: Arizona Historical Foundation, 1970), 16, 22–26; Needham, "Conscience of a Conservationist".

11. Barry Goldwater, *Where I Stand* (New York: McGraw-Hill, 1964), 45–46; Robert Dean, "'Dam Building Still Had Some Magic Then: Stewart Udall, the Central Arizona Project, and the Evolution of the Pacific Southwest Water Plan, 1963–1968," *Pacific Historical Review* 66 (February 1997), 81–98, esp. 97.

12. Howard Pyle interview by Jack August, transcript, November 9, 1982, 1, ASU-Oral-History; August, *Vision in the Desert*, 175–205; Dean, "'Dam Building Still Had

Some Magic Then,'" 97; Todd Andrew Needham, "Power Lines: Urban Space, Energy Development and the Making of the Modern Southwest" (Ph.D. diss., University of Michigan, 2006).

13. Board of Directors, Minutes of Meeting, July 20, 1964, November 19, 1964, vol.: "1964–1965," Board-Records; Lawrence Mehren, "Water: Arizona's Critical Asset," 11 *ABB* (February 1964), 3–9, esp. 3, 5; Frank Snell interview by James McNulty, June 20, 1989, transcript, 45–49, Arizona Bar Foundation Oral History Project: Arizona Legal History, Arizona Historical Society (Tucson); Pyle interview by August, 13–14; August, *Vision in the Desert*, 179–82, quoted 180.

14. Jack August Jr., "Old Arizona and the New Conservative Agenda: The Hayden Versus Mecham U.S. Senate Campaign of 1962," *Journal of Arizona History* 41 (December 2000), 385–412.

15. Data for League of Women Voters, folder 17, box 9, Mecham; [Mecham], speech notes, [1962], 1–2, folder 17, box 9, Mecham; [Mecham], untitled speech, [1962], 1, folder 23, box 9, Mecham; Mecham, draft statement for *Small Business Review*, [1962], folder 23, box 9, Mecham; [Mecham], "Mecham Talk to Phoenix Kiwanis Club," August 14, 1962, 1, folder 23, box 9, Mecham; [Mecham], untitled speech, [1962], 1, folder 23, box 9, Mecham; [Mecham], untitled press release, [1962], folder 23, box 9, Mecham.

16. Quoted August, "Old Arizona and the New Conservative Agenda," 390, 391, 393, 396, 397, 402, 403.

17. [Mecham], "Here Are the Facts," 1, folder 18, box 9, Mecham; [Mecham], draft letter to supports, undated, 2, folder 23, box 9, Mecham; Bill Becker, "Democratic Gain in West Expected," *NYT*, October 4, 1962, 39; "Goldwater Aide Pushes Campaign," *NYT*, September 2, 1962, 34; Bill Becker, "Arizona Matches Foes of 84 and 38," *NYT*, September 13, 1962, 22; Bernie Wynn, "Arizona" section of "How the West Will Go" feature, *LAT*, October 28, 1962, J2; "Senator Hayden Gains 7th Term," *NYT*, November 7, 1962, 34; Bill Becker, "2 Republicans Vie for Hayden Seat," *NYT*, July 29, 1962, 36; Stephen Shadegg, *What Happened to Goldwater? The Inside Story of the 1964 Republican Campaign* (New York: Holt, Rinehart and Winston, 1965), 50–55; Shadegg, *Arizona Politics*, 125–27; [George Fowler] to [Stephen Shadegg], [1962], folder Fowler, George (investigative reports), box unassigned, Shadegg.

18. Gerald Marvin Hermanson, "Urbanization of Agricultural Lands in Maricopa County, Arizona, 1950–1980 (master's thesis, Arizona State University, 1968), 26–54, quoted 52; quoted in Robert Autobee, *The Salt River Project* (Denver: Bureau of Reclamation History Program, 1993), 29.

19. Dean, "'Dam Building Still Had Some Magic Then,'" 81–82; Marc Reisner, *Cadillac Desert: The American West and Its Disappearing Water* (New York: Viking, 1986), 293–96, esp. 293, 296; Andrew Ross, *Bird on Fire: Lessons from the World's Least Sustainable City* (New York: Oxford University Press, 2011), 22–50.

20. Quoted in Spinney, "Municipal Government in Nashville, Tennessee, 1938–1951," 93; Kenneth Jackson, "Metropolitan Government versus Political Autonomy:

Politics on the Crabgrass Frontier," in Kenneth Jackson and Stanley Schultz (eds.), *Cities in American History* (New York: Alfred A. Knopf, 1972), 442–62; Abbott, *New Urban America*, 54–55, 172–84.

21. Bridges, *Morning Glories*, 152–59; Abbott, *New Urban America*, 54–55, 172–84.

22. Lassiter, *Silent Majority*, 52–54, 128, 297–98; Robert William Hildebrand, "Metropolitan Area Government: Miami, Nashville, and Phoenix in Perspective" (master's thesis, Arizona State University, 1974); Kruse, *White Flight*, 37–38, quoted 37.

23. Paul Fannin, "Governor Fannin's Speech: Rotary and Other Service Clubs of Wickenburg," September 18, 1962, folder 5, box 4, Fannin; "Arizona: Selected Tax Data and Trends of State Governmental Expense and Revenue," December 1962, folder 4, box 4, Fannin; quoted in Hildebrand, "Metropolitan Area Government," 92; "Over $22 Billion Taken In States' Taxes In 1963," *PG*, January 10, 1963, unattributed clipping, folder 6, box 4, Fannin.

24. *Record of Commission*, vol. 29: June 6, 1950–May 29, 1951, 420–21, Phoenix-Records; *Record of Commission*, vol. 30: June 5, 1951–April 29, 1952, 147, Phoenix-Records.

25. Hildebrand, "Metropolitan Area Government," 80–123, quoted 92; John Dale Wenum, "Spatial Growth and the Central City: Problems, Potential, and the Case of Phoenix, Arizona" (Ph.D. diss., Northwestern University, 1968), 80–123, quoted 113.

26. Wenum, "Spatial Growth and the Central City," 80–123, quoted 122, 131.

27. Board of Directors, Minutes of Meeting, September 15, 1952, vol.: "1952–1953," Board-Records; Board of Directors, Minutes of Meeting, February 19, 1951, vol.: "1950–1951," Board-Records; Hildebrand, "Metropolitan Area Government"; Bridges, *Morning Glories*, 154–55; Collins, *Emerging Metropolis*, 94–99, quoted 88; Wenum, "Spatial Growth and the Central City," 80–171, quoted 142–43; Konig, "Toward Metropolis Status," 82–115.

28. "What Annexation Can Do for You," May 24, 1961, folder 5, box 2, Mardian; Wenum, "Spatial Growth and the Central City," 133–44, quoted 132, 141, 143; Collins, *Emerging Metropolis*, 88–98; Konig, "Toward Metropolitan Status," 98–113.

29. Hilliard Brooke to Phoenix Citizens Living Outside the City Limits, undated, folder 8, box 1, Kantz; Board of Directors, Minutes of Meeting, November 20, 1950, vol.: "1950–1951," Board-Records; "Northwest Expansion Planned," *City Manager's News Bulletin*, August 4, 1951, 1; Wenum, "Spatial Growth and the Central City," 80–171.

30. Wenum, "Spatial Growth and the Central City," 133–44, quoted 134, 143; Collins, *Emerging Metropolis*, 88–98; Konig, "Toward Metropolitan Status," 98–113, quoted 105.

31. Wenum, "Spatial Growth and the Central City," 133–144, appendix B.

32. Ibid., 133–144; Collins, *Emerging Metropolis*, 88–98; Konig, "Toward Metropolitan Status," 98–13, quoted 109; "That 1959 Annexation," *AR*, December 6, 1975, A6; Don Bolles, "Charter Slate Opposes New Vote on Sales Tax Breaks," *AR*, December 4, 1975, A8.

33. Collins, *Emerging Metropolis*, 88–99, quoted 88.

34. Wenum, "Spatial Growth and the Central City," 149–71, quoted 157–159.

35. Ibid., 170–71; Collins, *Emerging Metropolis*, 94–99.

36. Collins, *Emerging Metropolis*, 94–99; Bridges, *Morning Glories*, 154–55; Konig, "Toward Metropolis Status," 82–115; Sam Mardian interview by Kristina Minister, March 13, 1988, audiotape, side 2, tape 6, Chamber-Interviews.

37. Bridges, *Morning Glories*, 154–155; Collins, *Emerging Metropolis*, 94–99; Konig, "Toward Metropolis Status," 82–115.

38. Advisory Commission on Intergovernmental Relations, *State-Local Taxation and Industrial Location*, 71–77.

39. Wright, *Old South, New South*, 173.

40. National Resources Planning Board, *Regional Planning Part XI*, 170; National Resources Planning Board, *Preliminary Statement, Regional Development Plan, Pacific Southwest, Region 8*, 218–19.

41. Margaret Pugh O'Mara, *Cities of Knowledge: Cold War Science and the Search for the Next Silicon Valley* (Princeton: Princeton University Press, 2005), esp. 1.

42. Advisory Commission on Intergovernmental Relations, *State-Local Taxation and Industrial Location*, 71–77, quoted 73.

43. Georgia State Chamber of Commerce, *1959 Industrial Survey of Georgia* (Atlanta: Georgia State Chamber of Commerce, 1959), 9, folder 7, box 187, Davis; Ronald Carrier, *Plant Location Analysis: An Investigation of Plant Locations in Tennessee* (Memphis: Memphis State University Press, 1969), 160.

44. Barry Goldwater, *Conscience of a Conservative* (Princeton: Princeton University Press, 2007), 74; Paul Fannin, "Federal Aid and Arizona Schools," November 27, 1959, 1, folder 3, box 21, Fannin; Royal Alderman, "Phoenix Revisited: The Electronic Boom Keeps Booming," *Western Electric News*, June 1959, 16–24, esp. 22.

45. Dean Smith, *Grady Gammage: ASU's Man of Vision* (Tempe: Arizona State University, 1989), 1–108.

46. Ibid.

47. Ibid., 51–108, quoted 86, 91.

48. Ibid., quoted 104; Ernest J. Hopkins and Alfred Thomas Jr., *The Arizona State University Story* (Phoenix: Southwest Publishing, 1960), 245–94, quoted 256.

49. Smith, *Grady Gammage*, 109–62, quoted 125; Grady Gammage to Sidney Osborn, January 28, 1947, in vol. 138, OPR; "Board of Regents of the University and State Colleges of Arizona," 1947, in vol. 138, OPR; Walter Bimson to Grady Gammage, June 30, 1952, in vol. 140, OPR; [Walter Bimson], "Memo re Tucson Meeting," in vol. 140, OPR.

50. Quoted in Western Management Consultants, Inc., *The Economy of Maricopa County 1965 to 1980*, 124.

51. Smith, *Grady Gammage*, 109–62; Daniel Noble, "Educating Industry to the Value of the Universities," October 11, 1961, 2–6, folder, 1, box 4, Fannin.

52. Robert Galvin, "Electronic Horizons," April 11, 1962, 4–5, folder 1, box 4, Fannin; Daniel Noble interview by Dick Lynch, September 26, 1976, transcript, 4–6, PHP;

Collins, *Emerging Metropolis*, 170–89, quoted 189; D. E. Noble to Mrs. K. Gammage, September 18, 1961, in vol. 225, OPR; D. E. Noble, "Motorola Reports Phoenix Progress," March 29, 1957, 6–7, 10, in vol. 234, OPR.

53. Administrative Staff of the Arizona State College at Tempe, "Higher Education for a Greater Arizona," in vol. 140, OPR; Hopkins and Thomas, *Arizona State University Story*, 288–90; Smith, *Grady Gammage*, 109–212.

54. J. A. N. Lee, "General Electric Corporation Computer Department," *IEEE Annals of the History of Computing* 17 (December 1995), 24–45; H. R. (Barney) Oldfield, "General Electric Enters the Computer Business—Revisited," *IEEE Annals of the History of Computing* 17 (December 1995), 46–55; Noble, "Motorola Reports Phoenix Progress," 7–9; Noble to Mrs. K. Gammage, September 18, 1961, in vol. 225, OPR; "State College at Tempe Foundation," April 17, 1956, 1–2, in vol. 229, OPR.

55. Frederick Marquardt interview by G. W. Johnson, November 15, 1978, transcript, 21–22, PHP; Collins, *Emerging Metropolis*, 170–87; Smith, *Grady Gammage*, 163–212, quoted 177; Hopkins and Thomas, *Arizona State University Story*.

56. Lewis Haas to Homer Durham, October 19, 1961, in vol. 1297, OPR; E. J. Demson, memorandum, undated enclosure with Walter Bimson to Grady Gammage, June 30, 1952, in vol. 225, OPR; E. J. Demson, "Memo of the Discussion and points of agreement reached at the group meeting with officials of Motorola, Inc.," undated, in vol. 225; "Minutes of the Arizona State University Foundation Advisory Committee on Engineering and Science," undated, 1–4, in vol. 225; Paul Fannin, "Governor Paul Fannin's Remarks at Unidynamics Division Dedication, Litchfield Park, Arizona," November 1, 1963, 1, folder 2, box 21, Fannin.

57. Alderman, "Phoenix Revisited," 22; "Summary of Engineers Registered in the Graduate School at Arizona State College," undated, in vol. 427, OPR; Daniel Noble to Governor Fannin, December 5, 1963, 3, folder 2, box 4, Fannin; "Governor Paul Fannin's Remarks at Unidynamics Division Dedication, Litchfield Park, Arizona," 1.

58. Walker, *Ghost of Jim Crow*, 3–10, 49–84; Michael Luger and Harvey Goldstein, *Technology in the Garden: Research Parks and Regional Economic Development* (Chapel Hill: University of North Carolina Press, 1991); Hodges, *Businessman in the Statehouse*.

59. Walker, *Ghost of Jim Crow*, 49–84; Hodges, *Businessman in the Statehouse*, 156–225.

60. Hodges, *Businessman in the Statehouse*, 196–97.

61. Hodges, *Businessman in the Statehouse*, 6–19, 156–225, esp. 187, 189–90, quoted 198.

62. Ibid., esp. 156, 177, 203, 204; Luger and Goldstein, *Technology in the Garden*, 76–99; O'Mara, *Cities of Knowledge*, 216–17; Cobb, *Industrialization and Southern Society*, 108.

63. Paddy Riley, "Clark Kerr: From the Industrial to the Knowledge Economy," in Lichtenstein, *American Capitalism*, 71–87; Clark Kerr, "The Multiversity: Are Its Several Souls Worth Saving?" *Harper's*, November 1963, 37–42, esp. 37–38, 41.

64. Minutes of the Meeting of the Education Committee, January 11, 1943, folder 4, box 30, SD; Minutes of the Meeting of the Education Committee, November 19, 1947, 3, folder 5, box 30, SD; Minutes of the Meeting of the Education Committee with the State College and Public Schools Advisory Group, April 15, 1948, folder 5, box 30, SD; Minutes of the Meeting of the Education Committee, September 6, 1949, 3, folder 5, box 30, SD; Panel Meeting of the Five Members of the Education Committee with Teacher Statements of San Diego State College, November 19, 1951, folder 5, box 30, SD; Minutes of the Meetings of the Education Committee, November 21, 1952, September 21, 1953, September 20, 1954, September 18, 1954, folder 5, box 30, SD; Education Committee Program of Work, February 20, 1956, folder 8, box 32, SD; Minutes of the Meeting of the Education Committee, April 8, 1960, folder 7, box 29, SD.

65. Harry Foster to O. W. Todd Jr., December 22, 1950, folder 3, box 26, SD; University of California Committee [Roster]; January 26, 1956, folder 14, box 92, SD; Organizational Structure of the Sub-Committee of the Chamber of Commerce Education Committee, [1956], folder 14, box 92, SD; Minutes of the University of California Committee Meeting, August 17, 1956, folder 1, box 92, SD; Notes on the University of California meeting, March 22, 1956, folder 1, box 92, SD; Arnold Klaus to T. C. Holy, April 3, 1956, folder 1, box 92, SD; R. H. Biron to T. C. Holy and Hubert H. Semans, February 21, 1956, folder 12, box 92, SD; "University of California, La Jolla Campus Expansion: History of Events to the Present," July 12, 1957, 1, 9, folder 1, box 92, SD.

66. Kenneth Lamott, "La Jolla's New University, Olympus on a Mesa," *Harper's*, August 1966, 82–88; Nancy Scott Andersen, *An Improbable Venture: A History of the University of California, San Diego* (La Jolla: UCSD Press, 1993), quoted 37 and 73.

67. Sheridan Hegland, "Regents OK U.C. Branch in San Diego," *Independent*, August 26, 1956, 1; folder 11, box 92, SD; Henry Love, "Scripps Institution Expansion Approved," *San Diego Union*, August 25, 1956, 1, folder 11, box 92, SD.

68. Quoted Andersen, *An Improbable Venture*, 92–95; John Galbraith, untitled speech, September 22, 1965, 1–2, folder 8, box 29, SD.

69. Advisory Commission on Intergovernmental Relations, *State-Local Taxation and Industrial Location*, 71–76.

70. National Resources Planning Board, *Preliminary Statement, Regional Development Plan, Pacific Southwest, Region 8*, 214–15.

71. "Notes on Mr. Carmichael's Speech in Knoxvlle, Tennessee—Sept. 3, 1966," folder 22, box 63, Carmichael; David Kaiser, "The Postwar Suburbanization of American Physics," *American Quarterly* 46 (December 2004), 851–88, quoted 871.

72. Needham, "Power Lines," 74–88, quoted 76.

73. Collins, *Emerging Metropolis*, 353–66, quoted 357; Board of Directors, Minutes of Meeting, April 20, 1953, vol.: "1952–1953," Board-Records; Needham, "Power Lines," 76–82, quoted 77–78; "Statement of the Case for the Phoenix Art Museum," unpaginated, folder 1, box 3, PAM.

74. "Statement of the Case for the Phoenix Art Museum"; Board of Directors, Minutes of Meeting, March 16, 1953, vol.: "1952–1953," Board-Records; Collins, *Emerging Metropolis*, 344–66.

Chapter 8. Industrial Phoenix

1. "Arizona Hitches Its Future to Ideas and Industry," *BW*, June 23, 1956, 114–28, esp. 114; Jacobson, "Phoenix Chamber of Commerce," 38.

2. Ballard, *Shock of Peace*, 32–51, 130–39; Schatz, *Electrical Workers*, esp. 8–10; Cowie, *Capital Moves*, 1–11.

3. Cowie, *Capital Moves*.

4. Abbott, *New Urban America*, 14–19; Advisory Committee on Intergovernmental Relations, "State-Local Taxation and Industrial Location," 6, 9; Leonard J. Arrington, *The Changing Economic Structure of the Mountain West, 1850–1950* (Logan: Utah State University Press, 1963), esp. 22–26.

5. Carrier, *Plant Location Analysis*, 5; James Clayton, "The Impact of the Cold War on the Economies of California and Utah, 1946–1965," *Pacific Historical Review* 36 (November 1967), 449–73.

6. Tom McKnight, "Manufacturing in Arizona," *University of California Publications in Geography* VIII (1940–1962 issue), 289–344; Western Management Consultants, Inc., *Economy of Maricopa County 1965 to 1980*, 94–101.

7. Western Management Consultants, Inc., *Economy of Maricopa County 1965 to 1980*, 94–101.

8. McKnight, "Manufacturing in Arizona," 290–311, quoted 311; Eileen Boris, "From Gender to Racialized Gender: Laboring Bodies that Matter," 63 *International Labor and Working-Class History* (Spring 2003), 9–13.

9. "Arizona State Board of Technical Registration," [1962], p. 1, folder 1, box 4, Fannin; Wright, *Old South, New South*, 173; O'Mara, *Cities of Knowledge*.

10. McKnight, "Manufacturing in Arizona," esp. 299; "Electronics Industry in Arizona," undated, 1–2, folder 1, box 4, Fannin; James Rork, "Establishments in Arizona Providing Products and Services Directly Involved in or Allied to Aerospace and Electronics Industries," December 1963, 2, folder 1, box 4, Fannin; James Rork to Paul Fannin, December 2, 1963, 1, folder 2, box 4, Fannin.

11. L. J. Crampton and Paul W. De Good Jr., *Industrial Location Survey: A Study of the Reasons Why Manufacturing Establishments Have Selected Sites in the State of Colorado Between 1948 and 1957* (Boulder: University of Colorado, 1957), 1–11, esp. 1; Joseph Bassi, "Where Earth Met Sky: The Creation of Boulder, Colorado as a City of Scientific Knowledge Production, 1945–1965" (Ph.D. diss., University of California, Santa Barbara, 2009); Stephen Leonard and Thomas Noel, *Denver: Mining Camp to Metropolis* (Niwot: University Press of Colorado, 1991), 220–26, 234–50, 336–37, quoted 241.

12. McKnight, "Manufacturing in Arizona," 293; Phoenix Chamber of Commerce, *1970 Directory of Scientific Resources* (Phoenix: Phoenix Chamber of Commerce, 1970); William Schriver, "The Industrialization of the Southeast Since 1960:

Some Causes of Manufacturing Relocation, with Speculation about Its Effects," *American Journal of Economics and Sociology* 30 (January 1971), 47–69; Carrier, *Plant Location Analysis*, 5–7; Georgia Department of Commerce, *Georgia's Gains Lead Nation* (Atlanta: Georgia Department of Commerce, [1955]), 1, folder 7, box 187, Davis; Cobb County Chamber of Commerce, "Cobb County Manufacturers and Industrial Roster," January 1969, folder 208, VF.

13. George Busey interview by Nancy Edwards, March 15, 1978, transcript, 7–9, PHP; John Colwell to [Boyd] Gibbons, July 23, 1959, folder 12, box 9, Fannin.

14. Lewis Haas to Barry [Goldwater], April 24, 1954, pdf 19, reel 30, CD 7, series VI, AHF-Goldwater; Goldwater to Haas, February 3, 1954, pdf 19, reel 30, CD 7, series VI, AHF-Goldwater; Haas to [Goldwater], January 22, 1954, pdf 19, reel 30, CD 7, series VI, AHF-Goldwater; Haas to [Goldwater], July 6, 1954, pdf 19, reel 30, CD 7, series VI, AHF-Goldwater.

15. Board of Directors, Minutes of Meetings, July 21, 1947, and October 20, 1947, vol.: "1947–1948," Board-Records; "Industrial Program Hits Full Stride," *WP* 3 (April 1948), 1.

16. "Chamber's Industrial Development Program Hikes City's Payroll," *WP* 3 (September 1948), 2; "Chamber's Industrial Campaign Paying Off," *PA* 4 (March 1949), 7; John T. Kimball, "Jobs Provided for 900 Persons," *PA* 5 (June 1950), 1; "What One Industry Means to Phoenix," *PA* 5 (July 1950), 2; J. Robert White, "Community Cooperation in Economic Development," 17 *ABB* (October 1970), 19–23, esp. 19, 20.

17. Board of Directors, Minutes of Meeting, March 15, 1954, vol.: "1953–1954," Board-Records; Board of Directors, Minutes of Meetings, July 21, 1947, October 20, 1947, vol.: "1947–1948," Board-Records; Frank Snell interview by G. Wesley Johnson, September 22, 1977, transcript, 6, PHP; Allen Rosenberg interview by Kristina Minister, March 28, 1989, audiotape, side 2, tape 11, Chamber-Interviews; Patrick Downey interview by K. Trimble, July 8, 1978, transcript, 6–10, PHP; Board of Directors, Minutes of Meeting, July 11, 1949, 4, vol.: "1949–1950," Board-Records; Ross, *Bird of Fire*, 116–47.

18. "Visit by Plant Locators Is Another First for Phoenix," *PA* 13 (November 1958), 3; "Headquarter Visits," *A Special Report for . . .* [Chamber newsletter], 1 (June 1968), 2, folder 2, box 1, Lewis-Roca; Board of Directors, Minutes of Meeting, June 17, 1958, vol.: "1957–1958," Board-Records; Phoenix Chamber of Commerce, *1970 Directory of Scientific Resources in the Phoenix Area*, unpaginated.

19. Rosenberg interview, side 2, tape 11; William Coerver interview by Nancy Edwards, November 8, 1978, transcript, 12–18, PHP; Downey interview, 9–11; "New Industry Plan Approved," *WP* 3 (January 1948), 2.

20. Minton Moore interview by Nancy Edwards, October 27, 1978, transcript, 1–4, esp. 2, PHP; [Herbert Leggett], "Bon Voyage," *AP*, November 1963, 1.

21. Andrew Needham, "Power Lines," 50–51; Lynne Pierson Doti and Larry Schweikart, "Financing the Postwar Housing Boom in Phoenix and Los Angeles, 1945–1960" *Pacific Historical Review* 58 (May 1989), 173–94, quoted 183; *Record of*

Commission, vol. 35: January 1, 1956–December 31, 1956, 356–57, Phoenix-Records; Downey interview, 9–11.

22. [Transcript—Luncheon meeting held at the Westward Ho Hotel], January 23, 1953, 4, 19–22, folder 3, box 9, Pyle.

23. Phoenix Chamber of Commerce, *What Phoenix and Arizona Have to Offer the Textile Industry* (Phoenix: Phoenix Chamber of Commerce, 1960), unpaginated.

24. Board of Directors, Minutes of Meeting, December 16, 1946, vol.: "1946–1947," Board-Records; Carl Bimson interview by Kristina Minister, April 14, 1988, audiotape, side 1–2, tape 7, Chamber-Interviews.

25. "Arizona Highways Magazine Devotes Issue to Phoenix," *PA* XII (February/March 1957), 1; "Arizona's Formula for Winning Friends and Influencing People," *AP*, March 1949, 2; quoted Robert J. Farrell, "*Arizona Highways*: The People Who Shaped a Southwestern Magazine, 1925 to 1990" (master's thesis, Prescott College, 1997), 6; E. S. Mancinellie to Howard Pyle, January 5, 1952, folder 11, box 67, Governor-Subject-Files.

26. Kelly, "Changing Face of Phoenix,"2–23, esp. 3, 10, 13; John Herbert, "Phoenix: Economic Capital of the Southwest Sun Country," *AH* 40 (March 1964), 29–46, esp. 23, 34, 37, 46; Raymond Carlson, "Portrait of a Bank," *AH* 32 (November 1956), 1; Joseph Stocker, "Valley National Bank: Financing American's Most Flourishing Frontier," *AH* 32 (November 1956,) 2–7, 34–39, esp. 3, 38, 39.

27. *Arizona Homes*, vol. 6, no. 2, September–October, 1955, esp. 22, 25.

28. "Home Builders Will Hold Married 'Queen' Contest," unattributed clipping, August 8, 1954, folder 6, box 1, series 1, AHBC; for rules and contest information see folder 13, box 2, series 1, AHBC.

29. "Mrs. Arizona Home Owner Named Here," *AR*, August 31, 1954, n.p., folder 13, box 2, series 1, AHBC; "150 Exhibitors Open Home Show" *AR*, February 13, 1955, n.p., box 2, folder 9, series 1, AHBC.

30. Martin, "New Millionaires of Phoenix," 25–26.

31. Abbott, "New West, New South, New Region"; Lassiter, *Silent Majority*, 23–68; Hodges, *Businessman in the Statehouse*, 70, 107; James Carmichael," "The South in Transition—The Opportunity and Future of Southern Industry," April 11, 1964, folder 14, box 63, Carmichael.

32. Matthew Lassiter, "Searching for Respect: From 'New South' to 'World Class' at the Crossroads of the Carolinas," in Bill Graves and Heather Smith (eds.), *Charlotte, N.C.: The Global Evolution of a New South City* (Athens: University of Georgia Press, 2010), 24–49, quoted 25.

33. Dieterich-Ward, "Mines, Mills, and Malls," esp. 208–27, quoted 227, n. 140.

34. William Deverell, *Whitewashed Adobe: The Rise of Los Angeles and the Remaking of Its Mexican Past* (Berkeley: University of California Press, 2004); Geraldo Lujan Cadava, "Corridor of Exchange: Culture and Ethnicity in Tucson's Modern Borderlands" (Ph.D. diss., Yale University, 2008), 77–184; descriptions of rodeos, dinners, and presents to visiting executives run throughout the Phoenix Chamber's inter-

nal newsletter and its committee and board of directors meetings, see any issue of *Phoenix Action!* or board of directors meeting minutes.

35. Cobb, *Selling the South*, 35–37; Prince, "History and Development of the Mississippi Balance Agriculture with Industry Program, 1936–1958," 114–26; Hodges, *Businessman in the Statehouse*, 33–40; Tennessee State Planning Office: West Tennessee Section, *Jackson-Madison County Industrial Site Survey* (Nashville: Tennessee State Planning Office: West Tennessee Section, 1974).

36. Dieterich-Ward, "Mines, Mills, and Malls," 101–3.

37. Schmidt and James, *Plant Relocation*, 130–31; Wayne King, "Atlanta Opening New York Office in a Move to Attract New Industry," *NYT*, February 11, 1977, A14.

38. Mid-South Progress Council, *An Invitation to Industry* (Memphis: Mid-South Progress Council, [195–?]), unpaginated; draft letter by Charles A. Collier, Wiley L. Moore, H. S. Dumas, and A. L. Zachary, February 19, 1948, folder 4, box 84, Sibley; membership roster, Georgia State Chamber of Commerce, folder 6, box 84, Sibley; Jim Montgomery, "Businessmen Alert to Political Issues," *Atlanta Constitution*, January 7, 1955, n.p., folder 6, box 84, Sibley; Memo: Community Data Reports to Area Chairmen, Local Advisors, Local Chamber Executives, January 12, 1955, folder 6, box 84, Sibley; Jack McDonough to Saythe Cambrell, December 7, 1954, folder 6, box 84, Sibley.

39. Quoted Herbert, "Phoenix," 23, 46; quoted Kelly, "The Changing Face of Phoenix," 10–11; quoted McKnight, "Manufacturing in Arizona," 316.

40. L. L. Stirland to Paul Fannin, February 7, 1962, folder 1, box 11, Fannin; quoted McKnight, "Manufacturing in Arizona," 316.

41. William Angel, "The Politics of Space: NASA's Decision to Locate the Manned Spacecraft Center in Houston," *Houston Review: History and Culture of the Gulf Coast* VI, no. 2, 1984, 63–82; materials on Phoenix's NASA bid, folders 1–2, box 4, Fannin.

42. Cullen Moore, "Arizona Industry in the Missile and Space Program," June 8, 1962, 6, folder 1, box 4, Fannin.

43. Jason Gart, "Electronics and Aerospace Industry in Cold War Arizona, 1945–68: Motorola, Hughes Aircraft, Goodyear Aircraft" (Ph.D. diss., Arizona State University, 2006), 120–35.

44. Ibid.; "Arizona Hitches Its Future to Ideas and Industry," 122–24; Daniel Noble interview by Dick Lynch, September 26, 1976, transcript, 3–4, PHP; Foorman Mueller interview by Nancy Edwards, May 26, 1978, transcript, 1–4, PHP.

45. John Shirer, "The Motorola Research Laboratory in Phoenix," *Arizona Business and Economic Review* 2 (February 1953), 1–4; King, "Toward Metropolis Status," 207–9; Daniel Noble to Governor Fannin, December 5, 1963, 1–4, folder 2, box 4, Fannin; "Arizona Hitches Its Future to Ideas and Industry," 122–24, quoted 124; Robert Galvin, "Electronic Horizons," April 11, 1962, 4, folder 1, box 4, Fannin.

46. Noble to Fannin, 2–3; Gart, "Electronics and Aerospace Industry in Cold War Arizona, 1945–68," 120–52.

47. Schatz, *Electrical Workers*, 7–9, 233–35, esp. 7.

48. Phillips-Fein, *Invisible Hands*, 87–114; typed copy "How's the Business Climate in Your Community?" *G.E. Monogram*, March 1958, folder 1, box 431, Sibley.

49. Lee, "General Electric Corporation Computer Department," 24–45; Oldfield, "General Electric Enters the Computer Business—Revisited," 46–55.

50. Oldfield, "General Electric Enters the Computer Business—Revisited," 46–55, esp. 49, 51.

51. Ibid., 46–55, esp. 51; Lee, "General Electric Corporation Computer Department."

52. Lee, "General Electric Corporation Computer Department"; Oldfield, "General Electric Enters the Computer Business—Revisited," 46–55, esp. 51; L. R. Boulware, "Politics . . . The Businessman's Biggest Job in 1958," typescript, May 21, 1958, 1, folder 453, box 18, Boulware; Phillips-Fein, *Invisible Hands*, 85–114; Rosenberg interview, side 1, tape 12.

53. Lee, "General Electric Corporation Computer Department"; Oldfield, "General Electric Enters the Computer Business—Revisited."

54. "Computers in Business," *ABB* 4 (September 1957), 1–6, esp. 4, 6; George Boyd to President Durham, "RE: Computer Negotiations," July 26, 1962, 1–2, in vol. 1159, OPR; G. Homer Durham, memo, March 6, [1962], 1–2, in vol. 1159, OPR; George Boyd to President Durham, "RE: Use of the G. E. Computer Center," July 27, 1962, 1–2, in vol. 1159, OPR; G. Homer Durham, memo, August 1, 1962, in vol. 1159, OPR; C. C. Lasher to G. Homer Durham, July 16, 1962, in vol. 1159, OPR; Alfred Thomas Jr. to Grady Gammage, April 1, 1958, in vol. 456, OPR; J. J. O'Brien and Gilbert Cody, "Memorandum Agreement," June 18, 1963, in vol. 770, OPR.

55. Quoted Herbert, "Phoenix," 23; Collins, *Emerging Metropolis*, 181–82; Lee, "General Electric Corporation Computer Department," 24–45, quoted 29; Oldfield, "General Electric Enters the Computer Business—Revisited," 46–55, esp. 52.

56. F. S. Hodgman to Frank Murphy and Wm. Reilly, [month and day missing] 1955, Board of Directors, Minutes of Special Meeting, September 8, 1955, vol.: "1955–1956," Board-Records; Bimson interview, side 2, tape 7; Snell interview by Minister, side 1, tape 11.

57. "Arizona Hitches Its Future to Ideas and Industry," 128; Robert Roe to Paul Fannin, December 9, 1963, 1–2, folder 2, box 4, Fannin.

58. Quoted Herbert, "Phoenix," 23; Robert Roe to Paul Fannin, December 9, 1963, 2, folder 2, box 4, Fannin.

59. Rice, "1958 Election in Arizona"; Guber, "Development of Two-Party Competition in Arizona," 35.

60. "More Important Job," *AR*, October 23, 1955, 6; Patrick Curran, "Tax Called Vicious," *AR*, October 27, 1955, 6; "Pulling Together," *AR*, October 29, 1955, 6; "Quick Action Asked on Sales Tax Spat," *AR*, October 21, 1955, 8.

61. Ernest McFarland, [untitled message to the legislature], October 24, 1955, 1–2, folder "Governor's Legislative Message File: 1955–1957," box 96, Governor-Subject-Files; Board of Directors, Minutes of Meeting, December 19, 1955, vol.: "1955–1956," Board-Records.

62. Shadegg, *Arizona Politics*, 197–99; Johnson, *Arizona Politicians*, 101–10, 158–67.

63. Shadegg, *Arizona Politics*, 80–84; Guber, "The Development of Two-Party Competition in Arizona," 68; Wolfgang Saxon, "Paul J. Fannin, 94, Who Served in Top Elected Offices in Arizona," *NYT*, January 17, 2002, B8; Board of Directors, Minutes of Meeting, March 19, 1951, vol.: "1950–1951," Board-Records.

64. Paul Fannin, "Man and Good Government," undated, 1–2, 6, 9, folder 6, box 21, Fannin; Fannin, "Speech Material—Government," undated, 1–2, folder 6, box 21, Fannin; Fannin, "Remarks of Governor Fannin at the National Sand and Gravel Association and National Ready Mixed Concrete Association Meeting in Chicago, Illinois," February 27, 1964, 6, folder 2, box 21, Fannin.

65. Shadegg, *Arizona Politics*, 80–110, quoted 102; Fannin, "Remarks of Governor Fannin at the National Sand and Gravel Association and National Ready Mixed Concrete Association Meeting in Chicago, Illinois," 6; quoted McCoy, "Desert Metropolis," 228.

66. Boyd Gibbons, "Who's [*sic*] Challenge?" April 25, 1964, 1, folder 2, box 11, Fannin; A. R. Kleindienst to Arthur Lee, July 27, 1964, with enclosure, folder 3, box 1, Fannin; McCoy, "Desert Metropolis," 236–37.

67. McCoy, "Desert Metropolis," 236–37; Paul Fannin, "The Governor's Office in Arizona," undated, 1, 3, 6, folder 1, box 1, Fannin.

68. Fannin, "The Governor's Office in Arizona," 5–6; McCoy, "Desert Metropolis," 236–37; Lewis Haas to Boyd Gibbons, undated, folder 6, box 5, Fannin; Boyd Gibbons Jr. to Lawrence Mehren, June 4, 1964, 1, folder 2, box 21, Fannin; Boyd Gibbons Jr. to Bill Rhodes, November 5, 1963, folder 4, box 8, Fannin; Konig, "Toward Metropolis Status," 198–203; Collins, *Emerging Metropolis*, 18–20, quoted 19; O. M. Sizer to Boyd Gibbons Jr., August 24, 1959, 1, folder 11, box 8, Fannin.

69. Lynn Robinson Bailey, *Bisbee: Queen of the Copper Camps* (Tucson: Westernlore Press, 1983), 135–50; Ray Helgesen to Boyd Gibbons Jr., February 10, 1960, folder 6, box 8, Fannin; Ray Helgesen to Boyd H. Gibbons Jr., October 25, 1960, 1, folder 6, box 8, Fannin.

70. Boyd Gibbons, "Report to Governor Paul Fannin on 'Prospecting' Tour to Los Angeles, December 2–5, 1959," undated, 2, folder 11, box 11, Fannin; McCoy, "Desert Metropolis," 230–38.

71. Ed Hazelton to Boyd Gibbons, January 16, 1961, folder 4, box 8, Fannin; Meeting Minutes enclosed with V. O. Allen to [Boyd] Gibbons, August 5, 1959, 2, folder 4, box 8, Fannin; Gibbons sent numerous copies of the same letter to industrialists he met, see copies in folder 4, box 8, Fannin.

72. Boyd Gibbons, "UNIDYNAMICS (Division of Universal Match Corporation) (Universal Match Corporation, St. Louis, Missouri): Litchfield Park (Goodyear), Arizona," undated, folder 2, box 11, Fannin.

73. Ibid.

74. Ibid.; Ben Brothers to Governor Fannin, December 3, 1963, folder 2, box 4, Fannin.

75. Fannin, "Governor Paul Fannin's Remarks at Unidynamics Division Dedication, Litchfield Park, Arizona," 1–3 (emphasis in original).

76. Robert Creighton to Arthur Lee, Personal and Confidential Re: Mr. Fannin's State Reorganization Address, October 29, 1963, 1–2, folder 4, box 1, Fannin; Ben Avery, "Not All Commissions and Boards Are Bad," *AR*, January 26, 1964, 24-A; "Fannin to Request Executive Changes," *AR*, January 17, 1964, 4 and 8.

77. Horace Phelps to Governor Fannin, September 26, 1962, 1, folder 1, box 11, Fannin; Confidential Memo: New Firms, 1959–1964, folder 2, box 11, Fannin; Boyd Gibbons Jr. to Lawrence Mehren, June 4, 1964, 2, folder 2, box 21, Fannin; Paul Fannin, "Arizona . . . An Invitation to Industry," undated, 1–2, folder: "'ARIZONA . . . An Invitation to Industry' (Rep. & Gaz. Ind. Dev. Project)," box 314, Governor-Files.

78. Cobb County Chamber of Commerce, "Cobb County Manufacturers and Industrial Roster," January 1969, folder 208, VF; Cobb County Chamber of Commerce, "The Major Firms of Cobb County," 1986, folder 208, VF; Cobb County Chamber of Commerce, "High Technology Industries in Cobb County," 1986, folder 208, VF; Cobb County Chamber of Commerce, "Cobb County Larger Employers," 1986, folder 208, VF; "Volkswagen of America; Porsche Audi; Combine Facilities in N x NW Office Park," *Impact* XVIII, no. 15, August 25, 1980, 1, folder 208, VF.

79. "Corporate Headquarters Center: A Progress Report," *Arizona Business* 24 (April 1977), 26–27; Luckingham, *Phoenix*, 177–220.

80. Lew Haas, "Phoenix," *ABB* 13 (January 1966), 13–14, esp. 14; "Corporate Headquarters Center: A Progress Report," *Arizona Business* 24 (April 1977), 26–27; Allen Rosenberg, "President's Report," *Phoenix* 19 (July 1965), 4–5; "News Letter [*sic*] to Office Building Committee," November 22, 1968, 1–3, esp. 1, folder 6, box 1, Lewis-Roca; "Office Building Committee Objectives," December 20, 1967, folder 7, box 1, Lewis-Roca.

81. "Greyhound Corporation Confirms Move to Phoenix," *DP* 3 (June 1971), 3

82. Ibid.; "Greyhound Impact on Economy Told," *DP*, 4 (February 1972), 11; quoted Luckingham, *Phoenix*, 187.

83. "News Letter [*sic*] to Office Building Committee," November 22, 1968, 1–3, esp. 1, folder 6, box 1, Lewis-Roca; "Office Building Committee Objectives," December 20, 1967, folder 7, box 1, Lewis-Roca; "Office Buildings Committee Membership List," folder 7, box 1, Lewis-Roca; Valley National Bank, *Arizona Statistical Review* (Phoenix: Valley National Bank of Arizona, December 1975), 27, 63; Valley National Bank, *Arizona Statistical Review* (Phoenix: Valley National Bank of Arizona, December 1989), 22, 31–32, 86.

Chapter 9. The Conspicuous Grasstops

1. Andrew Kopkind, "Modern Times in Phoenix: A City at the Mercy of Its Myths," *New Republic*, November 6, 1965, 14–16, esp. 14, 15, 16.

2. Bruce Schulman and Julian Zelizer (eds.), *Rightward Bound: Making America Conservative in the 1970s* (Cambridge, MA: Harvard University Press, 2008); Harvey, *A Brief History of Neoliberalism*; Phillips-Fein, *Invisible Hands*; Godfrey Hodgson,

The World Turned Right Side Up: A History of the Conservative Ascendancy in America (Boston: Houghton Mifflin, 1996); Bruce Schulman, *The Seventies: The Great Shift in American Culture, Society, and Politics* (New York: Da Copa Press, 2002).

3. Thomas Schaller, *Whistling Past Dixie: How Democrats Can Win Without the South* (New York: Simon and Schuster, 2006); Joseph Lowndes, *From the New Deal to the New Right: Race and the Southern Origins of Modern Conservatism* (New Haven: Yale University Press, 2008); Black and Black, *Vital South*; Michael Bowen, *The Roots of Modern Conservatism: Dewey, Taft, and the Battle for the Soul of the Republican Party* (Chapel Hill: University of North Carolina Press, 2011).

4. Katznelson et al., "Limiting Liberalism"; Friedman, "Exploiting the North-South Differential"; Lassiter, *The Silent Majority*; Kruse, *White Flight*; Crespino, *In Search of Another Country*; McGirr, *Suburban Warriors*.

5. Gene Burd, "The Selling of the South: Civic Boosterism in the Media," in David C. Perry and Alfred J. Watkins (eds.), *The Rise of the Sunbelt Cities* (Beverly Hills: Sage, 1977), 129–49, esp. 134; Lassiter, "Searching for Respect," 24–49, quoted 28.

6. Milton MacKaye, "The Cities of America: Phoenix," *SEP*, October 18, 1947, 36–37, 88–95, esp. 37 and 90.

7. [George Henhoeffer], "Arizona Industry Moves In," *BW*, December 13, 1952, 82–92, esp. 82, 84, 90.

8. "Squaw Dress Builds a $4 Million Industry," "Giant Valley Bank Gets Even Bigger by Swallowing Fastest Growing Rival," "Meet Arizona Highways, Unique State Publication," "'It's a Homer!'—for Mesa, Phoenix, Tucson Chambers of Commerce," "State's Tenth-Largest City Is Planned for Cactus Patch Near New Copper Mine," "Arizona's Dude Ranchers Ride a Golden Roundup," *WSJ*, March 9, 1953, 10–11.

9. "Arizona Hitches Its Future to Ideas and Industry," June 23, 1956, 114–128, esp. 118; Martin, "New Millionaires of Phoenix," 25–31, esp. 27; quoted in Needham, "Power Lines," 83, 85, and 86.

10. VanderMeer, *Desert Visions and the Making of Modern Phoenix*, 112; Bureau of the Census, *Census of Housing: 1970*, vol. 1, *Housing Characteristics for States, Cities, and Counties*, pt. 1, *United States Summary*, S22, S31, pt. 4, *Arizona* (Washington, DC: Government Printing Office, 1972), 62.

11. Raymond Arsenault, "The End of the Long Hot Summer: The Air Conditioner and Southern Culture," in Mohl (ed..), *Searching for the Sunbelt*, 176–211; Bureau of the Census, *Census of Housing: 1970*, vol. 1, *Housing Characteristics for States, Cities, and Counties*, pt. 1, *United States Summary*, S22, S31, pt. 7, *Colorado*, 62, pt. 11, *Florida*, 135, pt. 44, *Tennessee*, 82, pt. 45, *Texas*, 207, pt. 35, *North Carolina*, 98, pt. 6, *California*, 237, pt. 12, *Georgia*, 106 (Washington, DC: Government Printing Office, 1972).

12. Quoted in Needham, "Power Lines," 83; Martin, "New Millionaires of Phoenix," esp. 26–28.

13. "Holiday Schedules Arizona Feature," *PA* 6 (March 1952), 3; "Arizona: Industry Moves In," *PA*. 8 (January 1953), 2; "March Holiday Will Feature Phoenix," *PA*. 8 (August 1953), 6; "Wall Street Journal to Do Arizona Series," *PA*. 8 (February 1953), 6;

"Industrial Economy Publicized," *PA*. 11 (April 1956), 7; Board of Directors, Minutes of Meeting, February 16, 1953, vol.: "1952–1953," Board-Records; "Arizona: Industry Moves In," *PA* 8 (January 1953), 2; Board of Directors, Minutes of Meeting, February 15, 1954, vol.: "1953–1954," Board-Records.

14. "Leadership Does It," *Abilene Reporter News*, reprinted in *City Manager's News Bulletin*, July 12, 1956, 1.

15. Mark Adams and Gertrude Adams, *A Report on Politics in El Paso* (Cambridge, MA: Joint Center for Urban Studies of the Massachusetts Institute of Technology and Harvard University, 1963), V-26–V-27; quoted in Luckingham, *Phoenix*, 187.

16. Minutes of the Industrial Development Corporation Meeting, December 9, 1953, folder 7, box 41, SD; California State Chamber of Commerce, "Taxation of Raw Materials, Goods in Process or in Transit, and Finished Goods," March 1953, preface, folder 1, box 91, SD; Blake Johnson to Boyd Gibbons Jr., June 28, 1963, folder "Chambers of Commerce Out-ofState [*sic*] —Misc.," box 315, Governor-Files; Clayton, "Impact of the Cold War on the Economies of California and Utah," 456–57.

17. Clayton, "Impact of the Cold War on the Economies of California and Utah," 460; John Harter to Boyd Gibbons, November 21, 1963, folder "Chambers of Commerce Out-ofState [*sic*]—Misc.," box 315, Fannin; Minutes of the Meetings of the Industrial Development Committee, July 10, 1956, and May 12, 1955, folder 2, box 48, SD; Industrial Development Steering Committee, "Guide for the 1957 Industrial Development Committee Program," February 1957, 2, folder 10, box 47, SD; San Diego Chamber of Commerce, "Highlights—Industrial Department," [1962], folder 6, box 42, SD; Industrial Department, "Build Industrial Growth 1962 Program," 1, 3, folder 8, box 38, SD; Executive and Finance Committee, Agenda, February 9, 1962, folder 3, box 46, SD; B.I.G. Committee, Program of Work, 1964–1965, 1, folder 3, box 46, SD; Minutes of the Key Men Subcommittee, February 14, 1968, folder 4, box 46, SD; Barnes Chase/Advertising, "B.I.G. Industrial Development Program 1964–65," October 5, 1964, n.p., folder 1, box 12, SD; B.I.G. Executive Council Meeting, Agenda, December 18, 1963, folder 3, box 46, SD.

18. Frank Shaw to John Sibley, December 6, 1951, typescript with enclosure of Gordon H. Turrentine's remarks before an unidentified group meeting, 14, folder 3, box 83, Sibley; quoted Don Dedera, "Walter Reed Bimson: Arizona's Indispensable Man, Compleat Banker," *Arizona Highways* (April 1973), 26–29, esp. 27; Hopkins, *Financing the Frontier*, 200–204, 268–70.

19. Walter Bimson, "Talk Before Convention of General Insurance Agents of Arizona," October 15, 1948, 1, folder 238, box 29, VNB.

20. Ibid., 4–5.

21. Ibid.; Walter Bimson to Harry Miller, December 31, 1949, folder 360, box 37, VNB; Walter Bimson, "The Financial Problems of Small Business," [December 1949], folder 360, box 37, VNB; "U.S. Insured Loans Small Lines' Aims," *NYT*, December 7, 1949, 45, 47; "This Week in Washington," *WSJ*, July 13 and 27, 1953, 3; "President Gets Bill to End RFC, Set Up Small Business Agency," *WSJ*, July 30, 1953, 15.

22. Carl Flora to Walter Bimson, November 15, 1950, folder 360, box 37, VNB; R. B. Patrick to Walter Bimson, May 24, 1950, folder 360, box 37, VNB; Walter Bimson, untitled address at American Airlines luncheon, February 21, 1957, 4, folder 226, box 28, VNB; Walter Bimson, "Talk by W. R. Bimson, Alaska Bankers Association," June 2, 1957, 5, 10, folder 225, box 28, VNB.

23. Carl Bimson, "Handling Loans to Small Business," *Burroughs Clearing House*, January 1945, 18–20, 37–39, folder 934, box 68, VNB; Bimson, "A Banker's Participation in Public Affairs," February 12, 1960, in Carl Bimson, *Addresses of Carl A. Bimson*, vol. 9 (self-published, 1960), n.p., deposited at Arizona Historical Foundation (Tempe); Bimson, "Paying Our Way," May 17, 1960, in ibid.; Bimson, "Westward Ho!" May 20, 1960, in ibid.; Carl Bimson, "Formula for Frontier Financing," *Christian Science Monitor*, reprinted in ibid., 232–37, esp. 232, 236.

24. "Meet President Bimson," *Banking: Journals of the American Bankers Association* (October 1960), 1–7, folder 6, box 1, VNB; "Surtax or Chaos: Valley Bank Official," *AR*, April 7, 1968, 1-F and 6-F.

25. James Patrick, "The Certainty of Failure," February 14, 1968, folder 622, box 5, VNB.

26. "Current Developments," *AP*, October 1947, 1–2; "Both Federal and Local Taxes Continue to Set New Records," *AP*, October 1948, 2; "Current Developments," *AP*, August 1950, 1; "Happy Returns," *AP*, October 1951, 1; "As the Nation Goes, So Goes Arizona, in Presidential Voting," *AP*, October 1960, 3; "Liberalism," *AP*, October 1952, 1; "Bon Voyage," *AP*, November 1963, 1.

27. Keith Monroe, "Bank Knight in Arizona," *American Magazine* 140 (November 1945), 24–25,116–122, esp. 24, 25, 122.

28. Clark, "Brash Banker of Arizona," *SEP*, April 10, 1954, 22–23, 75–78.

29. Goldwater, "Whose Union, Whose Money, Who Is Boss," 14, loose in box 145, Shadegg.

30. Phillips-Fein, *Invisible Hands*, 87–114; L. R. Boulware, "Politics . . . the Businessman's Biggest Job in 1958," May 21, 1958, 1–2, 4, folder 453, box 18, Boulware (emphasis in original).

31. Boulware, "Politics . . . the Businessman's Biggest Job in 1958," in *Vital Speeches of the Day*, vol. XXIV, no. 19, 588 –93; "Politics Called 'Business of All,'" *AR*, May 25, 1958, unattributed clipping, folder 453, box 18, Boulware; "Politics Held Industry's Job," *AR*, May 22, 1958, unattributed clipping, folder 453, box 18, Boulware; "The Only Alternative," *AR*, May 23, 1958, 6, folder 453, box 18, Boulware; Boulware to J. Harvie Wilkinson Jr., July 17, 1958, folder 453, box 18, Boulware; Charles R. Sligh Jr. to Lemuel R. Boulware, May 29, 1958, folder 429, box 17, Boulware; Charles Johnson to Boulware, July 30, 1958, folder 429, box 17, Boulware; John D. Hoblitzell Jr. to L. R. Boulware, June 17, 1958, folder 429, box 17, Boulware; Carroll Reynolds to L. R. Boulware, June 26, 1958, folder 429, box 17, Boulware.

32. Ronald Reagan interview by Robert Goldberg, August 7, 1991, 1, Goldberg; Thomas Evans, *The Education of Ronald Reagan: The General Electric Years and the*

Untold Story of His Conversion to Conservatism (New York: Columbia University Press, 2007); Ronald Reagan, "Encroaching Control," March 30, 1961, 5, 11, 12, 17, folder 13, box 21, Fannin.

33. Goldwater to Boulware, December 10, 1971, folder 1040, box 38, Boulware; Goldwater to Boulware, September 22, 1980, folder 1040, box 38, Boulware; Goldwater to Boulware, April 27, 1978, folder 1040, box 38, Boulware; Goldwater to Boulware, June 13, 1983, folder 1040, box 38, Boulware; Boulware to Goldwater, June 20, 1983, folder 1040, box 38, Boulware.

34. Joseph Crespino, "Strom Thurmond's Sunbelt: Rethinking Regional Politics and the Rise of the Right," in Michelle Nickerson and Darren Dochuk (eds.), *Sunbelt Rising: The Politics of Place, Space, and Region* (Philadelphia: University of Pennsylvania Press, 2011), 58–81; Friedman, "Exploiting the North-South Differential."

35. Hodges, *Businessman in the Statehouse*, 1–17, 65–78; Luther Hodges to Clinton Anderson, May 30, 1945, folder 6, Hodges; W. Ray Bell to Hodges, with enclosures, October 13, 1948, folder 8, Hodges; Management Confidential Bulletin, "Mr. Hodges Completes Army Mission," December 7, 1948, 1–2, folder 9, Hodges; Hodges, "Personal Notes of Luther H. Hodges," May 29, 1950, folder 17, Hodges; Office of Economic Affairs Industry Division Memo, "Mr. Hodges' Itineraries, Firms and People Visited from His Arrival April 6, 1950 to June 6, 1950," undated, folder 17, Hodges; Houghston M. McBain to Hodges, November 16, 1951, folder 19, Hodges; Paul Kelly to George Santry, June 24, 1953, folder 51, Hodges.

36. Hodges, *Businessman in the Statehouse*, 18–78; "North Carolina: The South's New Leader" *Time*, May 4, 1959; Cobb, *Selling of the South*, 171–76; Bob Prentiss to Hodges, October 6, 1958, folder 205, Hodges; campaign materials and voter support: folders 1868–1872 and 1887–1897, Hodges.

37. Hodges, *Businessman in the Statehouse*, 65–78; Cobb, *Selling of the South*, 171–76; Hodges, untitled speech at Commercial Officer Convention in New Delhi, India, November 28, 1962, folder 1980, Hodges; Ned [Huffman] to Hodges, October 29, 1966, folder 1634, Hodges; Elizabeth Aycock to Mr. Haden, June 23, 1970, folder 2107, Hodges.

38. Orme Lewis and Paul Healy, "I Was the Great White Father," *SEP*, December 17, 1955, 36–37+, esp. 37; Orme Lewis to Mr. James G. McNary, December 29, 1955, folder 4, box 4, Lewis; [Illegible signature] to Mr. Secretary, January 10, 1956, folder 4, box 4, Lewis; A. Z. Nelson to Mr. Lewis, January 3, 1956, folder 4, box 4, Lewis.

39. Shermer, "Origins of the Conservative Ascendancy," quoted 696.

40. Quoted ibid., 698.

41. Ibid., 698–703.

42. Quoted ibid., 701–2.

43. Quoted ibid., 707.

44. Ibid., esp. 704–10, quoted 706.

45. John A. Andrew, *The Other Side of the Sixties: Young Americans for Freedom and the Rise of Conservative Politics* (New Brunswick, NJ: Rutgers University Press,

1997), 53–74; Goldberg, *Barry Goldwater*, 118–80; Phillips-Fein, *Invisible Hands*, 68–86, 115–49; Goldwater, *Conscience of a Conservative*, 17–32, 39–53, 63–80; Perlstein, *Before the Storm*, 3–42, 61–98.

46. Perlstein, *Before the Storm*, 99–488; Goldberg, *Barry Goldwater*, 149–240; Michelle Nickerson, "Moral Mothers and Goldwater Girls," in Farber and Roche, *Conservative Sixties*, 51–62; Phillips-Fein, *Invisible Hands*, 115–49.

47. Quoted Phillips-Fein, *Invisible Hands*, 143; Goldberg, *Barry Goldwater*, 149–240; Perlstein, *Before the Storm*, 99–488.

48. Quoted Phillips-Fein, *Invisible Hands*, 145; Harry Rosenzweig interview by Kristina Minister, March 27, 1988, audiotape, side 1, tape 13, Chamber-Interviews; Robert Novak, *The Agony of the GOP 1964* (New York: Macmillan, 1965); Stephen Shadegg, *What Happened to Goldwater? The Inside Story of the 1964 Republican Campaign* (New York: Holt, Rinehart and Winston, 1965).

49. Goldberg, *Barry Goldwater*, 241–338, esp. 116, 308, 330–32.

50. Barry Goldwater, untitled note: "This is for the Alpha File," undated, folder: "O'Connor, Sandra Day 1972–1994," box 14, Alpha Files, AHF-Goldwater.

51. Before Ruth Bader Ginsburg joined the Court, many scholars were most concerned with how O'Connor's sex influenced her decisions, see Sue Davis, "The Voice of Sandra Day O'Connor," *Judicature* 77 (November–December 1993), 134–39; Barbara Palmer, "Feminist or Foe? Justice Sandra Day O'Connor, Title VII Sex-Discrimination, and Support for Women's Rights," *Women's Rights Law Reporter* 13 (June 1991), 159–70; attention then shifted to O'Connor's experience in state governance, see Erwin Chemerinsky, "Justice O'Connor and Federalism" *McGeorge Law Review* 32 (Spring 2001), 877–954; Bradley W. Joondeph, "The Deregulatory Value of Justice O'Connor's Federalism" *Houston Law Review* 44 (Fall 2007), 507–51, which prefigured assessments of the post-1991 conservative bloc's views on federalism and regulation, see Mark Tushnet, *A Court Divided: The Rehnquist Court and the Future of Constitutional Law* (New York: W. W. Norton, 2005), 1–22, 249–318; Ruth Colker and Kevin M. Scott, "Dissing States? Invalidation of State Action During the Rehnquist Era," *Virginia Law Review* 88 (October 2002), 1301–86; Herman Schwartz (ed.), *The Rehnquist Court: Judicial Activism on the Right* (New York: Hill and Wang, 2002), 155–68.

52. Donald E. Boles, *Mr. Justice Rehnquist, Judicial Activist* (Ames: Iowa State University Press, 1987), 12–16, esp. 13.

53. Ibid.,16–17; U.S. Congress, Senate, Committee on the Judiciary, *Nominations of William H. Rehnquist and Lewis F. Powell, Jr.: Hearings Before the Committee on the Judiciary*, United States Senate, 92 Cong., 1 sess., November 3, 4, 8, 9, and 10, 1971, esp. 305, 307, 309.

54. U.S. Congress, Senate, Committee on the Judiciary, *Nomination of Justice William Hubbs Rehnquist: Hearings Before the Committee on the Judiciary*, United States Senate, 99 Cong., 2 sess., July 29, 30, 31, and August 1, 1986, 1152; Boles, *Mr. Justice Rehnquist*, 16–17.

55. Tushnet, *A Court Divided*, 10–24.

56. John Dean, *The Rehnquist Choice: The Untold Story of the Nixon Appointment That Redefined the Supreme Court* (New York: Free Press, 2001), 15–27, esp. 15–16.

57. Ibid., 34, 113, 129, 132; Boles, *Mr. Justice Rehnquist*, 5.

58. Committee on the Judiciary, *Nominations of William H. Rehnquist and Lewis F. Powell, Jr.*, 16–52, esp. 180, esp. 19.

59. Ibid., esp. 53, 69–72; Committee on the Judiciary, *Nomination of Justice William Hubbs Rehnquist*, esp. 1152–60, 324–25; Boles, *Mr. Justice Rehnquist*, 75–100, esp. 98–99.

60. Joan Biskupic, *Sandra Day O'Connor: How the First Woman on the Supreme Court Became Its Most Influential Justice* (New York: HarperCollins, 2005), 45–48, quoted 47.

61. Robert Van Sickel, *Not a Particularly Different Voice: The Jurisprudence of Sandra Day O'Connor* (New York: Peter Lang, 1998), 22–32; Biskupic, *Sandra Day O'Connor*, 7–29, esp. 28–29; Sandra Day O'Connor interview by Harriet Haskell, January 31, 1980, transcript, PHP; McFeatters, *Sandra Day O'Connor*, 22–46, esp. 46.

62. McFeatters, *Sandra Day O'Connor*, 47–52, quoted 47; Van Sickel, *Not a Particularly Different Voice*, 29–32; Biskupic, *Sandra Day O'Connor*, 22–69.

63. Biskupic, *Sandra Day O'Connor*, 22–69; Sandra D. O'Connor to Barry Goldwater, April 6, 1978, folder: "O'Connor, Sandra Day 1972–1994," box 14, Alpha Files, AHF-Goldwater; McFeatters, *Sandra Day O'Connor*, 52–53.

64. McFeatters, *Sandra Day O'Connor*, 1–18.

65. Ibid.; U.S. Congress, Senate, Committee on the Judiciary, *The Nomination of Judge Sandra Day O'Connor of Arizona to Serve as an Associate Justice of the Supreme Court of the United States*, 97 Cong., 2 sess., September 9, 10, 11, 1981, 2; Van Sickel, *Not a Particularly Different Voice*, 33–41.

66. Committee on the Judiciary, *Nomination of Judge Sandra Day O'Connor of Arizona to Serve as an Associate Justice of the Supreme Court of the United States*, esp. 57, 66, 102.

67. Tushnet, *A Court Divided*, 302; quoted John Jenkins, "The Partisan: A Talk with Justice Rehnquist," *NYT*, March 3, 1985, 32.

68. William W. Van Alstyne, "The Second Death of Federalism," *Michigan Law Review* 83 (June 1985), 1709–33; Jesse H. Choper, "The Scope of National Power Vis-à-Vis the States: The Dispensability of Judicial Review," *Yale Law Journal* 86 (1977), 1552–1621; Archibald Cox, "Federalism and Individual Rights Under the Burger Court," *Northwestern University Law Review* 73 (March–April 1978); Van Sickel, *Not a Particularly Different Voice*, 82–92, quoted 82–83.

69. Van Sickel, *Not a Particularly Different Voice*, 82–92; Tushnet, *A Court Divided*, 249–58; Van Alstyne, "The Second Death of Federalism"; Charles Rothfield, "Federalism in a Conservative Supreme Court," *Publius* 22 (Summer 1992), 21–31; Ruth Colker and Kevin M. Scott, "Dissing States? Invalidation of State Action During the Rehnquist Era," *Virginia Law Review* 88 (October 2002), 1301–1386; Linda Greenhouse, "The Supreme Court: Federalism; States Are Given New Legal Shield by Supreme Court," *NYT*,

June 24, 1999; Richard Fallon Jr., "The 'Conservative' Paths of the Rehnquist Court's Federalism Decisions," *University of Chicago Law Review* 69 (Spring 2002), 429–494; Sue Davis, "Rehnquist and State Courts: Federalism Revisited," *The Western Political Quarterly* 45 (September 1992), 773–782; Eleanor M. Fox, "Antitrust and Business Power," in Herman Schwartz (ed.), *The Rehnquist Court: Judicial Activism on the Right* (New York: Hill and Wang, 2002), 213–226.

Chapter 10. "A Frankenstein's Monster"

1. Chalmers Roberts, "Ex-Chief Justice of Arizona 'High Priest' of Ultra Group," *WPost*, December 20, 1961, A4; Roberts, "Ultras Drawing Impressive Financial Backing," *WPost*, December 21, 1961, A4; "Support in the Press Provides 'Ultras' with Respectability," *WPost*, December 22, 1961, A4.

2. Kopkind, "Modern Times in Phoenix," 14–15.

3. Sugrue, *Origins of the Urban Crisis*.

4. Abbott, *New Urban America*, 244–62; Smith, "Into the Political Thicket."

5. Self, *American Babylon*; Kruse, *White Flight*; McGirr, *Suburban Warriors*; Sugrue, *Origins of the Urban Crisis*; Darren Dochuk, *From Bible Belt to Sunbelt: Plain-Folk Religion: Grassroots Politics, and the Rise of Evangelical Conservatism* (New York: W. W. Norton, 2010).

6. Richard Hofstadter, "Paranoid Style in American Politics," *Harper's Magazine*, November 1964, 77–86.

7. California State Chamber of Commerce, "Interstate Tax Differentials as a Factor in Industrial Development (California Compared to Other States)," October 19, 1961, 1, 4, 7, folder 1, box 91, SD; Thomas Byrne Edsall and Mary Edsall, *Chain Reaction: The Impact of Race, Rights, and Taxes on American Politics* (New York: W. W. Norton, 1992); Bridges, *Morning Glories*, 176–204; Abbott, *New Urban America*, 214–43.

8. James Carmichael, "What Next?" April 29, 1946, 3, 6, 9, folder 22, box 62, Carmichael; *How to Plan a Business-Education Day* (Washington, DC: Education Department, Chamber of Commerce of the United States, [1950s]), n.p.; Phillips-Fein, *Invisible Hands*, 53–67.

9. Atlanta Chamber of Commerce, Minutes of Board of Directors Meeting, November 28, 1950, 1, folder 3, box 83, Sibley; Minutes of the Education Committee, March 26, 1952, folder 5, box 30, SD; Minutes of the Meeting of the B-E Day Committee, June 25, 1956, folder 2, box 14, SD; Program for Seventh Annual Business-Education Day, February 12, 1957, n.p., folder 9, box 14, SD.

10. Paul Fannin, "Message to the 25th Arizona Legislature, Second Regular Session," January 8, 1962, 10–11, folder 4, box 15, Fannin; Joseph Stocker, "Brainwashing the Classrooms," *Nation*, December 17, 1973, 653–55; Bethany Moreton, "Make Payroll, Not War: Business Culture as Youth Culture," in Schulman and Zelizer, *Rightward Bound*, 53–70.

11. Executive Committee, Minutes of Meeting, August 6, 1965, vol.: "1965–1966," Board-Records; Frank Snell interview by Kristina Minister, April 26, 1988, audiotape,

side 1, tape 10, Chamber-Interviews; Howard Pyle interview by G. W. Johnson, February 2, 1976, transcript, 32, PHP; Board of Directors, Minutes of Meetings, September 21, 1966, and June 21, 1967, vol.: "1966–1967," Board-Records; A. E. "Randy" Randall, "Across the Desk," *Dynamic Phoenix* 3 (April 1971), 7; M. A. Atkinson Jr. to Orme Lewis, October 16, 1962, folder 1, box 1, Lewis-Roca; "Members' Memories," *Phoenix* (July 1988), 61–68; "Phoenix Chamber of Commerce Board of Directors, 1963–1964," June 1963, folder 8, box 1, Lewis-Roca; "Long-Range Objectives for the Phoenix Chamber of Commerce," May 30, 1972, esp. 5, vol.: "1971–1972," Board-Records.

12. California State Chamber of Commerce, "Interstate Tax Differentials as a Factor in Industrial Development (California Compared to Other States)," October 19, 1961, 1, 4, 7, folder 1, box 91, SD; Subscriber, "Driven out by Taxes," *AR*, November 2, 1953, 6.

13. Darren Dochuk, *From Bible Belt to Sunbelt*; Lisa McGirr, *Suburban Warriors*; James Gregory, *American Exodus: The Dust Bowl Migration and Okie Culture in California* (New York: Oxford University Press, 1991); LaBau, "Phoenix Rising," 140–143.

14. Collins, *Emerging Metropolis*, 375–83, quoted 379, 381.

15. Ibid., 381–83, quoted 381.

16. Samuel Mardian, "Housing Code," typescript, May 9, 1963, 1–2, folder 8, box 11, Mardian; Executive Committee, Minutes of Meeting, April 24, 1968, 1–2, with enclosed "Housing Code Considerations" document, vol.: "1967–1968," Board-Records; Executive Committee, Minutes of Meeting, September 11, 1969, 2, September 19, 1969, 1, vol.: "1969–1970," Board-Records; Collins, *Emerging Metropolis*, 375–83.

17. Collins, *Emerging Metropolis*, quoted 383; on Nixon's New Federalism see: Robert Collins, *More: The Politics of Economic Growth* (New York: Oxford University Press, 2000), 98–165.

18. Brown, "An Analysis of the Phoenix Charter Government Committee as a Political Entity," 50–58.

19. "Who's Who on Stay American Committee's Ticket," *AR*, November 5, 1961, 22-A; Charlotte Buchen, "One Too Many Talks Led to Candidacy, Hanner Says," *AR*, November 4, 1961, 21, 25.

20. Michael Kazin, *Populist Persuasion: An American History* (Ithaca: Cornell University Press), 221–42.

21. Charlotte Buchen, "Pastor's Editorial Blasts SAC Group," *AR*, November 2, 1961, 1 and 12-A; "The Voter's Choice," *AR*, November 2, 1961, 6-A; "Misquoted, SAC Says on TV," *AR*, November 4, 1961, 12.

22. Bernie Wynn, "Phoenix Red Target, Candidates Say," *AR*, November 4, 1961, 19; "Williams Decries SAC's Statements," *AR*, November 2, 1961, 12-A; Wynn, "SAC Candidate Says Reds Plot Power Coup," *AR*, November 5, 12-A; Wynn, "Phoenix Red Target, Candidates Say," *AR*, November 4, 1961, 19; Buchen, "Pastor's Editorial Blasts SAC Group"; "The Voter's Choice"; "Misquoted, SAC Says on TV".

23. Sam Mardian, [campaign speech], n.d., 1, folder 9, box 11, Mardian; "Murphy Says SAC Attack Malicious," *AR*, November 2, 1961, 7; Jack Crowe, "Foes Lulling Voters, Say Charterites," *AR*, November 4, 1961, 19.

24. "The Voter's Choice"; "Udall Tags Opposition 'Irrational,'" *AR*, November 4, 1961, 19; "Issues for Conservatives," *AR*, November 13, 1961, 6.

25. "Right-Wing Slate on Phoenix Ballot," *NYT*, November 12, 1961, 45;Buchen, "Pastor's Editorial Blasts SAC Group,"; Johnny Johnson, "Fascists Belong on Extreme Left," *AR*, November 2, 1961, 6; Victor Riesel, "Inside Labor: Extremist Label Pinned On SAC," *AR*, November 4, 1961, 6.

26. Brown, "An Analysis," 57–58; Jack Crowe, "2½–1 Edge Tallied over SAC," *AR*, November 15, 1961, 1 and 7; Buchen, "One Too Many Talks Led to Candidacy, Hanner Says."

27. Warren Banner and Theodora Dyer, *Economic and Cultural Progress of the Negro, Phoenix, Arizona* (New York: National Urban League, 1965), 10–62; Whitaker, *Race Work*, 143–47; Nick Tapia, "Cactus in the Desert: The Chicano Movement in Maricopa County, Arizona, 1968–1978" (master's thesis, Arizona State University, 1999), 6–7; Chicanos Por La Causa to National Urban Coalition, "Program Proposal: Mexican-American Economic Development Activities," August 1970, folder 1, box 2, Lopez.

28. Flores interview by Edwards, 16–20, 25–28; Chiang, "Chinese Community in Phoenix, Arizona," 51–54; Tipton, "Men out of China," 352–53; Titcomb, "Americanization and Mexicans in the Southwest," 64–68; Melcher, "Blacks and Whites Together," 195–216; Whitaker, *Race Work*, 93–102.

29. Whitaker, *Race Work*, 118–24.

30. Ibid., 140–48, quoted 147.

31. Ibid., 140–48, quoted 147, 148; Flores interview, 16–25, esp. 20.

32. Flores interview, 16–28; Titcomb, "Americanization and Mexicans in the Southwest," 85–89; Tapia, "Cactus in the Desert."

33. Quoted in Chicanos Por La Causa, "Chicanos Por La Causa '69," 1969, n.p., folder 2, box 20, Lopez; Tapia, "Cactus in the Desert"; "Our History," Chicanos Por La Causa, Inc., http://www.cplc.org/about-us/history.aspx.

34. Chicanos Por La Causa to Southwest Council of La Raza, "A Proposal to Promote Political Education, Economic Development and Leadership Training," September 25, 1969, Lopez; Pete Garcia interview by Karen Smith, February 14, 1978, transcript, PHP.

35. Whitaker, *Race Work*, 173–99, esp. 176–79.

36. Collins, *Emerging Metropolis*, 64–67; "CG Blasts Basis of ACT Plea," *AR*, November 1, 1963, 19; Robert J. Early, "ACT Program Questioned," *AR*, November 4, 1963, 1; "ACT Forges Major Opposition Slate," *AR*, November 10, 1963, 28-A; "U.S. Aid Promised by ACT," *AR*, November 10, 1963, B1.

37. Collins, *Emerging Metropolis*, 64–67, quoted 66; "Hill Urges Tax Assessor for Phoenix," *AR.*, November 8, 1963, 19; "HEAR Ticket Entered Race Late; Places Stress on Conservatism," *AR*, November 10, 1963, A29.

38. Whitaker, *Race Work*, 167–68; Bridges, *Morning Glories*, 177; Brown, "An Analysis," 58–62; Joanne Smoot Patton, press release, November 4, 1963, folder:

"Rosenzweig: Government & Public Policy, Charter Government Committee, 1963" (2 of three), box: unassigned, Rosenzweig; "In a Nutshell" memo to all [CGC] candidates, folder: "Rosenzweig: Government & Public Policy, Charter Government Committee, 1963" (1 of three), box: unassigned, Rosenzweig; Patton, "Highlights of 1962–63," October 24, 1963, Rosenzweig; Patton, "Phoenix Growth History," October 24, 1963, Rosenzweig; Robert J. Early, "Graham Raps ACT," *AR*, November 5, 1963, 1 and 5; "Charter Government," *AR*, November 3, 1963, 6.

39. "Milton Graham Elected Mayor: Run-Off for Council Seats," *Weekly News Bulletin* 14 (November 14, 1963), 1, folder 2, box 42, Mardian; "Charter Government Candidates Elected," *Weekly News Bulletin* 14 (December 12, 1963), 1, folder 2, box 42, Mardian; quoted Whitaker, *Race Work*, 167; Brown, "An Analysis," 58–62.

40. Mrs. Joan Patrick, "Reader Criticizes Republic Editorial," *AR*, November 2, 1963, 6; James V. DeWitt, "ACT Candidates Offer No Program," *AR*, November 9, 1963, 6.

41. Whitaker, *Race Work*, 167–69; Collins, *Emerging Metropolis*, 66–69; VanderMeer, *Desert Visions and the Making of Modern Phoenix*, 240–42.

42. Frosty Taylor, "Klahr Zaps Charter Government in Speech," *Paradise Valley News*, January 19, 1974, n.p., folder 14, box 1, Lewis; "Review of C.G.C. Campaign Publicity & P. R. Agencies," July 29, 1965, folder: "Rosenzweig: Government & Public Policy, Charter Government Committee, 1963" (1 of three), box: unassigned, Rosenzweig; "Report by 1963 Chairman Charter Government Committee & Election (April 8–December 31)," undated, folder: "Rosenzweig: Government & Public Policy, Charter Government Committee, 1963" (1 of three), box: unassigned, Rosenzweig; Whitaker, *Race Work*, 167–69; Collins, *Emerging Metropolis*, 66–69, quoted 68; VanderMeer, *Desert Visions and the Making of Modern Phoenix*, 240–42; Marvin Andrews interview by Dean Smith, typescript, May 11, 1990, 9–10, ASU-Oral-Histories; John Driggs interview by Karen Smith, July 13, 1978, transcript, 1–8, PHP; Amy Silverman, "Old Glory," July 4, 2002, http://www.phoenixnewtimes.com/2002-07-04/news/old-glory/.

43. Richard Morin, "Candidate Poll Finds Most Back Ward Proposal," *AR*, November 2, 1975, 1, A-9; Richard Morin, "City Candidates Ignoring Issues, Observers Claim," *AR*, October 16, 1975, B-1, B-2.

44. "Keep City Hall Scandal-free, Candidate Says," *AR*, November 1, 1975, B-3; "Voter Rejection of Ward System Urged by Mayor," *AR*, November 2, 1975, B-1; Morin, "Candidate Poll Finds Most Back Ward Proposal"; Morin, "City Candidates Ignoring Issues, Observers Claim".

45. Mark F. Stearn, "Reverting to Mudslinging," *AR*, December 7, 1975, A-7; Robert F. Ehrlich, "Phony Growth Mania," *AR*, December 4, 1975, A-7; Sandra Mara, "Do We Really Want to Go Back?" *AR*, October 21, 1975, A-7; Don Bolles, "Candidates Begin Plans for Runoff," *AR*, November 6, 1975, 1, A-4.

46. Don Bolles, "Independents Will Try to Snap Charter 'Spell' on City," *AR*, December 7, 1975, 1.

47. Margaret Hance, Untitled Speech, typescript, [1974], n.p., folder 10, box 3, Hance; Hance, "Address to the CPBA," n.d., typescript, p. 3, folder 10, box 3, Hance;

Geoffrey E. Gonsher and Linda Upton to Mayor Hance, "Subject: City Activities 1976–1983," May 16, 1983, 1, 5, 6, folder 15, box 22, Hance; Hance, "Summary of Major Accomplishments," December 7, 1983, transcript, folder 15, box 22, Hance.

48. Luckingham, *Phoenix*, 179–85; Mrs. Leslie [Margaret] Kober interview by S. Laughlin, June 18, 1976, transcript, 16, PHP; "The Formation of Phoenix [40]," undated, esp. 3, folder: "Rosenberg: Government & Public Policy, Phoenix 40, 1975–1990," no box, Rosenzweig; "Phoenix 40: Long Range Planning Committee Recommendations," September 16, 1980, folder: "Rosenberg: Government & Public Policy, Phoenix 40, 1975–1990," no box, Rosenzweig; Phoenix 40 roster, "Early 1976," folder: "Rosenberg: Government & Public Policy, Phoenix 40, 1975–1990," no box, Rosenzweig.

49. Collins, *Emerging Metropolis*, 64–67.

50. Ibid.; "A Real Free-for-All," *AR*, November 6, 1975, A6; "'No' on Ward System," ibid., October 21, 1975, A-4; Joseph A. Pegnato, "Vote a Move to Democracy," ibid., November 1, 1975, A-7; Sandra Wilks, "A Right to Choose," ibid., November 1, 1975, A-7; Jana Bummersbath, "Freeway Initiative Is Approved by 54 percent," ibid., 1; "Unions Back Ward Election Plan," ibid., October 18, 1975, B4.

51. Quoted Ted Rushton, "District System: Ward Politics or Open Government? (The Answer Is in Your Garbage)," *Phoenix Magazine*, May 1985, 63–67, esp. 65; Luckingham, *Phoenix*, 221–30; Collins, *Emerging Metropolis*, 68–69; Bridges, *Morning Glories*, 194–200, quoted 195.

52. "Everybody Has Chance to Help Program of Industrial Growth," *San Diego Evening Tribute*, unattributed clipping, folder 7, box 9, SD; Mr. and Mrs. Lee Merchant to B.I.G., undated, folder 7, box 9, SD; Mr. and Mrs. P. Benedict to Business Reply Mail, September 2, 1961, folder 7, box 9, SD; S.D. resident to Sirs, undated, folder 7, box 9, SD; L. G. Egan to Norman Foster, September 24, 1961, folder 7, box 9, SD; occupant to [BIG], undated, folder 7, box 9, SD; one irate "X" San Diego citizen to [BIG], undated, folder 7, box 9, SD; Jacqueline McCaffrey to Sirs, undated, folder 7, box 9, SD; Iris Bascomb to B.I.G., undated, folder 7, box 9, SD; Oscar Q. Posthlawhistle to Sirs, undated, folder 7, box 9, SD.

53. Bridges, *Morning Glories*, 176–204, quoted 176.

54. Ibid., 176–204, quoted 197.

55. Abbott, *New Urban America*, 214–43; Ronald Bayor, "Models of Ethnic and Racial Politics in the Urban Sunbelt South," in Mohl, *Searching for the Sunbelt*, 105–23, esp. 105–8; Bernard, "Metropolitan Politics in the American Sunbelt," 73–76.

56. Kruse, *White Flight*, 180–93, quoted 180.

57. Ibid., 105–30, quoted 127.

58. Ibid., 194–95.

59. Quoted ibid., 197.

60. Ibid., 195–198, quoted 196, 197.

61. Ibid., 200–204, quoted 200–201.

62. Ibid., 128–30, quoted 129.

63. Ibid., 229–33, 251–61.

64. Ibid.

65. John Conlan interview by Gordon Sabine, August 12, 1992, transcript, PHP.

66. Quoted in ibid. 11, 19, 28.

67. LaBau, "Phoenix Rising," 140–147, quoted 142, 145, 149.

68. Orme Lewis to Sidney B. Wolfe, January 16, 1973, folder 15, box 5, Lewis; "Early Bird—1973," folder 15, box 5, Lewis; Stephen C. Shadegg to Laurens L. Handerson with enclosures, February 1, 1989, folder: "Fifty Years of Arizona Political and Judicial Recollections" by Laurens L. Henderson, Shadegg; Shadegg, *Arizona Politics*, 202.

69. LaBau, "Phoenix Rising," 26–28, quoted 28.

70. Shadegg, *Arizona Politics*, 125–26; Johnson, *Arizona Politicians*, 38–42, quoted 40.

71. "Jury Acquits Governor," *WSJ*, June 21, 1988, 38; quoted in Johnson, *Arizona Politicians*, 41; Alan Weisman, "Up in Arms in Arizona," *NYT Sunday Magazine*, November 1, 1987, 50+, esp. 59; Kenneth V. Smith, "The Resurrection of Evan Mecham," *National Review* 41 (May 1989), 42–43.

72. Johnson, *Arizona Politicians*, 38–42; Ronald J. Bellus, "Evan Mecham: Governing Arizona," *WPost*, July 17, 1987, A24; T. R. Reid, "Arizona's GOP Governor Ridiculed by the Voters," *WPost*, June 21, 1987, 3; Evan Mecham, "State of the State Address," January 11, 1988, http://www.kensmith.us/2009/05/state-of-state-1988.html.

73. Paula D. McClain, "'High Noon': The Recall and Impeachment of Evan Mecham," *PS: Political Science and Politics* 21 (Summer 1988, 623–38; Weisman, "Up in Arms in Arizona"; Thomas J. Knudson, "Arizona Torn by Governor-Elect's Plan to Drop King Holiday," *NYT*, December 23, 1986, A16.

74. Lindsey Gruson, "A Family Gathering Shows Split over Mecham Goes Deeper Than Politics," *NYT*, March 19, 1988, 6; William Schmidt, "Republicans Join the Roster of Arizona Governor's Foes," *NYT*, October 15, 1987, A20; Jon D. Hull, "Evan Mecham, Please Go Home," *Time*, November 9, 1987; quoted Johnson, *Arizona Politicians*, 42.

75. Associated Press, "Evan Mecham, Ousted Governor, Dies at 83," *NYT*, February 23, 2008; Smith, "Resurrection of Evan Mecham."

76. Snell interview by Minister, side 1, tape 10; Barry Goldwater to Walter Bimson, December 21, 1970, folder: "Bimson, Walter 1967–1971," box 2, Alpha Files, AHF-Goldwater; Goldwater to John Leach, November 15, 1984, 1–2, folder: "Pulliam, Eugene and Nina 1967–1984," box 15, Alpha Files, AHF-Goldwater; Walter Bimson to Barry Goldwater, January 11, 1971, folder: "Bimson, Walter 1967–1971," box 2, Alpha Files, AHF-Goldwater; Frank Brophy to Barry Goldwater, April 14, 1977, folder: "Brophy, Frank Cullen 1974–1980," box 2, Alpha Files, AHF-Goldwater.

Epilogue. Whither Phoenix?

1. Ken Silverstein, "Tea Party in the Sonora," *Harper's*, July 2010; Kevin Sack, "Arizona Medicaid Cuts Seen as Sign of the Times," *NYT*, December 4, 2010; Brigid Schulte, "In Arizona, Anyone Concerned Can Report Odd Behavior to Mental-Health

Experts," *WPost*, January 10, 2011; Hendrik Hertzberg, "Words and Deeds," *New Yorker*, January 24, 2011.

2. Jonathan Laing, "Phoenix Descending: Is Boomtown U.S.A. Going Bust?" *Barron's National Business and Financial Weekly*, December 19, 1988, 8+, esp. 32; Max Jarman, "Honeywell to Move 700 Jobs out of U.S.," *AR*, November 7, 2008; David Streitfeld and Jack Healy, "Phoenix Leads the Way Down in Home Prices," *NYT*, April 29, 2009; Ross, *Bird on Fire*, 12.

3. Quoted Ross, *Bird on Fire*, 162–63; Kate Galbraith, "Chinese Solar Panel Firm to Open Plant in Arizona," *NYT*, November 16, 2009.

4. Noam Scheiber, "Made Man," *New Republic*, August 20, 2008; Paul Alexander, *Man of the People, Revised and Updated: The Maverick Life and Career of John McCain* (Hoboken, NJ: John Wiley and Sons, 2008), 47–60; Matt Welch, *McCain: The Myth of a Maverick* (New York: Palgrave Macmillan, 2007), 39–56.

5. Scheiber, "Made Man"; Alexander, *Man of the People, Revised and Updated*, 61–120; Welch, *McCain*, 39–56; John McCain to Barry Goldwater, December 20, 1985, 2, folder: "McCain, John III 1978–1989," box 11A, Alpha Files, AHF-Goldwater; Goldwater to William Quinn, March 27, 1986, ibid.; Goldwater to Darrow Tully, September 10, 1984, ibid.

6. Scheiber, "Made Man;" Ewen MacAskill, "John McCain Wins Arizona Republican Primary," *Guardian*, August 25, 2010; Jason O'Bryan, "John McCain Coasts to Easy Victory in Arizona Senate Race," *Politicsdaily.com*, November 3, 2010; "Election Results 2008: Arizona," *NYT*, December 9, 2008..

7. Max Blumenthal, "McCain Mutiny," *Nation*, February 21, 2007; Welch, *McCain*, 71–204.

8. "Arizona Sends a Quayle Back to Washington," *Reuters.com*, November 3, 2010; Janie Lorber, "Shadegg Announces Retirement," *NYT*, January 14, 2010.

9. Bureau of Labor Standards, "Union Membership in Arizona–2011," March 24, 2011, www.bls.gov/ro9/unionaz.pdf; U.S. Census Bureau, "Arizona Quick Facts," http://quickfacts.census.gov/qfd/states/04000.html; Blumenthal, "McCain Mutiny;" Joseph Lelyveld, "The Border Dividing Arizona," *NYT Magazine*, October 15, 2006, 40–47, 84–86; Dawn Teo, "McCain's Home State Party Imploding, Plagued by Infighting and Scandal," *Huffington Post*, October 21, 2008; Sasha Abramsky, "Blue-ing the West," *Nation*, January 4, 2007; Robert Lavato, "Latinos Lean Left: Bringing Down the GOP's Big Tent," ibid., December 4, 2006.

10. David Sirota, "Ikea Joins the Race to the Bottom," *Salon.com*, April 15, 2011; Hertzberg, "Words and Deeds"; David Kocieniewski, "U.S. Business Has High Tax Rates but Pays Less," *NYT*, May 2, 2011; "A Setback for Arizona-Style Immigration Laws," *NYT*, April 13, 2011; Paul Krugman, "The Unwisdom of Elites," ibid., May 8, 2011; "Reform and the Filibuster," ibid., January 2, 2011; Tracy Gordon, "Unlock State Budgets," ibid., May 23, 2011; Emma G. Fitzsimmons, "Ohio Lawmakers Pass Anti-Union Bill," ibid., March 29, 2011.

11. Jay Heflin, "Gallup Poll Finds Majority Favor Ending Tax Cuts for the Rich," http://thehill.com/blogs/on-the-money/domestic-taxes/117995-new-poll-finds-americans-support-ending-tax-cuts-for-the-wealthy; "42% Say U.S. Corporations Don't Pay Enough in Taxes," http://www.rasmussenreports.com/public_content/business/taxes/august_2011/42_say_u_s_corporations_don_t_pay_enough_in_taxes; Megan Gibson, "Cairo Lends Support to the Protestors in Wisconsin—With Pizza," http://newsfeed.time.com/2011/02/21/cairo-lends-support-to-the-protestors-in-wisconsin-via-pizza/; Seth Freed Wessler, "The Far-Right Movement Behind Arizona Copycat Bills," http://colorlines.com/archives/2010/05/the_farright_movement_behind_arizona_copycat_bills.html; Barbara E. Hernandez, "Arizona Boycott Goes Viral as State's Tourism Industry Tries to Fight Back," http://www.bnet.com/blog/travel/arizona-boycott-goes-viral-as-states-tourism-industry-tries-to-fight-back/5845; Amy B. Means, "Doing Green Jobs Right," *Nation,* September 13, 2010; John Nichols, "AFL-CIO's Trumka Embraces All Workers—Including Immigrants," *Nation*, September 18, 2009.

Index

Page numbers in italics refer to illustrations

Acknowledgments

It took a village to finish this book. Countless friends, scholars, and family members have seen me through to this point. I am grateful to them all, especially the ones whom I forget to thank.

This project would not have been possible without the generous support of institutions and archives in and outside Arizona. I received much needed financing from the University of California's Labor and Employment Research Fund, the Charles Redd Center for Western Historical Studies, the Department of History at the University of California, Santa Barbara, and the University of Cambridge's Paul Mellon Professorial Fund. Archivists and librarians proved invaluable in their service and support, especially those at the George Meany Memorial Archives, University of North Carolina, Chapel Hill's Wilson Library, Emory University's Manuscript, Archives, and Rare Book Library, Cobb County's Central Library, San Diego State University's Special Collections and University Archives, University of New Mexico's Center for Southwest Research, the Nevada Historical Society, the Archives at the University of Colorado at Boulder Libraries, the Center for American History at the University of Texas, Austin, the Annenberg Rare Book and Manuscript Library, McFarland Historic State Park, the Arizona State Library and Archives, Phoenix City Hall, and the Arizona Historical Society. I am indebted to Julie Pace for this book's cover photo, which she took atop South Mountain to capture the sun setting over a plant once owned by Motorola. But I am also grateful to my research assistant Kelly Ball, who balanced her need to work and study at Emory with my constant requests for more material. The employees and managers of the Greater Phoenix Chamber of Commerce also deserve special thanks for allowing me unrestricted access to their records and the use of one of their offices to conduct research. The librarians at Arizona State University Archives and Special Collections made researching in the Phoenix summers a pleasure.

Chris Marín and Roann Monson alerted me to unknown, uncataloged materials and mercifully sneaked me into the librarians' ice cream social when I was at a particularly low, and overheated, point. Rob Spindler and Neil Millican were generous with their time when I searched for photographs. Arizona Historical Foundation's archivists went well beyond the call of duty. Both Susan Irwin and Linda Whitaker provided access to unprocessed collections and have been indispensable resources as I have struggled to track down records in other libraries and archives. Linda and her husband, Duane, have become wonderful friends, buying me dinners in Santa Barbara when they came through town and bringing me new treasures from AHF's rich collections. Linda has been a constant cheerleader and helped make sure that I finished this book.

Many senior scholars have been generous with their time and support. Alice O'Connor shepherded me through the early research on right-to-work laws. Paul Spickard proved an exceptional critic and fan as I labored to finish drafting the book. Matthew Lassiter provided extensive comments on the manuscript and answered countless e-mails when I was stuck. Mary Furner has been an inspiration as a historian and a teacher. Her thought-provoking and challenging questions have enriched my scholarship and thinking beyond measure. Nelson Lichtenstein's importance to my work is incalculable. He made a promise to read every word that I would ever write and has never wavered in that commitment.

I have also been lucky to find myself ensconced at innovative institutions, where I have found friendly peers and generous mentors. UCSB's Department of History and Center for the Study of Work, Labor, and Democracy attracted inspiring graduate students, most notably Jill Jensen, John Munro, and Leandra Zarnow, faculty members, like Laura Kalman, who helped me conceptualize the sections on Barry Goldwater's early Senate campaigns, and visiting speakers, including Thomas Sugrue, who later lobbied for my work's inclusion in this series and provided me with the feedback needed to prepare the book for publication. I also spent a productive year at Claremont McKenna College, where I had many wonderful students and benefited from the collegiality of Lisa Cody, Mary Evans, Stu McConnell, Albert Park, Jonathan Petropoulos, Arthur Rosenbaum, Daniel Segal, Diana Selig, Victor Silverman, and David Yoo. I am also indebted to the faculty and administrators at Loyola University Chicago, who hired me and then allowed me to spend two years at the University of Cambridge. Timothy Gilfoyle deserves special recognition for patiently waiting for me to decide to leave

California, offering me much needed guidance in editing my book, and supporting my request to extend my leave.

My two years as the Paul Mellon Fellow of American History were indispensable. Tony Badger, Lucy Delap, Michael O'Brien, Andrew Preston, Mike Sewell, John Thompson, and Betty Wood all welcomed me with open arms, lunch invitations, and lengthy explanations for navigating a new country, university system, and Cambridge's *lex non scripta*. I was both thrilled and relieved when Tony found the money in the Mellon research funds to pay for the book's illustrations. I was also honored when Andrew, with Tony's blessing, asked me to run the graduate workshop for American history, whose stalwarts (David Ballantyne, Jonathan Bronitsky, James Cameron, Kristal Enter, Zach Fredman, Adam Gilbert, John Heavens, Hannah Morgenstein Higgin, Ellen Horrow, Jonathan Koefoed, Stella Krepp, Sarah Matherly, Stephen Mawdsley, Ruth Martin, Asa McKercher, Elzelina Noomen, Amy Renton, Ardis Smith, Olivia Sohns, Tom Tunstall-Allcock, and Rebecca Wagner) helped me become a better teacher, writer, and researcher. The American History Subject Group's flexible expectations of my time afforded me the opportunity to speak at and attend conferences throughout the United States, the United Kingdom, and Europe. I spent my most pleasant Thursdays in London, where I enjoyed the company of Jonathan Bell, Jo Cohen, Erik Mathisen, Iwan Morgan, Kendrick Oliver, Kyle Roberts, Adam Smith, and Emily West at the Institute of Historical Research's American History seminar.

Fellow historians outside those institutions that I have, however briefly, called home have also been a part of this endeavor. Joseph McCartin was kind enough to read my manuscript and write letters on my behalf when I went in search of a contract. Kim Phillips-Fein has extended herself on my behalf for years. Tami Friedman has been generous with her time, wisdom, and knowledge. Nathan Connolly generously supplied me with research materials from the Miami Chamber of Commerce and provided helpful feedback as I struggled to compare the Sunbelt South and West. Andrew Ross never seems to miss a chance to tell people about my book, even before finishing his own project, *Bird on Fire: Lessons from the World's Least Sustainable City* (2011), on the turmoil in millennial Phoenix. I would also be remiss if I did not thank Daniel Amsterdam, Sven Beckert, Carl Bontempo, Andrew Wender Cohen, Joseph Crespino, Darren Dochuk, Dan Geary, Meg Jacobs, Jennifer Klein, Stephen Mihm, Christopher Nehls, Michelle Nickerson, Bryant Simon, Jason Scott Smith, Jennie Sutton, and Simon Szreter for their advice and support. The editors of the *Journal of American History*, the *Pacific Historical Review*, Oxford University Press, and University of Pennsylvania Press generously allowed me to use portions of my articles in this book. I also owe a great debt to Bob Lockhart, who shepherded me through the publication of my first edited collection and this book.

My friends and family also deserve special recognition. Gabriel Montaño first brought me to Phoenix in March 2000. That trip was an eye-opening experience for a born-and-raised northern Virginian wrongly convinced that her hometown's dynamism was unique. Lutz Lesshafft deserves a medal for holding my hand through the completion of the research and drafting of this book. His unwavering faith in me made me a braver person, one ready to leave California for Britain. Countless others in Arizona, California, Virginia, and Cambridge also deserve thanks for making the years spent on this project manageable, especially: Matthew Allen, Valerie Batterham, Terry Belanger, Justin Bengry, Matt Benton, Alison Borek, Cyrus Boyd, Jill Briggs, Kristen Brill, Andre Brown, Jessica Elliott, Mary Margaret Fonow, Karen Frank, Ela Frye, Athena Marie, Sarah Matthews, Jeff Miley, Heidi Marx-Wolf, Zena Moore, Chris Newfield, Duncan Odom, Holly Garcia O'Hearn, Todd O'Hearn, Ellen Rentz, Jack Clark Robinson, Catherine Salzgeber, Bianca Schmitt, Roland Schwarz, Klara Stefflova, Killarney Suniga, Sarah Watkins, Mike Wilson, and Warren Wood. But Josh Billings deserves special mention. He is largely responsible for reassuring me that I was ready to leave Britain. My life in Cambridge was fantastic before I met him but became sublime after our paths crossed. He even managed to make our concurrent return to the U.S. exciting, not formidable.

Kinship played a role in this book's completion. The Shermers—my father Bob, cousin Heather, aunt Angie, and uncles Ron and Don—have been a constant presence in my life. I have also found unyielding love and encouragement through a family that I have cobbled together along the way. No one could have a better mother than Virginia McConnell, who found more space in her heart for a young girl who was not her own than many would think possible, and Nelson Lichtenstein and Eileen Boris made a home for me in Santa Barbara. What started out as a club for University of Virginia exiles turned into a nurturing, encouraging, and much needed haven. I could not have made it through these past few years without all three of them.